CHARACTER DEVELOPMENT IN SCHOOLS AND BEYOND

CHARACTER DEVELOPMENT IN SCHOOLS AND BEYOND

Edited by
Kevin Ryan
and
George F. McLean

PRAEGER

New York
Westport, Connecticut
London

Copyright Acknowledgments

The sample study units used in chapter 8 are from *Values and Living: Learning Materials for Grades 7 and 8* by Clive Beck (Toronto: OISE Press, 1983). Reprinted by permission.

The epigraph by Gerald Grant quoted in chapter 5 is reprinted by permission of *Daedalus*, Journal of the American Academy of Arts and Sciences, "America's Schools: Public and Private," vol. 110, no. 3, Summer 1981, Cambridge, MA.

Library of Congress Cataloging-in-Publication Data

Character development in schools and beyond.

  Bibliography: p.
  Includes index.
  1. Moral education. 2. Character. 3. Moral education—United States. I. Ryan, Kevin. II. McLean, George F.
LC268.C34   1987   370.11′4   87-11753
ISBN 0-275-92191-3 (alk. paper)

Library of Congress Catalog Card Number: 87-11753
ISBN: 0-275-92191-3

First published in 1987

Praeger Publishers, One Madison Avenue, New York, NY 10010
A division of Greenwood Press, Inc.

Printed in the United States of America

The paper used in this book complies with the
Permanent Paper Standard issued by the National
Information Standards Organization (Z39.48-1984).

10 9 8 7 6 5 4 3 2 1

Contents

Preface
Robert Coles

For twenty-five years 1 have been working with children
in various parts of this country and abroad in hopes of
learning how they acquire their moral values, and very
important, how they try to live up to those values, if indeed they do so. At times 1 have been stunned by the
willingness of, say, small children from poor, uneducated
families to behave rather impressively, from an ethical
point of view, despite the overwhelming stresses and bur-
dens placed upon these boys and girls, not to mention
their parents. For instance (and 1 have many times mentioned this incident) 1 watched a six year old black child
go through mobs daily in New Orleans, be threatened, be
told she would be killed by the white segregationist men
and women who awaited her (during the autumn of 1960),
and yet she managed to walk past such people with poise
and dignity. 1 was trying to find out about her psychological adjustment (which turned out to be quite normal)
but 1 was not at all prepared, as 1 watched her closely
and listened to her every word, for what 1 learned (from
her teacher) she said as (escorted by federal marshals)
she passed those hecklers: "Please, dear God, forgive
them, because they don't know what they're doing."
    1 suppose we might be cynical about such a child's
capacity to connect her own considerable travail with that
of Jesus of Nazareth as He hung on the Cross, ready to
die. The child was only repeating what she heard in
church; she was obeying her parents, mouthing their pi-
eties--"coping" (that dreary, contemporary word) with her
considerable anxiety. True, she was fearful at times; and
true, she did find personal solace in the prayer she spoke
every day as she entered school, amid the screaming death

threats and curses—for months. But she also meant what she said, and was well able to explain her moral (as opposed to psychological motives). One day, for instance, as I asked her about "those people," whether she really did feel like praying for them, she responded with a question of her own: "Well, don't you think they need praying for?" The child had thrown the moral heart of the matter back at the doctor—had asked me, the grown-up and supposedly knowing child psychiatrist, to take a sharp look at my own values, purposes, ethical assumptions.

There are other children like her all over this country; in fact, boys and girls everywhere, by their very nature as human beings, have the capacity to ask questions, to wonder why, to take note of inconsistencies, to think of what might be as well as what is—and of course, what ought to be. Even as that black child showed her capacity for moral reflection, some of us wonder about many of our all too privileged children, who will never have to face screaming mobs, who won't experience poverty or the strain of racial prejudice—and who, not rarely, are nevertheless troubled, confused, morally adrift, hence the incidence of drug and alcohol abuse, of self-destructive behavior of all kinds, of visits to the offices of our suburban psychiatrists and psychologists. Even our bright and seemingly well-adjusted students are not necessarily decent and honorable individuals; as Walker Percy put it in The Second Coming, "they all get As, yet flunk ordinary living." Another shrewd writer, the poet and physician William Carlos Williams, reminded us that "smart isn't necessarily good," a paraphrase, really, of Ralph Waldo Emerson's distinction of one hundred and fifty years ago, between "character" and "intellect." A student of mine said as much recently when he offered this telling irony to me—that he "saw people get As in moral reasoning courses, and still behave very badly." He referred to their gossipy, smug, selfish ways—to his own, at times. I believe St. Augustine, long ago, dared face a similar moral paradox.

But that student and Ruby and indeed all of us who are students and teachers and parents will continue to pose such ironies to ourselves, one hopes and prays; and we all need to have, in that regard, the reflections of others, who have dared look at the question of "character," of moral knowledge and moral action, of the nature of moral purpose. We are fortunate to have, in this book, an important series of essays which will help us along

viii

enormously--give us plenty of reason to stop and consider
what we want morally for our children, for ourselves.
There has been an aching void in the literature of moral
reflection as it ought to apply to education, and this book
addresses that absence boldly and thoughtfully.

Robert Coles

Part I
The Context

1
Character Development:
The Challenge and the Model
Kevin Ryan and Thomas Lickona

Concern for the values and morals of the young is an enduring adult preoccupation. Down through recorded history, this worry about the character of the younger generation is evident. Concern, however, has never been enough to ensure that the young possess the type of character that can sustain the individual and society. Some societies have failed to transmit their values to the young, and this has often meant their swift decline. The rubble of history is mute testimony to this failure.

Societies, of course, must do more than merely survive. They must also grow--in their understanding of what it means to be a human community, in the range of opportunities they offer each member for full human development, and in their capacity to handle the new ethical problems wrought by technology and other social changes. In addition, they must learn to function as part of an increasingly complex world community, where global peace and justice demand ever increasing levels of cooperation. But whether the task is survival or development, any society ultimately depends for its success on the character of its citizens--on the extent to which a critical mass of its people hold, find their identity in, and act upon a shared moral vision.

Democratic societies have a special dependence on the virtue of their citizens. In the United States, for example, the Founding Fathers believed that universal schooling was needed, at least partly, because moral education was needed. Government by the people, where the people

themselves ensured a free and just society, required that
the people be good--possessed of at least a minimal understanding of and commitment to the moral foundations of
democracy. Those foundations included respect for law and
for the rights of others, voluntary participation in public
life, and concern for the common good. Loyalty to these
democratic values, Thomas Jefferson argued, must be in-
stilled at an early age.

Two centuries later, there are visible cracks in the
moral foundations of democracy. Ed Wynne, in Chapter 2
of this book, presents quantitative evidence that the conduct of United States youth, during the last 20 to 30 years,
is marked by two disturbing trends: (1) a rise in self-
destructive behavior (e.g., suicide, teen-age pregnancy,
and drug abuse), and (2) a rise in destructive behavior
involving others (e.g., juvenile crime and disorder in
schools). To these two trends, we would add two others,
equally troubling. The first is an attitude of "We're not
doing anything wrong." In a 1981 survey by the National
Organization to Prevent Shoplifting, for example, 50 percent
of the one hundred thousand youths aged 9-21 surveyed
said they had shoplifted, and most of those said they
would do it again. When a ninth-grade teacher of our ac-
quaintance asked how many had ever shoplifted, most
raised their hands. "Don't you think it's wrong to shoplift?" she asked. They answered, "We have a right to the
material things in life."

That answer points to a fourth disturbing change in
the moral values of the young, namely, a steadily growing
materialism. In 1970, according to the Cooperative Institutional Research Program at the University of California at
Los Angeles, 39 percent of U.S. college freshmen said that
"being very well off financially" was an important objective in going to college (Astin, The American Freshman,
1984). By 1984, that figure had risen sharply, to 71 percent. Meanwhile, less materialistic values had lost ground.
By 1984 only 44 percent of freshmen felt that "developing a
meaningful philosophy of life" was an important reason for
attending college, compared with 76 percent who thought so
in 1970.

Finally, behind this materialism may lie something
deeper still: a spreading privatism, a detachment from
community and commitment. That attitude, as Henry Johnson
argues in Chapter 3, strikes at the very heart of morality's
recognition of our interrelatedness and the claims we have

on each other. Privatism makes a virtue of selfishness.
It showed up in the findings of a recent book, When Dreams
and Heroes Died: A Portrait of Today's College Student
(1981), written by Arthur Levine for the Carnegie Council
on Policy Studies in Higher Education. On the basis of his
study of colleges and universities across the country,
Levine concluded that most of today's college students have
a "Titanic mentality." They think society is headed for
disaster, but they want to go first class. Their goal is
to make money, have status, and live well, not to better
the world as they find it.

BEYOND NATIONAL BORDERS

There is evidence, moreover, that no country has a
monopoly on these moral problems; they cut across national
borders. Here is a Canadian magazine (Donahue, 1984)
arguing the case for values education in the schools: 70
percent of Ontario's children, grades 7 through 13, use
alcohol; 33 percent of tenth-grade boys and 25 percent of
girls have had sexual intercourse, accompanied by rising
rates of teen-age pregnancy and abortion; suicide is the
second leading cause of death among teen-agers. Two
summers ago we joined philosophers, psychologists, and
educators in South America to share concerns and approaches to moral education. Here is what one woman,
head of a university department of education, had to say
about the state of moral affairs in her country:

> Moral values in my country are declining.
> It is a serious problem. First of all,
> more and more young people are living
> together without getting married so they
> can break up if they want to. Their
> children grow up without a secure situa-
> tion, and it has an effect. There is
> more crime among young people, and more
> dishonesty everywhere--in government, in
> business, among ordinary people. Part
> of the problem is people are spending
> more than they earn and need money to
> pay their debts. There is more material-
> ism--people are following a new life style.
> They think it will make them happy, but

it only makes them unhappy. And there
is more divorce, which never used to be
a problem.

CAUSES OF THE PROBLEM

How did we come to the present state of affairs?
In the United States, three social institutions have traditionally been responsible for shaping the character of the
young: the family, the church, and the school. However,
postwar United States, like many other nations, has seen
significant changes in all three of these institutions,
changes which in turn have had a major impact on their
teaching functions.

The Family

At a recent symposium on character development
sponsored by the American Educational Research Association,
the well-known sociologist James Coleman (1985) began his
comments with this statement: "I believe the causes of the
downward trends in youth character lie primarily outside
the school--in the changes that have taken place in the
American family."
Other observers echo that theme. John Agresto (1982),
a project director at the National Humanities Center in
North Carolina, writes of the erosion of family life and of
the family's function as moral educator, and traces that
erosion to values that have long been part of our culture:

> The same principles [that led to the de-
> cline of neighborhoods]--individualism,
> love of mobility and change, self-interest,
> self-fulfillment, and personal privacy--
> have weakened many of the bonds of the
> central moral teacher: the family. These
> principles, when pursued as the greatest
> of worldly aims, are antithetical to the
> persistence of vital family life. For ex-
> ample, it has become progressively harder
> for liberal countries, such as ours, to
> constrain divorce or insist that family
> life be peaceful and harmonious. . . .

> An emphasis on the principles of individ-
> ualism and private right hardly makes
> family ties "for better and for worse" a
> solid feature of our society (p. 156).

In the United States, one of two marriages now ends in divorce. Within the last decade, the number of single-parent households has doubled; more than one in five children now lives with only one parent. That one parent, typically the mother, frequently has a full-time job, plus all the household chores from preparing meals to getting the car fixed. She must struggle to find time for parental guidance and connecting with her children.

Even when there are two parents, family life must compete, as never before, with the demands of commitments outside the family. Two generations ago saw the father leave the home--often a farm or shop--to go to work. This generation has seen the mother leave the home. In 1970, 40 percent of married women worked outside the home; by 1980 it was 51 percent, and the projection is that by 1990 two of every three married women will be part of the work force (Smith, 1979). The last decade, moreover, has seen mothers of younger and younger children enter or return to the labor market (Hacker, 1982). What this means, quite simply, is that first the father and now the mother have less and less time to spend in face-to-face communication with their children.

There are still other changes: the trend toward smaller families, reducing the number of positive role models and support that brothers and sisters can provide; the fact that every year, one of five U.S. households moves, away from grandparents, away from long family acquaintances, and away from others who give children a sense of belonging and care enough to correct their behavior; the trend for parents increasingly to find their recreation apart from the family (Coleman, 1981); and, finally, diminished opportunities for children to contribute meaningfully to the work of the family, as they once could to the family farm or store.

There are certainly strengths in the modern family-- greater attention, for example, to the quality of interpersonal relationships in marriage, greater effort on the part of many parents to listen to children and to create relationships based on mutual rather than unilateral respect. And as a later essay in this book (Lickona, Chapter 10) makes clear, we are optimistic about the potential of families to contribute to children's moral development and help reverse the downward trends in youth character. But here we wish to note the very real changes in the family that threaten to undermine its crucial role in the moral education of the young.

The Church

The church not only speaks to our connection with our Maker, but is also a meaning maker. It addresses not only who we are, but what we ought to be and what we ought to do. By virtue of this concern, the church is directly involved in character development.

However, the exact place of religion in U.S. society is difficult to judge. We have often thought that if a visitor from outer space came to gather data on our society, landed in a motel and had only TV as a source of data, our extraterrestrial social scientist would have a very curious view of U.S. citizens, particularly concerning religion. The visitor would observe that the heroes of our TV shows have no apparent spiritual life. They are often caring, involved, and admirable people. But they belong to no church and seem totally untroubled by ultimate questions. In effect, our ideal citizens appear to live admirably without God.

Even the secular press has begun to note this phenomenon. Benjamin J. Stein (1985) observed recently in The Wall Street Journal that "on prime-time network television, there is virtually no appearance of religion at all." Stein wrote

> Whenever a problem requiring moral judgment appears--which is on almost every show--the response that comes is based on some intuitive knowledge of what is good and evil, the advice of a friend, a remembered counsel, or, more likely, the invisible hand of circumstance. When a cop goes bad and his partner must bring him in on "Hill Street Blues," there is no prayer, no ministerial consultation, no reference to scriptural precept. When a woman realizes she has sold her soul for

a car and a condo on any number of TV
movies, when a college student rethinks
his behavior toward women, none of their
analyses or actions has anything to do
with religious tenets of any recognizable
kind.
    With the exception of an occasional
attempt to put sex into the convent, such
as "Shattered Vows," religion and the appeal to religious values in decision-making
are simply invisible in prime-time television today (p. 5).

Does TV tell it like it is? Hardly. As Stein notes,
"In the gritty course of real existence, Americans spend
time and energy in the context of religious institutions
and religious precepts." Those precepts are often a major
factor guiding moral decisions.
    Fresh evidence of the role of religion in U.S. life
comes from a study carried out by Research and Forecasts,
Inc. (1981) at the request of the Connecticut Mutual Life
Insurance Co. The purpose of the study was to probe the
basic beliefs and core values of a diverse sampling of
Americans. In pursuit of that goal, the researchers conducted 2,018 hour-long interviews with 1,610 randomly
selected individuals. In addition, they sent an eight-
page questionnaire covering the same issues as the interviews to more than four thousand leaders in business, law,
education, government, the military, the media, religion
and science; 1,762 leaders responded.
    The researchers reported that they were quite sur-
prised by what they found. At the beginning of their report, "The Impact of Belief," they write: "In investigating
major aspects of American life . . . one factor that consistently and dramatically affects the values and behavior
of Americans is . . . the level of religious commitment"
(p. 6). The report goes on to say, "The impact of religious belief reaches far beyond the realms of politics, and
has penetrated virtually every dimension of American experience" (p. 6). The study found that

    Although less than half the public (44%)
    attend church frequently, three-quarters
    (74%) consider themselves to be religious.
    An equal number (73%) say they frequently

feel God loves them, and <u>nearly all</u> Americans (94%) say they experience this feeling
at least occasionally. Over half (57%)
the public report that they frequently engage in prayer (pp. 17-18).

Using a behavioral index of religious activities and
of the experience of religious feelings, the study also attempted to measure the depth of religious commitment. The
authors report that slightly more than one out of every
four U.S. residents can be termed "highly religious." The
report claims to have identified "a comprehensive and powerful group of Americans, approximately 45 million strong,
as intensely religious" and states further that such persons are "likely to vote often and to become highly involved
in their local communities" (p. 7).

Religion, then, is clearly a larger influence in
people's lives than one would gather from watching TV,
and that influence appears to be a force for participation
in public life. But there are other data that make the
picture more complicated. Wynne (Chapter 2) cites research showing a long-term decline in at least traditional
forms of religiosity among college students (though the
data do not go beyond the mid-1970s). In the 1970s,
while the general U.S. population rose by 11.5 percent,
the ranks of those professing membership in Christian or
Jewish congregations grew by only 4.1 percent (<u>U.S. News
& World Report</u>, April 4, 1983). The proportion of U.S.
residents attending religious services weekly dropped from
49 percent in 1955 to 41 percent in 1982. The proportion
agreeing that "religion is increasing its influence on American life" fell from 69 percent in 1957 to 38 percent in 1982. In
Canada, the United Church, the largest Protestant denomination there, finds Sunday School attendance barely a
third of what it was 20 years ago (Donahue, 1984).

Most observers, moreover, would agree that the
church's teaching authority has diminished significantly
from what it was two to three decades ago. The general
rebellion against established authority in the 1960s also
loosened the hold that religion had over the conscience of
young people. But in part, many believe, the church had
itself to blame for the loss of teaching influence. In the
1960s and 1970s, critics charge, the church stopped talking
about duty, devotion, and doctrine, and joined the cultural chorus preaching love, growth, and fulfillment. Re-

ligious education classes that once taught the catechism command to "know, love, and serve God," became indistinguishable from values clarification—a new movement which sought to have children look inward to themselves for value. Asked about her goals, one Sunday School teacher said, "We are teaching the children to grow, to become whole persons, to question, to choose values" (Kilpatrick, 1983, p. 24). This wholesale psychologizing of religion prompted one well-known psychiatrist (Menninger, 1973) to write a book entitled <u>Whatever Became of Sin?</u>

There is at least one more question one must ask in assessing the role of religion in contemporary moral life. If, as some studies show, religion is alive and well in today's society, then why is there a rising tide of materialism and privatism? The call of religion is to spiritual values and community, not to storing up treasures and retreating from commitments. It may be that we have always wanted God and a private prosperity at the same time. But any religion worth the name must put those values in tension.

Currently, almost 60 percent of U.S. citizens attend church or synagogue at least once a month (Stein, 1985). Whatever its past failures or present weaknesses, religion, like the family, is an enduring institution. As such, it has important potential for laying the foundations of our children's character development. Indeed, as several chapters in this book suggest, religion, with an eye to the ultimate, provides special reasons and resources for leading the moral life.

The School

By virtue of the fact that they hold our children for so much time during their formative years, schools have—or ought to have—a strong effect on the characters of the young. Indeed, schools in this country and around the world have traditionally been seen as institutions where the young received both cognitive <u>and</u> moral training. Schools have been the place where children were taught important lessons of good citizenship and membership in community. In the United States, adults have looked to the schools to transmit certain social values the nation both needs and prizes, values such as fair play, concern for excellence, respect for law and property, willingness to work hard, the ability to delay gratification, and a sense of service. In the nineteenth century and early part of this century, the school sought to instill these values in every way it could: through its rules and discipline, through the teacher's good example, and through its textbooks and curriculum. When children practiced their reading, for example, they typically did so through McGuffey Reader tales of heroism and virtue, like the one about "honest Charles," who was trusted (because he was known to be honest) to guard a salesman's oranges and who courageously repulsed "Jack Pilfer," the thieving bully who tried to steal them (Minnich, 1936).

With time, however, the moral consensus supporting this unabashed, old-fashioned character education began to break up. It did so under the hammer blows of several forces: Darwinism, which led people to see everything, including morality, as being in flux rather than fixed and certain; scientific empiricism, which, as in the case of the famous Hartshorne and May study (1928), seemed to show that moral behavior was highly variable, governed by external circumstance rather than by any consistent internal state that one could call "character"; and logical positivism, which permeated the universities and held that there were no objective moral truths—hence morality was a matter for personal choice rather than public transmission. The moral life came to be seen as a form of private life. In this climate, public schools retreated from their function as moral educators. Similarly, teacher education became increasingly technical, summoning teachers-to-be not to shape the values of tomorrow's citizens and leaders but only to transmit, with efficiency, a body of information and skills (Ryan, Chapter 14).

In the late 1960s and early 1970s, as both private and public morality seemed to be breaking down (as shown by a wave of scandals in all walks of life and increasing violence throughout society), there was renewed interest in the school's role as moral educator. The 1975 Gallup Poll turned up strong public support: fully 84 percent of parents of school-age children agreed with the statement that schools "should provide instruction that would deal with morals and moral behavior." Such general support, however, still left schools facing hard questions: What kind of moral instruction should they provide? Whose values should be taught, and how?

In the perceived absence of agreement about what moral content should be taught, the new forms of moral education focused on process: how to clarify one's values (values clarification), how to reason with greater complexity about moral conflicts (moral dilemma discussions), and how to make systematic moral decisions (values analysis). Each of these approaches made its own contribution to the revival or advancement of moral education, contributions which are reflected in this volume. But process without content didn't meet the whole need. Schools were still shying away from the crucial question of what students ought to value. Moreover, much of the new moral education, because it avoided the question of what are worthwhile human values, frequently fostered moral relativism. Teachers commonly began moral discussions with the statement, "There is no right or wrong answer" and ended with, "Make your own decision." Morality seemed to be a matter of personal opinion.

Ironically, at the same time schools were trying to stay officially value-neutral in the curriculum, they began, in their institutional functioning, to reflect and reinforce a substantive value shift in the wider culture. That shift is the growing emphasis on individual rights over and against civic responsibilities. Writing in Daedalus, Gerald Grant (1981) reports how this shift has not been lost on the young. A new student entering the Boston public schools would, Grant writes, "be handed 'the Book,' a 25-page pamphlet detailing student rights, with less than half a page on student responsibilities" (p. 141). He then goes on to describe how the pamphlet details an elaborate and exhausting process that teachers must go through to discipline a child and how many "protections" are built into the system for the student. Grant reports an incident he personally encountered while doing his study:

> A female teacher was still shaking as she told us about a group of students who had verbally assaulted her and made sexually degrading comments about her in the hall. When we asked why she did not report them, she responded, "Well, it wouldn't have done any good." "Why not?" we pressed. "I didn't have any witnesses," she replied (p. 141).

In schools that function like this, the traditional moral
authority of the teacher is reduced to a narrow, legalistic
authority. At best, students develop a strong sense of
their rights and a weak sense of their obligations; at
worst, they learn they can behave irresponsibly with im-
punity.

With one clear exception (Developing Character . . .,
1984), the recent critiques of U.S. education say little or
nothing about the schools' failures or promise as moral
educators of the young. That omission is itself part of
the problem. But there is every reason to believe that
the public still wants schools to help children become honest, decent, caring persons who are capable of leading
good lives in a troubled world. Indeed, in a fragile and
fragmented society, schools take on increasing importance.
Not every child has a stable and supportive home life; not
every child goes to church; but every child does go to
school. As this volume attests, we believe there is much
schools must and can still do, even in our intensely pluralistic age, to elevate the character of our children and our
nation.

In addition to the home, the church, and the school,
there are two other forces in the socialization of the young
that bear at least brief mention here. One is new; the
other is old, but has taken on new strength in recent
decades. These forces are television and the peer group.

Television

Two later chapters (Johnson, Sullivan) analyze in
depth the growing impact of the mass media as moral educator. Of all the mass media, television looms the largest.
The typical U.S. child watches TV for more than 30 hours
a week--more time than he or she spends with his or her
parents, playing with peers, attending school, or reading
books (Moody, 1980).

Neil Postman, New York University professor of communication arts, calls television "the first curriculum" because the typical high school graduate has spent more time
watching TV (fifteen to sixteen thousand hours) than going
to school (no more than thirteen thousand hours). Postman
reports that "television appears to shorten the attention
span of the young as well as eroding, to a considerable
extent, their linguistic powers and their ability to handle

mathematical symbolism. It also causes them to be increasingly impatient with deferred gratification" (U.S. News &
World Report, 1981, p. 43). Similarly, the National Institute of Mental Health report, Television and Behavior (1982),
surveying some twenty-five hundred studies during the
prior decade, documents a variety of negative effects of
television on children's cognitive and social-moral functioning. Postman also calls our attention to the fact that
"television is opening up all of society's secrets and
taboos, thus eroding the dividing line between childhood
and adulthood" (U.S. News & World Report, 1981, p. 43).
Allowing children full access to the seamier side of adult
life, Postman argues, flies smack in the face of what was
until recently part of our civilization's wisdom: that
childhood is a period of relative innocence, to be protected
and nurtured, a period necessary for children's healthy
development. The loss of that period was brought home to
us personally in a recent conversation with a kindergarten
teacher. Her five year olds, she said, now play "Guiding
Light" in the housekeeping corner. A typical play session
will begin with the children saying things like, "You're
pregnant by him," "You run away with her," and "You get
shot."

Clearly, television poses two serious threats to our
children's character development: first, it exposes them
to all manner of shoddy moral content (violence, law breaking, casual sex, infidelity, put-downs as humor, the idea
that things make you happy), which potentially affects
their perception of what is normal and appropriate human
behavior; and second, it further reduces, almost to the
disappearing point, the family talks, games, festivities,
and arguments through which children's socialization occurs and their values are formed.

The Peer Group

Young people have always gravitated to age-alike
groups. And peers have always offered the young important opportunities for moral growth: opportunities to interact on an equal footing, take the perspective of others,
face and resolve conflict, be part of a team, and experience the special bonds and challenges of friendship. But
in the past, adults were more likely to mediate peer influence: to keep track of whom kids were playing with and

what they were doing, to discuss values or behaviors they were picking up from playmates that didn't square with family values, to intervene to help solve a problem when an adult's help was needed, to talk with teens about the dangers of running with the wrong crowd, and to put restrictions (e.g., "No unsupervised parties") on a youngster's freedom when that seemed necessary.

As that kind of parental mediation declined for many children, a new kind of peer group influence arose: stronger than ever before and less tempered by adult values such as responsibility, prudence, and self-control. Schools also had an unwitting hand in the "liberation" of the peer group by reducing demands on students' time outside of school. A Nation at Risk (1983), for example, reported that U.S. high school students, on the average, spend only 4.5 hours a week on homework. Many teen-agers use their after-school freedom to work; an ABC television special, "Save Our Children, Save Our Schools" (1984), reported that 67 percent of U.S. high school students now hold jobs. Jobs have meant money in the hands of teen-agers, who now support, almost by themselves, whole industries. In this context, a distinctive youth culture has emerged with its own music, magazines, clothing styles, diversions, and values. Those values are often orthogonal to the values of deferred gratification, self-discipline, and service to others that have been part of the nation's tradition--and part of the moral heritage we want to pass on to our children.

One could argue that the weakening of traditional socializing institutions and the rise of new forces such as the media and peer culture are producing a new kind of character in the young. The data on increasing youth crime and suicide suggest the impact of the new influences and altered institutions. There is other evidence, however, that adults are still powerful figures in the lives of most youth. The February 6, 1984 New York Times reported the results of a Columbia University research project which studied, over an eight-year period, 300 adolescents of all social class levels in urban, suburban, and rural settings. The principal finding, which held up across five different states, was that teen-agers are more like their parents in their attitudes and values than they are like their peers (Collins, 1984). By itself, of course, that finding can be good news or bad news, depending on whether the values parents hold are ones worth emulating. But at the very least, this study offers hope. Despite all the competing influences, adults can still have a formative influence on the character of the young.

The present volume is written in the spirit of that hope. Our task has been to address three questions: How can schools (both public and private), the family, the community, the church, higher education, and even the mass media, contribute to the moral growth of the young? How can we educate so as to develop "full moral agency," that is, the kind of character that can translate moral knowledge and feeling into effective moral action? What obstacles confront us as we undertake such an enterprise?

The editors of a recent book, <u>Morality, Moral Behavior, and Moral Development</u> (Kurtines and Gewirtz, 1984), state that the current pluralism of psychological models of moral functioning reflects the ethical pluralism of the larger culture. It may no longer be possible, they suggest, to construct the kind of theoretical synthesis that inspires the support of a range of scholars. We were more optimistic when we undertook the present volume but soon found ourselves struggling with pluralism in our own ranks. We represent, for example, a variety of religious traditions. Ideologically, we run the gamut from neoconservative to neo-Marxist. Educationally, we differ on whether the ideal school looks more like a participatory democracy, with students helping to decide rules and policies, or more like the traditional school arrangement where adults make the rules and delegate limited, carefully supervised authority roles to students (such as tutor, monitor, or team captain). Psychologically, most of us subscribe to the general notion of "moral development"--the idea of a developmental progression, with later levels being more mature than earlier ones--but this, too, is challenged. Wynne (Chapter 4) thinks that "formation" is a more accurate metaphor than "development," and Beck (Chapter 8) rejects the notion of vertical development, arguing that adolescents are "as good at morals" as adults.

These theoretical differences underlie the wide range of character development strategies (teacher modeling, cooperative learning, direct moral instruction, moral discussion and debate, role playing, research on moral issues, teaching empathy through literature, study of the classics, self-esteem-building activities, reflective discussion of values such as friendship, work, health, and religion, "problem posing" the media, class meetings, cross-age tutoring, school assemblies, the school-wide just community, and community service and guided reflection on its meaning) proposed and illustrated in the various chapters. Beneath all this diversity, however, is a set of shared assumptions. These assumptions, we think, are the unifying threads that bind the different chapters into a whole and differentiate that whole from other approaches to moral education. These shared assumptions are:

1. Moral values are not relative, in the sense of being purely subjective or arbitrary; rather they are objectively grounded in human nature and experience. For example: To be fair, honest, and caring in our relations with others is to act in ways that are consistent with, and enhancing of, our essential human dignity. To be unjust, deceitful, and cruel is to act in ways that violate our essential human dignity. Philosophers speak of fundamental values such as justice, honesty, and love as being inherently and objectively good because they flow from the "constitutive human good"--that which constitutes or defines our very humanity. These values are what make us human. When we are faithful to them, we are faithful to our human nature--to what enables us to live and grow as individuals and communities.

2. Moral action is not due simply to rational or cognitive factors, but springs from moral personality, which includes affective qualities as well as intellectual processes.

3. Religion, defined as a stance bearing on ultimacy (What makes life worth living? What is our ultimate purpose and destiny?), is rooted in our human nature, and the working out of a religious understanding provides a foundation and support structure for moral development.

4. Current models of moral development and values education are not comprehensive enough to capture the full complexity of human character.

5. An adequate approach to moral education or character development must build on a comprehensive, integrative view of the moral agent, a view which does justice to the multidimensionality (thought, feeling, action) of the moral agent and its interactions with the moral environment; moreover, character development programs must include moral content (What values are worth holding?) as well as process (How should we reason about moral problems?) and be grounded in a nonrelativistic stance toward the human good.

6. The business of the moral life, to borrow from ethicist Daniel Callahan (1982), is to hold competing values in balance. We are, in our own society and in much of the Western world, only beginning to recognize and recover from an _imbalance_ created by a surge of "personalism" during the previous two decades. Philosophers (e.g., McLean, 1983) describe personalism as an ethos which gave rise to a "new subjectivity," a new respect and concern for the individual person.

Existentialism, through both literature and philosophy, contributed to this ethos by portraying persons as creating themselves through their freely chosen actions. From this new personalism came many good things: the civil rights movement with its concern for the freedom and dignity of all persons, a new respect for the child as a person, a heightened valuing of personal conscience (reflected in religion and theology), and a deeper appreciation of the idea of human development and the importance of enabling each person to develop his or her full potential (reflected by the growth of developmental psychology and the human potential movement).

But from this same personalistic ethos came a host of other, less positive changes: hostility to authority and rules, the notion that morality is entirely subjective, a "look out for Number one" individualism, and a general weakening of personal and social commitments. Prior to personalism, McLean (1983) observes, people were likely to view themselves as part of something that defined them—a member of a family, a son of the church, a citizen of their country—part of a community, an ongoing tradition that limited freedom (because it carried obligations) but supplied roots and identity and social purpose. When personal freedom became the reigning value, we experienced ourselves as able to choose our identity, our life-style, our values, our destiny—and saw any constraining influence as an intolerable restriction of our rights and individuality.

Now the challenge facing many societies is to construct a new balance: to reintegrate the person into community, to restore responsibility to freedom, and to recruit moral choice in the service of social values and goals. The effort to create a new moral balance shows up in all sorts of ways: less permissive child rearing, greater discipline in the schools, restoration of a core curriculum in our universities (part of an effort to rebuild a common culture), and a recovery of the place of traditional values and tested wisdom in the moral life. Part of the task of reconstruction is to ensure that the new trends are not reactionary but integrative: combining the deepened appreciation of freedom and individuality that is the positive legacy of personalism with an understanding of how to exercise freedom so as to enhance rather than undermine moral growth and community.

AN INTEGRATIVE VIEW OF THE MORAL AGENT

The chapters in this volume share, in addition to the above assumptions, an "integrative view" of the person as moral agent. This view or model (see Figure 1.1) holds, first of all, that human character involves the interplay of three components: knowing, affect, and action. Let us consider each of these in turn.

Knowing

Moral knowing begins with learning moral content: those values which constitute the moral heritage passed on from one generation to the next. Each new generation and each individual may alter or add to that heritage, but the heritage provides a foundation. In our own culture, that foundation typically includes values such as cooperation, courtesy, courage, fairness, honesty, loyalty, responsibility, religion, forgiveness, helpfulness, love, work, learning, democracy, freedom, equality, and respect (including respect for self, others, animals, property, and the environment). "Knowing" a value also means knowing what behavior it requires in concrete situations. What does "love" mean in terms of how you treat your little brother or sister? What does "respect" tell you to do when someone passes on information that is damaging to another person's reputation? What does it mean to be "helpful" when there's a new kid in your class who doesn't know his or her way around and doesn't have any friends?

Moral knowing includes moral reasoning. Reasoning asks, What are worthwhile values, ones that are for our good and the good of our fellows? Why are some values and their derivative actions good, and others bad? Why

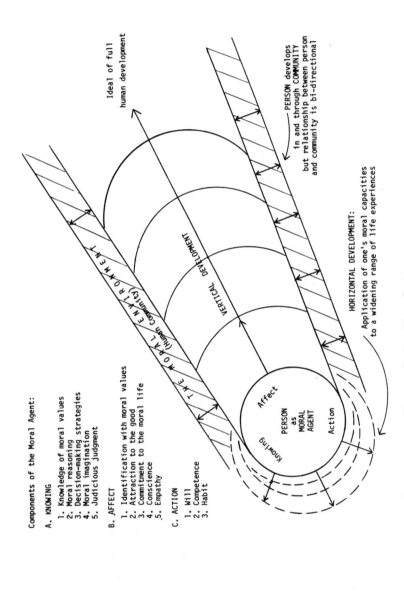

Components of the Moral Agent:

A. KNOWING

1. Knowledge of moral values
2. Moral reasoning
3. Decision-making strategies
4. Moral imagination
5. Judicious judgment

B. AFFECT

1. Identification with moral values
2. Attraction to the good
3. Commitment to the moral life
4. Conscience
5. Empathy

C. ACTION

1. Will
2. Competence
3. Habit

THE MORAL ENVIRONMENT (human community)

Ideal of full human development

VERTICAL DEVELOPMENT

HORIZONTAL DEVELOPMENT:
Application of one's moral capacities to a widening range of life experiences

PERSON develops in and through COMMUNITY but relationship between person and community is bi-directional

Affect

Knowing   PERSON as MORAL AGENT   Action

Figure 1.1   An Integrative View of the Moral Agent

is it important to keep a promise? Help around the house?
Share what you have with those in need? Why is it wrong
to cheat on a test? Shoplift from a store? Lie to your
parents? Moral reasoning also seeks to formulate principles (e.g., the Golden Rule, "Respect the rights and worth
of all persons") that help us to establish a hierarchy of
values and decide what to do when values conflict. What
principle should guide the eleven-year-old (Lickona, Chapter 7) whose friends take a package from someone's mailbox and then slough off the objection that "that's stealing"? What did loyalty and justice require of a German
citizen under the Third Reich? Of a U.S. soldier ordered
to shoot Vietnamese civilians at My Lai? What principles
should have guided Truman when he faced the decision of
whether to drop the atomic bomb on Hiroshima?

Moral knowing also includes cognitive strategies for
making decisions in a systematic way. Your best friend
in high school is pregnant and considering an abortion,
unbeknownst to her parents. What should you do? What
are your alternatives? The likely consequences of each
alternative? The moral values or principles involved?
What course of action would most likely maximize the good
consequences, minimize the bad, and still be faithful to
the important moral values or principles at stake?

Moral knowing, especially in complex matters, also
means becoming informed: trying to find out what's true
before you decide what's right. Consider, for example,
the proposal that the United States attempt to build an
outer-space "Star Wars" defense against the possibility of
Soviet attack by intercontinental ballistic missiles. Would
such a defense really work? What percentage of ICBMs
would it be able to intercept in an attack where the
missiles might number in the thousands? Does history tell
us anything about how the Russians would be likely to
respond to such a defensive initiative? Would they see it
as aggressive, putting the United States in the position of
being able to launch a successful first strike? Would they
be likely to react with an offensive buildup of missiles
that can be launched within the atmosphere (and thus out
of the range of the space shield)? Or are the Russians,
as some have charged, already moving to build a space
shield of their own? Clearly, neither ordinary citizens
nor experts can answer such questions with certainty.
But equally clearly, no moral judgment about how to proceed can be made without first trying to establish some
kind of an information base.

Moral knowing also depends, in a very important way, on moral imagination. Making a good moral decision—whether about how to help a pregnant teen-ager or how to prevent a nuclear war—requires that we project ourselves imaginatively into the situation, into the roles of the parties affected. Choosing the best course of action is only partly a matter of having the facts; it is also a matter of imagining what consequences might occur from this or that decision, and how it would be actually to experience those consequences. "Imagination," writes Elizabeth Simpson (1976), "invests meaning and saliency in persons and events" (p. 167). In Shaw's St. Joan, Simpson observes, "an elderly priest blames the repetition of evil in generation after generation on the failure of imagination; he himself had to actually see the young girl burned to realize the enormity of the act. He asks, 'Must then a Christ perish in torment in every age to save those that have no imagination?'" (Simpson, 1976, p. 167).

Finally, there is the quality of good judgment—what Aristotle called "practical wisdom"—that is indispensable to mature moral knowing. Philosopher Jon Moline (1982), proposing good judgment as a central goal of character education, argues, "If our students learn to be judicious or wise, it is likely that in the long run they will arrive at right answers" when they face hard moral problems (p. 197). We know, Moline says, what the qualities of wise judgment are: hearing both sides; avoiding hasty decisions whenever possible; seeking advice in decision making; considering how others have treated equivalent problems; trying to moderate the pressures of self-interest; giving special weight to the opinions of more experienced persons. As educators, Moline says, "We can describe such judicious traits to students, point out role models who have displayed them, and ask them to act in an equivalent fashion" (p. 198). We can also have young people practice being judicious when they make personal and group decisions. But however we do it, we should make the cultivation of a judicious style of judgment a basic objective of moral education.

Knowing moral values and what they require of us, reasoning about why such values are important and good (and how they differ from values which are not good), formulating moral principles to handle value conflict, systematic decision making, moral imagination, judicious judgment—these are the elements we see as constituting moral knowing. All must have our attention if we wish to educate for the full development of the cognitive side of moral agency.

Affect

Moral affect is broadly defined to include the whole range of factors, often neglected in discussions of moral education, that constitute the affective side of our morality. These affective factors are usually linked in some say to cognition but clearly go beyond it.

How deeply do we hold the values we say we hold? Do they lie at the center--or the edge--of our consciousness and personality? A half-century ago, McDougall (1936) argued that moral ideals are powerless unless they are rooted in a moral self. Elaborating on that idea, Blasi (1984) observes that for many people, being a just or honest or caring person is not part of the "essential self" that comprises their identity; hence those values are not powerful regulators of their behavior. But if, on the other hand, I do experience justice, honesty, or compassion as essential to my identity, then that identity becomes a strong motive for moral action consistent with those values. To act otherwise would be to violate my sense of who I am.

Do we love the good? In education for virtue, Kilpatrick (1983) points out, "The heart is trained as well as the mind, so that the virtuous person learns not only to distinguish between good and evil but to love the one and hate the other" (p. 112). That is why wise teachers have always looked to literature as a way to teach a sense of right and wrong. We can talk to children in abstract terms about deceit and hatred and loyalty and love, but when they come face to face with those qualities enfleshed in unforgettable characters, like the Wicked White Witch and the great and gentle Aslan in C. S. Lewis's Chronicles of Narnia (1970), they feel repelled by the evil and drawn, irresistibly, to the good.

How committed are we to living the moral life? Are we willing to do the right when it carries a cost? Does our conscience bother us (and how much?) when we betray a principle or fall short of an ideal? Do we have the capacity to feel the kind of constructive guilt that impels us to make amends and strive to do better? Do we have the ability to enter into another's suffering, the willingness to make ourselves vulnerable to another's pain?

Moral identity, attraction to the good, commitment, conscience, empathy--all these are part of the affective side of our moral selves. One could reasonably argue that these factors, taken together, constitute the larger part of our individual moral personalities. These affective factors, we submit, also constitute the essential bridge between moral knowing and moral action. Their presence or absence explains why some people practice their moral principles and others do not. Hence moral education which is merely intellectual--which touches the mind but not the heart--misses a core component of character.

Action

Moral action is the component of moral agency which brings knowing and affect to fruition. Moral action has three components: will, competence, and habit.

Will is what mobilizes our moral energy--the energy both to think through a problem and weigh choices and to act once the choice is clear. Will is what enables us to overcome--press through--inertia, anxiety, pride, or self-interest, to do what we know and feel is right.

Competence is also crucial. Good will alone will not assure effective moral action. To solve a conflict fairly, for example, we need skills of listening, communicating our view, and finding a middle ground. To aid a person in distress, we need to be able to conceive and execute a plan of action. Staub (1979), for example, found that children who had role played a series of situations in which one child helped another were subsequently more likely than children without such experience to investigate a distress cry from another room. Similarly, Huston and Korte (1976) report that "people who are capable of effective intervention and who feel competent to deal with emergencies are more likely than others to help" (p. 281). These findings suggest that moral competence may benefit from a general feeling of effectiveness as well as specific skills.

Finally, moral action, in many situations, also benefits from habit. Aristotle believed that morally good actions arise from a steady state of character, a deeply rooted disposition to respond to situations in certain ways. People who have good character, as Bennett (1980) points out, "act truthfully, loyally, bravely, kindly, fairly without being much tempted by the opposite course" (p. 130). Often they do not even think consciously about "the right choice." They are good by force of habit.

Habit begins in freedom, of course--with consciously made decisions to do the kind, courteous, or fair deed. An important part of our moral training, then, is developing good habits through repeated choices, habits that will serve us well not only when the going is easy but also when we are pressured, tired, or tempted. To recognize the role of habit in the moral life is to acknowledge what Aristotle argued: that virtue must be practiced, not merely known. The implication of that principle is clear: Character education, wherever it occurs, must provide many and varied opportunities for young people to act--to live out their developing values and ideals, and to reflect on what they value in light of their lived moral experience.

The three components of moral agency--knowing, affect, and action--obviously do not always work together. We may think that we should give more money to charity or more time to our children, but not care enough to do so; we may feel we have wronged a colleague or subordinate but be too proud to apologize; we may be distressed about a deteriorating situation in our marriage but lack the imagination or will to effect an improvement. But in any situation, full moral agency involves a unity of knowing (whether conscious or not), affect, and action.

AN EXAMPLE OF FULL MORAL AGENCY

As a brief example of fully functioning moral agency, we would offer an Associated Press story that appeared last winter on the front pages of many U.S. newspapers. The article reported an incident that happened on a downtown street corner in St. Paul, Minnesota, during near-zero weather. As a city bus stopped at the corner to pick up passengers, a middle-aged woman got on. Despite the bitter cold, she wore only a thin, tattered coat, no shoes, and socks that were nearly worn through. As she put her coins in the meter, a 14 year old boy got up from his seat, walked to the front of the bus, and handed the woman his shoes. "Here, lady," he said, "you need these more than I do." According to the bus driver who phoned in the incident, the woman accepted the shoes, and began to cry.

A simple act of human kindness, one person responding to another's need. And yet contained in that act, we
believe, are all three components of moral agency. This
young man saw a human need and made a judgment that
he should respond. Underlying that judgment, it seems
safe to say, was the value of helping, and moral imagination enough to appreciate what it must have felt like to
be out in a cold wave without warm clothing or shoes. It
seems equally clear that the boy was touched by the
woman's condition and felt impelled to act--affective responses that suggest a moral personality in which caring
lies at the core. Finally, this 14 year old took action.
Acting in this situation didn't require any special skill
but surely sprang from the virtue of helping, from a habit
of responding to others' needs. One can imagine that
there were many people on the bus who saw the woman's
need and even felt compassion for her, but lacking a
strong disposition to act (at least in this public situation),
they failed to take the initiative to help.

THE DEVELOPMENT OF THE MORAL AGENT

The fact that a 14 year old boy helped the woman
on the bus while many adults did not challenges facile
generalizations about "moral development." One could
offer other examples of how the moral responses of children often seem more direct and honest, more immediately
empathic, and less inhibited by social roles than the
moral responses of their elders.

Acknowledging that, we would nonetheless assert
that human persons, at least under favorable conditions,
do on the whole develop--toward a greater maturity, a
fuller realization of their humanity. It is evident that
people can and do develop physically, intellectually, socially, and spiritually. Our model holds that they develop
morally, too. (Even Beck, who in Chapter 8 challenges
conventional assumptions about development, states that
development occurs within the different periods of life.)
Moral development has been variously described by Piaget
(1932), Erikson (1961), Kohlberg (1981, 1984), Damon
(1977), Selman (1980), Gilligan (1982), Perry (1970), and
Knowles (in press). Some of these accounts have focused
on changes in the structure of moral knowing; others have
addressed affective or behavioral aspects of morality, such

as caring, identity, virtue, and commitment. Considered
together, these various accounts offer persuasive evidence
that people do in fact grow morally: toward greater ability to take and coordinate social perspectives, to balance
the needs of self and others, to imagine fully the situation
of others, to distinguish values which advance the human
good from those that do not, to construct moral principles,
to make moral decisions that are based on principle rather
than self-interest or social pressure, to judge judiciously,
to make and sustain commitments, to deal with moral ambiguity and uncertainty, to be aware of one's own moral
shortcomings, and to function in an integrated way that
seeks to bring conduct under the consistent dominion of
one's moral ideals.

All of this we might call "vertical development"--
the term which developmentalists use to describe growth
toward more differentiated, more integrated, more comprehensive ways of understanding and relating to the world.
In Kohlberg's (1984) scheme, for example, vertical development proceeds from preconventional to conventional to
postconventional or principled morality. But our model
asserts that there is another kind of development which is
at least as important as vertical development, and that is
horizontal development.

Horizontal development is the extension or application of a person's most mature capacities over a wider and
wider range of life situations. When horizontal development
is weak, a child may say in a moral discussion that "two
wrongs don't make a right" but then practice eye-for-an-
eye vengeance on the playground. An adult may rail
against dishonesty and corruption among politicians but
use a different standard when filling out his own income
tax. When horizontal development is weak, we may have a
moral capacity--moral reasoning, for example--but seldom
use it. It has been said that the greatest moral failure
in any society is not that people ask moral questions and
reach wrong conclusions but that they do not ask moral
questions. Moral education for horizontal development
seeks to develop persons who see the world through a
moral lens, persons for whom it is second nature to stop
and think, "Is this right?"

If we take the idea of vertical development seriously, we will provide educational experiences of increasing
variety and complexity, roles and responsibilities that
meet young people at the cutting edge of their development

and challenge them further. Elementary school students, for example, could be challenged by social roles, such as helping a classmate with his math, tutoring a child from a younger grade, leading a class meeting on how to reduce put-downs, or serving on a student council to prevent school vandalism. If we take the idea of horizontal development seriously, our commitment to fostering character will be wide as well as deep. In a school it would show up across the board: in the curriculum (in how many subjects do ethical questions get raised?); in instructional methods (do students work together as well as alone? do they reason and discuss as well as listen?); in classroom and school management (do students share responsibility for creating a good learning environment and solving problems that arise?); and in school relations at all levels (is there a whole-school climate of fairness and cooperation?).

Finally, our model of the moral agent says what we take to be obvious: that character develops in and through human community. We grow through membership. Roles to play, perspectives to consider, conflicts to resolve, commitments to fulfill, relationships to care about, responsibilities to juggle--these are the social matrix in which we live and have our moral being. Moreover, the relationship between the individual and community is best conceived not as one-directional (with the social environment shaping the person) but bidirectional: interactive, dynamic, one influencing the other. Translated into character education, this emphasis on community means that the family, the school, the church, the university must be human communities--interactive, participatory, making demands, providing support, challenging and helping youth to work together, think together, and take the risk and responsibility of relationships. This kind of participation in community provides obvious opportunities for intellectual growth, but it provides something deeper, too. When we interact with others in positive ways, we become attached to them, learn to value them--and eventually all people--as persons of worth and dignity, and come to know and feel from within our essential interdependence and responsibility for each other.

The chapters that follow vary in the attention they give to the different aspects of the moral agent, but all share the general model just described. Chapters are grouped in four sections. Part 1 of the book continues the context setting we have begun here. Wynne (Chapter 2)

presents long-term empirical evidence of downward trends
in youth character; Johnson (Chapter 3) tells us that if we
wish to form character, we must analyze and reckon with
the values of a relativistic and intensely pluralistic culture which will be the backdrop for whatever efforts we
undertake.

Part II, on the school, offers three views of how
public schools can best realize their potential as agents
of character development. Wynne (Chapter 4) summons
schools to avoid a focus on narrow cognitive learning and
individualistic concerns and to pursue instead "a vital
collective life." Prakash (Chapter 5) encourages communities and their public schools to persist in the struggle to
find genuine moral consensus in the midst of pluralism and
to provide a model to students of how to preserve mutual
respect while addressing differences. Power (Chapter 6)
proposes the democratic "just community" as a workable
way to generate moral consensus and felt community within
the high school and to overcome the privatism fostered by
big-school bureaucracy.

Part III centers on the classroom. Lickona (Chapter 7) describes an approach, scaled to the world of the
elementary schoolchild, that combines community building,
cooperative learning, moral reflection, and participatory
decision making. Beck (Chapter 8) proposes a junior high
school pedagogy which is "open but not neutral"--seeking
to explore values (concern for the needs of self, friendship, family, school) in a "joint inquiry" with students
while avoiding the fallacy that any judgment is as good
as any other. Starratt (Chapter 9) illustrates ten teaching principles, including the call to recognize and develop
our talents as "gifts for the community," principles which
he finds present in the "intuitive practice" of effective
moral educators in the high school classroom.

Part IV looks beyond the school. Lickona (Chapter
10) reminds us that morality begins at home, in the life
of the family, and describes what parents can do to capi-
talize on the special opportunities they have to develop
children's character. Hennessy (Chapter 11), while affirming the value of secular moral education in the public
school, argues that religious perspectives offer a deeper
foundation because they "deal with the deeper aspects of
our nature, our quest for the transcendental, for the will
of God." Sullivan (Chapter 12) calls attention to the rise
of television as a "moral miseducator," which feeds the

young "the myths of a commodity culture"; to combat its pervasive influence, he says, we must teach people to critique actively, not passively consume, media images, and values. Nicgorski (Chapter 13) challenges colleges and universities to return to their task of fostering ethical vision among their students, including those who will lead society and shape its moral quality. Ryan (Chapter 14) addresses a particular and crucial task of the college: the preparation of teachers who themselves model good character and have the commitment and skills to foster it in the young. Finally, in the epilogue, Thomas brings the pragmatic eye of an educational administrator of long experience to our collective analysis and prescriptions.

Emile Durkheim (1961), the great French sociologist, wrote in the earlier part of this century words that still speak to our condition:

> Society must have before it an ideal to-
> ward which it reaches. It must have
> some good to achieve, an original contri-
> bution to bring to . . . mankind. When
> individual activity does not know where
> to take hold, it turns against itself.
> When the moral forces of society remain
> unemployed, when they are not engaged
> in some work to accomplish, they deviate
> from their moral sense and are used up
> in a morbid and harmful manner (pp.
> 12-14).

Whether the moral forces of society are engaged in constructive work or turned toward destructive ends, we submit, is not a matter of chance. We can influence the character of society by influencing the character of the young. In our own age, widespread character education—both inside and outside of school—is not, to paraphrase Chesterton, an idea that has been tried and found wanting but one which has not been truly tried. The time has come to take up the challenge.

REFERENCES

Agresto, J. The American founders and the character of citizens. In E. Wynne (Ed.), Character policy: An emerging issue. Washington, D.C.: University Press of America, 1982, pp. 154-57.

Astin, A. W. The American freshman: National norms for
    fall 1984. Los Angeles: University of California,
    Higher Education Research Institute, 1984.

Bennett, W. J. The teacher, the curriculum, and values
    education development. In M. L. McBee (Ed.), New
    directions for higher education: Rethinking college
    responsibilities for values. San Francisco: Jossey-
    Bass, 1980, pp. 27–34.

Blasi, A. Moral identity: Its role in moral functioning.
    In W. Kurtines & J. Gewirtz (Eds.), Morality, moral
    behavior, and moral development. New York: Wiley,
    1984, pp. 128–39.

Callahan, D. Tradition and the moral life. The Hastings
    Center Report, December 1982, pp. 23–30.

Coleman, J. How do the young become adults?" In S. Elam
    (Ed.), Cream of the Kappan. Bloomington, Ind.:
    Phi Delta Kappa, 1981.

Coleman, J. Reflections on developing character. Unpub-
    lished remarks at the symposium on Developing Char-
    acter, annual conference of the American Educational
    Research Association, Chicago, April 1985.

Collins, G. Study says teenager adopt adult values. New
    York Times, February 6, 1984, p. B7.

Damon, W. The social world of the child. San Francisco:
    Jossey-Bass, 1977.

Donahue, P. The case for values education. Hamilton
    This Month, December 1984, pp. 21–24, 60.

Developing character: Transmitting knowledge: Sustaining
    the momentum for reform in American education.
    Chicago: Character, Inc., 1984.

Durkheim, E. Moral education. New York: Free Press,
    1961.

Erikson, E. The roots of virtue.

Gilligan, C. In a different voice. Cambridge, Mass.: Harvard University Press, 1982.

Grant, G. The character of education and the education of character. Daedalus, Summer 1981.

Hacker, A. Farewell to the family? The New York Review, March 18, 1982, pp. 37-41.

Hartshorne, H., & May, M. A. Studies in the nature of character. New York: Macmillan, 1928.

Huston, T., & Korte, C. The responsive bystander: Why he helps. In T. Lickona (Ed.), Moral development and behavior. New York: Holt, Rinehart, & Winston, 1976 .

Kilpatrick, W. K. Psychological seduction: The failure of modern psychology. Nashville: Thomas Nelson, 1983.

Kohlberg, L. Essays on moral development, vol. 1: The philosophy of moral development. San Francisco: Harper & Row, 1981.

Kohlberg, L. Essays on moral development, vol. 2: The psychology of moral development. San Francisco: Harper & Row, 1984.

Knowles, R. The acting person as moral agent: Erikson as the starting point for an integrated psychological theory of moral development. In R. T. Knowles, J. A. Mann, & F. E. Ellrod (Eds.), Psychological foundations of moral education. Washington, D.C.: University Press of America, in press.

Kurtines, W. M., & Gewirtz, J. L. Morality, moral behavior, and moral development. New York: Wiley, 1984.

Levine, A. When dreams and heroes died: A portrait of today's college student. San Francisco: Jossey-Bass, 1981.

Lewis, C. S. Chronicles of Narnia. New York: Macmillan, 1970.

34 / Character Development

McDougall, W. An introduction to social psychology. London: Methuen, 1936.

McLean, G. Moral education: A philosophical perspective. Unpublished paper at the International Seminar on Moral Education, Catholic University at Lima, Peru, 1983.

Menninger, K. Whatever became of sin? New York: Hawthorn Books, 1973.

Minnich, H. C. Old favorites from the McGuffey Readers. New York: American Book Co., 1936.

Moline, J. Classical ideas about moral education. In E. Wynne (Ed.), Character policy. Washington, D.C.: University Press of America, 1982, pp. 197-203.

A nation at risk: The imperative for educational reform. A report by the National Commission on Excellence in Education. Washington, D.C.: U.S. Government Printing Office, 1983.

Perry, W. G., Jr. Forms of intellectual and ethical development in the college years. New York: Holt, Rinehart, & Winston, 1970.

Piaget, J. The moral judgment of the child. New York: Free Press, 1965 (First published in English, London: Kegan Paul, 1932).

Research and Forecasts, Inc. The Connecticut Mutual Life report on American Values in the 80s: The impact of belief. Hartford, Conn.: Connecticut Mutual Life Insurance Co., 1981.

Save our children, save our schools. ABC Television Special, October 4, 1984.

Selman, R. The growth of interpersonal understanding. New York: Academic Press, 1980.

Simpson, E. A holistic approach to moral development and behavior. In T. Lickona (Ed.), Moral development and behavior. New York: Holt, Rinehart, & Winston, 1976, pp. 159-70.

Smith, R. Women in the Labor Force in 1990. Washington, D.C.: The Urban Institute, 1979.

Staug, E. Positive social behavior and morality, vol. 2: Socialization and development. New York: Academic Press, 1979.

Stein, B. J. TV: A religious wasteland. Originally published in Wall Street Journal, 1985. Reprinted in Focus on the Family, April 1985, p. 5.

Television and behavior: Ten years of scientific progress. A report of the U.S. Department of Health and Human Services. Rockville, Md.: National Institute of Mental Health, 1982.

U.S. News & World Report (TV's "disastrous" impact on children: Interview with Neil Postman), January 19, 1981, pp. 43-45.

U.S. News & World Report (A search for the sacred), April 4, 1983, pp. 35-44.

2
Trends in American Youth Character Development
Edward A. Wynne and Mary Hess

The word "character" is derived from a Greek word meaning "to mark," or "scratch." The derivation suggests the visible nature of the traits which comprise a person's character. And this element of visibility is a useful starting point for considering the matter of trends in U.S. youth character.

WHY VISIBILITY

As many of us recognize, the question of what constitutes "good character" is properly a subject of some controversy. Such controversy is not purely abstract. It can finally determine the framework of many practical problems, such as how to identify good character, how to measure it, and even how to manage schools, classrooms, and other youth-shaping entities so as to generate good character in the young. But, if we accept the concept of the visibility of character as a starting point, a certain foundation is established: We should be able to look around us and see whether children and youths display good character traits. Conversely, we should be reluctant to infer the existence of good character from the existence of internal states of mind.

Of course, the preceding discussion will lead us to recall some of the themes of behavioristic psychology. This approach stressed the study of observable conduct as the basic unit of psychological analysis. And that parallel has some logic. However, the concern with observable traits has a far more ancient background than behaviorism. Many institutions and character-oriented traditions--ranging from the Boy Scouts to Poor Richard and the Ten Commandments--have stressed the importance of right conduct. Conversely, these same traditions have often depreciated the significance of words without deeds; there are a number of benefits to the focus on conduct as the essence of character. These benefits should be briefly mentioned.

Conduct is visible, and can often be easily observed. And it is important that character traits be observable. We can only help try to form the character of the young if we have an efficient form of feedback. Thus, if we see someone steal (or "catch" them), we become able to rebuke them, punish them, or take other action. Or, if they are kind, we can thank them. Again, it is fairly easy to teach people to identify many forms of conduct; it is far harder to develop systems so different people may reach common conclusions as to someone's state of mind. But, without such common conclusions, people--like teachers in a school--cannot work together to form the character of others. These practical factors have much to do with the widespread acceptance of the traditional conduct approach to character. Indeed, the recent academic interest on states of mind as a main aspect of character development is probably partly due to the development of psychological instruments and techniques which allegedly accurately portray the state of mind of subjects. But, even assuming that such measures are valid, they hardly provide as expeditious feedback as can be generated by simply looking to see if students in a school are displaying courtesy to adults (and each other), or are vandalizing bathrooms.

Another relevant aspect of visibility is the traditional concept of "scandal." Formerly, scandal meant undesirable conduct which might tempt others to act likewise, or which might place a public institution into disrepute. It suggested the theme of bad example. The concept of scandal implied that special constraints should be applied to visible conduct--as compared with secret conduct, or undisclosed states of mind. The reality was that the social nature of potentially scandalous conduct could have more grave ramifications than private disorder. Thus it needs more careful monitoring. Finally, we must realistically consider that the good or bad character of others assumes most importance to us when it becomes visible. Virtuous or evil thoughts which are not acted on have only academic interest to most of us. In our world, time and energy are usually scarce resources. Therefore, it is understandable that many able and responsible people will not become concerned about the character of others until it is displayed through evident conduct.

It should be emphasized that the visible is not all. Any serious concern with character has to go beyond a naïve behaviorism. Thus, traditional character-building approaches were often also concerned with states of mind, and recognized that internal factors can significantly affect conduct. But, when traditional systems of character building tried to affect the state of mind of the young, they relied largely on didactic techniques, exemplary literature, and the study of role models. More introspective techniques, and exegetical analyses were reserved for persons whose virtuous conduct had already been demonstrated by the course of events. Thus, the Hindus encouraged mature adults, who had raised families, to abandon their homes and go into the forests or on the road, in a quest for deep knowledge; Aristotle implied that what he called political science would be taught only to persons over forty; and the formation processes of Catholic religious orders did not bring philosophy into play until the initiates had passed through lengthy trials as a novice.

Despite the traditional and practical merits of the visible conduct approach, some additional remarks are necessary regarding its use as a concept for looking at the character of the young. It is important to remember that words, themselves, constitute a form of conduct. Politeness, telling the truth in the face of temptation, verbally confronting liars or engaging in lying, are all verbal acts. Such acts constitute conduct. In fact, words often lead to more conduct--accepting justified punishment, withstanding coercion, or accompanying solicitous words with appropriate deeds. Finally, some people may fail to meet the obligations generated by their own public words. But, even where there is a gap between public words and deeds, the culpable party--who has orally taken a stand--has made himself vulnerable to various modes of retaliation. And so we generally recognized that certain responsibilities are tacitly generated by words; and acts which create responsibilities have ramifications for character development.

In sum, character is conduct, and the history of U.S. youth conduct is a form of the history of U.S. youth character. Now, there is a popular conception that contemporary youths are displaying especially poor character. For instance, "pupil discipline" was rated the top educational problem in the nation in 14 of the 15 annual Gallup polls of public opinion about education. (Interestingly enough, in the last poll, the second-rated problem was pupil drug use.) And most of us have heard a variety of "horror stories"--either first hand, or in the media--about delinquency and disorder among our young, especially around schools. But opinion polls and occasional anecdotes do not provide the sort of historical, comparative, long-term, hard data that are desirable for any serious discussion about patterns of youth conduct. And only with such data can we have an adequate base for analyzing our youth situation. For, as Lincoln said, in the opening sentence of his "House Divided" speech, in 1858, "If we could first know where we are, and whither we are tending, we could know what to do and how to do it."

Fortunately, a considerable body of reliable, long-term information about U.S. youth conduct is available. Much of this information is found in the national mortality tables. These tables annually disclose national rates of death by age and sex, for various specified causes. In a modern industrial country, such as the United States, we can assume that almost all deaths are noted and tabulated. Of course, there will be occasional exceptions to this principle, but the number of such exceptions is likely to be small. The rates are calculated in numbers of deaths per 100,000 persons in the age group; in other words, year-to-year comparisons can be made even though the absolute numbers of persons has changed over time.

HOMICIDE STATISTICS

We have available long-term trend data about rates of death by homicide for white males and females, between 15-24, from 1914 to 1983 (the year most recently available). The data disclose that the rate of male youth death by homicide is: (1) slightly below the highest point since we began compiling national statistics in 1914 (the high point was in 1980), (2) in 1980, it was 203 percent higher than the low of 1951, and (3) in 1980, it was 22 percent higher than the previous high years of the early 1930s. The precise pattern of these changes is presented in Figure 2.1.[1]

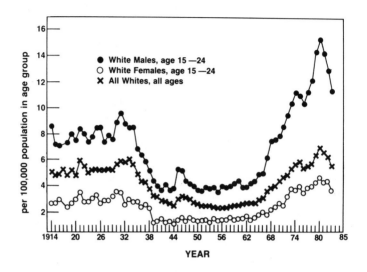

Figure 2.1   Homicide Rates for Certain Age Groups of U.S. White Adolescents, 1914–1983

The data discussed above refer only to whites. This system of tabulation was adopted in this presentation to focus on the conduct patterns of the majority population— the group least affected by poverty and racial discrimination. Presumably, this advantaged group would be less inclined to display character problems.

The death certificates of the homicide victims do not contain information about the murderers. Thus, we do not have details about who the people are committing these murders. However, the majority of murders are committed by persons familiar with the victim, and it seems likely that this applies to the young. Thus, the increase in youths' deaths by homicide represents a rise in murderous conduct by young persons. Surely this is a sign of character decline. We might also speculate that many homicides of young persons represent disorderly acts affecting both the murderer and the victim, for example, the murderer and "murdered" were drinking toether, or brawling. This is not to excuse the murderer. Still it suggests that youth murders often involve acts of collective disorder, as compared with the simple victimization of helpless innocents. The rate of increase in homicide for young whites (ages 15-24) is higher than that for all whites as a group. (Incidentally, the rate of increase in the homicide rate for young white females is nearly the same as that for young males, but the female homicide rate has started from a much lower base point.) Although we lack accurate national statistics about the pre-1914 homicide rates, it is notorious that crimes such as homicide are often related to trends such as urbanization. Thus, we may infer that the 1980 rate for young whites is at the highest point since the first European white settlements in this country in 1607.

SUICIDE STATISTICS

Another important youth mortality trend is disclosed in the statistics about youth rates of death from suicide. These data, in Figure 2.2, include all white males and females between the ages of 15-24, from 1914 to 1982 (the most recent year available).[2] They disclose that the rate of white male youth death by suicide is (1) near the highest point since we began compiling national statistics in 1914, and possibly at the highest point since 1607, (2) in 1977, it was 126 percent higher than the previous low year of 1944, and (3) in 1977, it was 78 percent higher than the previous high year of 1914. Unlike the homicide data--where both the youth and adult rates have tended to rise--the youth suicide rates have been rising while the adult rates have remained relatively stable.

Increased rates of death by suicide are a measure of character changes. Theoretically one cannot simply say that all young persons who commit suicide have serious character defects. One can imagine circumstances in which suicide is a rational and appropriate response by someone of strong character to some extraordinarily distressing circumstances, for example, to avoid a slow, painful death through cancer, or to shield another person from an intense pain. However, common sense indicates that there has been no notable increase in the levels of physical pain visited on our young, nor have our young been increasingly shouldered with enormous responsibilities or duties, for example, supporting their younger siblings. The more plausible conclusion implied by the suicide data is that

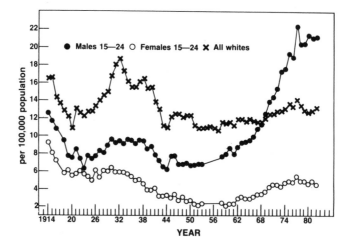

Figure 2.2   Suicides: 15-24 White, U.S., 1914-1982

contemporary young persons have essentially become less
adept at handling the moderate stress incidental to social
life.   In other words, the rising rates of youth suicide
undoubtedly represent a terrible tragedy.   But it would be
unrealistic to conclude that this increase is due to a vast
increase in powerful, crushing external demands placed on
adolescents, for example, extraordinary homework obligations, arduous household chores.   The changes in the adolescent suicide rate are probably more due to changes in
the psyches of successive cohorts of youths involved, as
compared with more strenuous requirements for conformity
placed on persons with relatively resilient psyches.   Youth
character has apparently become more fragile and less resistant to hardship.

OUT-OF-WEDLOCK BIRTHS

One other important official national statistic deserves attention: the rate of out-of-wedlock births.   This
rate is expressed in terms of the number of out-of-wedlock
births for each 1,000 unmarried females in the age group.
The first year for which national data are available
(broken down by race and age) is 1940.   Between 1940 and
1987, the rates of out-of-wedlock births for white females
between the ages of 15-19 increased 476 percent.   This

shift is also portrayed in Figure 2.3.[3] The data for the
most recent year, 1983, show the highest rate of adolescent
out-of-wedlock births tabulated so far. Although the rates
for white adolescents and all whites has also risen, the
adolescent rate has increased at a far faster pace.

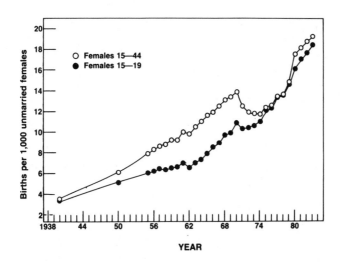

Figure 2.3   Out-of-Wedlock Births, U.S., 1938-1983

In considering the changes in conduct portrayed in
out-of-wedlock births, it is useful to realize that the years
from 1940 to 1983 were a period during which increasing
antibirth resources were made available to young females.
New contraceptives and techniques were developed, means of
distribution of these developments were elaborated, sex education courses were adopted in schools, and abortion was
made more widely available. Many observers, if they were
informed only about the antipregnancy and antibirth activities, would probably assume that the rates of out-of-
wedlock births would have tended to decline among the
young. Those observers would be wrong. Instead of declining, the rate of out-of-wedlock births increased to
probably the highest point in our history. Evidently the
social forces making for the increases in out-of-wedlock
births are peculiarly powerful.

PREMARITAL SEX

A synthesis of the research on the rates of engagement of adolescents in sexual intercourse is informative,
even though the studies involved do not use official statistics. The synthesis (see Figure 2.4) covered 18 separate
studies (by different researchers) of different groups of
young persons.[4] The studies were conducted for different
periods of time between 1958 and 1976. Not all of the respondents were unmarried. However, given the comparatively young age of the respondents involved (the oldest of
them were college undergraduates), it is likely that either
(1) the great bulk of them were unmarried, and/or (2) that
the proportion of married respondents probably stayed constant between the first and follow-up surveys. The surveys disclose a high pattern of overall consistency: There
was a steady increase in the proportion of youths who engage in premarital sex.

The connection between the increases in both out-of-
wedlock births and premarital intercourse is self-evident.
And the character implications of the out-of-wedlock births
are also clear. The typical perspective is that it is undesirable for an unmarried female to bear a child (or a
male to father such a child), since a one-parent family is
not an ideal foundation for child rearing. This perspective is especially valid with regard to adolescent mothers.
In other words, unmarried female adolescents who become
pregnant, and males who cause such pregnancies, are revealing serious character defects. They are not accepting
personal responsibility for the foreseeable outcomes of their
voluntary conduct.

In the abstract, the moral (or character-related)
implications of premarital intercourse among adolescents
may seem a more complex issue in our relatively permissive
era. However, the parallels between rising out-of-wedlock
birth and increasing premarital intercourse suggest there
is much merit to even the traditional secular wisdom--that
young persons are usually not able to handle the profound
implications of premarital sex. Thus, the contemporary
evidence argues for greater emphasis on youth premarital
abstinence: In general, it is wiser for unmarried young
people to say No, both in their individual self-interest,
and in the interest of potential out-of-wedlock children.
And such a pro-No approach is inherent in the concept of
good character development. Good character often is identified with the themes of self-denial and deferred gratification

Study	1958	59	60	61	62	63	64	65	66	67	68	69	70	71	72	73	74	75	76
Females in an intermountain-area university (Christensen and Gregg, 1970)	10%										32%								
Females in a midwestern university (Christensen and Gregg, 1970)	21										34								
Females ages 13 to 17 years in a Michigan town (Vener and Stewart, 1974)													16			22			
Females entering Yale University as freshmen, sophomores, juniors, or seniors (Sarrel and Sarrel, 1974)											25			75					
Females (white) ages 15 to 19 years, never married (national probability sample) (Zelnik and Kantner, 1977)														21					31
Females (black) ages 15 to 19 years, never married (national probability sample) (Zelnik and Kantner, 1977)														51					63
Females in a large southern state university (King et al., 1977)								21					37					57	
Females in a western state university (longitudinal study) (Jessor and Jessor, 1975)												51		85					
Females in a Colorado high school (longitudinal study) (Jessor and Jessor, 1975)												5		55					
Males in an intermountain-area university (Christensen and Gregg, 1970)	39											37							
Males in a midwestern university (Christensen and Gregg, 1970)	51										50								
Males ages 13 to 17 years in a Michigan town (Vener and Stewart, 1974)													28			33			
Males entering Yale University as freshmen, sophomores, juniors, or seniors (Sarrel and Sarrel, 1974)											33			62					
Males in a large southern state university (King et al., 1977)								65					65				74		
Males in a western state university (longitudinal study) (Jessor and Jessor, 1975)												46		82					
Males in a Colorado high school (longitudinal study) (Jessor and Jessor, 1975)												8		33					
Males and females age 15 in a lower-middle to upper-working class town in nonmetropolitan Michigan (Vener, Stewart, and Hager, 1972)													13			24			
Males and females age 15 in another lower-middle to upper-working class town in nonmetropolitan Michigan (Vener, Stewart, and Hager, 1972)													26			36			

© Pastoral Renewal, 1982.

Figure 2.4   Two Decades of Constant Increase: Adolescents Who Have Engaged in Intercourse

ILLEGAL DRUG USE

The illegal use of drugs and alcohol by adolescents is another important character-related trend to consider. Naturally, statistics about such conduct are not part of official records. But various measures are available.

One good resource is local surveys, anonymously asking students or other youths about their patterns of drug use. The San Mateo (Calif.) Department of Public Health conducted such annual surveys among the students in county schools from 1968 to 1977. Almost all of the students covered in the survey are white. To provide an adequate perspective on developments in the county, two tables are presented. Table 2.1 deals with marijuana use among either male or female students between the ages of approximately 12 and 17. (NA means no statistics are available.) Of course, there is a wide range in the frequency of marijuana use. Still, many of the students use it quite regularly; in 1977, 23.3 percent of the students covered by the survey reported that they used the drug 50 or more times a year.[5]

Table 2.2 deals with a different category of San Mateo students--the "nonusers." These are defined as students who have not used either alcohol, amphetamines, LSD, marijuana, or tobacco during the past year. As we can see, the proportion of nonusers has steadily declined, especially among lower-age groups and females. The lower half of Table 2.2 covers students who report "no significant use" during the past year--and the table and questionnaire precisely define what is meant by "significant use." As we can see, over the nine years covered, the proportion of those from all grades and both sexes reporting no significant use declined from 48.8 percent to 37.1 percent.[6]

California may be termed an untypical state, and San Mateo, an affluent suburban area, may be especially prone to drug problems. And the data stop in 1977. Because of these potential statistical deficiencies, it is also important to consider the trends in youth drug and alcohol use in a wider perspective. One means of acquiring such perspective is a series of surveys of an anonymous national sample of the high school graduating classes from 1975 to 1982.[7]

Table 2.1   San Mateo County, California, Surveys of Student Drug Use: Marijuana*

	MALES						FEMALES						STANDARDIZED RATE TOTAL GRADES 9-12	TOTAL RESPONSES
YEAR OF SURVEY	7th GRADE	8th GRADE	9th GRADE	10th GRADE	11th GRADE	12th GRADE	7th GRADE	8th GRADE	9th GRADE	10th GRADE	11th GRADE	12th GRADE		
Reporting any use of marijuana during preceding year.														
1968	NA	NA	26.8	32.3	36.9	44.6	NA	NA	22.9	28.1	31.7	31.9	31.9	18,774
1969	10.9	23.9	34.9	41.7	45.5	50.1	10.7	21.8	31.9	35.5	38.3	38.1	39.5	25,883
1970	9.8	22.8	34.0	44.9	48.9	50.9	7.2	16.7	31.9	42.1	42.6	44.4	42.5	35,148
1971	17.6	29.1	44.5	49.7	57.9	58.6	12.6	26.4	40.5	48.1	50.2	48.3	49.7	35,701
1972	17.1	33.2	43.9	51.8	59.5	60.7	13.2	29.3	39.0	49.2	50.8	52.9	51.0	31,251
1973	20.0	34.3	51.2	56.1	58.5	61.0	15.0	31.5	47.0	51.9	55.3	57.3	54.8	27,388
1974	22.7	37.7	48.6	57.3	59.4	61.9	18.0	33.3	47.8	54.6	56.7	58.2	55.5	28,232
1975	21.1	37.1	49.2	56.5	61.5	63.6	16.8	29.9	44.4	51.9	57.3	55.5	55.5	28,303
1976	21.7	36.5	47.8	57.5	61.8	61.1	15.6	32.4	46.1	54.4	57.9	56.0	55.3	20,848
1977	22.8	39.2	48.1	59.3	65.2	64.5	15.3	30.9	43.3	55.3	62.8	61.4	57.5	22,077
Reporting use of marijuana on ten or more occasions during preceding year.														
1968	NA	NA	14.3	18.1	22.5	25.6	NA	NA	10.6	14.9	16.7	17.4	17.5	18,774
1969	4.1	11.6	20.2	25.6	30.2	34.0	1.7	7.4	18.1	21.2	23.2	22.4	24.4	25,883
1970	2.7	10.2	19.6	28.8	34.1	34.2	1.4	6.9	16.2	26.3	26.2	28.2	26.7	35,148
1971	5.3	14.6	26.2	33.3	42.3	43.3	4.1	12.3	23.0	31.0	32.9	30.5	32.8	35,701
1972	5.8	17.2	26.8	36.8	41.3	44.9	4.6	14.1	23.0	32.2	35.7	35.3	24.5	31,251
1973	6.7	16.3	31.9	39.6	43.4	45.4	5.2	14.8	27.0	32.9	36.6	37.8	36.8	27,388
1974	8.4	20.1	29.9	39.1	42.9	47.0	5.6	14.5	29.3	35.6	38.9	38.8	37.7	28,232
1975	6.9	17.9	29.5	36.9	43.8	45.4	5.0	13.3	25.2	33.6	38.6	37.2	36.3	28,303
1976	7.2	17.7	27.0	36.7	43.1	41.8	4.5	14.8	24.5	34.6	39.8	36.0	35.4	20,848
1977	7.8	18.2	27.0	38.0	46.7	47.7	4.2	12.7	21.8	33.4	41.9	40.3	37.1	22,077
Reporting use of marijuana on fifty or more occasions during preceding year.														
1968	NA	NA	NA	NA	NA	NA	NA	NA	NA	NA	NA	NA	NA	18,774
1969	NA	NA	NA	NA	NA	NA	NA	NA	NA	NA	NA	NA	NA	25,883
1970	NA	NA	11.4	19.2	20.3	22.0	NA	NA	7.2	14.0	14.4	15.3	15.9	35,148
1971	NA	NA	17.2	23.2	23.5	31.9	NA	NA	11.6	17.0	19.4	18.5	21.1	35,701
1972	NA	NA	15.9	25.5	27.8	31.6	NA	NA	12.4	19.1	21.1	20.2	21.7	31,251
1973	3.3	9.8	20.3	27.9	31.3	32.4	2.3	7.5	14.2	18.8	21.5	20.4	23.4	27,388
1974	4.0	11.4	19.6	26.3	31.4	34.2	2.3	7.8	17.4	22.0	22.4	22.8	24.5	28,232
1975	3.3	9.6	19.9	24.0	29.6	30.7	2.4	7.0	13.7	18.9	23.0	20.9	22.6	28,303
1976	3.9	9.8	17.0	24.3	29.8	30.0	2.2	7.6	13.5	19.2	24.6	21.3	22.5	20,848
1977	4.0	11.1	16.3	24.6	31.2	34.3	2.0	6.8	11.6	19.4	24.6	24.2	23.3	22,077

*Cumulative levels or use reported by junior and senior high school students, 1968-1977, by school grade and sex of respondent, specific rates per hundred responses.

Table 2.2   San Mateo County, California, Surveys of Student Drug Use: "The Non-Users"

Levels of "no use" and "no significant use"*** of any or all of the following substances: alcohol, amphetamines, LSD, marijuana and tobacco reported by junior and senior high school students, 1968-1977 by school grade and sex or respondent, specific rates per hundred responses.

YEAR OF SURVEY	MALES						FEMALES						STANDARDIZED RATE TOTAL GRADES 9-12	TOTAL RESPONSES
	7th GRADE	8th GRADE	9th GRADE	10th GRADE	11th GRADE	12th GRADE	7th GRADE	8th GRADE	9th GRADE	10th GRADE	11th GRADE	12th GRADE		

Reporting that they had experienced no use of any of the specified substances during the year preceding the survey:

YEAR OF SURVEY	MALES 7th	8th	9th	10th	11th	12th	FEMALES 7th	8th	9th	10th	11th	12th	STD RATE 9-12	TOTAL
1968	NA	NA	24.4	24.1	19.7	15.7	NA	NA	33.4	26.4	22.1	20.2	23.2	18,774
1969	36.6	29.1	26.4	19.1	15.4	12.4	47.8	36.2	30.4	24.6	20.9	17.9	20.9	25,883
1970	39.9	27.8	25.6	18.0	15.3	14.4	47.9	35.6	28.7	19.1	18.1	16.1	19.4	35,148
1971	35.1	24.7	19.0	17.8	12.8	12.3	46.7	30.2	23.6	19.2	16.6	15.7	17.1	35,701
1972	32.8	21.7	18.2	14.1	11.5	9.4	42.3	25.7	20.1	15.9	15.2	12.4	14.6	31,251
1973	21.0	16.5	13.3	11.2	10.9	10.7	27.3	16.0	15.4	12.7	12.3	10.3	12.1	27,388
1974	21.2	13.7	12.1	12.7	9.8	8.5	24.1	16.7	13.6	12.5	10.2	9.3	11.1	28,232
1975	23.4	17.0	13.1	10.5	10.0	8.6	29.5	16.8	14.7	11.2	10.1	9.7	11.0	28,303
1976	25.5	18.1	14.6	11.1	8.4	10.7	32.4	19.5	15.7	12.0	10.1	8.8	11.3	20,848
1977	24.0	16.2	12.3	10.3	8.5	7.4	30.2	20.9	14.3	11.1	8.3	7.3	9.9	22,077

Reporting that they had experienced no "significant use"*** of any of the specified substances during the year preceding the survey:

YEAR OF SURVEY	MALES 7th	8th	9th	10th	11th	12th	FEMALES 7th	8th	9th	10th	11th	12th	STD RATE 9-12	TOTAL
1969	NA	NA	56.9	48.5	40.5	32.8	NA	NA	60.3	56.9	49.2	45.5	48.8	25,883
1970	80.9	65.1	57.5	46.4	39.2	36.7	84.8	71.2	61.0	49.4	43.4	44.2	47.2	35,148
1971	74.2	58.6	50.5	43.3	34.2	30.7	80.5	64.6	52.4	45.9	43.1	42.3	42.9	35,701
1972	71.4	55.3	48.6	39.6	34.4	27.2	77.2	59.7	51.6	42.6	38.9	36.5	39.9	31,251
1973	68.0	52.6	42.1	36.3	32.4	29.8	73.6	55.6	46.7	42.3	37.7	35.5	37.8	27,388
1974	68.7	50.7	45.3	35.1	31.3	27.3	71.2	56.1	44.4	39.9	36.4	31.7	36.4	28,232
1975	71.7	57.0	46.0	37.8	31.8	26.2	75.9	60.0	46.6	40.1	35.9	32.5	37.1	28,303
1976	74.7	59.4	51.6	41.3	31.4	29.8	79.1	59.5	49.0	38.0	34.8	34.6	38.8	20,848
1977	73.5	59.7	49.1	39.4	30.3	25.1	79.4	63.3	49.3	40.3	33.4	30.5	37.2	22,077

***Significant use: Alcohol—ten or more occasions; Tobacco—ten or more occasions; Marijuana—ten or more occasions; LSD—three or more occasions; Amphetamines—three or more occasions.

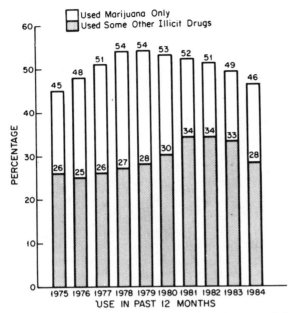

Figure 2.5   Trends in Annual Prevalence of an Illicit
              Drug Use Index (All Seniors)

       The figures presented are not quite as high as
those from San Mateo––63 percent of the San Mateo seniors
used marijuana in 1977, while the national figure for that
year was 51 percent.   Still, the San Mateo and national
trends display many parallels.   We should also recognize
that trends in adolescent drug use are somewhat variable.
Thus, the national survey revealed that reported use of
hallucinogens (e.g., PCP, LSD) declined from 16.3 percent
in 1975 to 10.3 percent in 1982, while the use of cocaine
rose from 9 percent in 1975 to 17.3 percent in 1985.   But
despite these variations, the statistics only disclose the
relative stabilization of adolescent drug use at historically high levels.   It is true that the statistics do not go
back beyond 1975, but a simple inquiry can demonstrate
the nature of the long-term changes regarding drugs and
the young.   Just ask any adults over forty whether it was
possible or easy for them to purchase either marijuana or
cocaine when they were high school seniors.   Eighty-five
percent of the 1985 class reported that it was "fairly
easy," or "very easy" for them to get marijuana; the comparable figure for cocaine was 48 percent.   One can be

confident that the comparable figures for the period before 1959 were far lower.

The character-related implications of this increased youth drug and alcohol use are clear. Persons using drugs are comparatively disengaged from the realities around them. But good character is developed, and applied, through engagement. Furthermore, drug use is essentially a way of pursuing immediate gratification, by means of escaping reality, and withdrawing into a private fantasy world. Indeed, as Nicgorski and Ellrod have pointed out, the Aristotelian tradition of ethics gives great emphasis to the importance of habits such as self-discipline for maintaining character. We have to manage ourselves so as to stay engaged with events around us. Drug and alcohol use also constitute illegal conduct, per se--and, indeed, many youths engaged in such usage also encourage others to become violators, or even go further and sell illegal substances to other youths. Finally, it is notorious that many irresponsible and criminal acts are committed by youths under the influence of drugs and alcohol. We can thus conclude that the long-term rise in youth drug use represents an objective decline in youth character.

DELINQUENT CONDUCT

The adolescent crime rate is also an indicator of youth character. Statistics about changes in the levels of crime must be considered with caution. It is notorious that changes in reported crime rates may be attributed to other causes than a real increase in actual crimes. For example, the changes may be partly due to changes in police arrest or tabulation policies. Still, long-term trend data and statistics making comparison among different age groups can be instructive. Figure 2.6 presents such data for all persons (including blacks) for the years 1932 to 1983 (the most recent year available) and for the specified age groups.[8] The statistics have been weighted to allow for shifts in age group size. It is evident that these rates have increased remarkably, especially for younger groups over the years portrayed. For instance, between 1930 and about 1982 the rate for the group age 26 and over increased 13-fold, the rate for the group ages 18-24 increased 79-fold, and the rate for the age groups under 18 increased 100-fold. Undoubtedly, these increases reflect the effects of a variety of trends, for example, better record collection, more formalized police procedures. But it is noteworthy that the greater rates of increase occurred in younger age groups.

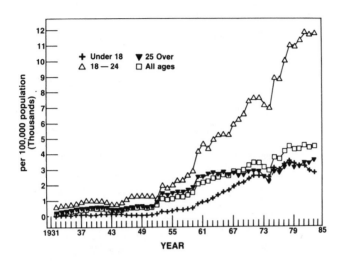

Figure 2.6   Arrest Rates by Age for U.S., 1932-1983

Apropos of delinquency, it is also pertinent to consider information about changes in students' conduct in and around schools, since these institutions are our most important youth socialization institution. Understandably, developing precise information about such trends is difficult; changes in patterns of conduct in individual schools over the years may be just as much a function of neighborhood changes as compared with changes in conduct among students from approximately similar family backgrounds. Still, even when this qualification is accepted, there are a variety of data sources which permit us to make some generalizations about student conduct trends on a national basis. Rubel, who has tried to most carefully analyze these statistics and derive trends, concluded that the level of in-school disorder that had evolved (by 1977) was at the highest point in the twentieth century.[9]

One researcher in the field of school discipline told me the following anecdote to portray the situation. During 1982, he was walking through the halls of a high school in a large Eastern city, accompanied by the chief

of security forces for that school district. My friend noticed a student smoking a marijuana cigarette. He said
to the chief, "You saw that. Aren't you going to do anything about it? There's one of your guards standing right
over there." The chief replied, "What do you recommend I
do? Don't you realize that my staff has to save their
energies for more important problems?"

TEST SCORES

Another national development reflecting on youth
character that should be considered is the long-term decline
in the levels of measured cognitive learning in students.
Of course, cognitive knowledge, per se, is not synonymous
with good character. But acquiring such knowledge is
often associated with character traits, such as application
and persistence. Thus, significant decline in measured
knowledge might be interpreted to signify a change in the
character traits possessed by successive cohorts of youths.
The test score decline can be portrayed through a variety
of measures. First, there are the changes of the scores
attained by test takers on the Scholastic Aptitude Test.
That test is a standardized written objective examination
administered annually to a high proportion of college-
oriented high school seniors. The test score patterns in
this test between 1963 and 1985 are outlined in Figure
2.7.[10]

	Verbal			Mathematical		
	Male	Female	Total	Male	Female	Total
1967	463	468	466	514	467	492
1968	464	466	466	512	470	492
1969	459	466	463	513	470	493
1970	459	461	460	509	465	488
1971	454	457	455	507	466	488
1972	454	452	453	505	461	484
1973	446	443	445	502	460	481
1974	447	442	444	501	459	480
1975	437	431	434	495	449	472
1976	433	430	431	497	446	472
1977	431	427	429	497	445	470
1978	433	425	429	494	444	468
1979	431	423	427	493	443	467
1980	428	420	424	491	443	466
1981	430	418	424	492	443	466
1982	431	421	426	493	443	467
1983	430	420	425	493	445	468
1984	433	420	426	495	449	471
1985	437	425	431	499	452	475

Figure 2.7   SAT Score Averages for College-Bound Seniors,
1967-1985

There are also a variety of other aptitude tests.
Some are taken by college seniors interested in post-
collegiate academic work, while others are taken by high
school seniors in lieu of the Scholastic Aptitude Test.
Waters and Lawrence calculated the annual average rates
of score decline (or increase) for these tests for the years
for which national data are available. Their calculations
for these tests (including the SAT) are presented in Figure 2.8.[11]

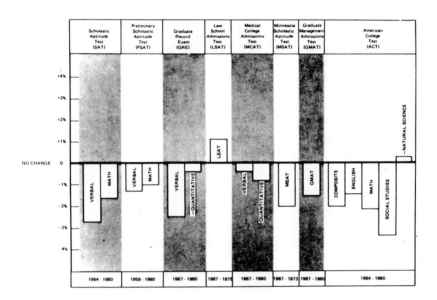

Figure 2.8   Aptitude Measures. Vertical axis: mean
              change per year.   Horizontal axis: mean
              proportion of a standard deviation per year.

The scores on various standardized objective achievement tests are another objective measure of pupil learning.
These tests are administered to students at different grade
levels as they pass through elementary and high school.
Waters and Lawrence also tabulated (Figure 2.9) the annual average rates of decline (or increase) for these
scores on a different test between the dates recited in
Figure 2.7.[12]

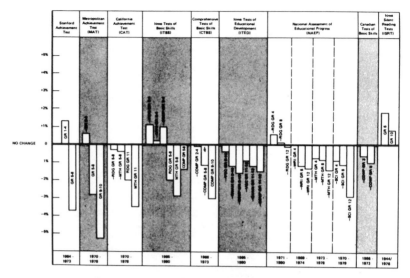

Figure 2.9   Achievement Measures. Vertical axis: mean
change per year. Horizontal axis: mean proportion of two standard deviations per year.

The interpretation of the significance of these declines
has been a topic of some controversy.[13] Aptitude tests, after
all, are not administered to a true sample of the student
population, but only to students who hope to attend certain
colleges and graduate schools. However, the achievement tests
while not administered to all students, are administered to
relative cross-sections of students. And their patterns of decline are essentially congruent with those of the aptitude
tests. Waters and Lawrence, whose analysis seems the most
thorough, concluded that there has been a steady incremental, nationwide decline in levels of pupil learning which
slowed down—but did not stop—in the late 1970s.

In conclusion, it is appropriate to remark on the noteworthy—and distressing—internal consistency of the statistics
presented. The rate of youth arrests rises—and the rates of
youth homicide and drug use also rise. Premarital sex increases, and so do out-of-wedlock births. A great many forms
of youth disorder increase, and measures of learning outcome
decline (is it any surprise that disordered youth do poorly
in school?). Whatever one's questions are about the accuracy
of any particular measure of disorder presented, it is evident
that the shifts in each measure tend to increase the credibil-
ity of all the others.

DISCUSSION

The conclusions and implications of the material presented in this chapter are both self-evident--and ambiguous. The character of typical U.S. youths has substantially declined over the past 20 to 30 years. This is not to say that all of our youths are displaying poor character. But it does mean that the overall level of poor character has dramatically increased. It is obviously desirable to devote more thought and energy to improving school (and college) policies that shape youth character. This is not to suggest that improving character-related education activities is the entire solution to the complex challenge before us. And here is where the matter of ambiguity arises. We do not know all of the causes of our problem, nor all the "solutions." Indeed, even if we knew many solutions, we might not be able to put them into effect. But despite our imperfect knowledge, there are some general themes that should be kept in mind.

First, we should note that certain general trends did not typify the period from the mid-1950s to 1980--the era of most character decline. To be specific, the following things did not happen:

- Per student expenditures for education did not decline.
- There was no decline in state or federal expenses for social welfare.
- There has been no increase in the standards of moral conduct expected of the young.
- The formal qualifications of teachers did not decline.
- The general standard of living did not decline.
- The nation has not been continuously affected with political stress--the late 1950s were notoriously quiescent, and the presidencies of Ford, Carter, and Reagan have not engendered dramatic unrest.

The point of the preceding list is that the decline of youth character is not evidently connected with many popularly alleged "causes"--the underfunding of education or social welfare programs, the oppression of the young, the spread of poverty, or general political stress. It is also significant that there are patterns of change which did increase or intensify throughout the entire period of character decline. In other words, the following things did happen:

- The average length of attendance of young people in school and college has increased, and educational institutions have become larger and more bureaucratic.
- Urbanization and suburbanization have increased.
- Per capita real income has increased.
- Family size has decreased, and both one-parent, and two-parent working families have increased.
- Youth exposure to mass media has increased, and the content of that media has changed.
- Popular values have increasingly shifted in favor of "self-actualization," and most education institutions have abandoned the principle of in loco parentis.
- There has been increased judicial sympathy with protecting the rights of accused persons.
- The subject matter presented to students in schools has become inherently less sympathetic to causing students to have appropriate feelings about traditional values.

The exact connection between the preceding persistent trends and the youth character debate is problematic. Still, a certain gross correlation is evident: The abandonment of traditional values, and their replacement with new, more individualistic ones, has been associated with the spread of youth disorder. This correlation would not simply justify the readoption of traditional approaches regarding the young, nor the rejection of more contemporary ones. Still, it does generate a certain intellectual obligation for proponents of more "open" approaches. Putting it bluntly, things (measured by conduct changes) have been getting worse as the influence of the new has spread. Promoters of more open approaches toward the young must recognize the implications of this parallel: In justifying their innovations, they must offer some theory as to why things have been getting worse while the force of tradition has declined, and the influence of openness has grown. In other words, by many measures, youth conduct was at its "best" in 1955--suicide, homicide, drug use, out-of-wedlock births were all at far lower rates than today. If traditional approaches toward the young were so bad, and more open ones better, why have things kept getting worse as we have moved further from the old and into the new? Don't the data suggest that further moves toward untraditional moral education will lead to even more youth self- and other-destruction?

This is not the place to settle some of the cause-and-effect questions just raised. For the moment, it is sufficient to recognize that the youth character situation is in a bad way. Schools are one of the important institutions of our society which can help to correct the problem. Obviously, schools alone cannot "solve" the problem. No single social institution can produce such an effect. But each such institution--the family, schools (and colleges), the government (at all levels), the media, the churches, and other community institutions--all have important and constructive roles to play. It is time for them to become more strongly engaged. A first step can be to examine the character of our young--to look carefully at day-to-day conduct--and see what can be done to help it change in more wholesome directions.

NOTES

1. U.S. Public Health Service, National Center for Health Statistics, Homicide in the United States, 1950-1964, Series 20, No. 6 (Washington: Government Printing Office, 1967), and personal communication, 1986; U.S. Public Health Service, Death Rates by Age, Race and Sex, United States, 1900-1953, Homicide, 43(31) (Washington: Government Printing Office, 1956).
2. U.S. Public Health Service, National Center for Health Statistics, Suicide in the United States, 1950-1964, Series 20, No. 6 (Washington: Government Printing Office, 1969), and personal communication, 1986; U.S. Public Health Service, Death Rates by Age, Race and Sex, United States, 1900-1953, Suicide, 43(30) (Washington: Government Printing Office, 1956).
3. U.S. Public Health Service, Vital Statistics of the United States, 1973, Natality 1 (Rockville, Md.: National Center for Health Statistics, 1973), and personal communication, 1986.
4. Kevin F. Perrotta and Kevin N. Springer, "A Revolution in Premarital Sex," Pastoral Renewal 6(12) (June 1982), pp. 92-93.
5. San Mateo County, Department of Public Health, Report: Survey of Student Drug Use, 1977 (San Mateo County: Department of Public Health and Welfare, 1977).
6. Ibid.
7. Lloyd Johnston, Jerold G. Bachman, and Patrick M. O'Malley, Highlights of Student Drug Use in America,

1975–1985 (Washington: Department of Health and Family Services, 1986), p. 37.

8. U.S. Bureau of the Census, Statistical Abstract of the United States, 1980 (Washington: Government Printing Office, 1980); Historical Statistics of the United States from Colonial Times to 1970 (Washington: Government Printing Office, 1975); Population Estimates by Age, Sex and Race, 1900–1959, Series P–25, No. 311 (Washington: Government Printing Office, 1973); Population Estimates by Age, Sex and Race, 1960–1970, Series P–25, No. 519 (Washington: Government Printing Office, 1973); Population Estimates by Age, Sex and Race, 1968–1977, Series P–25, No. 721 (Washington: Government Printing office, 1978); Population Estimates by Age, Sex and Race, 1976–1979, Series P–25, No. 870 (Washington: Government Printing Office, 1981).

9. Robert Rubel, The Unruly School (Lexington, Mass.: Heath/Lexington, 1977).

10. College Board, National Report on College Bound Seniors, 1985 (New York: College Board, 1985).

11. Brian K. Waters and Janice H. Lawrence, "Military and Civilian Test Score Trends (1950–1981)," presented at the annual meeting of the American Education Research Association, New York, April 1981.

12. Ibid.

13. For examples of this controversy, see e.g., Willard Wirtz, On Further Examination (New York: College Entrance Examination Board, 1977), and Paul Copperman, The Literacy Hoax (New York: William Morris, 1978).

3
Society, Culture, and Character Development
Henry C. Johnson, Jr.

OUR MORALISTIC AGE

As the "prime time" program fades into the commercial, our attention is artfully drawn to a new set of images: A popular television personality, carefully selected for the age and status of the target population, lovingly fondles two high-tech copying machines that will, the images assure us, make our harried lives easier, and therefore better. As the 30-second spot closes, the camera tightens on the hero's face as he delivers the "clincher": "The Canon PC 10 and PC 20, for the most important person in my life-- me!" Having delivered this undisguised moral maxim, the video hand moves on, perhaps back into the "provocative" program we have been watching but more likely into another "message" about what we "owe" ourselves, "need," or "ought to have" in order to live better, fuller, and, above all, more "exciting" lives.

We live in a moralistic age, an age drenched with symbols and images urging our commitment to a bewildering variety of moral principles. We live in a media-dominated age, an age in which the symbols, images, and principles that give us our sense of being part of a larger society are largely presented by the media. We are in fact becoming a society created by the media. By the term media I mean all that vast array of agencies, techniques, and enterprises that <u>address</u> us, that <u>speak</u> to us with messages designed to tell us who we are, to structure our ideas, and to govern our lives. That is, to say

the same thing, to develop our character or habitual dispositions to think and act, to believe and value. I do
not mean merely the new video churches. These agencies
are outspokenly homiletical. I mean all the agencies:
television, radio, the movies, the rock music industry, the
new style press; and all their ramifications, right down
to pornography, bumper stickers, T-shirts, and punk hair-
cuts.

The media are not alone in this function, of course.
A baffling set of social groups and networks, institutions,
and other forms of social life present the moral content
necessary for any coherent society to exist. The media
are particularly significant, however, because of the growing power and the explicitness of their moralizing activity.
They also uniquely manifest the complicated social and cultural matrix within which the moral domain has its meaning
and function. It is to the general character of this matrix
of beliefs and values as a whole, which is articulated
through all our social structures and arrangements, that
this chapter points. Subsequent chapters will discuss particular aspects of it in detail. If our concern is for
character formation, especially through some sort of deliberate educative process, we dare not ignore this matrix
as the fundamental context of our efforts. It provides in
a significant degree the conditions and the definition of
our task.

In a simpler age moral and ethical recommendations
were clearer and more homogeneous, and the process of
nurturing character might easily be informal, virtually
unself-conscious. But merely teaching what is agreed upon
as good and true and beautiful, and teaching children how
to identify and resist bad examples no longer suffices.
Ours is not a Dickensian world in which life is a morality
play with all the characters clearly labeled. Our moral
world is complex and often contradictory in the extreme.
Hence, it has become a conscious problem in which the task
is to disentangle ourselves from the welter of contradictory
and unreflective moral assertions that assault us and our
children on every side. Thus, paradoxical as it may
seem, it is the abundance rather than the absence of
moral content that poses the problem. The solution, then,
is not merely asserting the truth--a truth which in our
society may be regarded as only one more strident voice
in a cacophony of moral imperatives--but enabling all of
us to sift and winnow the multitude of moral maxims and

principles which are hurled at us in an uncritical and socially irresponsible manner.

THE SOCIOCULTURAL NATURE OF CHARACTER

Character development is a social and not an individual process, because being human is a social not an individual phenomenon. Even for those who believe, as I do, that we are given a singular personal identity by the direct act of God, our development, the particular realization of our common nature as human beings, is still a social process. There is no such thing as a solitary, a private, human being. The ethical domain arises out of this fact. Indeed, the term ethics is one of a family of terms. Taken together, they demonstrate the full weight we must give to this fundamentally social presupposition of any form of human character development. In its Greek roots, the term ethikos signifies the characteristic conduct of a people or a community. Their ethos is the set of customs, moral and nonmoral, that both shape and manifest this character. Because we must grow and develop together as a people and in a community, we require the development of an ethike techne, or moral art, by means of which we can live together.

As William James pointed out, if there were but one of us, if you or I dwelt alone in a "moral solitude" with no other sentient beings to consider, we would require moral considerations or principles only to achieve a unity in our private life and development.[1] But that is not the case. We live in a social world of multiple needs and desires, claims and counterclaims that are real but conflicting and that introduce a problem of obligation and call for ethical thinking. We are interdependent and therefore mutually responsible to one another. Our physical interdependence is, one would suppose, obvious. But there is much more--a moral interdependence which is prerequisite not merely to survival as an organism but to our achievement of the normative notion of humanity. To be human means, for example, to be free to act. But freedom for me puts a claim upon others. To be human means to be able to act in the real world. But that puts a claim upon others not to misrepresent the world--i.e., not to lie by bearing false witness about the world. And, of course, if others are to be able to be human, the same claim is

made upon me. Unless we give ourselves to understanding
and honoring these mutual claims and accepting our interdependence, none of us shall be able to attain the humanity we individually seek. Again, if these claims were
simple or their resolution obvious, we would need no ethical art; but they are not. Hence, not only principles but
ethical skills are necessary for seeing, understanding, and
judging what is right and good for one and all, together.
To seek privacy of conduct and a moral estrangement from
others is the most dangerous and deceptive of goals. Yet
it seems to be precisely this thread of privacy that ties
together the current moral patchwork.

THE AMERICAN TRADITION, PAST AND PRESENT

None of us is born into an abstract moral universe.
We have both a concrete ethical context and a concrete
ethical history. Without denying the moral continuities
which bind the very notion of humanity across times and
places, it is important to recognize that the concrete locus
of our efforts at character development is in the United
States and within the historic U.S. social-moral tradition.
The main outlines of this tradition are clear. Although
serious arguments and qualifications may be raised about
our purity of intention and single-mindedness in performance, there is little doubt about our proclaimed goals.
We set out as citizens to seek a society characterized not
only by simple justice for the individual but some sort of
equality for all. The achievement of this, we have continued to believe, rests not merely upon efficient political
mechanisms but on a further moral commitment to freedom
and openness as the necessary presupposition to rationally
ordered social and individual life. Our commitment to
these moral principles is most clearly evident not so much
in our often spotty practice as in the fact that these are
the practical presuppositions of our most important social
and cultural institutions. Because these institutions rest
upon a moral base, and not one of coercive power, these
institutions are delicate, fragile, easily twisted, and even
perverted. But, at least in the tradition, our institutions
and arrangements have also been held to fall under the
judgment of overarching moral commitments, bound by principles not to be nullified by individual interests or even
the caprice of political majorities.

Traditionally, this array of institutions and principles has rested upon a cultural foundation comprising a limited theological and/or metaphysical consensus and a much more explicit moral consensus rooted in a natural law ethic. The whole enterprise could be functionally sustained only by a citizenry of a certain moral character-- i.e., not a private morality but a reasonably homogeneous disposition to act and be judged in terms of certain fundamental moral principles. To be a virtuous people, a people of character, was believed to be the necessary condition of a free and just society. And that character was public, meaningful, authoritative and (of particular importance for our purposes) teachable. Horace Mann called the whole business the "laws of reason and duty," to which it was the duty of schools and teachers to introduce their students.

As a consequence of this tradition, education in this nation, as everywhere else, was centered in moral formation or character development. But times and situations alter. Neither society nor education could remain the same. What was clear to the point of self-evidence to the members of a simpler society rapidly became murky indeed with the advent of conditions not only unforeseen but perhaps unthinkable from an optimistic Enlightenment vantage point. Even as the Founding Fathers were putting the finishing touches upon the "first new nation" (to use Seymour Martin Lipset's apt description) and grounding it on fundamental principles of rationality and morality, certain social and cultural forces were already at work. And these forces would at least severely test, if not render highly dubious and problematical, the very grounds upon which we had built. We can touch on only some of these forces, but their impact and persistence can hardly be doubted. They have come to set for us a new context.

Perhaps the most salient of these changes was the industrial revolution and its closely linked urban and technological revolutions. When Adam Smith (by trade a moral philosopher, we sometimes forget) ushered in a new social and economic world upon the radical presupposition that wealth need not be discovered but could in fact be caused, his motive was sound: The then increasingly visible poverty of the many could be alleviated by the deliberate production of plenty. But whatever his intent, his economic analysis provided a foundation for a radically new moral justification for unfettered greed and avarice beneficial to the few. It made plausible the morally corrosive conclusion that social justice and equity would require no conscious moral effort but would come automatically from the operation of the "invisible hand," which would transmute individual covetousness into social benefit. The ability to produce wealth rested in turn on the extension of a division of labor, the moral and educational effect of which we will examine in greater detail. Suffice it to point out here that the resulting fragmentation of work in the classical sense, of the community, and ultimately of the person, can hardly be underestimated in its effect on our lives. Smith's essentially benign intents were soon forgotten; his system, if it ever came to exist at all, did not achieve the socially beneficial goals he sought. But the new mode of social, economic, and moral life which he set free from its classical theological and philosophical constraints underlies virtually every society we encounter today.

The evidence is all around us. As John Kenneth Galbraith has pointed out, under the onslaught of the industrial age, cities ceased to be seats of government and the flowers of culture and instead became themselves impersonal machines for the production of goods.[2] As the well-kept factory stores each commodity in its place, so our cities stored labor and material, not in places most advantageous for the nurturing of human life but in logical utility for the productive process. Public goods and services followed suit--if any real concept of the public existed by the time full-scale urbanization was under way. In earlier, smaller, and more comprehensive communities there was much that needed to be and could be shared. Mutual responsibility and interdependence were facts in constant view. But soon the paradoxes of contemporary life began to emerge fully. Each atomized instrument of the production process--i.e., those who once were persons-- became both more interdependent and more estranged, more dependent on the public and more privatized and individuated. Whole "communities"--local "aggregations" might be the better term--and even regions ceased to be self-sufficient social-moral communities and became instead segregated resources in a process whose corporate mind and will was situated elsewhere. (The same is now true of whole countries, caught in the web of a political economy which is more the extension of the old factory system than a subsistence system for a world household.) The intercommunication presupposed by a dispersed factory system

rapidly developed, but our sense of personal isolation and
disintegration also became pandemic. We were soon in
touch with everybody, but knew nobody, including ourselves.

The technological revolution further enhanced this
paradoxical process of disintegration in the midst of coercive unification. As the tool, which was once the extension of a person, was replaced by the machine, of which
the worker became the extension, the locus of choice and
rationality became the machine and the system, not the
person. The intelligence of the industrial "operative" (to
use the quaint term once assigned to the machine tender)
became increasingly unimportant. The need for rational
moral choice once thought to underlie the process of providing for others faded from consciousness. Work became a
quantity of effort and it could be sold for a price. It
was directed not by one's personal intent but by the process which possessed one. The crucial bond between
thought and action, between self and consequences, became
so attenuated as to be meaningless for all but the few. A
sense of "powerlessness," "anomie," "ennui"--terms newly
coined to describe our condition--and the loss of any but
an assigned functional identity became highly visible
characteristics of ordinary life. They are now the chief
topics of the human conversation. And with them came an
enormous sense of enforced irresponsibility. "I only work
here," says the clerk when we return a piece of shoddily
made and fraudulently advertised merchandise to the point
of purchase, which is no longer likely to be even the
point of production, let alone the maker himself. No one
is in charge; no one is responsible; no one need consider
the questions that arise. The system, the company, the
corporation does not change its mode of operation, it brings
in behavioral scientists to help the workers accommodate
to the process and to manipulate consumers into accepting
the results.

One could go much further in discussing the evils
of a mass society: There is its excessively bureaucratic
structure. There is its transiency, its rootlessness. There
is our social and cultural fragmentation, which is often
extolled as pluralism when it is only a least common de-
nominator neutrality. Even religion has privatized and
secularized itself into a technique for individual meaningfulness, a contradiction in terms. The companion of our
largely mindless work is now an opiate leisure that does
not restore us for creative activity but shields us from the

truth about both the world and ourselves. On MTV (the video rock music network) an image jockey recently signed off with these words of hope: "It's Sunday, and as we creep into the work week you can keep us [MTV programs] like a carrot in front of your nose, to remind you that there is a weekend coming up!" Like the MTV week, each day rings not to evensong but to the brewer's "Miller-time," not to prayer and meal and family but to tavern or disco or cocktail party.

To repeat, we could discuss such things and their obvious relation to what we, as persons, are and can become. But that is not the purpose of this chapter. Many have drawn our attention to the discontents of our civilization, and other contributors to this series will provide the disciplined analysis that we need as we seek to distinguish appearance and reality. Many will, however, quite rightly object that not every aspect of modern life is evil. For many—and, one would hope, potentially for all—there have been incredible gains in nutrition and health, a previously unimaginable lightening of the effort once required for mere survival, and an ease and rapidity of communication that has heightened our moral sensitivity in some not unimportant respects. We can, if we will, come face to face with war and hunger and racism and other forms of human exploitation. We have a surfeit of things and conveniences and high culture at our fingertips. Good things have resulted. None of us would very cheerfully exchange our lot for that of our primitive forebears or the widespread bondage of earlier times. But the equally apparent moral problematic of our time has a lesson for us. Things, even good things, are not in themselves redemptive. Their goodness, their beneficial potential, depends upon their moral use, which is just the point. The question before us, then, is simply, what has become of that clear world of reason and duty, that set of institutions presumably based on reflective thought and moral character, that can shape and order our goods and our lives? It is surely not strange that, given the changes that have accompanied our potential progress, moral formation or character development has been called up as the critical need. For, if there is no ethikos, no characteristic conduct of a people—in part because there is no people—and if the ethos is chaotic and contradictory, can there be any character formed, any ethike techne conveyed to help us choose and follow the good?

EDUCATION AND THE LOSS OF CHARACTER

Once taken for granted as the heart of any educational program, moral education in general has been particularly problematical since the turn of the century. As
the call for moral development increased due to the double-
edged thrust of our progress, any firm basis for moral
formation appeared to grow increasingly doubtful. Character education or development, once the term of choice,
became particularly problematical. We began to doubt that
human action was in principle rational, let alone govern-
able by moral principles. In a massive, three-volume
study entitled the "Character Education Project" (H. Hartshorne and M. A. May, Studies in the Organization of
Character, 3 vols. [New York: Macmillan, 1928-39]), the
very notion that there could be any such thing as charac-
ter--any persistent disposition to act according to moral
principle in a variety of situations--was emphatically de-
nied. The conclusion of the study's principal authors,
Hartshorne and May, was that what human beings do is to
act according to the specific norms of groups with which
they are closely identified. Thus, if Suzy's particular
Scout troop (not the Girl Scouts in general) happens to
put a premium on honesty, Suzy may be honest with them,
or possibly on other occasions when members of her troop
are present, but it does not follow that she will not crib
her examinations at school or lie to other people.

The issue is complex, of course, but Hartshorne and
May's study rests upon certain presuppositions about human
behavior that made their methods and their conclusions
likely to be confirmed. They shared with many of their
contemporaries in research the belief that human action
was best conceived in crudely naturalistic terms. Any
particular behavior was thought to be learned in specific
situations, as it produced results satisfying to the individual, and it would be repeated only in response to situations sufficiently alike to call for that behavior. Learning
thus becomes essentially atomistic, situation-specific, and
little if at all related to any general form of reasoning.
Hence it will do no good to teach moral principles--if
there are any, a philosophical issue that was undergoing
much scrutiny at the time as well--or to hope that such
principles, if taught, will produce any general form of
recurring behavior we could call general conduct or character. Human beings are bundles, so to speak, of specific

acts and their specific consequences. We are not persons
with minds and wills that have some identity and characteristics that transcend these immediate and particular
occasions. Moral education would necessarily mean, in
that case, attaching rewards or punishments to specific
acts, largely through the approval or lack of approval of
peers or authority figures of some sort. Human actions
are not governed by rules or reasons, are not responses
to moral analysis and are not the result of any personal
moral effort or act of the will in the old-fashioned sense.

The source of this practical skepticism was also
complex. Much of it owed its authority to the work of
Edward Lee Thorndike, an educational psychologist who
believed that the conclusions of Darwin led necessarily to
the belief that human action has no "inside," so to speak.
An angry "person," for example, is not a mysterious entity
that gets mad and expresses itself through a body; the
body is all there is--an organism that responds to threats
by snarling, striking out, or what have you. Hence,
thousands of years of effort at forming the "inside" of
persons, by presenting the truth or attempting to inspire
good behavior, had been entirely misguided and understandably ineffective.

This approach to human action and learning had a
great appeal, especially to public school administrators
and teachers. It was simple, clear and readily cast in
the form of methodological "do's" and "don'ts" for the
classroom. It appeared to be value-free, requiring no
commitment (indeed, probably forbidding any) to any ultimate moral or ethical principles. Time and much more research and reflection have, however, shown that such an
approach to human nature in general and to moral development in particular need not be regarded as the sole realistic and scientific way of looking at things. Such crude
Darwinisms, with their atomistic and mechanistic perspective on human action, have themselves largely been relegated to the museum of the past. More adequate, holistic
psychologies, capable of comprehending much more of the
obvious richness and complexity of human personal and
social life, are available. (Some were available back
then as well, but they were passed over, especially by
educators.) Notions of person and character, and analyses
of human behavior in terms of reason and even will, now
compete quite actively with the tired behaviorisms of the
past. That is important, because without such concepts,

any form of moral education or character development will
be largely impotent—either relegated to an abstract philosophical realm without an adequate moral psychology to
link it with action in the world, or redefined in crude
psychological terms that will empty it of any real meaning.

SOCIETY AND CHARACTER FURTHER EXAMINED

Before continuing our examination of some of the
most salient characteristics of our contemporary social and
cultural situation, a brief summary of our argument to
this point may help the reader. The moral and ethical
dimensions of our experience are intimately related to and
bound up with our present social and cultural world.
That is not to say that the moral and ethical principles
which we take to govern this aspect of our lives are merely derived from these situations or contexts. Our moral
and ethical concerns are, however, called up by the fact
of our relatedness and interdependence as social beings.
The notion of character, as some consistent meaning and
direction in our lives, although sometimes discredited by
educators bemused by an egregiously defective analysis of
human behavior, is as crucial for any coherent social
world as it is for our becoming genuine persons. It is
also an important concept under which to consider moral
and ethical conduct developmentally.
    Our aim as educators is to help persons become
moral persons in the full sense. Our aim cannot be to
make them moral, of course; that would be self-contradic-
tory. Nor can we be content to enable them to make occasional ethical judgments. If our aim is character, not as
the merely negative prohibition of certain proclivities but
as a positive notion of consistent being and acting in the
real world, as the realization of the growing potentialities
of a coherent self, we cannot avoid taking account of the
concrete social and cultural matrix in which character develops. It is necessary, then, to consider in more detail
some key aspects of this social and cultural matrix that
seem to be particularly important for the realization of
these educational aims. As a first step, we must examine
in greater depth the crucial moral relation between self
and community and the paradoxical position we are now
in—a situation in which we simultaneously seek a private
individuality and decry the loss of community.

Any society rests, for its successful operation, on the expectation of reasonably consistent, coherent behavior on the part of its members. Our choice of friends and allies, or our wariness of some persons, rests upon our ability to make some general assessment of what they are, what they are likely to do. When I bring my new automobile into the service station run by a long-trusted operator, I do not expect him to fill my tank with water and sugar, even if he has been encouraged to do so by someone who happens to have it in for me and who has offered to make it worth the operator's while. The very notion of a meaningful life for any of us would be unthinkable if the behavior of others were not significantly different from that of my cat, who will, it is quite clear, take what he prefers in the situation. In a free, democratic society, these expectations are both particularly crucial and necessarily moral, because the institutions and forms of life are themselves founded on the rightness and goodness of certain ways of acting. Furthermore, these ways of acting presuppose both that there are real and legitimate claims upon all of us and that we have the freedom to act in accordance with a notion of value that is more than personal and private self-interest.

A recent rock lyric has as its repeated theme, "no promises, no demands." It strikes me that this phrase represents the current view—and the "thread" I mentioned—about as clearly as any few words can. But such a world, private to the point of being solipsistic, could not exist, at least as a human world. The philosopher Gabriel Marcel has argued that one of the uniquely human aspects of life is in fact just this characteristic of promising one another.[3] In a touching passage he sketches a situation most of us have encountered. A friend, mortally ill of a particularly distasteful disease, presses his claim upon us. He asks us to promise to visit again. We promise to do so—knowing that we ought to do so, knowing that we can do so, and knowing that we will not want to do so when the time comes. Our promising, which we know is no prediction since we may well fail to keep that promise, shows that we can and do have the freedom to "bind" the future. It would be unthinkable to say: "Perhaps I'll come to see you day after tomorrow—if the situation arises such that it would be to my advantage, satisfy some deeper biological instinct," or what have you! It is possible of course, in the sense of not being logically refutable, that

the whole human world we are put in touch with through
history and philosophy and literature, and through religion, has been totally false and misleading. But, as
Whitehead once remarked, when our philosophical theories
render well-attested human experience incredible, it is
probably time to give up the theories, not become cynical
about our experience. And it is morally sensitive action
of the sort Marcel describes that we have found in ourselves, and talked about, since the human conversation
began.

   We can also find this sense of wider moral awareness in a very different tradition. One of this nation's
more interesting philosophers, now unfortunately largely
forgotten, Josiah Royce, frequently wrote about what he
called the "religion of loyalty."[4] (It is perhaps worth
noting that he came to these very different conclusions in
the early years of this century, just when others were
finding the mechanization of human life the only plausible
alternative.) Royce chanced to notice an account of the
death of one Ida Lewis, who had kept the Lime Rock Light-
house in Narragansett Bay for 50 years. Although she had
participated in the saving of some 18 lives during her
tenure, it was to her 50 years of routine service, isolated
but not private, that Royce pointed. Hers was a life with
a "steady call upon daily fidelity," to use Royce's tren-
chant phrase. She was loyal not to fame or self in the
selfish sense, but to a wider community (which she rarely
saw) and to a "cause." She honored, steadily over time,
a commitment which brought about a spiritual unity, one
in which individuals were united in a life the meaning of
which transcended their separate meaning as individuals.

   Without this faithful consciousness of something beyond ourselves, and larger than this moment, there is
nothing human even for the individual. "Left to ourselves,"
says Royce, "we live not only narrowly but inconsistently."
"Self-will," he insists, "left to itself, means self-defeat."
Even when we cannot choose our situations, we can choose
how we live them, and it is what we build on the whole
and over the long run which makes self and society not
only good but possible. The warp and woof of a truly
human social world is the characteristic behavior of its
people, our character, and not our momentary inclinations,
however free we may feel when we follow them. Character,
Royce says in effect, is a "spirit suited not only to great
occasions" (those infrequent heroic moments such as Ida

Lewis had) "but to every moment of reasonable life, and not only to any one or two callings, but to all sorts and conditions of men."

What I am proposing, then, is that (from many perspectives) we require as human beings membership in a morally sensitive community. The possibility of such membership, however, has been radically diminished by developments in our social and cultural milieu. But the need for it is attested by our very discomfort in this situation and the remedies we so obviously seek. One method of resolving the problem is to attempt to escape from it. This flight very often takes the form of a romantic fugue in which, having lost real community, we desperately try to create some sense of community and identity by forming some close personal attachment with some "significant other" (as fashionable psychological jargon puts it). Strong emotional attachment to someone, sometime, is at least a temporary antidote to the lack of belonging and the accompanying fear of life which is so easily experienced in a dehumanized world. Sexual union in particular is, one might say, one form of instant identity and community, but it is also usually ephemeral and ultimately disappointing. It is no remedy for those for whom the sexual passions are either not yet, or no longer, the center of life, although we appear to be busily trying both to hurry up and prolong them. Such a strategy is not new nor is my interpretation novel. Matthew Arnold, in the mid-nineteenth century, contemplating a world which, under the onslaught of new forms of thought, appeared to many to have lost its larger meaning, was forced to sigh in response, "Ah, love, let us be true to one another!" Why? In the conclusion of "Dover Beach," he explains.

> For the world, which seems
> To lie before us like a land of dreams
> So various, so beautiful, so new,
> Hath really neither joy, nor love, nor light,
> Nor certitude, nor peace, nor help for pain,
> And we are here as on a darkling plain
> Swept with confused alarms of struggle and flight,
> Where ignorant armies clash by night.

Much of the same can be said of the minicommunities we try to form to take the place of the larger communities and institutions that once provided us with a stable

and meaningful direction for our lives. Not only the com-
munes of the once feared "hippies," but the vast array of
support groups and other therapeutic associations we are
bidden to join are similar examples of the human need to
be together. Yet they are little more satisfactory. They
are partial, not comprehensive. They seem to suggest that
we can "go it alone," or "take charge of our lives" by
ourselves once we have resolved some particular problems.
They also come and go, leaving us once more alone and
exposed to an impersonal and hostile world. The fact is
that the lives of all of us are too closely bound together
by a thousand real ties, economic, political, even biological, for the creation of such palliatives to offer any remedy when, to adapt Robert Bolt's dialogue in "A Man for
All Seasons," common moral principles are all laid flat
around us and there is no place to hide from each other.
We cannot flee. Our only hope is to accept the situation
and teach ourselves and our children to lead principled
lives, to develop character consciously, in terms of the
present human condition.

WORK, FAMILY, AND GROWING UP RESPONSIBLE

One aspect of human life which has provided a
common moral structure is, as I have already suggested,
our work. The central role of work in human life has
long been recognized, and its importance for understanding the relationship of self and community is crucial.
When Aristotle begins his examination of the state and
community "in their first growth and origin" in his Politics,
their starting point is the union of male and female, "a
union of those who cannot exist without each other."[5] This
necessary union, he insists, is not merely biological but a
condition of human life as a whole; "it is characteristic
of man" he says, "that he alone has any sense of good
and evil, of just and unjust, and the like, and the association of living beings who have this sense makes a family and a state." Thus, he strikes the same note we have
been considering. Both family and community are morally
as well as physically interdependent. And, because the
issue for human life is not merely its quantity or duration
but its quality, it is the moral and ethical dimension
which makes it human in its most fundamental sense. In
discussing the family, perhaps without noticing it himself,

Aristotle makes a crucial point when he quotes approvingly the poet Hesiod "First house and wife and an ox for the plough." The ox and the plough are the instruments through which the family sustains itself physically. But what is important to consider for our purposes is that even the most primitive community requires three things: a place and interdependent persons and a common task, a mutual work to be done. That is to say, there is in this proto-community not merely people and things but a dynamic, purposeful functioning, which is its end. For the family, this common task is at first subsistence, but for the larger and more perfect community at which the family itself aims, the common task is to achieve those higher levels of activity of which human nature is capable.

The point I want to make is that it is in this common constitutive activity, their proper work, that family and community are fully realized. It is in part in these shared tasks and the structure and meaning they bring to our lives that we as human beings find in an important respect our meaning and identity. It is also one of the most important places where we gain the sense of moral responsibility to one another. Aristotle is out to make his case against the Sophists, who held that the state—any community—was a mere convention held together by power and desire. If the Sophists (of that day or this) are right, which they are not, the community—others—have no real claim on us. Through this common work, however, the community voices its claims on us and provides us with the possibility of achieving what we can only achieve together, a mutual human life.

Now all this has a great deal to say about work and good work, in the generic sense, as participation in socially relevant activity intended to make us all human. If Aristotle has put his finger on an important aspect of the matter, and if this mutual activity is radically altered in its character, at either the family or the community level, then we are likely to be in for trouble. The meaning of our lives, and our identity as persons, including our sense of interdependent moral responsibility, may simultaneously be so attenuated that there may be left only the hunger for them, and the pain of their loss that our diminished humanity still suffers. That does not, indeed, seem very far from what has actually happened to us, as not only Aristotle but a host of perceptive philosophers and social critics of a very non-Aristotelian sort have also argued: Hegel and Marx in the last century, for example; social prophets such as Schumacher and Ellul in our own day, not to mention Marcel or Jean-Paul Sartre. Consider again what has become of our "work." From that innocent, primitive division of labor that Adam Smith found crucial for causing wealth by increasing production has come an atomization that divides not only the task but ourselves until, paradoxically, we become ever more dependent upon others and yet less and less closely related to anyone. Having lost the sort of work that could help make us persons, we find ourselves functions; and, far too often, when we cease to function, we cease to be.

Precisely as our work has lost any very clear and moral relationship either with the primary family community or with any genuine wider community of human ends, our sense of disintegration and estrangement within the hollow shell that remains of these communities has increased. Consider what is left of the family. In most cases it has long since lost any common task of providing cooperatively for its own subsistence. Recently its virtually sole mutual task has been begetting and raising children. But in many cases even that is now gone either through the rejection of childbearing in toto or by delegating the function of childbearing or childrearing to others—something now seen by many as a "right," which society is obliged to honor so that both partners may find their individual fulfillment as they choose, usually in their separate ways. It is not, any longer, a union of two people who cannot live without one another. There being no community in and through the work, we suddenly do not know who we are, or even if we are. Our chief preoccupation is then to find ourselves again, to contrive ways to relate, and to ask each other, or anyone else we can find, whether we are really living. Any number of novels, slick or pulp periodicals, or "soaps" make this abundantly clear. With no community in the work, there is no communication that arises in shared tasks. We stare at each other with a debilitating self-consciousness and try desperately to "relate," failing to see that meaningful relationship arises, at least in part, through common human work.

Having then less and less reason to stay together, less and less meaningful common work, the marriage relationship itself must now be given some reason and meaning. One must be invented. But the invented ones have little power over us and little power to hold us together. We are left with only a prolongation of the romantic search, which ought to end with a satisfying and stable relationship that grows and deepens in scope and quality but which in fact is perpetuated until we are out of breath and mind: What will help? Another partner? Another therapist? Another "interpersonal" technique? Another "job," which is, of course, not the same as work! Something must be able to help, and each day's talk show, or "news" broadcast, or popular magazine, usually has one to propose. But they do not avail us much.

A closely related phenomenon is the youth culture. Easily forgetting the pain and confusion and emptiness that our children necessarily share with all of us who are caught up in this situation, we bewail the irresponsibility of youth. There is an irresponsibility that has now reached alarming proportions, often characterized by cruelty to one another and terrorism to the vulnerable. But what is "youth" now? An empty period between the dependency of childhood and the hoped for meaningfulness of adulthood, though we have already found reason to believe that to be a meaningfulness more of promise than fact. In this empty interval (filled only by a mythical world created, at considerable profit, by adults in the hope of holding their children until they and we are ready to incorporate them) there is little meaningful activity, little reason to be responsible, because little the young can do makes any real difference to anyone or anything. Taking out the garbage or mowing the symbolic suburban lawn may have some meaning, but hardly enough to sustain the personal and moral growth we desire.

What we now call the "youth culture" is a very recent business, of course. Roughly up to the conclusion of World War 11, there was simply childhood and adulthood, with little in between. The later years of childhood were a period of transition and preparation, not for prolonged adolescence but for the community of effort that lay ahead. When my own family moved from the city to the suburbs, time was already hanging heavy on the hands of the "kids" who were living in an unreal community. Our elders were beginning to talk about youth centers and other things, so that we would have "something to do"--since we had no work. None of this, nor the make work we were sometimes given, fooled us very much or satisfied us. For this reason, l greatly preferred the farm on which l spent long periods of time. lt was structured by a clear, socially

relevant, and highly interdependent task! It was the
kind of meaningful and morally educative work that Dewey
defined as social activity with "a real motive behind and
a real outcome ahead."[6] As a small child I had watched
that task daily. In my imagination and play I rehearsed
my future participation in it, in the hope that on some
glorious day I would be invited into it! When, for example, the day came that I was first asked to drive a team
of horses, with a genuine responsibility in that community
of work, the sense of being responsible was overwhelming.
So was the conviction of participation in a meaningful way
of life and a resulting identity among those I had watched
over the years exercise that "steady call on daily fidelity"
of which Royce spoke.

Do not misunderstand me. That place and that
world and that time were not perfect. Nor, probably, is
any return possible. They were not halcyon days, nor
was that farm an arcadia to which we can now run if we
choose. These were the Depression and post-Depression
years and the seeds of the coming social and economic de-
struction had long been taking root. But rural life was
then still something of an exception--still communal, still
dependent in some measure on cooperation and the extended
family, still coherent. Now, as I drive through the same
country, the great farmsteads are going or gone, replaced
by "agribiz" and the division of labor that accompanies
that mode of production. The totality of action and
thought necessary for the individual farmer of old is now
replaced by the array of specialists, thoroughly mechanized,
who come to plow or harvest or otherwise "process" what
is not theirs--or, sometimes, not anybody's, in a manner
of speaking. I am not, of course, suggesting that farm
life was the only sort of structure through which social
moral development--character--may be understood or
achieved. But it illuminates in an important way the
sense in which a community in the work, when that work
is in at least some sense whole and socially relevant,
draws one into a moral context within which development
can occur. If we no longer have it, we must address that
fact directly, because we cannot escape its consequences
until we find some other way.

In contrast to that world, as in the youth culture
with "nothing to do," we can only fill in the void. Principally, we rely on two ingredients: the first is entertainment: the bizarre world of rock or disco, the movies,

sports, or body-building, for example. The second is schooling, and ever more schooling. And when that becomes boring and unreal, we fill that in turn with entertainment, so that even higher education often becomes little more than a further prolongation of adolescence, in special staging areas, through an extension of the same empty youth culture, replete with "nudie flicks" in the dormitories and concerts and lectures by the ersatz folk heroes of the day, to keep the customers happy.

PRIVACY AND PLURALISM

I will turn now to two rather more subtle problems we have mentioned that seem to me also to be crucial sociocultural elements in the context of contemporary moral development. First, the very notion of freedom has undergone a revolution with enormous impact especially upon the young. Again, this revolution has not just suddenly appeared; its roots are easily carried back to the nineteenth or even the eighteenth century, perhaps even further. But the fact of this revolution now appears very starkly in its pervasiveness and the power of its effect. That revolution is the interpretation or translation of freedom as privacy. In contrast to the classical view of freedom as the opportunity to realize one's humanity through commitment to something higher or larger or transcendent; in contrast even to the considerably less robust view of freedom as the right to an almost atomic individuality but one within at least some context of moral relation that characterized the laissez-faire liberalism of the last century; the present popular notion of freedom is just that "moral solitude" which William James says is not available to us. We need see ourselves related only to those we happen to care about, or even to no one else at all. As could be expected, this private world now includes the notion of private acts that, one is taught to believe, affect no one but oneself. Gone is the crucial conviction that what I do with or for myself, even in my secret thoughts and actions, is related to others, all others. We no longer believe that my self is not my own; it is not something which lives and breathes by itself or to itself. Furthermore, this notion of private selves and private acts makes possible in turn a shrinking of the moral universe, which we find attractive because within its diminished confines we may at least feel very moral. I may feel obliged to treat my wife or my children or my intimate friends with some ethical consideration--though not even that is necessary; it is a matter I may choose if I wish--but not the starving child overseas or the unattractive neighbor next door. It is my life, my body, my property, my "thing," my self. I may give it or share it, but that is a question of convenience or inclination, not of necessity or principle.

Another related factor in the contemporary moral climate is the widespread conviction that political pluralism is a philosophical justification for a crude relativism. In a society in which there are only private worlds, there can be no universal moral context or principles. In a society in which we permit or even encourage difference, including difference of opinion, the conclusion is sometimes invalidly drawn that any or all acts and ideas stand on the same footing. Consequently none can be held to transcend individuals or groups--except, of course, the principle that we are all equally entitled to believe or do what we like. But, the political principle that there are good reasons for permitting difference, for encouraging (not just tolerating) something we have come to call pluralism, does not entail the further epistemological principle that all notions are equally true or good. To hold such a view is to remove any moral justification for pluralism itself, not to mention such presuppositions of our society and culture as we have already mentioned--viz. honesty and openness and justice. The freedom that we must affirm is the freedom to be both tolerant and committed to certain ethical and epistemological principles. Without that freedom probably no society, and certainly our society, has any meaning at all.

THE TROUBLESOME TROUBADOUR:
THE MEDIA IN AMERICAN LIFE

The primary agency that has at least hastened if not actually brought about this revolutionary new "society" and "culture" is, I believe, what we now call the media. By the media, as I have said, I mean those particular instrumentalities that address us, speak to us, sometimes claiming to allow us to speak to one another. I include television, the popular music industry, the movies, the popular press and probably even much of the legitimate theater of our time. We sometimes refer collectively to at least a portion of these instrumentalities as the communications industry. But surely here the word <u>communications</u> has suffered a profound change in the process. Its primitive logic presupposes some sort of human unity through rational interchange. What it creates at present is a unity of exposure that pretends to represent an engagement with reality. It induces, however, not a healthy interaction among persons but a privatized passivity. Through the media, so to speak, the more we become one by attachment to a new technological umbilical cord, the more radically separate we grow. While claiming to mirror our world and our life ("give us 18 minutes and we'll give you the world" proclaimed one 24-hour news channel), the media in fact coerce us to believe, without thought, in a cartoon of self and reality. Representatives of the media frequently bewail their being made into whipping boys for the ills of modern life, but it is difficult to deny that both the form and the content of our purported communication system raise the most serious questions.

How is this accomplished? The crux of the matter lies, I believe, in the fundamental form of the process. The media, as I have defined them, might better be known in another popular term as the image industries. They provide symbols and images, attach them to persons, events, and ideas, and then broadcast them to the folk. This process necessarily entails judgments of fact, meaning, and value on the part of authors, producers, and sponsors, but the object in view is to procure receptivity, not to engender critical, reflective response. Thus, reactionary conservatism, as supposedly characteristic of the blue-collar class, is projected through "All in the Family." The paradigmatic image of the conservative is the image of Archie Bunker: stupid, bigoted, sexist, domineering, antagonistic to the young, but of course highly entertaining. He is already part of our popular language: now any conservative is an "Archie Bunker," with all the cultural content and emotional baggage that goes along. The image is universal: all conservatives are Archie Bunkers; all Archie Bunkers are conservatives. Conservatism is not a philosophical concept or a political proposal, with a capacity for truth or error or complexity. Through the "magic of television" it is an image you laugh at but mustn't like or be like. What is "good" is attached to an attractive image; what is "bad" is attached to an unattractive image. The normative concept fades out; the emotionally or ideologically driven image remains. The viewer's role is to watch and to accept, not to respond critically. That would lower the program's entertainment value and seriously limit its commercial viability. Even the nightly news, with its affected stance of objectivity and the issue-oriented talk shows are primarily the creation and manipulation of images for the purposes of entertainment. Controversy, provided that it is emptied of tedious analysis and reflection, is good (and very profitable) entertainment.

It is sometimes alleged that this media content is somehow the new heroic (or antiheroic) literature of our time. But the largely dreary cartoons of humanity that pour from these media represent only a new secular hagiography (bestiary?) for us to sample at random as our taste or mood may dictate. Needless to say, there are exceptions, though they seem to grow less and less frequent. But, on the whole, this content is overwhelmingly directed to and for that private world of private acts we have been considering. The perfect symbols are the "walkman" craze and the new private music-television cassette player, which will circulate still more widely and "personally" the images of one particular subculture. In the media world, value questions of the most complex and important sort are not questions for complex moral analysis but questions of personal life-style; and when it comes to matters of style and taste, there can, as Cicero said, be no dispute.

The difference between the new entertainment industry and the educative role of classical literature, drama, and poetry is perfectly clear. The persistent focus of the latter on human life as the occasion for complex moral analysis is virtually impossible to deny. In that literature (and our history making as well) we are brought together into a human community that transcends time and place, through an internal analysis of real and possible human actions mediated through art. (Even when Flaubert broke precedents and introduced us to Madame Bovary, it was not to image wicked women as vulnerable and attractive but to face us with the issues posed by a world and a character we were creating for ourselves.) The artfulness of the classical literary medium, now largely abandoned in our schools, drew us in to participate rather than merely to watch, and to grow in our humanity rather than merely to exchange one shopworn mask for another.

As John Dewey--surely no traditionalist--pointed out, the literature we studied enabled us to conduct an imaginary "rehearsal" of the nature and effect of the traditional moral wisdom on our own future aims and acts.[7]

The curious rock culture that has flickered and crackled into being represents a particularly powerful and alarming manifestation of the phenomena we have been considering. The retreat of the young (and many of the not so young) into a private world of music, now with visual images even more concretely attached in rock videos, is a baffling and disturbing development. Apart from the occasional assertion of some social complaint--most frequently about boring work, boring teachers, or the terrors of environmental desecration or nuclear weapons--the form and content of this music is in large measure exclusively private, virtually to the point of narcissism. It is an only thinly disguised appeal for a make-believe drug culture, crudely sensual, aggressive to the point of violence, exploitive of others, and generally socially divisive and destructive. The lyrics and visuals, produced at enormous cost and with the highest technical sophistication, self-righteously attack every institution in sight, with special attention to church and school. That all this is taken with high seriousness by some of their elders fools few of its artists or its consumers. The message to satisfy oneself, at whatever cost to others, is clear and compelling and often aimed at the very young. And its impact is undeniable. As O'Shaughnessy wrote: "We are the music-makers, /And we are the dreamers of dreams . . . we are the movers and shakers / Of the world for ever, it seems."[8]

The new media culture, and especially the rock culture, is also a call to hero worship, except that now the heroes are principally those who entertain us. It is perhaps crucial to have heroes, especially during adolescence when one is trying to envision what one is to become. And, if we do not have genuinely close relations with anyone (through family, work, or community) the need for heroes becomes even more compelling. By becoming imaginatively related to one or more heroes, some sense of meaning and participation may be created. All of this might be well and good except that both in performance and in person the new entertainment-world heroes (including the sports figures who loom so large) are in most cases simply empty, morally disreputable cartoons of what human nature can and should be.

Because of the incredible cost and complexity of the
media, the power of the very few who control their content
is now enormous.   The principal format, television, is not
a medium of communication either accessible to or responsive to the people, especially in the local community.   Having largely driven out other, "colder" mediums of communication, to use Marshall McLuhan's categorization, television
(and radio) reign supreme.   Nothing can compete in drawing crowds of listeners and viewers--as opposed to readers
or discussants.   Print is dead or dying.   Our forefathers
and mothers wrote to and for each other, in letters and
newspapers, tracts, and broadsides.   The inexpensive modern technology of printing could make a continuation of
written, reflective communication possible, of course, but
its impact has been reduced virtually to nil.   Hence, the
relative handful of writers, producers, and salespeople
who together engineer and mastermind the electronic media,
have an access to and an influence on our lives without
previous parallel.   The notion that they generate the content of the media out of the fundamental levels of life in
the United States, and its meanings and values, is naïve
in the extreme.   They exercise the power of characterizing
ourselves to ourselves as they see fit, restrained only by
the homogenization necessary for commercial acceptance at
a national level.   The fact that we necessarily accept it,
without any social control except the specious freedom to
tune out, is taken to indicate real agreement.   That conclusion may be doubted.   But what cannot be doubted is
the impact of those who control the images, tell the stories,
and sing the songs in any culture or society.   The relation of this phenomenon to the process of deliberate formation of character, to ethikos and ethos and to the possibility of any rational, reflective ethike techne cannot be
doubted either.

SCHOOLING AND THE DEVELOPMENT OF CHARACTER

One could build a superficially plausible argument
that, given the social and cultural context I have sketched
in, the media represent the new school, the new form education must take, willy nilly, in the world of today.   Some
have so argued, but their arguments fail for a number of
reasons, at least if we hold to the notions of schooling
and educating that we have historically maintained.   Edu-

cation, for at least twenty-five hundred years in the West, has been focused through some normative conception of the general development of human nature in a coherent social and cultural relationship. There can be little doubt that we live in the midst of an information-creation-and-transmission explosion, largely through the agency of the media. But the dissemination of information is not of itself educative. The prevailing motives for this distribution are in no sense educational. As Professor Sullivan will demonstrate more conclusively in Chapter 12, the motive that governs the media is not general but particular--sometimes almost random--and in most cases commercial rather than social or moral. Furthermore, if the society and culture are themselves chaotic or even contradictory--and the media both convey and foster this incoherence--their impact can hardly be educative.

Schooling, on the other hand, represents an attempt to institutionalize an educative process in a concrete social setting. It has presupposed the ability to create ideal, controlled communities distinct from the real world--a world always thought to be in need of perfecting if not reforming. In a simpler age, access to a wider world, through the provision of information and access to the chief vehicles of the culture (principally through the medium of print, of course) fell largely within the school's control. A number of factors have, however, dramatically altered the school's status as an effective nexus between past and future, between society and culture, and between the individual and his or her larger society. Once again, not the least have been the media. In their present form, their pervasiveness and psychological impact far outrun the school's ability to guide and control even in the best of circumstances. On the other hand, the effect of the media--unless they were themselves to be centralized and bureaucratically controlled, as in some Orwellian society--is at best haphazard and therefore they are incapable of exercising any positive, coherent schooling function.

If the media cannot provide a new school or educational process, but may be capable of rendering the old one largely ineffective, where does that leave us? The situation is considerably more complex than I have just suggested. Since the seventeenth century in this country, the primary agency for educating the young has been not just the school, of course, but the local community, including family, church, and schooling (where and as needed).

Space precludes our considering more than one or two important respects in which we must clarify and revise our thinking. The other chapters in this series furnish more extensive and more adequate analysis. For now, I would like first to emphasize only that the school still represents a wider social context for the child and a potential introduction to a still wider one. That is to say, entry into the educational process in the form of schooling moves the person from the essentially narrow and falsely homogeneous nature of individual and family-centered experience. Provided it chooses to be a genuine community that mediates a yet wider world to the individual, the school can help the child become conscious of that wider community that is the source of his or her meaning in important respects. That expanded awareness also puts us in touch with those larger moral and ethical claims upon us that I have argued are central to character development.

Secondly, whatever else the school is being asked to do, one of its central and indispensable aims is to make possible critically intelligent, reflective living. No other human institution has this as a principal aim. If the school's other social baggage makes the comprehension or effective accomplishment of this aim impossible, that situation must be changed. A crucial element in this is the previously examined change in the social and cultural conditions that surround the school. Where (perhaps) we could once be content with merely conveying a reasonably coherent culture, we must now prepare students to live in a complex and often contradictory culture. In this context, the problem is not nearly so much to gain information about, or access to, a wider world and culture as how to organize and weigh, in a responsible and critical fashion, the flood of social and cultural content that washes over all of us daily. That is not, of course, to say that life does not have many more dimensions. But the deliberate cultivation of intelligence, through the power of critical reflection, is one task that is principally the school's and the central concern of no other institution. The task of the school is to enable the student to develop a perspective from which to deal with the environing culture and society, not simply to mirror it.

To live intelligently and reflectively necessarily entails the ability to be intelligent about the moral content of all human culture and society--that is, all human

living, including one's own conduct toward self and others.
It is not necessary to inject moral content or ethical questions into the study of history or literature or science,
they are there already, because there are moral and ethical dimensions in every sort of human experience as it is
lived. Deliberately to reduce human experience to neutral
terms, so that that subject matter drawn from it no longer
represents a form of moral experience, is to destroy simultaneously both the educational content of any area of study
and the principal element in anything that can be called
human life. The educator's calling is to enable students
to recognize this moral content (in relation, of course, to
other relevant and appropriate elements of content), and
to be as morally intelligent and reflective as they are
scientifically intelligent and reflective or physically skillful. War, for example, does not merely raise moral issues; its study does not merely permit us to inject moral
questions; war is a moral issue. War is a form of human
relationship and the central question that makes human
relationships is precisely their moral content. Nor is this
a question of some doctrinaire, illicitly imposed "ideology,"
as some social scientists might term it, with the implicit
warning that we'd best be careful about dealing with such
issues and stick simply to the "facts." Although justifications for particular human actions may be categorized by
social scientists as mere ideology--they are not so considered by their advocates, of course--the question of the
form and quality of human relations is not itself a partisan or ideological issue. On the other hand, the frequent
tendency to reduce the study of international politics to
terms of self-interest, on the view that such an analysis
is not ideological but somehow objective, scientific, and
value-free, is probably an ideological commitment only
thinly veiled as neutral scholarship.

Education and schooling, I have argued, are moral
enterprises in themselves. This is true first of all because
if any educational goal is being pursued that goal is normative, not merely descriptive, and consequently rests ultimately on a justification in terms of value principles.
Furthermore, the school is a form of human community,
both the life and task of which are also moral questions
and rest on moral principles. But there is more. School
life itself involves all the moral relations we have previously discussed, and they should be consciously considered by
all participants in that community. Finally, the school's

central pedagogical task, the development of critical reflective intelligence, also rests upon moral commitments to
truthfulness, openness, justice and equity, among others.
These need to be consciously considered, not buried as
silent presuppositions that are never directly confronted.

"BUT, WHOSE VALUES?"

Discussions of moral education in schools are usually
met with an ultimate challenge in our "pluralist" society
and culture: "But, whose values are you going to teach?"
As the reader may have sensed, I have been working my
way toward the solution of this final difficulty. I have
been attempting to show that human life is a moral question. Insofar as education and schooling have as their
object human life, human society and culture in their fundamental sense, that content is intrinsically moral and
ethical. Because these moral and ethical questions are not
partisan or ideological and hence they can be dispensed
with only at the price of removing not only the principal
educative content of schooling but humanity itself. The
moral and ethical issues (and today much specifically
moralistic content) are an inescapable aspect of all human
life and experience. There can be no question about our
right to bring this to the attention of our students and to
require them to deal with moral issues with the same reflective, critical intelligence that we require them to address other issues and elements in our culture and society.
They need to learn how to think them through in moral
terms and to learn what moral action might be.
That will, however, require moral content, not just
an abstract skill of moral analysis. Surely that will
transgress the boundary of indoctrination. Not so. Just
as it need not invent moral questions, the school need not
invent the moral content open to investigation by the student any more than the school is called upon to invent
the subject matter of physics or mathematics. That moral
content (though admittedly it is more complex and more
controversial than the content of the safer, conventional
disciplines and skills) is also there, in the human moral
conversation that has gone on for as long as human history. The question is not the right or obligation of the
school to select or impose any set of moral principles, but
the obligation of the student to consider the moral issues

and his or her right to bring to bear on those issues, at
the highest possible level, the moral wisdom that is available in our ongoing culture. The issues are there; the
sources used are likely to reflect the diverse cultural and
social backgrounds of students. If this engagement with
moral issues and moral content is done publicly--that is to
say, in the school as an open community of inquiry--it
will represent the positive potential of the pluralism we
cherish rather than the dessicated, least common denomina-
tor neutralism so frequently encountered. The teacher's
role in this process of confronting the moral reality of
human life is not to impose but to aid the student in
bringing to bear on the moral content of any area of
human inquiry the various traditions of moral understanding and analysis that are an objective part of the student's
own (and our common) heritage. The task is not to indoc-
trinate but to guide these activities of inquiry and communication by the moral criteria implicit in the educative
process itself and in faithfulness to the school's function
as an important social (and hence moral) institution in its
own right.

AND, WHAT ABOUT RELIGION?

All this applies equally to the even thornier issue
of religion. Neither religious motives nor religious content
need be excluded from the process of critical intellectual
and moral development, even in public schools. I see no
reason why Catholics or Mennonites or Jews should be deprived of the right to bring to bear their unique and important traditions of moral analysis, linked as it is to
their distinctive theological principles and religious experience, on the personal and social moral issues which
our world thrusts upon us all in common. It will, of
course, be the correlative duty of Unitarians or of Luther-
ans (or, indeed, of Moslems or Buddhists) as religious
traditions and communities, to prepare their own students
for this process. (This is a task which at least most religious communities do not accomplish with much effectiveness at present but which they could, and I think should,
take up again.) Nor is this contrary to the Constitution
or the dictates of the Supreme Court. The thrust of the
Court's recent decisions is that the public school has neither warrant nor power to become a church--i.e., to become

an institution dedicated to exercising religious practice or
serving as an agency for deliberate conversion. The public school is to remain a school, but the school's function
of critical study of common traditions and the use of their
content in understanding and dealing with our common
problems, cannot legitimately be twisted to prohibit free
access to religious traditions as objects of study or
sources of thought.[9] Furthermore, to stay away from religion is to make much of our past and present unintelli-
gible. Religious illiteracy is not the highest form of pluralism. It is a very dangerous form of ignorance from
the perspectives of believer and nonbeliever alike.

Those schools that are free, in our system of government, to commit themselves outspokenly to live out their
theological and moral heritage, ought, I also believe, be
at pains to see that their students can also explore at
least something of the variety of moral and religious traditions which are present in our common human history.
This is a contribution to the public good in which they
have a claim and a responsibility, without any necessity
of imposing the view that all commitments are either alike
or equally valid.

The question of religion and its relation to both
public and independent schooling requires a great deal of
re-examination. I can here but scratch the surface. The
issues on all sides are both real and serious. In the
first place, as we have noted, the existence of schools
under openly religious auspices has been guaranteed since
Pierce, the 1922 Supreme Court decision which terminated
prolonged and repeated attacks on their legitimacy. (The
grounds set out in that crucial decision are in fact of
peculiar force in our present concern for moral development: The state has no power to force the family to abandon its values as a basis for education, although the
state--that is to say, we as citizens in common--does have
legitimate interests of its own which we are entitled to
ask any process of schooling to take into account.) But
the mere freedom to be unique does not by itself create a
unique character for religious (or any other nonpublic)
schools. Without a genuinely distinctive content, methodological principles, and forms of life, such schools will
produce mere division rather than provide for the enrichment of either the individual or what could be a genuinely
pluralistic society.

The notion of a one best system of universal, mandatory, publicly controlled education has in fact never been realized. It was a particular goal envisioned by the Yankee school platform articulated by Horace Mann, but the elite have never accepted it, and religious communities have, as we have just noted, been free to reject it. Perhaps, then, we should straightforwardly consider a pluralistic educational system of the sort that prevails in many other societies. Yet, the stakes are extremely high, socially and politically, and people of goodwill and intelligence can and do differ on this matter. Given our chaotic social and cultural context, however, and the necessity of social and cultural consensus for any educational process, the case for encouraging such subcommunities as have the distinctive grounds and the cohesive commitments necessary to educate has some compelling reasons.

There is, finally, one very fundamental question that confronts the educator in the Christian tradition. Much of what we have been discussing may, on solidly traditional religious grounds, be accused of a fatal flaw: the notion that character is merely a personal intellectual achievement, and that it can be achieved by some antiseptic, pedagogical technique in an institutionally sterile setting. From at least some theological perspectives, character, in its full sense, is a divine gift, a grace to be received and exercised only within a community of faith. Such a religious notion of character is not in content necessarily incompatible with, let alone inimical to, the notion of character grounded in the common good we need to fashion in a free, plural society. We may, however, doubt that it can be fully achieved in terms of so religiously neutral a context and process. Our human past (for some three thousand years) offers little promise that positive moral growth comes to full fruition at the hands of philosophers, or social engineers, or even the efforts of morally literate and committed teachers by themselves. The list of pedagogical failures here includes such dedicated moral educators as Socrates, Plato, and Aristotle, to name only the best known. If goodness comes fully, not by human effort alone, but only by grace and within a community of faith, we may indeed lack the necessary grounds for optimism.

There are, of course, many other questions both practical and substantive that lurk under the brevity of our discussion. Because they cannot be raised or resolved here does not mean that such questions do not exist or are unimportant. One of the most demanding is the task of preparing teachers and curriculum developers who are really competent to accept responsibility for character development. Another is the fact that our whole institutional organization and operation of schooling will have to be re-examined if the development of character is to be removed from its peripheral position. That we can do something about such issues seems to me, however, beyond question. The need exists. Given our social and cultural situation, it appears to be critical. The opportunity does not have to be made; it also exists in the very educational and social tradition within which we live. What more do we require, at least to begin?

NOTES

1. "The Moral Philosopher and the Moral Life," in Essays on Faith and Morals (New York: Longmans, Green, 1943).

2. The Age of Uncertainty (Boston: Houghton Mifflin, 1977); (see especially Chapter 11).

3. Being and Having, Katharine Farrer, translator (Westminster, England: Dacre Press, 1949), pp. 47-56.

4. "The Religion of Loyalty," Lecture V in The Sources of Religious Insight (New York: Scribner's, 1912).

5. Politics Book I, Chapter 2 (1252a-1253a) in W. D. Ross, translator, The Student's Oxford Aristotle, Vol. VI: Politics and Poetics (London: Oxford University Press, 1942).

6. The School and Society (Chicago: University of Chicago Press, 1899). Also printed in Reginald D. Archambault (Ed.), John Dewey on Education--Selected Writings (New York: Modern Library, 1964), pp. 297-300.

7. Human Nature and Conduct--An Introduction to Social Psychology (New York: Modern Library, 1957), pp. 145-46, 178-86.

8. William Arthur Edgar O'Shaughnessy, "Ode." He continues:

> One man with a dream, at pleasure
> Shall go forth and conquer a crown;
> And three with a new song's measure
> Can trample a kingdom down.

9. The best sources are Engle et al. v. Vitale et al., 370 U.S. 421 (1962) and School District of Abington Township v. Schempp, 374 U.S. 203 (1963).

Part II
The School

4
Students and Schools
Edward A. Wynne

The topic of this chapter is the relationship between students and schools, and character development. This topic is of critical importance to our concerns. However, before considering the matter in some detail, we must acquire a general perspective. Otherwise, our vision will stay trapped within a small slice of the present, or we will confront important issues with a severely limited foundation. And so we must approach the issue by flank attack.

ABOUT HISTORY

The problem of transmitting good character is inherently complex because young human beings have longer periods of dependency than almost any other species. This dependency permits them to learn elaborate skills, and requires adults to surround them with intricate systems of instruction and nurture. Almost by definition, all cultures develop such systems to shape and protect their progeny. The central aim of these systems has been to transmit good character to the young. And, throughout history, and even in prehistoric societies (according to anthropological research), deliberate thought has been directed at managing such systems for education and socialization.

A large body of philosophy and lore--starting perhaps with Socrates and Plato--has evolved regarding the management of character development. Much of this knowledge is still studied, and even applied, in our own era.

This intellectual continuity is understandable; certain constant problems arise through all education systems. In sum, in our era any analysis of education for good character should be strongly colored by historical perspectives; most education systems (even into the twentieth century) gave greater priority to character as an education goal than to cognitive learning, and we should make use of this experience.

Despite the value of such traditional knowledge, special problems confront persons who try to apply its approaches in contemporary education systems. Modern schools are historically unique environments. This uniqueness does not destroy the worth of traditional insights. But such insights need to undergo analysis and adaptation before they can be applied. A first step in such analysis is to consider deliberately what is meant by the "unique nature" of modern schools and colleges.

For most of human history and prehistory, there were no such things as schools and colleges. Instead, there were relatives, elders and intimate servants who helped to inform the young. Sometimes, such persons assumed a formal status, and undertook roles such as tutors, pedagogues, or mentors. But even in such instances traditional process of education was mostly informal and personal. When we hear remarks about Plato's "school," we must realize that the school was comprised more of disciples than students: a small group of young and middle-aged men who chose to associate with some master—and who were accepted by him—to learn via informal discourse. Terms like "school" represent an effort to impose our contemporary perspectives on a very different situation. Most traditional insights regarding character development in the young assumed that such development would be fostered via close, constructive relationships between youths and adult mentors. The most important aim of such relationships was to transmit moral values both by example and instruction. This assumption was even transferred to vocationally structured situations, where patterns such as master/apprentice were applied. This does not mean that the optimum was always attained. Exploitation of the young is not only a modern problem. However, whatever the variations which occurred in reality, the model envisaged nurturant intimacy. Such intimacy required persisting relationships between significant adults and the maturing young.

It is true that much of the traditional literature about character formation was developed by persons largely concerned with the training of young aristocrats--and may not appear to be directly applicable to our era.   But anthropological research has demonstrated that, even among more typical youths, the principles articulated in such philosophies were, in practice, applied generally to the young in a somewhat diminished form.   A lovely story to this effect is found in the Introduction of Margaret Read's Children of Their Fathers (New York: Holt, Rinehart and Winston, 1986).   The anthropologist describes meeting a young native elementary schoolteacher (from the tribe she was studying) while walking through the bush. The teacher was conversant with English.   The teacher, while walking, was simultaneously reading a book.   The anthropologist asked, "What is the book?"   It was Plato's Republic.   The teacher observed that the book had many good ideas about forming children, and that those ideas were complementary to those traditionally practiced by his tribe.   And the succeeding ethnographic study supports the tribesman's conclusion.

Schools, with paid teachers and formal groups of pupils, began to evolve as significant institutions during the late Middle Ages.   But their influence on the young during such earlier eras was quite limited.   Only small proportions of the potential "market" were enrolled. Classes in early schools were often age- and abilityheterogeneous, and pupils were frequently called on to assist less able peers.   The general shortage of resources also compelled teachers to assign pupils to perform maintenance, and other chores.   The lengths of enrollment were usually quite brief.   The size of individual schools was typically small; often there was only one teacher, presenting a variety of subjects.   Many of these schools were managed by, or subservient to, religious institutions.   As a result, their teachers, and the subject matter presented, naturally tended to focus on character-relevant topics.   In sum, early schools typically could have only a modest influence on character, largely due to the limited length of pupil enrollment.   Furthermore, due to the special nature and intimacy of those schools, that influence would be akin to that recommended by the classic procharacter tradition.

These various forces making for congruence between schools and character development persisted in the United

States well into the twentieth century. For example, William Torrey Harris (1835-1909), a leading Hegelian philosopher, was strongly sympathetic to such approaches, and successively served as superintendent of St. Louis public schools, and U.S. commissioner of education. And some people may remember reading recollections of older adults--in sources such as Reader's Digest--about the benign influence on them of the teacher at their one-room school. Part of the reason for such influence was the mentor-like relationship possible in a one-room school, where one teacher might instruct a continuing group of students for three to eight years. Undoubtedly, criticisms can be directed at the curriculum limitations of such a situation: One teacher might not have the knowledge to cover the variety of material which should be presented during such a prolonged period. But there is no doubt that the character influence of such an adult on pupils could be very strong.

TWENTIETH-CENTURY SCHOOLS

During the later nineteenth century, a number of changes began in society which, gradually but decisively, altered the nature of U.S. schools. These changes had important implications for the management of pupil character development. Urbanization increased. This meant that larger numbers of pupils lived within walking distance of any one school; as a result, individual schools could efficiently be made larger, employ more teachers and enroll more pupils. Society, in general, became more wealthy. Thus, more children could spend longer periods of economically unproductive time attending schools. U.S. society became more religiously heterogenous. As a result, it became necessary for schools to base their value rationales on (at first) nonsectarian Christianity, then essentially on deism, and finally, on purely secular principles. The subject matter taught in schools also became more elaborate, and more specialized teachers were needed. And the principle of age- and knowledge-differentiated classes became more widely followed, partly due to the modern learning psychologies. Finally, the importance of economies of scale and staff specialization was further legitimated by the spread of industrialization and mass production. Within a comparatively short historical period, the modern school became the modal education institution.

The differences between this institution and its various predecessors are noteworthy. Compared with its predecessors, the modern school contained more pupils and teachers; had more cognitively oriented subject matter; had more transitory relationships among pupils, and between pupils and particular teachers; enrolled its pupils for longer periods of time; was more likely to be a rationalistic and secular institution; and was less subject to direct parental influence. Ironically, applying "traditional" perspectives, the contemporary school is less effective than its predecessors in forming good character—and, at the same time, more pupils are enrolled in it for longer periods. Despite such shifts, character development in the traditional sense remained a substantial formal goal of elementary and secondary education up until about the 1930s. The changes in school organization affected the character development techniques applied. Still, these techniques stressed pupil conduct, as well as cognitive and conceptual learning. In effect, a type of cultural lag occurred: schools—and the ideas affecting schools—became less effective in shaping pupil character; however, efforts were still made to adapt old principles to the changed environment.

This brief analysis is congruent with the data presented in Chapter 2. Those data show that, by objective measures, youth disorder has been steadily increasing. Simultaneously, as just argued, schools have absorbed more youth time, and become less effective in forming good character. The spread of "bad" schools is a significant cause for the rise in youth disorder. It is about time for us to consider proposed changes in school structure and policy which might correct this distressing situation.

In assessing such proposals, we should display a special sympathy for prescriptions derived from traditional patterns. After all, for the immediate past we have obviously been applying school policies derived from nontraditional perspectives: Speaking frankly, their track record does not appear too good. We should also strive to escape from the thralldom of "presentism." In a literal sense, we cannot turn the clock back. But this does not mean that some former values and practices, now practically abandoned, cannot be resurrected. There are obviously cyclical elements in history. The only interesting question—regarding turning the clock back—is whether some phenomena are semicyclical or not. Incidentally, evidence

will be presented here to emphasize that what is "the
present" is a matter of debate. Many schools, while not
receiving faddish attention, still apply numerous traditional procharacter practices. The present is really a
very heterogeneous mix.

We can better assess the value of traditional approaches if we characterize them as reflecting a particular school of psychology.

THE DOMINANT CONTEMPORARY PSYCHOLOGY

Certain implicit psychologies dominate contemporary
education. For the purposes of simplicity, they might collectively be termed Zeitgeist. They help determine the
structures of relationships which appear in schools among
teachers, among students, and among teachers and students.
It is incongruent with the traditional psychology which
was applied in earlier, procharacter, environments. Until
we see the discrepancies between these past and present
psychologies, we cannot engage in appropriately restruc-
turing school policies and practices. Among the special
characteristics of the Zeitgeist are

- The assumption of the innate goodness of human nature.
  As a result, great weight is given to self-expression,
  fulfillment, and free choice. Simultaneously, the value
  of external controls, punishments, rules and authority
  is depreciated. In effect, the concept of development
  has been substituted for that of shaping, or formation.
- Priority is given to the attainment of individual, personal aspirations. Conversely, making sacrifices on the
  behalf of a group, or being gratified through some collective success, is given little weight.
- Supreme satisfaction is attributed to the attainment of
  immediate goods, services, and intimate personal relationships. Remote rewards or recognition--fame, historic
  remembrance, entitlement to a desirable afterlife--are of
  little consequence.
- Immediate, public expressive conduct is held in low regard by prestigious persons. Some license and status
  is granted to "certified" artists, or groups of adolescents.
  However, typical adult citizens are not expected to participate in routine or frequent religious or communal activities which have a high expressive content.

For example, the evident fact is that students, without
appropriate structure provided by adults, typically engage
in disorderly or unconstructive conduct. But this "fact"
will not convert believers in the Zeitgeist into supporters
of discipline and external structure with regard to the
young. Instead, the believers will point out exceptions to
the data--for example, disorder does not always occur
when structure is withdrawn. The believers will propose
new ways (minus the assertion of authority) which they
contend will diminish the disorder. If the new ways are
tried, and they don't work, believers will find flaws in
the particular applications, and urge further experiments.
If the disorder still persists, believers will contend that,
as a matter of moral right, firm authority cannot be applied against student disorder; such application is immoral,
and will also warp the students' adult life. They may
also contend that a little disorder--visited on other children, not their own--is not so terrible. And so on.

The Zeitgeist is not consistent with all which may
be termed "modern psychology." For instance, the later
thinking of Sigmund Freud, as articulated in Civilization
and Its Discontents, is replete with pessimistic remarks
about the character of human nature. In passing, Freud--
an evident atheist--observed that "man is the wolf to man."
And Berelshon and Steiner concluded a vast survey of
psychological research by remarking on man's immense
capacity for self-deception, and for substituting his aspirations for his perceptions. Such psychiatrists, and psychologists, would ridicule educational approaches founded
on freeing students to make their own judgments, or which
gave significant weight to the pursuit of immediate gratification. They would propose that human life survives only
through the constant collective social control and suppres-
sion of our aspirations for omnipotence and animal release.

This sympathy for group life does not imply a denial of real individual differences, and the need for
schools to respond to such variations. All groups--from
football teams to families--must foster some level of diversity to operate as efficient collectives. Such diversity permits a division of labor. Durkheim pointed out that appropriate diversity can therefore foster group productivity
and cohesion. Furthermore, all individual talents ultimately attain fulfillment through engagement with others.
Thus, individual development ultimately must be assisted
by group engagement. However, groups cannot persist if

their members frequently engage in random, or undisciplined conduct. So assisting individual development through group processes means that some aspects of development must be constrained or monitored. Otherwise, groups cannot be born and persist--in the interest of all developing individuals.

None of this is to imply some Manichean polarity between individualism and group life and authority. As we know, groups, and persons holding authority over groups, are capable of inordinately evil conduct. But, to my mind, all previous serious psychologies (perhaps excluding the early Rousseau) took the inevitability of group life as given: The group surely possessed tragic potential but, in the most literal sense, it was a fact of life. The critical flaw underlying many modern education practices is the assumption that students can be provided with education without ensuring that they are sited into vital groups, under constructive adult general supervision. The assumption is a flaw because such unsited students will either form misdirected groups on their own, and/or engage in self- or other-destructive conduct.

POLICIES WHICH REJECT THE ZEITGEIST

General principles have been identified and defended. It is time to apply those principles to identify and explain school policies which can foster good character development among students. Such policies should be founded--to the extent practicable--on the principles of what I call traditional psychology, and which now might be termed common sense. Even in our era, such policies are not operationally novel. Much of the current, effective school research demonstrates that many public and private schools have been applying anti-Zeitgeist policies. The only original element of my proposals is to state that these deviant, but successful, schools are doing something which is philosophically and scientifically sound. To amplify my point, appropriate descriptive materials about so-called "traditional" procharacter approaches now being applied in schools will be interspersed in the succeeding text. The materials are derived from a report, developed in 1982-1983 by Ed Wynne on well-run Chicago-area public and private schools.

The policies to be proposed cannot be reflexively adopted in entirety by all schools, for a variety of reasons.

They will be recited in this text as if they were a menu.
Then, users may make choices or imaginative adaptations,
depending on the limitations of their different circumstances.
Such limits may be due to policy conflicts among staff (or
parents), union contract provisions, architectural constraints, or many other inhibitors. Incidentally, legal
constraints may arise (in some public schools) about proposed policy changes, for example, adopting a relatively
strict dress code. But groups of public school parents
can choose to waive rights to protest such matters, if
they want such an option for their child. Thus, subschools
or other units can be formed, where faculty, pupils, and
parents commonly commit themselves to apply principles
which cannot be imposed on objectors. It should be emphasized that, on the whole, resistance to my proposals
will be more due to habit and ideology, rather than lack
of funds. Money may help smooth the way to initiate certain innovations. However, day-to-day school operation
under my proposals should not be any more expensive than
at present, and probably not so costly.

The revised school should give considerable stress
to the development of vital collective life among students.
Adult control should be maintained over that life, so it
proceeds in wholesome and constructive directions. Depending on the developmental level of the students involved,
the nature of adult control will be more or less explicit,
and intrusive. Control will also be exercised by older
pupils over younger pupils--also subject to sensitive adult
supervision.

"Vital collective life" means that the student groups
will have real--although limited--responsibility and authority. Some students will assume positions of leadership,
and be given consequential power. Groups will also be
encouraged to engage in expressive activities, involving
matters such as singing, ceremonies, the recitation of
oaths, and the wearing of identifying badges, or clothes.
To put the matter directly, the groups should be assisted
to develop a spirit akin to that of the traditional Boy (or
Girl) Scouts.

Something should be directly said about the role I
propose for pupil authority, and the general concept of
student authority. In many modern schools, students have
little or no authority, beyond determining the pace at
which they will do their own work. In more traditional
education structures, students exercised diverse forms of

limited authority and influence over others: as tutors (determining the rate of others' learning), in assignments as monitors (supervising pupils' obedience to rules), as members of clubs and councils (participating in collective decision making), or on teams (monitoring the conduct of other players).

Some adults may view such "authoritative roles" as trivial. At the same time, these critics decry the total lack of authority of most pupils. And such critics then overreact, and propose potentially inappropriate authority for the young, for example, assessing and criticizing nuclear power policy, community activism, so-called students' rights in schools. Many such activities either are boring and sterile to pupils--after the novelty is gone--or exercises in covert adult manipulation. There was quite a push--largely adult stimulated--for such intrusive activities by students some ten to fifteen years back. It has now subsided. This is understandable. Covert adult manipulation which does not relate to youth needs is a potent trigger for youth cynicism. It is unfortunate that this eclipse of activism has not led more educators to recognize the real need students have for adult-guided youth authority.

> In a suburban public junior high school, the student council undertook many projects for worthwhile ends. They organized fund-raising activities, planned special days for appreciation for school employees (e.g., Secretaries' Day, Nurse's Day), helped teachers to organize field trips, and otherwise made themselves useful. It was plausibly estimated that the average council member spent 200 hours a year in such activities.[1]

In many modern schools, these student groups should be self-selected, with the choices (whether to join) being made by the parents and, sometimes, the pupil. The responsibilities assigned to the groups might be varied: cleanup around school, hall guards, tutoring, fund-raising, (minor) maintenance, ceremonial functions, and intramural and intermural sports. These activities may seem trivial or uninteresting to some adult ears. However, we should keep in mind the psychological principle articulated in

Tom Sawyer. Remember how Tom--applying nineteenth-
century psychology--transformed painting the fence into a
glamorous and desirable activity by making it a scarce
and prestigious good?

Much depends on how skillfully an activity is presented. Indeed, in our day, millions of high school students work hard to be permitted to join athletic teams,
and risk their necks. There's nothing inherently valuable
to such activities. It's simply a matter of how things
are managed so prestige is--or not--attributed to players.
Furthermore, many schools now do incidentally engage in
activities such as I propose. They have athletic teams,
junior ROTC, cheerleading, drama groups, and a variety
of equivalents. And the adults assisting such activities
believe--correctly--they are performing an important service to the young. The problem is simply that we need
more of such activities, more students need to be involved
and--here's the next challenge--the activities need to be
integrated into school academic programs.

A ghetto public elementary school provided the following self-report, which was verified by a site visit:

> A current problem at the school involves
> the "refinement" of girls into young ladies.
> Frequently, those not directly involved with
> schools assume that boys constitute greater
> discipline problems. This is not necessar-
> ily true. Girls can frequently be more
> devious, can get into fights, and generally
> cause more restlessness and insecurity in a
> class. At our school several programs have
> been undertaken to present to our girls a
> positive image of womanhood and to build
> feminine self-esteem and character.
>
> In general, our staff attempts to treat our
> middle and upper grade girls as young
> ladies. The attitude with which each staff
> member and the male students treat them is
> very important. They are addressed as
> "young ladies" and the traditions of chival-
> ry are employed as much as possible.
>
> The girl cheerleaders are the pride of our
> school. Their outstanding record is testi-
> mony to the support which they are given.

Our school annually holds a cheerleaders
and basketball luncheon for participants
and parents at which members of both teams
are recognized and given individual trophies.

Finally, Ms. Ollie Sims, our counselor, runs
a charm class for upper grade girls. Ms.
Sims is herself a model, and highly qualified to teach good grooming. In the after
school class, she stresses dress, make-up,
poise, good grooming, posture, etiquette
and many other factors which contribute to
a young lady who has pride not only in
her appearance, but in her character as
well.

The overall program we believe, is working.
There still are the petty fights and disagreements which take place. These are
dealt with in fairly stern measures, as
has been the tradition at our school. But,
in the case of the girls, we attempt to
counsel them regarding the manner in which
they are demeaning themselves. We also
emphasize the contempt in which they are
held by their peers, rather than allowing
them to deceive themselves into believing
that their peers respect them. The most
critical cases are invited to join the charm
class.[2]

Such activities need to be a part of the academic
program because academics are an important part of the
business of any effective school. If collective activities
are segregated from academics, a critical message is being
given: Academic activities are the really important thing
for ambitious students.

Today, in most U.S. schools, academics are approached almost entirely as individualistic activities. Individual students are given particular assignments or tests,
or are asked to work alone on their personal activities,
and are allotted grades or scores solely on the basis of
their personal output. All of this seems natural. However,
it is really in contrast to most adult employment, and
many other historic and even contemporary (foreign) educational patterns. In most environments, the important

work of the world--which is not academic learning--is done
by groups, and people who work as part of groups. There
are work units, teams, shops, offices, production lines,
and departments. The individuals in each of these entities coordinate their efforts with each other, to get a total
job done.

School is a highly atypical institution, because a
student can receive high praise and satisfaction while the
unit--his class--does very poorly. The significant characteristic of the many in-school group activities 1 proposed
earlier is that they treat individual students as parts of
vital collectives: There's not much sense in being a good
musician in a poor band, or a good hall guard when the
rest of the guards don't care. Students in vital collectives strive to do their parts well in their own self-
interest, and for the good of the group. "Their part" inevitably includes trying to make other group members also
do well; and other group members simultaneously care
about the performance of our hypothetical student member.
Effective groups give stress to caring, supportive member-
to-member relationships, and improving the overall performance of the group. In contrast, typical modern classrooms provide adult-designed grading and reward systems
which stress, to students, devil-take-the-hindmost attitudes.

From a report about a large suburban high school:

> The school has an 85 white/15 black stu-
> dent body. It has conducted a number of
> activities designed to encourage student
> racial integration. There was a high de-
> gree of pupil racial integration in the
> lunchroom; there were only a few tables
> which strictly were black, and many were
> racially mixed.

There are many instances of school patterns which
strive to focus on more group-competitive approaches. In
earlier U.S. schools, there were traditions of contests between classes and schools over academic achievement, for
example, spelling bees, one class versus another, fraternity (and sorority) members helped one another before ex-
ams--in both licit and illicit ways. In England, the students in prestigious public schools were expected to uphold
the academic prestige of their "houses." In the Lancas-
terian tutorial schools, widely copied in nineteenth-century

United States, rows of students competed against each other to display collective academic excellence. Contemporary U.S. researchers, such as James S. Coleman and Robert Slavin, have devised, and widely disseminated, deliberately tested team learning exercises, covering typical cognitive materials. Today, in the socialist countries (such as the USSR and Cuba) much stress is given to developing both supportive and competitive relationships among groups of students. Indeed, their education systems give as much priority to student character as did the public schools in Victorian United States. And, in Japan, with its strong academic press, elementary schools are deliberately managed to maintain high levels of cohesion among pupils at different ability levels. The patterns of academic assignment and grading which exist in many U.S. public schools in the mid-1980s were not decreed by God. They are the product of particular circumstances and concepts, which need not--and will not--indefinitely persist.

RECOGNITION SYSTEMS

Schools which value both cognitive learning and group cooperation must maintain recognition systems which are concerned with both factors. Thus, students should be rewarded for both individual (or formally cognitive) and interpersonal skills. And "interpersonal skills" covers matters such as group commitment, tact, communication, honesty, and planning. Such a recognition system may involve some form of grade which aggregates both the cognitive and cooperative elements. Or there may be two types of "grades," or recognition: one for academics, and one for cooperation. But the important thing is that both grades must have significant weight. Putting it starkly, someone who did not accumulate sufficient recognition for cooperation might, on graduation, receive a limited diploma, which signified the student was intelligent, but self-centered. Or, perhaps, students who satisfy both criteria will graduate with honors. The mechanics are important, but the concept is simple. The school will give just as much priority to evaluating a student's participation as a group member as in evaluating his or her role as an individual academic learner. Students may still have the right to be loners, just as people do in adult life. But being a loner is, at best, a neutral status--both Hitler and Christ might be described as loners. The only certitude we can offer about being a loner is that it is personally costly. We can offer no assurance that individual loners will be particularly good or bad. We should not unduly glamorize a very problematic status.

A Chicago Catholic elementary school was described as follows:

> Each classroom, each month, was asked to designate its "best citizen." The names and photos of these designated students were conspicuously posted outside the principal's office, near the front door of the school. By April, about sixty pupils' names were displayed by the door. The principal also remarked that the school provided a variety of badges, ribbons, notes to parents and other devices to stimulate constructive changes in pupils.[3]

The mechanics of carrying out team-learning approaches in particular contemporary schools are not always simple. This is especially true in departmentalized schools, with teachers who have moved toward subject specialization. Questions arise about pupil scheduling, the nature of homeroom policies, reorganizing curriculum, communication with parents, and the development, monitoring, and maintenance of appropriate group relationships among students. None of these matters are insoluble. After all, such questions are the everyday business of scout masters, church group leaders, coaches, parents in larger families, and almost all adults who supervise other employees. But the proposed changes do call into question some of the assumptions underlying contemporary school patterns. This chapter is not the place to explicate the important topic of mechanics. Serious readers are invited to examine some of the literature I have referenced; many of these writings are designed for reading by administrators and teachers.[4]

SCHOOL SPIRIT

Discussion about student collective life must also turn to the matter of school spirit. Thoughtful adults will subscribe to remarks about the importance of community in

human life, and then foolishly make deprecating remarks
about matters such as pep rallies, school mascots, home-
comings and the like. Such critics fail to realize that
the noble concept of community, in day-to-day life, dis-
tills down to innumerable small, emotionally laden actions
and symbols, which take people "where they are." When
we are dealing with children and adolescents, school spirit
is simply the traditional educator term for the formal concept of "community." And, whenever adults treat the concept of promoting school spirit as juvenile, they are simultaneously unsympathetic to the creation of wholesome community in schools. Without widespread adult support, it
is not surprising that many schools lack wholesome spirit.

School spirit enriches school collective life by
stressing the importance of intragroup concerns. Thus,
students are instructed to care about each other, as co-
citizens in the same school. And to be proud, and responsible, about the reputation of their school. This
means they become less self-centered and more other-
centered. School spirit also enhances ties between students and faculty, and among faculty. "Spirit" signifies
that these persons take pride in their common membership
in a noteworthy community. Such developments enhance
the ability of faculty to provide wholesome models and
counsel for the students.

One Chicago area suburban middle school sent out
the following welcoming letter to its students, which ap-
pealed to their collective pride:

Dear Student,
Hello! You have been lucky enough to be
scheduled to come to Nathan Hale Middle
School. Hale Middle is by far the best
Middle school in the U.S.A. I know you
have been looking forward to starting your
1982-83 school year, and we are looking
forward to having you.

Hale Middle School students are the best
behaved, the most energetic, the most
school spirit minded, students in the entire
district.

Hale School will reach new heights of excellence this year, with the cooperation of
everyone of you.

Give it your best shot, think excellence,
and welcome to Nathan Hale Middle School.[5]

The precise mechanics of fostering school spirit depend on many variables. But most of the variables are
subject to deliberate, intelligent, manipulation. Winning
athletic teams are helpful, but not necessarily central.
First priorities are: (1) the recognition, by the adults in
and around the school, that school spirit is a matter
worthy of high priority, and (2) adult willingness to act
in ways that expressively communicate to pupils, for example, attending games, participating in pep rallies, wearing
school colors, having responsible "fun" with pupils, singing
the school's alma mater with gusto. We must recognize
that educators lead children and adolescents, and not
philosophers or computers. After satisfying the foregoing
two priorities, it is necessary to consider a number of
subsidiary factors, and manage them to enhance spirit:
the school newspaper, assemblies, school colors, homecom-
ings, press releases publicizing school achievements, a
school song, the general elevation of school ceremonial life,
the fostering of responsible fun involving faculty and students, the enlistment of support from alumni, and the spot-
lighting of noteworthy incidents in school or community
history. Just like Ton Sawyer getting his friends to paint
the fence, schools acquire spirit if dedicated, clever
adults decide that's what they want to have happen.
    We should also recognize the importance of school
spirit to good teacher performance. Research has frequently demonstrated the sense of isolation which afflicts many
educators. Perhaps the spread of this malaise is part of
the cause for the decline of pupil school spirit; conversely,
as teacher spirit improves, equivalent efforts may be made
to heighten pupil spirit. Obviously, educators must work
on these concerns simultaneously.
    In a Chicago public school, the regular bulletin to
parents included the following story:

When Rudy Vogel, a teacher who is about
to retire, went to attend the December 21st
assembly, he thought he was going to see
a Christmas program. He was surprised
and very touched to see the beautiful program which the students had practiced
secretly to perform in his honor. His fam-

ily had been invited to attend, and all
were moved by the speeches and songs prepared to honor him. Mr. William Smith,
the principal, presented Rudy with a
plaque commemorating his service. Mr.
Vogel's speech of thanksgiving expressed
his deep feelings as he responded to the
applause of students and staff members.[6]

THE GOALS OF MY HYPOTHETICAL SCHOOL

Readers may muse about the goals toward which the
collective activities of my hypothetical school are aimed.
But my school is not largely hypothetical--it was derived
from field research. Thus, 1 can talk about the goals
which have been pursued in the public and private schools
1 have observed which apply traditional approaches. Essentially, these goals are:

- For staff and pupils to treat each other humanely,
- To cause pupils to attain high levels of cognitive learning, and good character,
- For the school to be of simple, direct service to the community in its immediate area,
- To encourage students to strive for significant personal
success in life--considering their varied innate abilities,
- To encourage students to apply--in general--the same
attitudes toward other citizens as they do among school
citizens.

Some readers may have more ambitious goals for
their hypothetical schools, for example, to teach students
how to create a new and better society, or to critique the
nation's role in the world. But, 1 confess, 1 find such
views unrealistic at the level of elementary and secondary
education. A little history can amplify my conclusion.
During the Great Depression, George S. Counts (1889-1974),
a prominent U.S. scholar, wrote Dare the School Build a New
Social Order? (New York: J. Day, 1932). Interestingly enough
Counts, in his other writings, was highly sympathetic to developmental approaches, and the need to respond to pupils'
"innate" interests. The later political experiences of Counts,
and his activist associates, demonstrated the ridiculousness
of posing such "daring" questions about elementary and

secondary education in a complex, democratic society. Their proposal ended up as an exercise in utopian political irrelevance. Contemporary schools have immense problems working at internal community building. The "modest" objectives 1 have sketched above are ambitious enough for the rest of this century.

So far, my proposals to improve student character have generally been positive in tone. But collective life, and character development, is not only concerned with affirmative elements. There is also the matter of prohibition. Groups cannot be effective unless their members suppress certain forms of misconduct. Putting it succinctly, schools which hope to develop pupil good character must (1) decide what forms of conduct (which realistically may occur in their school) are undesirable, (2) prohibit such misconduct through clear, direct statements, (3) widely circulate such statements among teachers, students, and parents, (4) provide for incremental, simple, unpleasant punishments for misconduct, (5) ensure that violators are identified, and appropriately punished, (6) aim to enlist all community members, including pupils, in the process of code enforcement, (7) try to understand, and reform, persistent violators, and (8) be prepared to "exile" unreformed violators to other environments, and, if appropriate, provide them with occasions to develop insight and display contrition.

PREDICTABLE RESISTANCE

It is appropriate to recognize that the measures proposed will be received with coolness, or hostility, in some influential quarters. Indeed, such resistance may be even more of an obstacle to carrying out the proposed innovations than mechanical barriers. And that is why the introduction to this chapter gave such weight to the topics of history, psychology, and philosophy. The introduction emphasized that what is now taken as the education norm is, historically speaking, relatively novel. And the opinions which run counter to the proposed innovations actually have a relatively thin public base. These opinions run counter to the attitudes which are typical in many adult environments: job sites, families, athletic teams, many traditional religious orders, and the armed services.

The opinions are discordant with conclusions of most citizens and parents. For example, these informed observers have consistently rated pupil indiscipline as the paramount problem facing public schools. The opinions are discrepant with implications of the data, in Chapter 2, about increasing youth disorder. Those data reveal that the application of individualistic education has been apparently related to the spread of that disorder.

There is also inconsistency with the day-to-day practices followed in many contemporary public schools which have been formally found extra-effective.

Finally, the opinions are even incongruent with long-term trends in pupil cognitive performance. Systematic tests have generally revealed that, as the level of school funding has steadily climbed, and permissive attitudes in schools have become more prevalent, measured pupil learning outcomes have declined or, at best, recently stabilized.

Educators who choose to try to run more group-oriented schools will not really be bucking the tide. They will simply be responding to the facts confronting them. Those who choose to stay focused on self "what-have-you" and narrow cognitive learning are really the ones who will be trapped in the past.

NOTES

1. Reports derived from E. A. Wynne, Chicago Area Award Winning Schools, 1982-1983 (Chicago: College of Education, University of Illinois, 1983).
2. Ibid.
3. Ibid.
4. M. Read, Children of Their Fathers (New York: Holt, Rinehart & Winston, 1986).
5. Wynne, Chicago Area Award Winning Schools. See, e.g., R. E. Slavin, Using Student Team Learning (Baltimore: Center for the Study of Schools, 1980); E. Aronson, The Jigsaw Classroom (Beverly Hills: Sage, 1978).
6. Ibid.

5

Partners in Moral Education: Communities and Their Public Schools

Madhu Suri Prakash

> The teacher has the sublimely delicate task
> of marrying the small-group loyalties neces-
> sary for productive learning to the large-
> group loyalties of the broader community
> and of universalistic principles.
>
> David Seeley, Education
> Through Partnership*

The partnership of school staff and community, like other
social relationships, has been shaped by the times, the
cultural and political milieu within which it has been
forged and sustained. In the dynamic interaction between
the two primary socializers, the goal of an educative alliance continues to be, in the manner of many ideals, elusive and slippery. Too often, the mismatched partners in
this marriage either fail to communicate, or one or the
other dominates disproportionately, threatening the ends
that require mutually supportive cooperation.

This chapter begins with an examination of some of
the significant historical transitions in this partnership.
The three interrelated factors that have radically affected
the nature of this relationship are increases in the scale
of the educational system, the rise of professionalism, and

---

*From Education through Partnership: Mediating
Structures and Education (Cambridge, Mass.: Ballinger,
1981), p. 233.

119

standardization of curricula. These are responsible for
reducing the participation of parents and community members in the educational process. This chapter explores
the hindrances to cooperation posed by these factors. It
also studies the difficulties raised in the face of pluralist
differences. Having identified the hindrances, it moves
positively toward several possibilities for fruitful forms of
cooperation between communities and their public schools.

CHANGING CONTEXTS FOR MORAL EDUCATION: FROM FAMILIAL NURTURE TO PROFESSIONALIZED SCHOOLING

Historians provide rich accounts of the nuances, the
shifts and swings in the evolving interaction between
schools and their communities. Descriptions of the democratic localist model of public schooling in the last century reveal educators constrained into almost complete
acquiescence to the values and goals of the local community or its dominant members upon whose pleasure they
served. Ralph Hartsook's "interview" for a teacher's job
in Indiana vividly illustrates both the limits on the educator's autonomy, as well as the reduction of education to
socialization in the context of one of the earlier designs
of public schooling:

Want to be a school-master, do you? You?
Well, what would you do in Flat Crick
deestrick, I'd like to know? Why, the
boys have driv off the last two, and licked
the one afore them like blazes. . . .
They's pitch you out of doors, sonny,
neck and heels, afore Christmas.

"You see," continued Mr. Means, spitting
in a meditative sort of way, "you see, we
a'n't none of your saft sort in these dig-
gins. It takes a man to boss this deestrick.
Howsudever, ef you think you kin trust
your hide in Flat Crick school-house, I
ha'n't got no 'bjection. . . . Any other
trustees? Wal, yes. But as I pay the
most taxes, t'others jist let me run the
thing."[1]

On another, more gentle note, the "perfect and un-
spoken consonance between families and schools" is captured in portrayals of the school teacher who, "virginal,
pure and caring, lived in the homes of the schoolchildren's
families," and taught their values and morals in the one-
room schoolhouse. Her "classroom teaching was an extension of the child's parenting."[2]

> Here the teacher herself often a mere slip
> of a girl, a young teacher wrestles with
> her slightly younger contemporaries, boards
> with members of the school board, is chap-
> eroned by the entire community of which
> she is one, and finally marries a member
> of that community--or goes on teaching for-
> ever happily, with at least one attributed
> romance to give her dignity and pathos.[3]

In a continent of change and transition, the community's schoolmarm was yet one more bulwark against the
loss of identity or freedom threatened by "the melting pot."
Little wonder that the democratic localists vehemently opposed the very notion of exposing their children to the
trained products of normal schools, a "Prussian importation
to raise the spectre of a cadre of Whiggish teachers learning and then imposing state defined doctrines."[4]
Despite all precautions taken by communities Catholic and Jewish, German, or French, "state-defined doctrines" did finally succeed in making their way in, aided
and abetted by the steadily growing power of professionals,
the "experts" of child development, who replaced the devoted loyal spinsters of local communities. The certified
teacher, slowly perhaps, but very steadily, continued to
shift allegiance from the communities' values, desires, and
aspirations to the ethic of professionals, the officially
recognized "scientists" of child rearing.
The mystique of the scientific educator remained essentially untarnished into the middle of the twentieth century and quiescent communities were disposed to accept
the judgments of their "betters" regarding the appropriate
ways in which children should be shaped intellectually
and morally. But amid the scandal of declining test
scores, with fewer and fewer scapegoats or legitimate excuses for failures, the difficulties of keeping the professional pedestal upright have continued to grow. Communi-

ties, which earlier had accepted the official diagnosis of
their inferiority have, after the moral revolts of the 1950s,
found sufficient self-affirmation to begin to reject their
assigned role of subservience, demanding instead to have
their voices heard, their values respected.   Blacks and
Amish, Bethel Baptists and Hare Krishnas, fundamentalists
and Catholics, each have asserted their rights to bring up
their children within their own values.   And liberal jus-
tices, sympathetic to demands for autonomy, have supported many such requests as legitimate, and long overdue.
   No longer secure in their science, school administrators and experts are resorting to "a low profile, out of
the cross-fire of conflicting demands."[5]   The "controversial"
has been nervously dumped and "the basics" has been
limited to skills which can be computed on "objective"
tests--an appeasement of a public which wants solid out-
puts for the inputs purchased by their tax dollars.   In
the era of privatization of religion and morals, moral education, never an uncontroversial subject even at the best
of times, has become "a dirty word"[6] within the institution
of public schooling.   A supposedly "neutral" process is
now resorted to in response to the state's demand for

> Competence in the processes of developing
> values--particularly for the formation of
> spiritual, ethical, religious and moral
> values. . . . (The responsibility of the)
> school: a. knowledge of the diversity of
> values, b. skill of making value-based
> choices.[7]

"Values clarification" have become the magical catchwords,
the latest supposedly pluralistic solution in an era where
hardly any cultural group will tolerate having its values
ignored for those of the mainstream.

A FRACTURED PARTNERSHIP: PUBLIC
SCHOOLS LOSE THEIR PUBLIC

> The great paradox in American education
> today is that only the privates have a
> public in the classical sense.
>   Gerald Grant, "The Character of
>   Education and the Education of
>   Character"

Beleaguered professionals, freshly chastised by dis-
regarded clients for past insensitivities, "re-visioned" by
revisionist analysts "excavating for conspiracies," lack
some of their earlier power to do harm. Unfortunately,
the same circumstances also rob them of the trust and confidence, the essential moral authority, to do much good.
There are other ironic twists to be found in the current
U.S. context. An informed, articulate, and discerning
clientele could provide new challenges, important for up-
grading and maintaining quality control. Yet, if the pro-
ducer has the obligation of pleasing all, and the clientele
is too divided to formulate any agreement, the compromise
to create a product which satisfies everyone is likely to
degenerate into something that satisfies no one. So public
schools, condemned for not being liberal enough, nor sufficiently conservative, not atheistic enough and neither religious, bombarded on all sides, paralyzed by criticism,
try to stick it out in some narrow niche, safe from disagreement. But this, too, will not do today in an era in
which public schools, as the "modern secular churches,"
are supposed to provide salvation from all social miseries--
including political corruption and urban crime. With expectations high, such circumspect withdrawal provides only
more ire and disillusionment.

Public school personnel mourn the absence of public
support. At the same time the public decries the absence
of institutional responsiveness. Many parents resort to
private schools in the hope of finding an intellectual and
moral climate that supports their own sensibilities. Because the decision to send their children to private schools
reflects a conscious choice, parents are more prone to accept the moral authority of private school staff--an acceptance too often withheld from their public school counterparts. This helps to make the task of moral education
more feasible in the setting of private schools.

Discussing this feasibility, Grant identifies two
kinds of freedom that distinguish private schools from public institutions.

> The private schools have two kinds of free-
> doms that are not present in the same way
> in the public schools. The first of these
> might be called "freedom from." The pri-
> vate school is not encumbered by that
> thick external layer of constraints and

policies that has contributed to the technicist and adversarial culture in many public schools. The second freedom might be
called voluntarism, or "freedom for." That
is, private school parents are not just flee-
ing public schools or engaged in white
flight, although some are. Most seek the
ethos or tradition that the particular
school represents. That tradition is usually a way of talking about character, and
represents some agreement about which virtues are most worth having. A primary
function of private schools is to make visible an otherwise invisible collectivity, to
draw together a public that shares similar
preferences. The private school is both a
symbolic and an actual representation of
valued moral and intellectual goods.[8]

The task of leadership in creating "the positive
ethos" necessary for "the education of character," Grant
concludes, is made easier in the context of the private
school.

The leaders of such schools are chosen because they exemplify those values; they
are "the best of us," persons capable of
symbolizing the tradition and of drawing
others into it. Leaders are supposed to
have the wisdom to choose teachers who
represent the tradition. They must be able
to evoke shared commitments and to lead
others in fuller realization of the valued
goods of the community. The quality and
character of the teachers are believed to
make a great difference.

Conditions of work in the public setting create a
different breed of leaders.

The leader is not selected as an instantia-
tion of particular virtues but for competence
in interpersonal skills, fairness in enforcing rules, and strength to withstand
conflict. . . . Whereas the head of a

private school is largely a symbolic communicator with the external public (in fact,
must continually re-create and sustain that
public), the public school principal must
be a skilled advocate within a bureaucracy.
The principal in a public setting can be a
mere satisfier, presiding over the rule system, the guardian of process with no vision
of desired outcomes. Personal charisma
earns some an extra measure of authority
that enables them to create a semblance of
community within a bureaucratic system.
But the relentless temptation in an environment of competing and often aggrieved interest groups is to abandon any effort to
achieve transcendent ideals by which all
could be bound and to fall back into the
role of a passive agent of process.[9]

Not surprisingly, the values clarification curriculum
of moral education, marketed as a scientific process for
dealing with values, proved to be the most popular among
public-school teachers. Painlessly easy to implement, the
avowed "neutrality" of values clarification promises safety
from parents safeguarding their "privatized and subjectiv-
ized" morality.[10] Only slowly is the ruse of the neutrality of this approach to moral education being found out.[11]
Meanwhile, caught in the rift between neutral staff and
irate parents, students increasingly are left to their own
devices and the pressure of their adolescent peers to freely
"hierarchize their values" any way they wish.[12] In the
vacuum created by defensive or absent adults, the creators
of "prime time" find easy access for suitably shaping the
characters of their current and potential consumers. With
great urgency, concerned observers remind us: "Today in
the inner city and suburbia alike, a wild manchild who
is without a supportive culture raises hell in our schools.
Uprooted, he cannot be shaped. Only a community of
friends, family and others in whom he recognizes his economic and emotional dependence can provide the soil for
his education."[13]

Toward Conjoint Action

> Evils which are uncritically and indiscrimi-
> nately laid at the door of industrialism and
> democracy might, with greater intelligence,
> be referred to the dislocation and unsettle-
> ment of local communities. Vital and thor-
> ough attachments are bred only in the inti-
> macy of an intercourse which is of neces-
> sity restricted in range.
>
> John Dewey, The Public and Its Problems[14]

The need for a new kind of partnership between public schools and their communities has repeatedly and forcefully been articulated over the last two decades,[15] especially prompted by the increased alarm over the "distancing
centralization" and the dehumanizing large scale of school
bureaucracies. The central problem of these "worlds
apart"[16] remains that of creating an integrated, consistent
environment of caring adults, effective in nurturing the
moral character of learners through the formation of civic
virtues.

It hardly needs reiterating that there is no simple
or quick solution to mend the rupture between schools and
their communities. Only in poor humor (or from wretched
habit?) could one propose that yet another service bureaucracy—of specialized official intermediaries—be created to
weave new ties between these split worlds. Schools need
to become "convivial" institutions. How? For some, the
solution lies in nothing short of smashing all "the manipu-
lative and compulsory institutions of the right."[17] Less
revolutionary prescriptions remain sensitive to the social
and political costs of anything as drastic as a "deschooled
society." It is urged, instead, that we strive for the
more amicable and feasible compromise of softening the
hard edges of bureaucratic structures, making them more
pliable and responsive to local communal conditions. A
new type of institutional incumbent is required to operate
such transformations successfully—one whose efficiency is
defined nonquantitatively in terms of the sensitivity and
creativity to forge and sustain ties with the "real people"
being served.

On the other side of the fence, a less inchoate public which is supportively active (as distinct from debili-
tatingly and aggressively critical) must be formed. Indi-

viduals need to sharpen their skills in creating informal
"mediating institutions"[18]-- a contervailing power to, as
well as a mutually supportive structure for, the formal
public institutions. The United States has an old and admired tradition in the art of coalescing. It stirred admi-
ration among visitors of the last century, such as de
Tocqueville. The voices of interest groups which are far
from silent today is proof that, though many forces still
tend to "eclipse the public," the associative spirit is far
from dead. There is abundantly rich, raw material for
the creation of communal organizations which can provide
essential links in democratic self-management.

Efforts at forming effective partnerships exist in
the U.S. educational experience. In Two Worlds of Childhood, Bronfenbrenner records the nature and achievements
of Head Start programs for bringing the community's
"people back into the lives of children and children back
into the lives of people." Senior citizens, youth street
gangs, among others, are the types of potential nonprofessional educators shamefully underutilized by the school
bureaucracy today, according to Bronfenbrenner. In the
resulting moral vacuum, children are deprived of the
models as well as the reinforcement important for pursuing
those superordinate goals which require the extension of
the individual's world to include the interests and well-
being of the whole group. Inspired by similar notions, in
"A Community of Believers," Crimm (Daedalus, Fall 1981)
records the moral achievements of the community of Atlanta
as it rises en masse to address the problems of learning
in a large school district. Lightfoot, in Worlds Apart,
richly portrays the advantages black parents have brought
to the moral well-being of their children and the climate
of the school by participating in its governance.

A telling illustration of the enormous untapped educational resources of our communities is available in the
experiment with mentally retarded persons recorded in Two
Worlds of Childhood, which reveals also the limits of professional institutionalized nurture. In the study conducted
by Harold Skeels, female inmates of a state institution for
the mentally retarded were allowed to take care of a
group of institutionalized three year olds, also retarded.
Each "mother" was trusted with the responsibility for one
of the children.

A control group was allowed to remain in
the original--also institutional--environment,

a children's orphanage. During the formal
experimental period, which averaged a year
and a half, the experimental group showed
a gain in I.Q. of 28 points (from 64 to 92),
whereas the control group dropped 26 points.
Upon completion of the experiment, it became possible to place the institutionally-
mothered children in legal adoption. Thirty
years later, all 13 children in the experimental group were found to be self-support-
ing, all but two had completed high school,
with four having one or more years of college. In the control group, all were either
dead or still institutionalized.[19]

Evidence that even the minimally educated or "edu-
cable" can be so effective should prod official educators
as well as uninvolved citizens to become more sensitive to
the possible contributions of adults who are not allowed to
teach simply because they are not officially certified to do
so. Demonstrating the same point in Deschooling Society,
Illich discovered potential teachers even among school
dropouts. To take one instance, in 1956 the influx of
Puerto Ricans created a dire necessity for Spanish-speaking
staff members in the parishes of New York. Announcements
were made over a Spanish radio station for persons from
Harlem whose native language was Spanish. Although some
of those who responded were school dropouts, within a
week this group was trained to use the U.S. Foreign Service Institute (FSI) Spanish manual designed for use by
linguists with graduate training. Six months later, each
one of the parishes had staff members who could communicate in Spanish.

In another urban area, Bronfenbrenner identifies a
similar success story about the school that transformed its
local toughs, the "Golden Bombers," into guardians and
teachers. Invited to participate, these adolescents took on
the jobs that parents were not available for: conducting
children through traffic, taking them on outings, and reading aloud to them, among other things.

Communities have members who may know more than
teachers do about local vegetation and forms of animal
life. They would be the ideal persons to take students to
local forests and rivers, farms, and gardens to share
their self-taught skills on a regular basis. Again, in

<u>Two Worlds of Childhood</u>, we hear of cases of young and old nonprofessionals trusted with the responsibility of sharing their interests and insights with children during Head Start weekends. While these activities helped move the school out into the community, Crimm's article indicates ways to move the community into the school. In Atlanta, the local banking group has provided schools with banking equipment for teaching students its use. Regional artists have loaned their paintings to school buildings, in addition to sharing their skills and artistry. Executives from companies in town are scheduled to teach students on a regular basis. Social studies classes are made richer by the lectures of local attorneys.

Unfortunately, scheduling an occasional guest lecture seems to be the only gesture most teachers currently make in their attempts to involve surrounding communities in the formal educational process. Employees of Planned Parenthood or counselors are called in to speak to students about some aspects of human sexuality. Owners of local industrial plants in the neighborhood are brought in to inform students about the skills and strengths considered desirable for certain occupational categories. Members of political organizations sporadically drop by to share some experiences.

Such attempts on the part of teachers do help to reduce the separation of schools from their communities. However, they are limited in scope--mere nods of acceptance--rather than full-fledged recognition of the fact that local communities abound in educational resources. These consist of problems to be addressed, as well as resourceful, energetic, politically courageous role models who rise above the mass of apathy and use the opportunities provided by democratic processes.

The poor use of outsiders is not an anomaly, but one aspect of the mind-set generated by the professionalization of education, according to which the most serious business of educating must remain the monopoly of those trained in schools of education. Consequently, the community guest lecturers are allotted their slots at the periphery of the curriculum. They are a pleasant "addition," but remain quite dispensable resource persons, whose presence is nothing more than a mild peppering designed to break the monotony of business as usual.

Although difficult to achieve, the very notion of business as usual needs to be transformed if we are successfully to overcome the officious bureaucratic boundaries established between the local public and our public educational institutions. These boundaries are sustained by the absence of mutual trust between professionals and public. Professionals are pushed into staking out their own turf by a public which is both hostile and passive, overly critical while relatively uninvolved. By separating themselves and narrowing the possibilities for successful education, professionals in turn exacerbate the public's distrust. Students are the ones to suffer most the effects of these artificial barriers.

On the one hand, these boundaries have reduced the challenges we present to our students into mere "school problems"--artificial, contrived, and too often simple-minded questions that students immediately recognize as something quite apart from the challenges of life in the real world. On the other hand, they preclude parents and the nonprofessional public from the moral responsibilities of educating the young. While it is claimed that adults today are more egocentric than in the past,[20] this phenomenon cannot be dissociated entirely from their reduced responsibility for child rearing. This, in turn, is exacerbated by the encroachment of professionals into areas of care previously shared by the extended family and neighborhood. For many young persons this means less than desirable role models outside the schools; while inside the building, the relative artificiality of school settings robs them of contexts that arouse the moral emotions and develop the moral imagination. For the more dogged and determined as well as those drawn to abstract and theoretical explorations, school tests become necessary though irrelevant, or at best interesting sets of hurdles that must systematically be overcome for graduating into real life. Schools teach many in this group only the prudent (as distinguished from the moral) ways of moving ahead. For those less ambitious or competitive or abstraction oriented, the irrelevance poses an insurmountable barrier to learning. As the latter continue to lag behind increasingly, they lose their moral respect both for themselves and the adults who continue to "imprison" them in "meaningless" routine. Considering this situation in his time, Dewey noted that the moral loss generated by such school settings was at least as much as the intellectual.[21]

How can the educational curriculum be expanded to make genuine room for learning both inside and outside

the school building? What kinds of projects can more
fully engage the nonprofessional public in the development
of students? What moral challenges can we present to the
young so that they are not lost in the great gulf between
real-life problems and test questions on chapters covered
during the week?

The brute reality of life is such that none of us
need go further than our communities in order to discover
genuine problems demanding moral attention. Not many
localities are entirely free of unemployment, hunger, or
child battering, or of public buildings and parks and
roads which demand repair; no community remains unthreat-
ened by nuclear war, pollution, and ecological imbalances.
One important root cause for the growth of such problems
is that most adults believe these defy understanding or
solution by the efforts of ordinary persons; only specialists and scientists possess the faculties and expertise required for dealing with them. As most choose to leave the
tasks of governance to functionaries or politicians, a common problem that threads its way through all of our communities is the low quality of democratic participation. Unfortunately, this moral apathy can be attributed in part
to schools where we learned to sit for hours and years on
end, protected from the harder task of identifying and confronting complex problems. It should be predictably hard
to break out of habits of passivity inculcated over the
years of one's development.

In what ways do we fail adequately to participate
in democratic government? What specific problems riddle
our communities? How can the average person best utilize
the democratic machinery to put pressure on state representatives and senators? What sorts of measures or steps
can the individual take to make his or her contribution
toward reducing the arms race? What are the particular
connections between that race and the specific forms of
local ills--of unemployment, of nutritional deficiency among
the poor, of polluted rivers? What sorts of letters can we
write, what kinds of protests can we mount to make our
views heard in redressing injustices both large and small?
What can persons, young and old, do to "make a difference"?

Each one of these questions expresses a moral as
well as an intellectual concern that could generate an educational project. In pursuit of answers, students must
acquire the methods of inquiry taught by different disci-

plines. They need to acquire the skills of social and
physical scientists. In search of answers, they must
learn how to formulate questions, manage interviews, initiate conversations, follow a lead, locate and pin a
source. These tasks demand practical as well as theoretical skills. In learning to speak in their own voices, students must move also toward the mastery of different literary styles. To consider the right questions and envision
the right answers, they have to be touched by the spirit
of sympathy, concern, and goodwill that defines persons
of moral character. While in no way limited in their potential for intellectual stimulation, communal questions and
projects hold far greater promise for moral stimulation.
Not mere abstract or make-believe, they concern the trials
and tribulations, the pain and happiness of real individual
persons with whom one meets and talks. Their reality and
concreteness contain antidotes to the threat of moral detachment posed by pure abstraction and by the years spent
in merely theoretical investigations.

To understand and address these problems, students
must contact persons who are already engaged in ameliora-
tive action: parents involved in social service, citizens
helping the aged and handicapped, political lobbyists who
fiercely reject the idea of dumbly sitting on their haunches
"waiting for Godot" from state and national capitals to
resolve the latest or the ongoing crisis. Such communal
projects demand student initiative (as distinct from teachers' invitations); they possess the potential for directing
schoolchildren to a variety of role models who are likely
to know far more about practical details than do teachers.
Indeed, such challenges to inquiry also force schoolteachers
to continue their own education by, for instance, learning
how to take social or political action. Like their academic
counterparts in universities, teachers are prone to be more
adept in theory than in practice. Consequently, through
exposure to others, students will have the dual benefits of
role models exemplifying theoretical as well as practical
competence.

From the perspective of bureaucratic managers, such
community projects threaten procedures established for
monitoring and control. They are too messy to maintain
safe accountability: They cannot be neatly measured in
terms of classroom hours spent in instruction and learning,
textbooks and chapters read, and students examined. They
require forms of flexibility that, <u>Horace's Compromise</u>[22]

reveals, we are too afraid to entrust to our teachers and principals. This lack of trust also explains the orderly wall built between school and town: Only those who have gone through the professional mill will be allowed to handle our children. Despite its advantages, the uniformity of this mill ultimately creates the poverty of school experiences. Fearful of taking risks, not willing to pay for the expense, we manufacture a standardized learning package which cheaply and safely closes our children off from the promise and possibilities of ventures outside the school building.

Can the community become an effective moral educator? Yes, but only if the formal and compulsory system will open its doors wider. This involves more than a peripheral alteration of rules. It requires nothing short of an overhauling of our concepts of effective curricula, scheduling, monitoring, and testing. We need to have greater faith in our students and members of the public who possess no education diplomas.

THE CHALLENGE OF PLURALISM: A COMMON SCHOOL OR THE VOUCHER SPLIT?

Recently, liberals have expressed considerable alarm over the new waves of conservative interest groups that have moved quite forcefully into the public domain, influencing legislation in all aspects of U.S. life. In the area of education, conservative communal participation has been directed at the design of curricula, school library policies, disciplinary measures, and religious instruction, among others. Brodinsky, with liberal dismay, documents the vigor and power of such group action:

> The New Right creates a new organization about every 30 days on national, state, or local levels. Some die quickly and are replaced by others. A recent count by the National Education Association (NEA) showed 67 major national organizations promoting ultra-right causes and working against the public schools. The number of local groups under the influence of the New Right is incalculable. Hundreds, possibly thousands, of "concerned-citizen,"

"parents-for-school-decency," "parents-who-care" groups promote right-wing ideologies for specific objectives--be it the elimination of a course or the banning of a book.

Helping to promote the various causes of the New Right is a network of national, state, and local agencies. A variety of interlocking and mutually supporting organizations, which have as their aims: developing and propagating "model" legislation for states; promoting prayer in public schools; promoting creationism; censoring textbooks and school library books; ending unionism and union tactics in education; promoting the interests of Christian schools; cutting taxes and school expenditures; nurturing conservative ideas; fighting "secular humanism" in public schools; and channeling corporate gifts and funds into colleges and universities that promote "free enterprise."[23]

Liberals find unpalatable many of the goals on the agenda of conservative communal action, for some of the New Right demands threaten hard-won liberal moral victories which have helped generate greater equality and freedom for previously disadvantaged groups. Yet, in spite of the alarming dimensions of this communal action, there are aspects which seem commendable even to the opposition.

For one, the active indignation of conservatives over the moral climate (or, lack of it) in public schools in particular and in the country in general reveals that, contrary to the gloomy prognosis of social analysts mulling over the debilitating effects of modernity, the spirit for self-government survives. It exists, despite long, tiring commuter lines, the deadening monotony of the assembly plant, the alienating character of gargantuan organizations, the rigid machinations of petty bureaucrats, the empty jargon of such technocrats or experts as human engineers, and labor power planners. Furthermore, this indignation reveals also that at least some modern parents and communities are no less concerned for their progeny than were earlier generations.[24] In the political arena, the time seems ripe for the conservative reminder that no group and its government can flourish without at least some minimal shared conception of the good life. For some liberals, as Dworkin argues, the governance of political life must rest on a neutrality in matters of morality. The government must not interfere with the lives of people as long as they do not harm others.[25] Translated into curriculum for the schools, this impoverished concept of political morality has given us a hollow, anesthetized "education" progressively empty of moral content and an increasing threat to the formation of community-minded individuals. For such a conception goes against the very spirit of communal dispositions and attitudes.

There is yet another way to view the positive dimensions of the conservatives' efforts to shape the moral climate of their schools, their communities, and nation. They provide a fresh challenge to liberals, prodding them to explore more deeply their moral-political concepts of the good life as well as the moral and intellectual education essential for sustaining it. The results of renewed inquiry and deeper understanding should generate some sparkling debate between proponents of competing conceptions of education. In the midst of heightened dialogue, it will be hard to allege that Johnny's education is left completely to the certified professional teacher. More generally, the care of one generation for another, vividly displayed through genuine dialogue and active participation, is not without immense pedagogical merits. It provides valuable lessons in moral education to learners in the schools of a democracy; it captures the moral essence of social life where full, free, and equal participation in self-governance is heavily prized.

Dewey's search for a politically and morally vital public led him back to the towns and villages where face-to-face communities could be found. It was here, he argued, through personal contact, sustained and strengthened through conversation, debate, and joint action, that moral sentiments might properly be nurtured. Rooted in the humane tradition of the community, the learner's moral imagination could be enlarged by the educator to form more universal attachments. Family attachments could be extended to communal ones, laying the foundations from which individuals would take off imaginatively to include the other people of the world.[26]

It is said, and said truly, that for the world's peace it is necessary that we

understand the peoples of foreign lands.
How well do we understand, I wonder, our
next door neighbors? It has also been
said that if a man love not his fellow man
whom he has seen, he cannot love the God
whom he has not seen. The chances of regard for distant peoples being effective as
long as there is no close neighborhood experience to bring with it insight and understanding of neighbors do not seem better.
Democracy must begin at home, and its home
is the neighborly community.

(There) is something deep within human
nature itself which pulls toward settled
relationships. Inertia and the tendency
toward stability belong to emotions and
desires as well as to masses and molecules.
That happiness which is full of content
and peace is found only in enduring ties
with others, which reach to such depths
that they go below the surface of conscious experience to form its undisturbed
foundation. One knows how much of the
frothy excitement of life, of mania for motion, of fretful discontent, of need for
artificial stimulation, is the expression of a
frantic search for something to fill the
void caused by the loosening of the bonds
which hold persons together in immediate
community of experience.[27]

Underlying the prescriptions for a partnership is
the premise that public schools exist within communities
which, while divided by many differences (including those
between liberals and conservatives), are fundamentally
united at a deeper level by some basic systems of values.
These shared values make possible a shared existence
which the young must be raised to sustain, strengthen,
and improve. Among the common values is a conception of
tolerance which demands respect for others, even when
their chosen beliefs, values, and life-styles diverge widely from one's own. Thus, the shared value of pluralism
at one level permits, at another, a pluralistic diversity--
an acknowledgment of regard for all the incredible differences which makes each one of us distinct and unique.

Pluralism, so understood, is not a morally empty concept. On the contrary, it implies the existence of a number of values:

> the minimal order required for dialogue, the willingness to listen to one another, respect for truth, the rejection of racism (or openness to participation in the dialogue), as well as those transcendent values that shore up the whole society--a sense of altruism and service to others and respect for personal effort and hard work. Without such agreement, one does not have a public, but a kind of radical relativism; not pluralism but mere coexistence.[28]

However, pluralism, as asserted by many today, robbed of its ethical connotations, is wielded as a sledgehammer to smash any notion of a shared morality, any form of consensus. Divisiveness is all that "pluralism" is seen to connote. Reflecting on the implications of holding such a conception, Raywid analyses

> the diminishing allegiance among Americans to the broad universals as to value and belief that must ground a genuinely "common" school. Instead, we find large numbers clinging more closely to particularist values not shared by other identity groups. And simultaneously, we find a heightened unwillingness to "go along" quietly with the rest--not just pluralism, but an <u>obtrusive</u> pluralism. (Obtrusive) pluralism makes the idea of the "common" school far less viable than before. Differences in perception, belief, and priority have become too pronounced to prove compatible with an education program geared to instilling common knowledge, beliefs, and values.[29]

The threat of an "obtrusive pluralism" is quite obviously not limited to the extinction of the public school. It is designed to drive a wedge between liberals and conservatives, fundamentalists and atheists, "moderns" and "traditionalists," precluding the possibility of a level of shared political existence based on a common public morality. In the clamor announcing the differences between personal or group moralities, the integrative framework of a public moral outlook is altogether ignored. Yet obtrusive pluralism forces us to ask ourselves once again what moral core binds us and sustains a shared existence. A mere prudential pact is clearly too tenuous and fragile for reliable, binding agreement. We are best cautioned again by moralists who portray for us the underlying raw brutishness of life and relationships which do not rest on the strong foundations of some form of moral consensus.

A closer look uncovers the essential irony of today's "obtrusive pluralism." Many of the minorities and interest groups, announcing the independence of their moral outlook from that of "the mainstream," fail to discern that the guarantee of their "freedom to be different" is best safeguarded by the existence of shared pluralist values that they implicitly disregard by denying a consensus. Admittedly, this consensus has conveniently been manipulated by groups in power to ignore interests they have had a moral obligation to respect. Yet, acknowledging the legitimacy of such long-ignored rights and privileges has not required a transformation of an earlier moral convention, but rather a fresh and deeper understanding of an existing code and its more consistent application.[30]

Much of this agreement is apparent even today upon closer inspection of the criticisms that conservatives and liberals hurl at each other as they attempt to influence policy for institutions, including public schools.[31] It is clear that community members, whether classified as "the New Right" or "Liberal Elitists," are equally concerned about the failure of schools to develop moral and intellectual virtues. Parents of neither political leaning take kindly or cavalierly the existence of vandalism, theft, cheating, and rudeness.

Undeniably, there do exist deep disagreements too. Books that one group of parents choose to burn are clearly favored by others. While some urge candid discussions of sexuality, others express a preference for more reticence on the subject. Corporal punishment provides another bone of contention. And, while avowed agnostics shudder at the idea of the reintroduction of some form of prayer in school, the devout despair of an "education" untouched by the religious spirit. This disagreement has touched off others: The "creationism vs. evolutionism" conflict and the bitter dialogue over the MACOS curriculum.[32]

What is the appropriate solution to this concomitant existence of consensus and conflict in values? (See Chapter 3.) It is clear that strategies tried earlier are neither desirable nor feasible, for the modern moral challenge facing the schools is to offer a solution which does not involve imposing exclusively the moral and religious values of one cultural or religious group while forcefully ignoring competing others.

Vouchers are considered a panacea by some--not only as a cure for bureaucratic ineffectiveness, but also as a just pluralist strategy for honoring differing moral sensibilities and incompatible world views. By guaranteeing more choice, vouchers should encourage more "voice" and "loyalty"--aspects of communal participation, conspicuous in their absence today.[33]

Others seriously question the results of this solution, viewing it instead as a divisive cop-out. Behind the prima facie amicability of the voucher route, they discern an intolerance, the rejection of a generous and peaceful compromise under the same roof. Vouchers serve to emphasize incompatibilities clouding over the moral consensus of which we need to remind ourselves as well as the young. Vouchers rob us of an extremely valuable symbol of our commonness by essentially wiping out the common school, claim some. Proponents of voucher plans reject this grim diagnosis.

Responding to the provoucher rationalization that schools of choice do not threaten the consensus, champions of the common public school conclude differently. Leery of the upheaval of vouchers, they urge a compromise within the common school. A more diversified curriculum, they claim, can appropriately respond to the differences while demonstrating that "the unity of society must be based on a consensus which is deeper than the party conflicts"; that "toleration would not have been possible in the long run if the various religious traditions did not show that they shared a certain consensus in spite of their differences." Inspired by the belief that "contradictory viewpoints can actually enrich a consensus,"[34] supporters of the common school emphasize the educative potential of an environment where contradictions and conflicts coexist. Indeed, such a context should keep alive a dialogue, essential for stimulating a deeper understanding of the alternative moral traditions. They remind us of an important educative function of the school: not mere socialization, the replication of an existent form of communal existence, but of its regeneration and improvement through a continuous exposure to new ideas.

Unfortunately, the common school has not always proved to be such a fertile environment. In the recent past, dissent has been squashed in favor of "single vision." The professional technicist's narrow vision has replaced that of the dominant nineteenth-century elites. Past failures, however, do not rule out the present potential of an arena where, through advisory committees, community members extend and deepen the existing consensus. Indeed, public schools can provide a model to their younger members, revealing how adults successfully exhibit mutual respect in settling differences.

Settlements, though not always easy, are feasible. For example, a period of silence grants the religious opportunity to pray and to agnostics the freedom to reflect on appropriate objects of choice. Books can be found which neither sacrifice aesthetic merit nor offend more sensitive parents. The attitudes and preferences of parents to programs like MACOS could be accommodated through the inclusion of optional courses.[35] A similar solution seems feasible with regard to sex education.

Undoubtedly, not all disagreements can be settled by a compromise. In the interests of education, certain demands may have to be ruled out altogether. For example, whether the creationist theories can be included as scientific is not, it seems, a matter of free choice.[36] The judgments of professionals here must temper the hopes and wishes, not to mention the biases and bigotry, of a particular community. There must be room for professional autonomy. This needs, however, to be re-created so as freshly to define the nature of professional freedom that is compatible with an extended understanding of the educational responsibilities of communities.

Earlier on, we saw how attempts to placate and compromise resulted in a "watering down," a school "solution" with few moral merits. Whether vouchers or the common school provide the best solution, it is difficult to predict. However, to learn from past mistakes in this case is to search for genuine "means"--a communal search for some middle ground between competing interests and miseducative

extremes. Through embarking on such a moral quest, a
community provides the best guarantee for success in the
moral education of its youth.

NOTES

1. Edward Eggleston, The Hoosier School Master
(New York: Hill & Wang, 1957), pp. 1-2; as quoted in
Michael B. Katz, "From Voluntarism to Bureaucracy in
American Education," Sociology of Education 44 (1971), p.
309.
2. Sarah Lawrence Lightfoot, Worlds Apart (New
York: Basic Books, 1978), p. 15.
3. Margaret Mead, The School in American Culture
(Cambridge, Mass.: Harvard University Press, 1951), p. 7;
as quoted in Lightfoot, Worlds Apart.
4. Katz, "From Voluntarism to Bureaucracy in
American Education," p. 307.
5. David Tyack and Elizabeth Hansot, "Conflict
and Consensus in American Education," Daedalus, Summer
1981, p. 14.
6. Madhu Suri Prakash, field notes for "An Eth-
nography of Clydesdale Central School."
7. Goals in Elementary, Secondary and Continuing
Education in New York State (The University of the State
of New York, 1974); as quoted in Martin Egar, "The Conflict in Moral Education; An Informal Case Study," Public
Interest (1981), p. 62.
8. Ibid., p. 144.
9. Ibid., pp. 144-45.
10. For an incisive analysis of the paradox of public schooling in the liberal era of "private moralities,"
see Emily Robertson, "Private Morality and Public Schooling," presented at the MASPES meeting, Spring 1983.
11. Martin Eger provides a case study recording
the horror with which some parents in New York State responded to the curriculum of values clarification taught in
their children's school. See "The Conflict in Moral Education: An Informal Case Study." Another critical analysis
of values clarification is available in Rick Ellrod's "Contemporary Philosophies of Moral Education," in George T.
McLean, Frederick E. Ellrod, David L. Schindler, and
Jesse A. Mann, "Act and Agent: Philosophical Foundations
for Moral Education and Character Development" (Washington: University Press of America, 1986), Chapter 1.

12. Urie Bronfenbrenner discusses this pattern of socialization in Two Worlds of Childhood--U.S. and U.S.S.R. (New York: Simon & Schuster, 1972), Chapter 4.

13. Malcolm Provus, "In Search of Community," Phi Delta Kappan 54 (1973), p. 658.

14. Epigraph from John Dewey, The Public and Its Problems (Athens, Ohio: Ohio University Press, 1927), p. 212.

15. See, for example, Ronald Campbell and John Ramseyer, The Dynamics of School-Community Relationships (Boston: Allyn & Bacon, 1955); Miriam Clasby, "The Community Voice in Public Education," Social Policy (1977); Leslie H. Cochran, L. Allen Phelps, and Linda Letwin Cochran, Advisory Committees in Action (Boston: Allyn & Bacon, 1980); Mario D. Fantini, Marilyn Gittel, and Richard Magat, Community Control and the Urban School (New York: Praeger, 1970); Leonard Fein, The Ecology of Public Schools: An Inquiry into Community Control.

16. The character of the rift between these two worlds is very astutely and sensitively portrayed by Lightfoot in Worlds Apart.

17. For a provocative discussion of "convivial institutions vs. institutions of the right" and of returning the task of education to the deschooled community, see Ivan Illich, Deschooling Society (New York: Harper & Row, 1983).

18. Michael Novak, "Mediating Institutions: The Communitarian Individual in America," Public Interest (1982).

19. Bronfenbrenner, Two Worlds of Childhood, p. 140. For more extensive discussions of the actual and potential contributions that different communal groups can make, see Bronfenbrenner, Two Worlds of Childhood, especially Chapters 5 and 6; Alonzo Crim, "A Community of Believers," Daedalus (1981); Lightfoot, Worlds Apart; Illich, Deschooling Society.

20. Gerald Grant, "The Character of Education and the Education of Character," Daedalus (1981), p. 149: ". . . parents appear to be less altruistic, with 66 percent feeling that 'they should be free to live their own lives even if it means spending less time with their children,' and 63 percent say they have the right to live well now 'even if it means leaving less to the children.'"

21. John Dewey, Moral Principles in Education (Carbondale, Ill.: Southern Illinois University Press, 1975), p. 22.

22. Theodore Sizer, Horace's Compromise--The Dilemma of the American High School (Boston: Houghton Mifflin, 1984).

23. Ben Brodinsky, "The New Right: The Movement and Its Impact," Phi Delta Kappan (1982), p. 88.

24. However, for an insightful discussion of the latest hypocrisy of family faddism, see Sally Helgesen, "Theoretical Families," Harpers (1982).

25. Ronald Dworkin, "Liberalism," in Stuart Hampshire, ed., Public and Private Morality (New York: Cambridge University Press, 1978). Contrasting the conservative viewpoint with the liberal ones, Dworkin describes the former's support for "the virtuous society. A virtuous society has these general features. Its members share a sound conception of virtue, that is, of the qualities and dispositions people should strive to have and exhibit. They share this conception of virtue not only privately, as individuals, but publicly; they believe their community, in its social and political activity, exhibits virtues, and that they have a responsibility, as citizens, to promote these virtues. In that sense they treat the lives of other members of their community as part of their own lives." (pp. 136-37)

26. This idea has also been strongly articulated by Emile Durkheim, Moral Education (New York: Free Press, 1961). In his discussion of the second element of moral education--attachment to the social group, Durkheim discusses the role of the school in expanding the scope of this attachment, extending it gradually from the immediate family to the whole of humanity.

27. Dewey, The Public and Its Problems, pp. 213-14.

28. Grant, "The Character of Education and the Education of Character," p. 148.

29. Mary Anne Raywid, "The Blurring of the Fringes: From 'Dangerous Organizations' to 'Obtrusive Pluralists,'" Educational Leadership (1977), pp. 498-99.

30. David S. Seeley, Education Through Partnership: Mediating Structures and Education (Cambridge, Mass.: Ballinger, 1981), Chapter 13.

31. For a critical dialogue between liberals and conservatives, see Phi Delta Kappan (1982).

32. See Raywid, "The Blurring of the Fringes," for a discussion of the controversy touched off by MACOS/ Man: A Course of Study, a program that is "unique and absolutely outstanding. It effectively brings sophisticated

concepts, inquiry skills and values to a level where 10 and 11 year olds can deal with them" (p. 6). The program was developed by Jerome Bruner and the Educational Development Center with the assistance of the National Science Foundation.

33. Analyzing the nature of ideal communal participation, Seeley discusses the significance of the elements of choice, voice, and loyalty.

34. These three quotations come from Reinhold Niebuhr, "Without Consensus There Is No Consent," Center Magazine (1971).

35. Raywid urges this solution in "The Blurring of the Fringes."

36. For an important insight on resolving the "creationism vs. evolutionism" debate, see Huston Smith, "Evolution and Evolutionism," Christian Century, July 7–14, 1982.

6
School Climate and
Character Development
Clark Power

INTRODUCTION

In his recent effort to retrieve Aristotle's <u>Ethics</u> as an alternative standpoint for doing contemporary moral and political philosophy, Alasdair MacIntyre calls attention to
Aristotle's use of the pronoun "we" in addressing his
Athenian students. As MacIntyre describes Aristotle's
voice, "It is magisterial and it is unique; but it is also
a voice that seeks to be more than merely Aristotle's own.
'What do we say on such and such a topic?' is a question
that he continuously asks, not 'What do I say?'"[1]
MacIntyre goes on to identify Aristotle's collective voice
with that of the best citizens of the Athenian city-state.
We can begin to grasp the significance of Aristotle's collective voice by comparing it with the individualistic voice,
typical in our own society. Our inability to say "we" in
making moral prescriptions reflects a lack of a genuine
moral consensus and sense of moral community.

In this chapter I propose that we examine whether
our schools reflect the kind of moral community Aristotle's
ethical instruction presupposed or whether they reflect a
privatistic society fostered by the bureaucratic organization of work and politics. I will take as a starting point
for this exploration MacIntyre's suggestion that at the
heart of any moral community is the ability to speak for a
group's shared norms and values or for a genuine moral
consensus. In the first part of this chapter I will suggest through a case study that the Aristotelean communal

context for doing character education is regrettably absent in the typical large high school. This absence of a school climate, characterized by a commitment to fairness and community, prevents students from forming the kinds of attachments and commitments which lead to a developed sense of moral obligation and loyalty. In the second part of this chapter I will present the just community approach to character education, developed by Kohlberg and his colleagues, as one way of promoting a positive moral climate through participatory democracy.

PRIVATISM IN CONTEMPORARY SCHOOLING

A Case Study

Follow, if you will, how a typical disciplinary problem gets handled in a large public high school. Timmy, a sophomore, cuts his fifth consecutive English class. His teacher, Mrs. Smith, reports the cut to the assistant principal, Mr. Jones, who keeps the attendance records for the sophomore class. Mr. Jones has been busy most of the day supervising lunch periods and patrolling halls and corridors. Although the student handbook states that he should have had a conference with Timmy after his third class cut, Timmy's case is low on his list of priorities. Racial tensions, drug dealing, and vandalism take up much of his time and concern. He does, however, manage to see Timmy the next morning. Timmy is sullen and uncommunicative. Mr. Jones tells him that for the next two weeks he will have no free periods but must report to the study hall. He warns him that after two more cuts he is liable for suspension from school.

Timmy goes to English class that day but cuts the next four. Mrs. Smith complains that Timmy should have been suspended. Finally Mr. Jones arranges another conference with Timmy but first asks Timmy's counselor, Mrs. Russell, for advice. Mrs. Russell confesses that she has not seen Timmy in over a year because she is swamped with helping students apply for college and counseling a few students with exceptionally difficult emotional problems. Before Timmy sees Mr. Jones, she manages to talk to him briefly. She does not get much further with Timmy than to find out he has a "personality conflict" with Mrs. Smith. She then tries to help Timmy to see that cutting class may jeopardize his future. She promises she will look into having Timmy switched into another English class; but Mr. Jones reminds her it's too late in the semester for that. In his second meeting with Timmy, Mr. Jones "lays down the law." He threatens suspension but Timmy pleads for another chance and promises to go to class.

Some commentary on the preceding scenario from the perspectives of the individual actors will complete our case study. Mr. Jones, the assistant principal, is torn between Mrs. Smith's demand for law and order and Mrs. Russell's plea for understanding. He hates always being in the middle but accepts it as part of his job. Mrs. Russell is critical of teachers like Mrs. Smith for sticking to the letter of the law. She finds they often fail to consider the storms and stresses of adolescence and problems at home, such as divorce and alcoholism. Mrs. Smith just wants to do what she does best--teach English. She tries to keep order in the classroom and she expects the administrators and counselors to support her.

Timmy is not at all interested in the conflicts the adults in the school are having over his case. He does not like Mrs. Smith's class because it is held right after lunch and he and his friends usually smoke marijuana at lunch time behind the school. He resents the fact that Mrs. Smith is one of those teachers who goes by the book and reports all of his cuts. Some of his friends have been skipping their classes and have never gotten caught. Most of Timmy's peers could care less about his cutting. Some think he is wasting his time in school and that it will eventually catch up with him. Others think the English class is boring and if he can get away with not going why shouldn't he? A few students in Timmy's class resent the fact that he seems to be "getting away with murder."

Divisions within the School Culture

What does this case tell us about moral community and character education? First, let us note that Timmy perceives the obligation to go to class as being imposed by Mrs. Smith and Mr. Jones. The cutting rule is something they demand. As far as he is concerned, he says, "I would like to cut and if it doesn't hurt me, why should it bother anyone else? Who cares? It's my business."

Timmy fails to take a "we" perspective on the cutting rule. He defends his "right" to decide whether or not to cut class. Of course, we know that his decision to cut class was not his alone. Timmy's peers were pressuring him to cut class and hang out with them. This case reveals a split between the adult and student cultures in the school.

The split becomes problematic from the standpoint of discipline when the students regard the rules of the schools as part of the adult culture and follow their own peer group norms which may run counter to the expectations of the adults. The bureaucratization of the school only exacerbates the split between the adults and the students by dividing the adult culture into administrator, counselor, and teacher cultures. Clearly Mr. Jones needs support from Mrs. Smith, Mrs. Russell, Timmy, and his friends. Such support can come when school rules and punishments reflect the will of a unified community.

The split within the adult culture, as I have depicted it, is based on a division of labor which separates the functions of teaching, administration, and counseling. While the division is not absolute, it is extensive enough to create certain tensions and misunderstandings. More importantly, given such a division of labor, discipline is understood as a form of social control or behavioral management and not as an expression of a shared morality. Durkheim warned us about this view of discipline eighty years ago:

> People conceive of school discipline so as
> to preclude endowing it with such an im-
> portant moral function. In reality, however,
> the nature and function of school discipline
> is something altogether different. It is not
> a simple device for securing superficial
> peace in the classroom--a device for allow-
> ing the work to roll on tranquilly. It is
> the morality of the classroom, just as the
> discipline of the social body is morality
> properly speaking.[2]

Discipline as Behavioral Management

In order to better understand the rule of an administrator-disciplinarian in a large high school and the im-

plications this role has for building community and character education, let us carefully analyze Mr. Jones's role as
disciplinarian. If we were to ask Mr. Jones to evaluate
the way he handled Timmy's case, he would probably admit
that he should have tried to see Timmy sooner. He would
excuse this delay by pointing out that he had more urgent
problems to attend to and that he was so deluged with
cut slips. He may even humbly suggest that another system of monitoring class attendance might work better and
call a meeting of other administrators and a few teachers
to work one out. Mr. Jones may also admit that he lacked
a good punishment for Timmy. Taking Timmy's free time
away was difficult to enforce and not very onerous. Suspension entails arranging a formal hearing with Timmy's
parents, a lot of trouble for a problem as common as cutting class. Besides, for many students suspension means
a personal holiday from school. What kind of deterrent is
that?

Mr. Jones's practice of discipline has four major
shortcomings. First, moral criteria do not enter in any
significant way into his evaluation of what is good preventative or punitive discipline. Second, the time and
energy he puts into his job are focused on the instrumentalities of maintaining order and enforcing rules to the
neglect of the effects these measures may be having on
school climate. Third, Mr. Jones does not significantly
involve the other staff and students in making and enforcing rules. This creates a situation in which staff and
students regard rules and punishments as external controls
imposed by school authorities isolating Mr. Jones from
both groups. Fourth, Mr. Jones sees no educational import
to what he is doing and therefore he is unaware that he
may actually be miseducating students.

Discipline and Fairness

Let us examine these shortcomings in more detail.
First, Mr. Jones did not use moral criteria in evaluating
his administration of discipline in his school. By that I
mean he was more concerned with reducing the incidence of
undesirable behavior than he was in the fairness of the
rules, sanctions, and disciplinary methods he employed.
Mr. Jones may object that a concern for student rights and
fairness can be counterproductive because it leads to more
permissive rules and weakens the discretionary power of
the administrator to enforce what rules the school does have.

Theodore Black, a former New York state regent, takes this common-sense position in his book, Straight Talk About Education.[3] He cites court decisions, which uphold students' rights for due process and which challenge schools to demonstrate that equal treatment is given in the punishment of minorities, as contributing to the erosion of discipline in the school. For Black, educators have only two alternatives: discipline or disruption. Discipline requires a strong authority unencumbered by the red tape of procedural justice and checks on even-handedness in punishment. The rights of the disrupters should not be allowed to interfere with the rights of those students who want to learn.

Must discipline and fairness to the accused be seen as mutually exclusive? It is difficult to imagine how any kind of authority can be effective, short of the authority of a police state, unless that authority is perceived as fair. Instead of equating procedural justice with the functioning of our legal system, which often becomes ensnared in the adversarial process and in legalism, we can make discipline more just by establishing rule-making and rule-enforcing procedures which involve the relevant parties in moral discussion and participatory decision making. But some may object that such procedures, no matter how simple, would tie up administrators, teachers, and students in continuous meetings and hearings and take time away from the classroom. There is no doubt that these procedures take time. However, the time spent in these meetings could and should be construed as character education. Is there any guarantee that these procedures would lead to a decrease in school crime and disruption? This is the bottom line for most administrators, as I have illustrated with Mr. Jones. Actually there is some empirical support that democratic participation can develop internal commitment to group norms, leading to a reduction in rule breaking.[4]

Discipline and Its Ends

Now let us proceed to the next shortcoming of discipline--the priority given to the instrumentalities of its practice over its ends. In dealing with the problem of class cutting Mr. Jones emphasizes how best to keep records. This is not an unusual response. In dealing with other problems, such as stealing and vandalism, administrators typically resort to such tactics as guards and watchdogs, electronic surveillance, and warnings to students not to bring valuables to school. In focusing on the means rather than the ends of a particular policy, they assume that the ends of the policy can be easily defined. In the cases of cutting and stealing the goals are taken to be the elimination of undesirable behaviors. Little if any thought is given to other possible ends of discipline, such as student moral reasoning or the school's social climate. Nor is sufficient attention given to the possibility that certain tactics may undermine these ends. Often administrators act as though the means of eliminating human problems should be similar to the means of eliminating nonhuman problems. In this respect, buying locks, hiring guards, and posting crime bulletins is similar to scattering rat poison or replacing a leaky valve. The relevant questions focus on finding the cheapest and most effective way of controlling the problem rather than on examining how these remedies may influence students' sense of the school as a community of persons.

Discipline as a Collective Undertaking

The third shortcoming I identified concerns the lack of involvement of staff and students in the making and enforcing of rules. As I have previously suggested, participatory decision making is a way of making the disciplinary process more fair and more effective. Our analysis of Timmy's case indicated that part of his problem had to do with peer pressure which can run counter to the expectations of the adults in the school. If Timmy and his peers had been involved in making the rule, they would have had a better understanding of what it entailed and why it had to be made. They would have had some impact in fashioning it, and thus they could have genuinely spoken of the rule as "ours" (the students' and the staff's), instead of "theirs" (only the staff's).

Democracy, while important for the building of a community of shared norms and values, is not necessarily the only means for doing so. The Durkheimian approach to moral education and the similar collectivist model employed in the Soviet Union rely on additional strategies. Essential to any approach, emphasizing the need to build a moral consensus or a powerful community, is that members of a group are willing to submit to the authority of the group (however that group authority is determined) and that they feel a strong sense of attachment to the group.

Durkheim termed submission to the authority of the group, the spirit of discipline, the first element of moral temperament. For Durkheim, discipline is basically constraint: the constraint of consistency or regularity in the performance of moral duty and the constraint of yielding to the authority of moral precepts which take priority over all other nonmoral concerns and personal inclinations. Durkheim referred to attachment to the group as the second element of moral temperament. Attachment to a group, whether it be family, the workplace, or country, brings with it a sense of fulfillment and happiness. Attachment to a group also evokes a sense of altruism or willingness to sacrifice for others. With these two elements of moral temperament, discipline and attachment, Durkheim brings together two of the essential characteristics of any ethic: the right which commands and the good which attracts.

Crucial to Durkheim's approach is that the elements of moral temperament are formed within a certain social context, a context which promotes a strong sense of communal attachment. As Durkheim explained,

> When . . . morality has yet to be established, when it is still nebulous and unformulated, then to achieve this end we must have recourse to the active and imaginative forces of conscience, rather than to purely conservative forces—since it is not a matter of conserving anything. While we must certainly not lose sight of the need for the disciplinary element of morality, the educator should apply himself first and above all to evoking and developing this morality [attachment]. . . . It is necessary to involve individuals in the pursuit of great collective ends to which they can devote themselves; to train themselves to cherish a social ideal; for the realization of which they may someday work.[5]

The way educators help students to cherish social ideals is to introduce them into an attractive, cohesive school community. Durkheim said that we need to give children that taste of the pleasure of saying "we," rather than "I," so saying "we," the child is aware that supportive, de-

pendable community is behind him or her.[6] In order to
develop the pleasure of saying "we," educators must deliberately call students' attention to the "spirit of the class"
or "pride in the school" and seize upon whatever events
draw members of a class or a school together as occasions
for furthering their collective consciousness.

All too often we make the mistake of equating the
school spirit with the momentary feeling of cohesiveness
right after winning a close game. We fail to grasp the
connection between the experience of group solidarity and
the cultivation of social responsibility. Durkheim reminds
us of the importance of fostering a shared sense of identification with the school community, not only through school
sports, but also through other kinds of events which arouse
common sentiments, whether they be a classroom discussion,
a cooperative project, a shared aesthetic experience, or a
morally praiseworthy action. The Durkheimian moral educator "lies in wait" for these opportunities to build and
express the unity of the group.

Discipline presents another opportunity for community
building. When a relationship between discipline and attachment to a community is established, discipline becomes
both a means of conserving and strengthening community
and an expression of the life of the community. We may
think of the norms of discipline as including rules pro-
scribing actions, such as cutting class, stealing, fighting,
and drug use, and informal norms prescribing actions,
such as norms of participation, trust, caring, and collective responsibility. Upholding these norms is a means to
the end of establishing a community. Symbolically, these
norms express or make visible the shared sense of community.

Disciplinary problems arise when there are breakdowns in community. The stronger the community the less
likely those breakdowns will occur. When they do, a
sense of community supports the rehabilitative dimension
of the disciplinary process. When Mr. Jones brought Timmy
to his office, he hoped to deter Timmy with his sanctions;
but we have noted that the sanctions lacked the kind of
impact Mr. Jones would have liked. The solution to the
problem of punishment is not to come up with more horren-
dous punishments but to abandon the whole notion that the
primary purpose of punishment should be deterrence. Durkheim offers another way of viewing punishment: as an expression of the sentiment of disapproval, based on a moral

154 / Character Development

evaluation of the act. The power this expression has for
changing the person who broke the rules depends upon the
strength of the community. If the community really matters to a member, then their disapproval will matter also.
If not, then their disapproval will be a matter of indifference. In our example, Timmy could care less about Mr.
Jones's disapproval, because he is not a representative of
a common school community. His peers, however, generally
support or ignore his behavior; and their opinions are
what really count. If the school were a community, then
Timmy's peers might share Mr. Jones's expectations for
class attendance. Timmy might also feel some attachment
to the school and care about being a good member. At
Mr. Jones's instigation or their own, peers could thus
pressure Timmy to bring his behavior in line with the community's norm. This disciplinary process could also have
a salutary effect on Timmy's peers by reminding them of
the attendance rule and reasserting the authority of that
rule.

When discipline is handled in this collective way,
Mr. Jones can no longer think and talk about school rules
as if they belonged to him or to the staff. Durkheim made
it clear that adults in the school should not act as if the
source of their disciplinary authority comes with their
superior size, age, wisdom, status, or capacity to reward
or punish. He suggested that the relationship between educators and the school rules and ideals should be analogous
to the relationship between the priest and God. Both
should be "instruments" and "intermediaries" of a greater
reality. While this analogy has difficulties, it does make
it clear that the rules of the school are suprapersonal and
not the mere reflection of the wishes of an adult authority.
Both the adult and the student are members of the same
community. Both are bound by the rules of that community.[7] Aristotle makes a similar point in his Ethics, noting that personal commands, even though they may be fair,
do not have the force of reasonable rules and may be
counterproductive by provoking the resentment of the subordinate:

> The man who is to be good must be well
> trained and habituated. . . . this can be
> brought about if men live in accordance
> with a sort of reason and right order, pro-
> vided this has force--if this be so, the

paternal command indeed has not the required force or compulsive power (nor in
general has the command of one man, unless
he be a king or something similar), but
the law **has** compulsive power, while it is
at the same time or rule proceeding from a
sort of practical wisdom and reason. And
while people hate **men** who oppose their im-
pulses, even if they oppose them rightly,
the law in its ordaining what is good is
not burdensome.[8]

In criticizing the failure to involve students in the
making and enforcing of rules I have moved from criticizing a failure to be democratic to a criticism of a failure
to build communal support for school rules and their enforcement. I have suggested that democracy and community
building should complement each other; however, I have
shown that community building along the lines Durkheim
envisioned may be possible without democracy.[9] The key
to the Durkheimian approach is that the adult educators
in the school community have the skill and sensitivity to
be group leaders who function with the support and confidence of the group. When we grasp the essence of the
Durkheimian approach to community building and discipline,
it becomes obvious that on the whole our schools are not
organized to encourage that kind of adult group leadership. Mr. Jones, who has the responsibility for discipline,
lacks the close, continuous relationship with Timmy and his
classmates to foster community. Mrs. Smith and Mrs.
Russell are also handicapped by a lack of continuous contact.

Discipline as a Process of Moral Education

Now let us consider the fourth and final comment I
have on Mr. Jones's method of discipline--that it is miseducation. By that I mean that Mr. Jones is unintentional-
ly teaching Timmy a moral lesson which will stand in the
way of rather than promote Timmy's moral development.
Mr. Jones is teaching Timmy that he must be good or he
will be punished, either through the sanctions of the school
or through the "natural consequences" of his behavior.
This pragmatic, instrumental justification for moral action
is Stage 2 on Kohlberg's stages of moral judgment (Appen-
dix A). I do not wish to imply that Mr. Jones is reasoning

at Stage 2. His own moral justification for deterrence may be at a higher stage (4 or 5). However Mr. Jones thinks of deterrence, the communication he gives to Timmy is Stage 2. This communication will not challenge Timmy's moral understanding since Timmy's stage of moral reasoning is already at least Stage 2. What Mr. Jones does, then, is confirm that Timmy's existing interpretation of why he should follow the rule--"because you might get caught and punished"--is correct. Similarly the tactics of surveillance and threat which Mr. Jones employs as "preventative measures" convey a Stage 2 message.

This first kind of miseducation concerns the moral content which we communicate to students when threats and punishments become the primary means of controlling their behavior. A second kind of miseducation concerns the sense of responsibility fostered when students are placed in roles which shield them from taking responsibility for each other and the school, as a whole. I have noted that Timmy's classmates do not try to help Timmy to come to class or feel particularly responsible for Timmy's problem. The general student view is that Timmy's behavior is his own business. Mr. Jones and Mrs. Russell confirm this view by keeping their meetings with Timmy private.

Further support for the impression that cutting class is a private affair is given in the way Mrs. Russell handles Timmy's case. The focus of her approach as a counselor is to help students who have disciplinary problems to see that breaking the rules is not in their best interest. While Mrs. Russell is willing to excuse Timmy, she also wants him to come to understand that cutting class could ultimately jeopardize his future. She does not find much value in artificially punishing Timmy for cutting class by sending him to study hall or by suspending him because she thinks that the harm he is doing to his future is punishment enough. As Timmy's counselor, she must make him aware of the natural consequences of actions so that he can make the best decision about his future. If Timmy decides to cut class, then he must be willing to live with the consequences of poor grades. Mrs. Russell does not address the question of whether Timmy should consider the consequences that his actions have for others and the class as a whole. Furthermore, in her psychologizing about the cause of Timmy's problem and its solution, little or no attention is given to a sociological interpretation and intervention. Mrs. Russell acts as though one-

on-one therapy is sufficient for handling behavioral problems, although she may complain that there are not enough
counselors to go around. She does not consider the problem presented by Timmy's peer group and by the school's
organizational framework.

A more sociologically oriented approach to discipline
seems necessary if students are to develop a sense of responsibility for the welfare of the school community. The
need for developing this sense of responsibility is illustrated in the following excerpts taken from a class discussion about making an agreement that would require students to enforce a rule against stealing. This discussion
is particularly revealing because high school students in
general recognize that stealing is a serious, intrinsically
immoral action, while they generally regard such actions
as class cutting and marijuana and alcohol use as less
serious, conventional violations. The adult discussion
leader presented the class with a situation which had recently occurred in the school. A student left his portable
tape recorder in his locker and forgot to lock it. Another
student passing by stole the tape recorder and later
bragged about it to his friends.

Leader: Should his friends express their disapproval?

Mary: I'd say you'd better not brag about it. You'd
better shut your mouth or you'll get caught.

Sally: If somebody is going to be dumb enough to bring
something like that into the school, they deserve
to get it stolen. If you aren't together enough
to lock your locker, then what can you expect.
If somebody is going to steal, then more power
to them.

Leader: Is that what other people think? It's ok if you
can get away with it?

Many students: No, stealing is wrong.

Leader: Well then, do you have a responsibility in a situation like this to try to talk the thief into returning the stolen goods?

Mary: You can't put pressure on students like that.

Bill: You can't ask that.

Mary: This school is responsible for enforcing rules.
We are teenagers. We have our own responsibility,

but we can't be responsible for totally everything. It's totally ridiculous to put it on the
students.

Bill: Yeah, the kids come here to learn, not to patrol
the hallways. They come here to go to school.

Mary: We are the ones who are teenagers. The teachers are grown up. They are the big people.
They are supposed to control the students in the
school. We are here to learn.

Todd: You shouldn't steal. But the way society is,
everybody does it . . . [Expressing disapproval]
depends on a lot of things--[like] who is whose
friend. It depends on what they want to do. . . .
Let them take the risk of losing a friend or let
them not say anything.

This exchange is quite revealing and by no means
atypical. I would like to call attention to four points.
First, there is a gap between students' acknowledgment
that stealing is wrong and their passive acceptance of its
occurrence. Since, as Todd put it, "everybody steals,"
few members of the school, including the staff, feel a
sense of moral outrage or disappointment when stealing
occurs. Second, this complacency about stealing constitutes a form of support for it. The students reacted in
ways which protected the thief; and Sally even condoned
stealing, as a fitting response to the foolishness of bringing something of value to school. Third, Sally's willingness to excuse the thief while blaming the victim illustrates
the strength of the privatistic norms of self-protectiveness
and mistrust and the lack of any collective sense of mutual trust or care. Fourth, the students refuse to accept
responsibility for rule enforcement, as incompatible with
their status as teen-agers and students and as destructive
of their friendships. While we may feel sympathy for
Mary's claim that asking students to share responsibility
for enforcing rules places great pressure on them, are we
to maintain that adolescents should feel no responsibility
in this area? Moreover, need there be a conflict between
adolescent loyalties to their peer friendship groups and
loyalty to the school as a whole? For Aristotle such a
conflict would indicate that something was lacking in their
conceptions of friendship and the school society. He

viewed the bonds of friendship as necessary for making the polis or larger societal associations possible.

My final point about miseducation has to do with a failure of schools to develop in students a habit of active, democratic participation. The fact that the staff generally make the significant decisions about school life and discipline leads students to develop habits of passivity and acquiescence. Such habits may be functional within certain bureaucratic contexts. However, such habits run counter to the principle of democratic participation, which underlies our society, and to our conception of the developed moral conscience, as one which actively seeks to discern the right and the good in active collaboration with others. Unfortunately, in many of our schools we teach about political democracy in the social studies class but our practices of schooling are far from democratic. John Dewey pointed out that this segmentation of democracy into a narrow, political realm posed a great threat to our democratic political structures:

> Whenever democracy has fallen it was too
> exclusively political in nature. It had not
> become part of the bone and the blood of
> the people in the conduct of life. Unless
> democratic habits are part of the fibre of
> a people, political democracy is insecure.
> It cannot stand in isolation. It must be
> buttressed by the presence of democratic
> methods in all social relationships.[10]

The context for these remarks by Dewey is a plea for greater teacher participation in decision making as well as for student participation. How are teachers to help students to form democratic habits, if their workplace, the school, discourages the faculty's exercise of democratic participation? How is democracy to become a part of the "bone and blood" of our youth if it is not a vital part of their school experience?

THE JUST COMMUNITY APPROACH

In the first section of this chapter 1 focused on the lack of a collective "we consciousness" in high schools as a problem for the moral education and offered some ex-

planation for why such a collective consciousness fails to
develop. In this section I will outline an approach to
character education which explicitly sets out to form collective norms and values: the just community approach.
The just community approach is oriented to the building of
community through direct democratic participation in making
decisions about matters of discipline and school life. I
have already indicated a need for democracy and community in our schools. Now I will indicate what the just
community approach can do, by providing some examples
taken from experience in several alternative schools and
one large, traditional high school which have applied this
approach. I will proceed by enumerating some general
features common to all of these schools and commenting on
the extent to which these features promote the establish-
ment of a collective consciousness conducive to character
development.

School Size

     The size of the school is a crucial prerequisite for
effective community building. Debates over school size oppose the material benefits large schools offer of greater
resources (better libraries, labs, and athletic facilities),
specialized services, and cost-effectiveness to the social
benefits small schools offer of more continuous and frequent
staff and student interactions, a stronger sense of cohesiveness, and a greater opportunity for participation in
school activities. Research dating from Barker and Gump's
classic, Big School, Small School, indicates that a greater
percentage of students in small schools participate in
school activities, hold positions of responsibility, and feel
challenged academically and socially, than do students in
larger schools.[11] Furthermore, these studies indicate that
large schools have the most detrimental effect on academically marginal students.
     One way of resolving the dilemma of school size is
to divide the large high school into smaller living-learning
units. To date, the majority of the just community alternative high schools have been schools within schools. They
offer a core curriculum of at least social studies and
English. The students generally take their language, and
more specialized math and science courses, in the larger
high school.

Role Sharing

Within the smaller school setting the need for bureaucratic organization and specialization is considerably
less. In the just community schools, teachers, counselors,
administrators, and students share to a degree the responsibilities of teaching, counseling, and leadership.
Since the schools are democratic, decisions which affect
the school as a whole are brought to the community for
discussion and resolution. Generally these decisions have
to do with disciplinary rules on fighting, stealing, vandalism, attendance, and drug use, and with policies affecting the quality of social interaction in the school, for
example, attempts to bring about greater racial and ethnic
integration. The staff resolve matters which call for their
particular expertise, such as deciding the academic curriculum, although student input is encouraged. All staff
members have responsibility for advising a group of about
12 students, a structure similar to the traditional homeroom. In these groups the adult leader does much of the
work that school counselors would like to do but find they
do not have the time to do. They meet regularly with
their students and monitor their progress academically and
socially. They also lead discussions to prepare their
groups for the weekly democratic meeting of the entire
school and to deal with the particular concerns of those
whom they advise.
In these settings the teachers find their primary
allegiance shifts from the department to the smaller school
unit. This allows for greater interdisciplinary cooperation
and for a concern for the curriculum as a whole. Departmental affiliations are maintained but they do not have
their former significance. The teachers generally experience far greater autonomy and responsibility in the small
democratic school than in the larger school because the
range of decisions they make is larger and their influence
on policy making is far more direct.

The Democratic Structure

At the very heart of the just community approach is
the weekly democratic meeting, called the community meeting. During this meeting problems of school life and discipline are discussed and voted upon. All members of the

school, students, support staff, faculty, and administrators have a vote. Direct participatory democracy has the advantage over representative democracy of including all students in an educational and community-building process. Ironically, many of the students who do not participate in representative student governments are the alienated and isolated youth who could most profit from such experience.

The community meetings serve three important functions in the school. First, they help to govern the school. Second, they provide a rich opportunity for moral discussion in which various points of view are elicited, reasons are given and examined, and a consensus is sought. Third, they act as community-building rituals in which the life of the group is renewed through participation in a common event.

The practice of high school democracy draws criticism from two very different positions. There are those who base their opposition on a fear that the immaturity and inexperience of adolescents will lead to decisions harmful to the school society and the best interests of students and staff. On the other hand, there are those who claim that the staff subtly undermine attempts to establish genuine democracy because they use their superior status, power, and persuasive ability to manipulate students subtly.

In the ten years I have been working with the just community approach I have found that while these critiques point to possible dangers, these dangers can be avoided with proper planning, training, and institutional safeguards. The most serious problem raised by student immaturity that I have seen came during the first community meeting of one of the alternative schools, Cluster School. The agenda was to decide on afternoon course offerings. A student proposed making afternoon classes optional. The motion was seconded and a vote immediately taken. As the students gleefully rushed out of the meeting Kohlberg blocked their exit, claiming that they had only taken a straw vote and that the real vote would follow during the next meeting after there had been a discussion. Kohlberg looked back on this first meeting as a valuable illustration for the Cluster staff that a laissez-faire approach to democracy would not work. Not only were the students immature, but a significant number of them (about 40 percent) had had a history of disciplinary problems, especially truancy, prior to joining Cluster. The Cluster staff adjusted to this situation by holding a staff meeting prior

to each community meeting.   During this time they planned
the agenda for the next community meeting, anticipated
what issues might arise, agreed to make sure certain issues did arise, and exchanged views on how they should
act in adviser group and community meetings in order to
assure that the discussions and decisions were worthwhile
from the perspectives of moral and community development.
The staff then met students for small group discussion in
adviser groups.   Finally, all met in the community meeting.   There adviser group reports were shared, a discussion ensued, and a straw vote was taken after all the
major points of view had been expressed. Following the
straw vote, those in the minority were given the first opportunity to argue their position further.   These procedures
effectively eliminated snap decisions, like the one making
afternoon classes optional.

Now critics of staff manipulation might find that
these procedures give too much influence to the staff and
render democracy little more than a charade.   Those of us
working with the just community approach would not deny
that staff members wield great influence in a high school
democracy.   Nor would we deny that they can and do abuse
that influence at times.   Nevertheless, we have found that
the democratic process itself imposes limits on the staff.
Time and again we have seen students reject staff proposals either because the staff member did not link his or
her proposal to the shared ideals of a democratic community or because the staff proposal was out of touch with
the existing moral atmosphere of the community.

In order to have influence in a democratic community, staff must clearly put the ideals of democracy and
community before their personal opinions and desires.
Furthermore, they must be patient with the limited progress a community can make in the realization of its goals.
For example, as a way of dealing with the problem of
stealing in the Cluster School, Kohlberg advocated that if
all attempts to get the thief to return the money failed,
then each member of the community should chip in to make
restitution.   This policy presupposed that Cluster members
shared norms of caring, trust, and collective responsibility.   Cluster members did not adopt collective restitution
as a response to stealing incidents during the first year
of the school before these collective norms had formed.
However, during the second year of the school some advocated the proposal as their own.   After a stealing incident

in which $9 was taken from a student's purse, a student
speaking for her adviser group said in a community meeting, "It's everyone's fault that she don't have no money.
It was stolen because people just don't care about the community. . . . [They think] they are all individuals and
don't have to be included in the community. Everybody
should care that she got her money stolen . . . and we
decided to give her money back to her."[12] This proposal
for collective restitution was agreed to in the meeting because by the second year most students cared about the
victims of thefts and wanted to do something to restore
trust.

Community-Building

Schools do not spontaneously become communities,
even with the right kinds of institutional structures.
Community building requires interaction over time. The
process is slow. Progress is not inevitable and regression is always possible. In the analysis and evaluation
of community 1 have undertaken with Kohlberg and colleagues, we consider a number of related aspects of group
life, which we term "moral atmosphere."[13] First, we focus
on the formation of a collective consciousness. When group
members initially begin to discuss problems and propose
solutions, they can only speak for themselves as individuals. Only after agreements have been reached can they
truly begin to speak for the group as a whole. As a
group faces more and more issues together, common norms
and values become salient; members see the implications
their decisions in one area have for those in another.
For example, in the first year of Cluster school, students
gave their personal opinions about why or why not an attendance rule should be made. They did not see any connection between their attendance rule and other rules about
drugs and stealing; nor did they see how attendance related to issues of communal friendship and racial integration. Two years later they saw all of these issues as relating to their participation in the life of a community.
They spoke with confidence in affirming the presence of
collective values of participation and caring.
In noting how a collective consciousness builds as
individuals' norms develop and then become interrelated,
1 would like to call attention to a second aspect in the

formation of community, an acknowledgment of the community as a terminal value. Participation, trust, and caring are important norms because the life of the community depends upon living up to these norms. In the case study we noted how the students and staff have a largely pragmatic, instrumental view of the school as an institution. They tend to value it for how it helps to prepare students for either the next step of schooling or the job market. They often fail to see the school as a community, having an intrinsic worth. Thus they justify rules about class attendance, stealing, and drug use solely in terms of how they benefit the individual. In the just community school, an emphasis is placed on the communal association as an intrinsically valuable social end in addition to other individual ends, such as cognitive and moral development and job preparation.

A third aspect of our analysis concerns the extent to which members of a community commit themselves to upholding the shared norms and values of the group. In Cluster's first year a lenient attendance rule was made which allowed ten cuts. When students exceeded the number of cuts, there was little concern. Two years later a "no cut rule" was enacted. This new rule expressed a new commitment to take attendance seriously. As one student put it, "If you have a certain amounts of cuts . . . I feel it gives you excuses, because I do that myself. But if you have an obligation to fulfill, then you have to face up to it and if you don't after a certain amount of time; then I guess you don't belong here." When students cut without any excuse, they appeared before the community and often received what we called a "community pull-up" from other students: "I want to say it directly to you, because you know what you are supposed to do. I just want to say that with your probation I want to see you participating in our classes and taking care of business." This exhortation is based on a sense that there is a collectively shared norm of participation. "You know what you are supposed to do." Furthermore, the student doing the exhorting feels responsible for seeing that this shared norm is upheld. Giving a verbal "pull-up" was not the only kind of response students made to the violation of community rules. They also volunteered to help students to get to class, for example, by going by their homes to make sure they got to school on time. The practice of discipline in the just community schools, when it was its

most effective, combined a sense of seriousness in upholding the shared norms of the community with a demonstra-
tion of care and responsibility for the individual community member.

A final aspect to our analysis of the community is
the moral adequacy of the group's collective norms and
values. A strong sense of collective commitment does not
guarantee a moral community. Indeed, in our society we
have a great fear that a strong, collectivist society will
violate basic human rights and destroy individual creativity and critical awareness. The democratic structures of
the just community school safeguard and promote criticism
and individual initiative. In the democratic meetings we
place great stress on attending to the moral justifications
for policies and on the need for continuous rational examination of those justifications. I noted that such a concern for moral justification was lacking in Timmy's case
and is typically absent in the disciplinary process. Thus,
we have found those students from large public high schools
typically perceive the rules and disciplinary practices of
their schools at a lower moral stage than do the students
from the just community schools.[14]

THE APPLICABILITY OF THE JUST
COMMUNITY APPROACH

I began this essay by raising a fundamental problem for moral education--the lack of moral community in
our schools--and then proceeded to offer a possible solution: the just community approach. At this point I am
in a position similar to one I first found myself in eight
years ago when the alternative high school projects were
still in their infancy and our research had barely begun.
During presentation by some of us working with the just
community approach in Cluster school, a former commissioner of education politely acknowledged that he was sympathetic with our work but he skeptically challenged:
"Will it play in Peoria?" There are at least three problems raised by this question. First, is there sufficient
interest and commitment in schools, which are not closely
affiliated with universities, to expect that teachers and
administrators will abandon conventional notions of schooling and adult authority and embrace a democratic, communitarian approach? Second, can an approach originating

in small, alternative high schools, whose staff and student body chose to be there, be made applicable to the large high school? Finally, does the approach require such extensive staff training and consultation as to put it beyond the reach of most schools?

At that time we were too concerned about immediate problems in Cambridge to worry about Peoria. Furthermore, those of us involved in just community projects questioned whether the worth of our experiments ought to be judged by their ability to be mass produced and circulated. In our view if we could establish and maintain even a few of these schools they would offer a provocative and significant alternative to the status quo in U.S. secondary education and could become a catalyst for future reform.

Eight years later, with the just community approach playing well in the original sites without any university-based consultation, we can begin to think about how well the approach can play on the road. Indeed, a number of recent attempts have been made to adapt elements of the approach to more conventional public and private high school settings in the form of town meetings, disciplinary and fairness committees, and teacher-adviser programs. Interest in the just community approach has generally grown out of practical concerns about violence, school crime, student alienation, cheating, and racial and ethnic tensions. Insofar as educators feel that their schools do not have adequate social structures for dealing with these concerns, they are prepared to explore a more radical approach to school life and discipline. While radical compared with some educational reforms, the just community approach is, nevertheless, rooted in a long tradition. Central to that tradition is the notion that education ought to prepare one for citizenship in a moral society. In the best of the U.S. educational tradition, preparation for citizenship has entailed preparation for participation in a democracy.

In the first chapter of this volume, Lickona and Ryan presented an "integrated model" which attempted to draw from the best of a tradition of philosophical, psychological, and educational concern for character education. Their interest in developing such a model grew out of dissatisfaction with certain methods of character education which they thought to be incomplete and/or unbalanced in some sense. The case study I described in the first part of this chapter is, I believe, a good example of a disci-

plinary approach which fails to meet the criteria of an integrated model. The cognitive, emotional, agenic, and
communal dimensions of the integrated model were all attenuated in an approach which selectively concentrated on
producing effective behavioral control. Timmy, the student
with the cutting problem, was not dealt with as a moral
person belonging to a community of moral persons but as a
problem to be managed by a variety of professionals, each
given a limited authority over the various segments of
Timmy's school life. The English teacher teaches Timmy
English, the history teacher teaches him history, and so
forth. The counselor counsels him when he has a psychological problem; and the administrator disciplines him
when he breaks a school rule. But who helps Timmy to
live as a complete person in a group with other persons?
Who teaches Timmy to think for himself, to make decisions,
and to consider the concerns of others?

In the just community approach the responsibility
for character education rests on no individual, department,
guidance center, or administrative council. The responsibility belongs to everyone. Obviously this raises problems
for schools in which interdepartmental dialogue is almost
nil. An integrated model for character education demands
an integrated school, not just in a mixture of racial and
ethnic groups but in a dialogue among staff members. Of
course, that kind of integrated dialogue must include the
students too, not just as passive onlookers but as involved
agents.

The thrust of this chapter has been to find a place
for character education in the climate and discipline of a
school. Students quickly become cynical of approaches to
character education which advocate ideals in the classroom
which seem unrelated or even contradictory with practices
in the school. Furthermore, any serious attempt to reach
both the cognitive and affective dimensions of the person
in an educational program must deal with real-life moral
decisions and actions and not simply with hypothetical or
historical cases. Ironically, our experience teaching classroom moral discussion techniques indicates the practicality
of a more ambitious and integrated approach to moral education. Kohlberg reports that he and Fenton once trained
teachers to do hypothetical moral discussion in their social
studies courses.[15] About half of the teachers successfully
applied their instruction during the research phase of the
project, which was to assess the effects of moral discussion

on students' moral reasoning. A year later, after the research had concluded, Kohlberg and Fenton returned to
find that not one teacher continued to do moral discussion.
Kohlberg quips that while the operation was a success "in
that the research showed the moral discussion technique
did promote significant moral judgment development, the
patient had died." The hypothetical moral discussion approach, while effective in the eyes of the researchers, was
not relevant to the teachers, who were looking for approaches more directly related to their particular curricular goals and who were more concerned about improving
student behavior. We responded by adapting moral dilemmas to the curriculum and by looking to the just community
approach as a way of bridging the gap between judgment
and action. Thus, although it is more demanding and ambitious, we think the just community approach has a much
better chance of succeeding in the long run than other,
less integrated approaches.

On this optimistic note, I hasten to add a conclud-
ing reflection on the problems of proceeding from grand
theories to practice in education. We typically think that
excellence in education largely depends on the quality of
teachers and administrators and on the curriculum. Thus
we ignore the students' input into the process. Those of
us who have worked with the just community approach
have learned that significant progress only comes about
when everyone assumes responsibility for the school. Sometimes this requires that we scale our ideals to fit the
realities of the school society and adolescent development;
always this requires that we regard students less as passive recipients of instruction and more as coworkers, fellow builders of a community. Perhaps the logo the Cluster
school students created for their school expresses this idea
best. It depicts a crew of workers busily constructing a
makeshift schoolhouse. The building is only half-finished
and what has been built seems in need of immediate repair.
Yet the schoolhouse is theirs. And even though they know
their cohort of students will not finish it and they suspect
no future cohort ever will, they persist in their labor, en-
joying their fellowship, and learning to live as morally
responsible adults.

NOTES

1. Alasdair MacIntyre, After Virtue (Notre Dame, Inc.: Notre Dame Press, 1981), p. 138.

2. Emile Durkheim, Moral Education: A Study in the Theory and Application of the Sociology of Education, trans. Everett K. Wilson and Herman Schnurer, ed. Everett K. Wilson (New York: Free Press, 1973), p. 148.

3. Theodore Black, Straight Talk About Education (New York: Harcourt, Brace, Jovanovich, 1982).

4. Clark Power and Joseph Reimer, "Moral Atmosphere: An Educational Bridge Between Moral Judgment and Moral Action, in New Directions in Child Development: Moral Development, ed. William Damon (San Francisco: Jossey-Bass, 1978).

5. Durkheim, p. 102.

6. Ibid., p. 240.

7. Ibid., p. 155.

8. Aristotle, Nicomachean Ethics, in The Basic Works of Aristotle, ed. Richard McKeon (New York: Random House, 1941), 1180a, 14-24.

9. For an application of some of Durkheim's collectivist principles of moral education which do not involve democracy, see Chapter 4. While I have acknowledged some of the positive aspects of this kind of approach, I am, nevertheless, opposed to it as being an unacceptable form of indoctrination.

10. John Dewey, "Democracy in the Schools," in Intelligence in the Modern World: John Dewey's Philosophy, ed. Joseph Ratner (New York: Modern Library, 1939), pp. 720-21.

11. Robert G. Baker and Paul Gump, Big School, Small School (Stanford, Calif.: Stanford University Press, 1964); Thomas Garbarino, "The Human Ecology of School Crime," in Theoretical Perspectives on School Crime, vol. I (Hackensack, N.J.: New Gate Resource Center, 1978).

12. Power and Reimer, pp. 108-9.

13. These categories for assessing community are more technically discussed in Ann Higgins, C. Power, and L. Kohlberg, "The Relationship of Moral Atmosphere to Judgments of Responsibility," in Morality, Moral Behavior and Moral Development, eds. William Kurtines and Jacob Gewirtz (New York: Wiley, 1984), pp. 74-109.

14. Higgins, Power, and Kohlberg, p. 104.

15. Lawrence Kohlberg, "The Just Community Approach: Theory and Research," in Moral Education: Theory and Application, eds. Marvin Berkowiz and Fritz Oser (Hillsdale, N.J.: Erlbaum, in press).

16. Lawrence Kohlberg, "Moral Stages and Moralization: The Cognitive Developmental Approach," in Moral Development and Behavior: Theory, Research and Social Issues, ed. Thomas Lickona (New York: Holt, Rinehart and Winston, 1976), pp. 34-35.

Table of the Six Stages of Moral Judgment[16]

Level and Stage	Content of Stage		Social Perspective of Stage
	What Is Right	Reasons for Doing Right	
LEVEL I--PRECONVENTIONAL Stage 1--Heteronomous Morality	To avoid breaking rules backed by punishment, obedience for its own sake, and physical damage to persons and property.	Avoidance of punishment, and the superior power of authorities.	Egocentric point of view. Doesn't consider the interests of others or recognize that they differ from the actor's; doesn't relate two points of view. Actions are considered physically rather than in terms of psychological interests of others. Confusion of authority's perspective with one's own.
Stage 2--Individualism, Instrumental Purpose, and Exchange	Following rules only when it is to someone's immediate interest; acting to meet one's own interests and needs and letting others do the same. Right is also what's fair, what's an equal exchange, a deal, an agreement.	To serve one's own needs or interests in a world where you have to recognize that other people have their interests, too.	Concrete individualistic perspective. Aware that everybody has his own interest to pursue and these conflict, so that right is relative (in the concrete individualistic sense).
LEVEL II--CONVENTIONAL Stage 3--Mutual Interpersonal Expectations, Relationships, and Interpersonal Conformity	Living up to what is expected by people close to you or what people generally expect of people in your role as son, brother, friend, etc. "Being good" is important and means having good motives, showing concern about others. It also means keeping mutual relationships, such as trust, loyalty, respect, and gratitude.	The need to be a good person in your own eyes and those of others. Your caring for others. Belief in the Golden Rule. Desire to maintain rules and authority which support stereotypical good behavior.	Perspective of the individual in relationships with other individuals. Aware of shared feelings, agreements, and expectations which take primacy over individual interests. Relates points of view through the concrete Golden Rule, putting yourself in the other person's shoes. Does not yet consider generalized system perspective.

Stage	What is right	Reasons for doing right	Social perspective of stage
Stage 4—Social System and Conscience	Fulfilling the actual duties to which you have agreed. Laws are to be upheld except in extreme cases where they conflict with other fixed social duties. Right is also contributing to society, the group, or institution.	To keep the institution going as a whole, to avoid the breakdown in the system "if everyone did it," or the imperative of conscience to meet one's defined obligations (Easily confused with Stage 3 belief in rules and authority).	Differentiates societal points of view from interpersonal agreement or motives. Takes the point of view of the system that defines roles and rules. Considers individual relations in terms of place in the system.
LEVEL III—POST-CONVENTIONAL, or PRINCIPLED Stage 5—Social Contract or Utility and Individual Rights	Being aware that people hold a variety of values and opinions, that most values and rules are relative to your group. These relative rules should usually be upheld, however, in the interest of impartiality and because they are the social contract. Some nonrelative values and rights such as life and liberty, however, must be upheld in any society and regardless of majority opinion.	A sense of obligation to law because of one's social contract to make and abide by laws for the welfare of all and for the protection of all people's rights. A feeling of contractual commitment, freely entered upon, to family, friendship, trust, and work obligation. Concern that laws and duties be based on rational calculation of overall utility, "the greatest good for the greatest number."	Prior-to-society perspective. Perspective of a rational, individual aware of values and rights prior to social attachments and contracts. Integrates perspectives by formal mechanisms of agreement, contract, objective impartiality, and due process. Considers moral and legal points of view; recognizes that they sometimes conflict and finds it difficult to integrate them.
Stage 6—Universal Ethical Principles	Following self-chosen ethical principles. Particular laws or social agreements are usually valid because they rest on such principles. When laws violate these principles, one acts in accordance with the principle. Principles are universal principles of justice: the equality of human rights and respect for the dignity of human beings as individual persons.	The belief as a rational person in the validity of universal moral principles, and a sense of personal commitment to them.	Perspective of a normal point of view from which social arrangements derive. Perspective is that of any rational individual recognizing the nature of morality or the fact that persons are ends in themselves and must be treated as such.

Part III
The Classroom and Its Curriculum

7

Character Development in the Elementary School Classroom

Thomas Lickona

DEVELOPMENT DURING THE ELEMENTARY
SCHOOL YEARS

Our younger son Matthew has always been a snuggler, part of his larger affinity for contact with people. When he was in the first grade, for example, his progress toward getting off to school was often agonizingly slow, delayed by his taking every opportunity to make contact of some kind--crawling on your lap at the breakfast table for a long hug, engaging you in extended conversation about some problem or detail that he "had to talk about," and so on.

Then one spring morning, not long before he turned seven, Matthew woke us up at 5:30 A.M., an event without precedent. There he stood, showered, fully dressed, hair combed. He was all ready for school, he announced, and was going out to the kitchen to fix himself some breakfast. He was obviously immensely pleased with himself. After breakfast, he insisted on leaving early for school and on walking the several blocks by himself, without the heretofore much-desired company of his seventh-grade brother. I watched him cross the street and then break into a run, never looking back.

This by no means became a regular pattern--most school mornings we continued to fight the clock--but I knew I had witnessed one of those developmental moments we cherish as parents. As he launched himself off to school that morning, Matthew was supremely happy, altogether "sealed up" in a new kind of self-sufficiency. That assertion of self-sufficiency, says Robert Kegan in The Evolving Self (1982), signals a new stage in ego development, the emergence of "the imperial self." The continuing, often exaggerated differentiation of this newly independent self, punctuated by regular protests of unfair treatment by adults, is much of what the elementary school years are about.

Margaret Gorman, writing in The Psychological Foundations of Moral Education (Knowles & McLean, 1986), reminds us that this new independence is very much a public affair and at bottom an expression of competence ("See, I can get off to school without the slightest bit of help"). This is an "age of extraversion," a time of great activity, of Erikson's drive to master things and to display the mastering self. Elementary schoolchildren want to be competent--in school subjects, in sports, in social roles--but what is more, they want to be known to be competent. Hence the appearance of a concern with how one is viewed by others. When Matthew was in the third grade, he came home one day and told us that it was important at school to "have a reputation." "Why?" I asked. "I don't know," he said, "it just is. . . . Everybody needs a good reputation for something. Take Bret Pritchart. He's good, he's smart, and he's strong. Now, that's the example of a perfect kid." That year Matthew, absolutely straight-faced, proclaimed that his New Year's resolution was "to be perfect."

As adults, we may smile at all of this, but it is serious business for kids. Through achievement and the recognition of achievement by peers, teachers, and parents, schoolchildren develop a sense of themselves--a self-concept which is the sum total of the things they can do. A natural expression of this way of experiencing self is competitiveness, wanting to do more things and do them better than the next kid. In this way, children of this age put themselves under a lot of pressure and as a result can be extremely hard on themselves and on each other. They are quick to say "I'm no good" when they do not succeed at something, and they are easily humiliated by any kind of public failure. And, at least partly because they are not fully secure about their own competence, they are notoriously intolerant of incompetence in their peers. Spend some time on an elementary school playground and you will wince at how children routinely heap scorn ("You

stink!") on age-mates who have the misfortune to make an
error in a game or otherwise fail to measure up.

Cliques also begin to form during the middle elementary school years. Membership in one of these peer
groups is both a source of approval for competence ("You
make the grade") and a badge of social success ("We like
you"). Those within the inner circle, as it is known at
my son's school, frequently affirm their coveted status by
denigrating those who lack it. Says a fifth-grade teacher:
"The name calling in my class is constant. Boys who
aren't tough or athletic get called 'fags.' The three
Japanese children in the class get called 'egg roll' and
'wonton soup'; one Japanese boy became terrified to come
to school. Boys also call girls names--'fat,' 'pancake
face,' and the like." Such name calling is often accompanied by the exclusion of those who are "different"--from
games at recess, conversation at lunchtime, and social
groups in the classroom. Children's reputation for cruelty
at this age is well deserved.

This kind of cruelty, however, is not the inevitable
by-product of this developmental period. Developmental
tendencies always interact with and are modified, for better or for worse, by environmental influences. Television
violence and put-downs; a lack of discipline, love, and
emotional security in the home; a culture that emphasizes
look-out-for-No. 1 competition; a school that fails to teach
caring and cooperation--all these factors exacerbate the
negative side of the developmental thrusts of this period.
But it is also true, as I hope to show, that teachers can
fashion environment, set expectations, and provide moral
instruction that channel the natural thrusts of elementary schoolchildren toward socially constructive ends--
and further development.

Happily, even in the heyday of the drive for competence and callous competition, other developmental forces
can be marshaled to check these excesses and foster the
growth of character. In the cognitive realm, children are
increasingly capable of what Piaget calls "decentering"--
keeping more than one factor in mind at a time. That
means a better ability to consider alternatives and consequences when solving a problem. In the realm of social
perspective-taking, Selman (1980) documents the enormous
progress children can make in learning to put themselves
in the other person's shoes: moving from egocentrism to
focusing on one other person's viewpoint, to considering

two viewpoints in a dyad, and then to being able to mesh the needs of the individual and the group.

In the realm of moral judgment, Kohlberg's work (1981) shows that children, by the end of the elementary school years, can at least begin to apply the Golden Rule, to understand why trust and mutual helpfulness are essential to human relationships, and to desire to be a "nice person" by living up to the expectations of significant others and the nudge of conscience. Kegan (1982), to return to the realm of ego development, charts the transformation of the overly autonomous imperial self into the more fully integrated "interpersonal self" as the child negotiates the persistent demands of his or her social world.

Thus elementary schoolchildren, like their counterparts at later developmental levels, are a constellation of strengths and weaknesses, their vices being an excess of their virtues. They are independent and competitive to a fault, overly eager to succeed, easily hurt by failure or insult, yet so often insensitive to the ways they hurt others. For all of that, their minds and moral potentialities are rapidly unfolding.

GOALS OF CHARACTER DEVELOPMENT DURING THE ELEMENTARY SCHOOL YEARS

Given what is happening developmentally with elementary schoolchildren, what are reasonable goals for their moral education? Three broad goals, I believe, stand out:

1. To promote children's development away from egocentrism toward relations of cooperation and mutual respect;
2. To foster the growth of full moral agency--a capacity for moral judgment, feeling, and action (so that children know the right, want to do it, and are able to translate knowledge and feeling into effective moral behavior);
3. To develop, in the classroom and the school, a moral community based on the values of fairness, caring, and participation.

Classrooms and schools dedicated to these three broad goals would seek to develop in children the following specific qualities:

1. A self-respect that derives feelings of worth not only from competence but also from prosocial behavior toward others;
2. Social perspective-taking ("How do others think and feel?" "How does my behavior affect the group?");
3. Moral reaoning ("What is the right thing to do?");
4. Knowledge of culturally important values, including procedural values (such as reasoned argument, tolerance of differences, and democratic processes) and substantive values (such as honesty, compassion, and justice);
5. The skills (e.g., communicating, problem solving, and coordinating actions) of cooperating with others toward a common goal;
6. Character traits (habitual ways of responding) such as fairness, kindness, truthfulness, and a generalized respect for others;
7. An openness to the positive influence of adults as socializing agents.

A word in defense of this last objective, since 1 believe the others, to one degree or another, depend on it. If you have seen The Miracle Worker, the soul-stirring play about Helen Keller, you will remember what 20-year-old Annie Sullivan finds when she arrives at the Keller household. At age seven, Helen is blind, deaf, and dumb, but she has succeeded in tyrannizing the adults around her. She smashes and destroys objects that displease her; she crams her food into her mouth with both hands; if anyone tries to correct her, she flings herself on the floor and thrashes violently--and her parents give in to the tirade. Annie Sullivan's first attempts to teach the intractable Helen, one of which ends when Helen stabs her with a pin, make one thing unmistakably clear: Helen will not learn anything until she accepts and submits to Annie's authority over her. As this insight dawns upon Annie one night in her bedroom, she enters the following in her journal: "Obedience is the gateway through which knowledge enters the mind of the child." Annie Sullivan proceeded to require and to get that obedience from Helen, and the rest of the story is known to us all.

Now, few of us want to foster in children a slavish obedience to authority; that is the stuff of which good Nazis are made. But the imperial self in elementary schoolchildren these days includes an increasing disrespect for adult authority and hostility to its influence. Here, for example, is a fifth-grade teacher in an affluent suburban school district: "On the playground l find kids more resistant to adult intervention. If you try to break up a fight, they argue with you and then throw another punch as they walk away. That didn't used to happen."

That kind of attitude on the part of children is one factor behind the rising tide of discipline problems that are driving many teachers from the profession. If you have been in elementary schools lately, you know that the latest approach to this problem, one which is rapidly gaining in popularity, is something called "assertive discipline" (Canter & Canter, 1976). This system is nothing more than teachers laying down the law and punishing the lawbreakers. By itself it represents inadequate moral education--it does not treat children as if they have minds--and it is not even a fully satisfactory approach to controlling behavior. But assertive discipline does recognize a basic fact: that children do need to be controlled, do need to be socialized, before they can learn anything, moral or otherwise, and that this process requires adults who have confidence in their legitimate authority and are not afraid to use it in appropriate ways. Obedience on the part of children (following directions, listening, being open to the wisdom and guidance of the teacher) may not be the only gateway through which knowledge enters the mind of the child, but it is one of the first.

A MODEL OF MORAL EDUCATION IN
THE ELEMENTARY CLASSROOM

How do teachers, confident in their authority to establish behavioral norms and hold children accountable to them, go about pursuing the specific educational goals l have listed above? l believe teachers benefit from having a model that can guide decisions about what to do in the classroom, one that offers a map of the territory of moral education. The model depicted in Figure 7.1 offers one such map, derived from my work with elementary school-teachers over the last 14 years. This model says to the teacher: "To do an adequate job of moral education--one which has a chance of real impact on a child's developing character--you should have four things going on in your classrooms: (1) building self-esteem and social community;

(2) cooperative learning and helping relations; (3) moral reflection; and (4) participatory decision-making." Taken together, these four processes embrace both the formal academic curriculum and the "human curriculum" (rules, roles, relationships) that make up the life of the classroom.

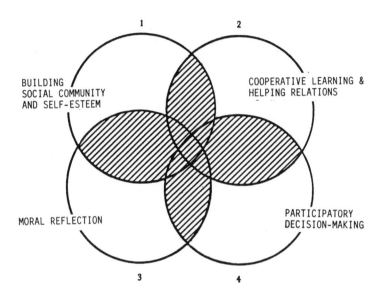

Figure 7.1   Model of Moral Education

Figure 7.1 shows these four processes as overlapping spheres, since any one process, done well, frequently involves the others at the same time.   To flesh out this model, three questions need to be addressed: (1) What is meant by a given process?   (What does it mean, for example, to "build self-esteem and social community"?; (2) Why is that process an important part of moral education?; and (3) How does a teacher do it?
    Let me consider each of these processes in turn.

Building Self-esteem and Social Community

    To build self-esteem in the elementary school years is, first of all, to foster the sense of competence and mastery which is at the core of the child's self-concept. Second, it means to teach children to value themselves as

persons, to have the kind of self-respect that will enable
them to stand up for their rights and command respect
from others. To build social community means to create a
group which extends to others the respect one has for oneself. More specifically, it means to develop a class in
which students come to (1) know each other as individuals,
(2) respect and care about each other, and (3) feel a
sense of membership in and accountability to the group.

Self-esteem is important to character development
because morality begins at home, with valuing your own
person, and because it is easier to love your neighbor if
you love yourself. Social community is important because
it contributes to self-esteem—partly by creating a norm of
mutual respect that inhibits the put-downs by which children undermine each other's self-esteem, and partly by
helping children to feel known and positively valued by
their peers. Social community is also important because
it supplies a vital affective dimension to moral education,
a flow of good feeling, that makes it easier for children
to be good, easier for them to cross the bridge from knowing what is right to doing it. Teachers who take the
trouble to build positive "group feeling" know at least intuitively that developing virtue is an affair of the emotions as much as it is an affair of the mind. Finally, a
supportive classroom community provides, for an increasing
number of children, a surrogate "family" that helps to meet
important emotional needs not being met at home.

How does a teacher foster self-esteem and social
community? For elementary schoolchildren, since demonstrating competence is so high on their developmental
agenda, self-esteem requires having opportunities to succeed and have their successes recognized by others. Knowing this, teachers of younger grades often hang for each
child a strip of construction paper titled "I Can . . ."
under which the child enters his or her competencies
("read," "write my name," "ride a bike," etc.) as the
year goes on. Viewed as contributing to a positive self-
concept, children's intellectual and other achievements are
not unrelated to character development but a foundation
for it.

A third-grade teacher describes the difference that a
measure of recognition can make for a child: "At the beginning of the year, I try to find out something that's
unique or special about each child. It can be anything—
a hobby, a physical skill, an award they won the year

before, something they made that they're proud of--as long as it's important personally to the child as an individual. I then make this something important to me. I stress to the child how important it is to me and that it's something just the two of us share. When the child knows I value this something highly, he begins to value himself more highly."

Frequently, elementary-school teachers also use public affirmation, similar to that described by Starratt in Chapter 9, to bolster self-esteem. A student teacher, for example, noticed that many of her sixth-grade students had negative views of themselves. So, she says, "I wrote a note to each child stating one of the characteristics in the child that I admired. I also asked the children to please write back to me what they liked about themselves. They were so excited about these notes that we discussed them at our 'Ups and Downs' circle time. Subsequently, I observed that many students displayed to a greater extent the positive characteristics that had been identified through our note exchange and group sharing."

Wise teachers begin, on Day 1 of the school year, to foster self-worth and social bonds. Two teachers who team teach second- and third-graders in Brookline, Mass., greet children when they arrive in September with this message: "All of us will be together for 180 days. It will be much happier for everyone if we get along and are able to cooperate. We don't expect you to like everybody, but we do expect you to respect each other and to take care not to hurt anyone. During the first several weeks of school, we'll be helping you learn the skills you'll need to cooperate and to show respect for others."

This orientation is then followed, over the weeks, by simple activities enabling children to get to know each other: playing a game, solving a puzzle with someone you don't know very well, writing down all the ways you and a new partner are alike and different, and so on. The teachers comment: "Through the course of the year, a sense of trust develops. Children begin to reinforce the ideas and abilities of others; they support one another in difficult times. This doesn't happen overnight. It grows slowly and must be openly encouraged."

When students of any age are asked, "What's the best thing about school?" they typically answer, "My friends." The need for friends is never stronger than it is in elementary school; witness a child's chief worry--

"Will I be able to make friends?"--when he or she has to move to a new school. It is hard to feel good about yourself and happy in school if you don't have a real friend there, and hard to feel part of the group if there are none you can count as friends. So in fostering self-esteem and social community, teachers would do well to pay attention to this basic need of children.

One way to do that is to discuss issues of friendship--What are some ways you can try to make friends with people? What if you're a new kid in school? Why do people need friends? What does it mean to be a good friend? Another way is to structure the social life of the classroom so as to maximize children's opportunities for positive interactions with others. A fourth-grade teacher had a system of rotating "learning partners"; every three weeks pupils got a new partner with whom they worked at least once a day on an assigned task. A fifth-grade teacher found she could reduce the prevalence of cliques in her class by having a seat lottery at the end of every week (desks in her room were contiguous, arranged in a large rectangle). The drawing meant that each week, each child was almost sure to have two new neighbors-- and a chance to make new friends.

It is in this context--building community and self-esteem--that many of the values clarification activities have legitimacy. Most values clarification strategies involve two things: clarifying one's own thoughts, feelings, values, and significant experiences (What are ten things I love to do? Three things I'm good at? Something I would like to accomplish in my life? A time when I felt good about myself for doing what I thought was right?), and then disclosing the product of that clarification to someone else. Adults who have participated in such activities can attest to the mutual respect and even closeness that these exercises can create in a surprisingly short time. Similarly, when children disclose what is personally important to them--and when those disclosures are listened to with respect--self-worth and social community are both enhanced.

Such activities can also put teachers in touch with the special needs of individual children. One fifth-grade teacher, using an exercise from Values and Teaching (Raths, Harmin, & Simon, 1978), made up blank "telegrams" bearing the incomplete message "I urge you to _____," and instructed her students each to "send" a telegram to a real person in their lives expressing a real feeling or

concern. Wrote one ten year old boy: "To my real Dad,
who I have not seen for 6 or 7 years: I urge you to
visit me for a summer or a weekend or even just a day."
Comments his teacher: "It made me cry when I read this.
I resolved to spend more time with this boy, in the hope
of helping him secure his desire or at least express/resolve
his pain."

When others give us their time, their attention,
their friendship, we are better able to say to ourselves,
"I am worthwhile. I matter to somebody else." Feeling
good about ourselves, we have an easier time being good
to others. That basic truth underlies this first and most
fundamental process of moral education: fostering the
self-esteem of the individual in and through human community.

Cooperative Learning and Helping Relations

Social community will be "thin" if students come together to share thoughts and feelings in circle time, but
spend the rest of the day working individually on academics. The second process of moral education, cooperative learning and helping relations, says students must
work together as well as talk together. If we want them
to develop the skills and spirit of cooperation—essential,
as Ed Wynne (Chapter 4) points out, to their adult lives—
we must make cooperation a regular feature of classroom
life.

Roger and David Johnson, in their book Learning
Together and Alone (1975), identify three classic learning
patterns: cooperative (where we function interdependently,
my success helping yours since we have a common goal);
competitive (where we are adversaries, my win being your
loss); and individualistic (where we work independently,
my success or failure being unrelated to yours). Cooperative learning, the Johnsons submit, should not replace the
other two modes, each of which has its own value in developing a student's potential and pursuit of excellence.
But cooperative learning should have what it rarely does:
the status of an equal partner in the teaching-learning
process. In support of that contention, the Johnsons cite
a spate of studies indicating the assorted benefits, academic as well as sociomoral, of cooperative classroom work:
heightened student enthusiasm for the task at hand, in-

creased academic productivity, improved self-image, greater empathy for others, and greater racial harmony in schools undertaking integration.

Teacher testimony echoes the research. Here is Debby Boyes, a third-grade teacher, who began cooperative learning in the simplest way--by assigning a task to partners:

> I gave each pair of children a record
> sheet with measuring activities on it. All
> of the questions revolved around the chil-
> dren themselves and their playground:
> How far can you jump on the sidewalk?
> How far apart can you spread your feet?
> How high can you reach on the building?
> How long is the teeter-totter? I suggested
> that when one partner jumped, the other
> mark off the leap with chalk, and that
> way they could measure each other's jumps,
> stretches, and so on.
>
> The children were laughing, relaxed, and
> extremely busy. Those who got mixed up
> on their measuring were helped by their
> partner or another twosome. They agreed,
> argued, rechecked their calculations, and
> looked to me with a lot of pride.

Some elementary teachers use the whole academic curriculum as a vehicle for developing cooperation. One way to do this is described by Sister Paul Barno. In science, her fourth graders worked in pairs to construct and balance mobiles. In art, they drew group murals and designed and decorated a quiet "meditation corner" for the classroom. But the crowning achievement came in social studies where the whole class collaborated on a unit on Mexico as their contribution to the school's "Festival of Many Lands." Sister Barno writes:

> The children were excited to work on this
> project. They eagerly settled into their
> tasks, were able to talk out most disagree-
> ments, and objected if one person tried to
> take over. As they worked on maps, charts,
> and displays of people, places, and things,
> it was encouraging for me to hear them

discuss new points of view, reconsider
their own, and alter their first opinion.

The fruit of our labors included an enriching day on which many parents joined us
as we discussed what we learned, danced,
ate tacos, and broke piñatas. The children
were able to view their efforts on TV and
in the newspapers. More than this, we all
felt a new unity among us that this cooperative experience had made possible.
One tangible result was a change in a
little boy who had not been well-accepted
before. His mother is a Mexican. Eddie,
who had rarely offered answers in class,
participated readily in this project. He
instructed us in life in Mexico, since he
had visited there. On the final day of
the project, his family came in with Mexican gems and silver, and Eddie proudly
wore a toreador's costume made by his
mother's hand.

This teacher's "Many Lands" project points out the
clear connection between cooperative learning and social
community. Curriculum content alone will not necessarily
move children to accept those who are different and value
those differences. Sister Barno succeeded in generating
mutual respect among her children--and a new appreciation
of Eddie--because she combined the content of her unit on
Mexico with the process of cooperative learning. Social
studies became social development.
    Let me hasten to add that all is not always sweet-
ness and light when teachers set out to make cooperative
learning part of their classrooms. Often the first attempts
are sabotaged by children's well-established habits of individualism and competition. One fourth-grade teacher,
for example, set up cooperative math groups, hoping children would help each other, but soon found them bickering
in a tense atmosphere of group-against-group competition
("Come on, stupid, you're gonna make our team lose!").
Teachers come to appreciate the formidable range of social-
moral competencies required for productive small group cooperation: taking the perspective of coworkers, communicating effectively, respecting and integrating the ideas of
others, dividing labor, making compromises, and coordinat-

ing actions toward a common end. These very skills (far harder to develop than, say, adding sums or punctuating a sentence) are, of course, the raison d'être for cooperative work in the classroom. But they will not develop unless the teacher is committed to a long-range effort in this area and prepared to monitor, support, and help children evaluate their fledgling cooperative efforts.

Cooperation is also made easier when children learn to support each other. A fifth-grade teacher instituted a practice called "appreciation time," a short session at the end of each day when class members could tell something that another person had done that they appreciated. At one meeting, for example, one girl said, "1 appreciate Julie for loaning me some paper when 1 forgot mine. All 1 did was say 1 didn't have any, and she offered me some of hers." A boy said, "1'd like to appreciate Stan for helping me study for my spelling test. That was the first time 1 ever got 100!" This teacher reports that appreciation time became the single most popular activity in her classroom, all the more impressive when one recalls that children this age, left to their own devices, typically trade insults rather than compliments. Besides fostering mutual regard and helpfulness among classmates, group appreciation also teaches children to do publicly what many adults find difficult to do at all: give and gracefully receive positive feedback.

Many teachers foster helping relations in the classroom by taking a further step: using class problem-solving meetings to crystallize feelings of community and interdependence into a clear sense of collective responsibility. Often such meetings address a problem which affects many or all class members: too much noise, people not helping with clean-up, students taking or otherwise abusing others' property, and so on. But collective responsibility means more; it asserts that we are our brother's keeper, that even if only one person is having a problem, it's everybody's problem. If there's a new boy who doesn't have friends or know his way around school, that's a class concern. If one person has had her lunch money stolen, that's a class issue. A kindergarten teacher found, in fact, that her children listened and interacted best in their circle meetings when she posed the question, "Who has a problem they would like other people to help them solve?"

Many cooperative learning activities foster the kind of cooperation that serves the immediate mutual interests of the cooperators (as when students do a group project or study for a test together). Other strategies foster cooperation that involves helping another (as when one student teaches another, or the group helps an individual member solve a problem) with the expectation that the help-givers will eventually receive similar help in return. Different from both of these, however, is a third kind of cooperation: working together to help someone without the expectation of reciprocity. This form of cooperation gives children opportunities to help others without thinking, "What's in it for me?" It thus takes cooperation beyond the boundaries of self-interest and into the realm of altruism.

Let me give a case in point which shows how teachers of even young children can begin to develop this kind of altruistic cooperation. A second-grade teacher, who for several weeks had been using class meetings and cooperative learning to build moral community, read her class a story about a man who lived in a circle of love. When he asked another person to come into this circle, the person refused. Instead of being hurt or discouraged, the man said, "Well, if you won't come into my circle of love, I'll just have to make it bigger so it will go around you!"

In the discussion that followed, the teacher asked the children if they would like to be in a club. She reports:

> The children responded to this idea with
> enthusiasm. After much brainstorming, we
> decided to name our club "The Love Circle,"
> after the story. We made badges out of
> circles with the word LOVE in the center.
> On the opposite side of the badge, each
> person wrote one way he or she promised
> to help the club in the way they lived,
> and shared this with a partner. Each
> month we try to think up a special way to
> enlarge our love circle. This month it is
> putting on a play for the people in the
> nursing home down the road from our school.

We can all think of similar stories of schools which have nurtured compassion and service. Sixth graders in a lakeside community in central New York studied their town's

water shortage during a summer drought--interviewing officials to determine the severity of the problem, for exam-
ple--and published in the local newspaper the results of
their research, including a list of many ways to conserve
water. When Matthew was a first grader, teachers in his
school discussed the famine in Cambodia with the students;
they decided to have a sale to which children donated old
toys and games, proceeds to go to the relief effort. A few
years ago, when the city of Atlanta was being terrorized
by an elusive child murderer, schoolchildren across the
country wrote to send their concern, their prayers, or
money they had raised to support summer camps for Atlanta's black children. During the Christmas season,
children in some classrooms are made aware of their community's effort to raise money for poor or tragedy-stricken
families, and have the opportunity to contribute from their
allowances to a class donation.

In these and other ways, children can learn that
there's a bigger world out there, that a lot of people in
it are hurting, and that we should do what we can to
help them. This is not to suggest that we should inundate
children with information about all the wars, famines,
natural disasters, and other tragedies of the world; their
young minds and emotions aren't ready to handle that.
But at least some early exposure to human needs beyond
their own group and to the idea and importance of being a
concerned citizen will sow the seeds from which a mature
social consciousness can eventually grow.

The need to begin early to foster enlightened cooperation and altruistic service is underscored by the
sociopolitical context that currently confronts us. We seem
to live in an increasingly Hobbesian society in which personal selfishness masquerades as life-style, politics becomes the clash of narrow interest groups rather than the
care of the common good, and cooperative problem solving
is a vanishing art. All manner of people now run to the
courts to settle conflicts that used to be solved through
communication, reasoning, and compromise; it is no accident that in the United States the number of lawyers is
increasing more than twice as fast as the general population. There are, as always, complex sociological currents
afoot to explain such social changes, which may be partly
irreversible. But we would do well to remember the counsel of anthropologist Ashley Montagu: "Cooperation, not
conflict, has been the most valuable form of behavior for

human beings taken at any stage of their evolutionary history." And if we wish to strengthen a cooperative ethic on a societal scale, we should strive to make it part of the characters of children as they live and work in the small society of the classroom.

Moral Reflection

The third process crucial to moral education in the elementary school years is moral reflection. "Reflection" here is intended to cover a wide range of intellectual activity: reading and thinking; discussion or debate about moral matters; explanation by the teacher (e.g., of why it's wrong to make fun of a handicapped child); and first-hand investigation and experience which increases children's awareness of the complex ecosystem to which they belong and which they must learn to care for. Of all the processes of moral education, moral reflection is aimed most directly at developing the cognitive, rational aspects of the moral agent. At the same time, however, this more self-consciously rational aspect of character development can be carried out in such a way as to foster a union of cognition and affect, so that children come to feel deeply about what they think and value.

To show how this can be accomplished, let me share with you an account of one school's effort to make caring the unifying theme of its academic curriculum (for a much fuller account, see the summer 1983 issue of Moral Education Forum). The Fieldston Lower School is a private elementary school in New York City. Its program for socio-moral education is intended to help children: (1) learn about the interdependence of all living things, (2) identify, affectively, with other people and with the world around them, and (3) develop, as a consequence of their learning and identification, a sense of obligation to nurture, protect, and respect all life.

A series of articles by the staff of the school (Moral Education Forum, 1983) describes how this vision becomes educational practice. The curriculum includes a wide variety of experiences both within and outside the school, all designed to help children appreciate and identify with the peoples and other living things they are studying. The principal speaks, for example, of the school's commitment to understanding environmental issues:

We want our children to understand and
respect the balances in nature, to respond
to the needs of living things, to support
and consequently to value life. Our third-
graders become gardeners, and our 5's and
6's become the caretakers of butterflies
and birds. Each fourth-grader adopts one
tree on the campus and studies it throughout the school year, learning its seasonal
cycle. They map the campus, label the
trees, and plan a nature walk. We do
this so our children will come to see themselves as part of and responsible for the
natural world around them. Our curriculum
takes note of seasonal changes because all
living things, plants, animals, and humans,
are affected by their environment. In the
fall an Indian garden, planted by last
year's third-graders, is harvested by our
current third-graders, and the children
learn how the gift of the land yielded corn,
beans, and squash to the Woodland Indians. (Cole-Farris, 1983, p. 12)

A fifth-grade social studies teacher describes how
she uses the Middle Ages as the core of her curriculum in
that grade. This historical period is an ideal developmental match for children aged 10-11, she explains, because
their concerns are a microcosm of medieval themes: (1) the
struggle for power, yet need for protection (corresponding
to the social system of feudalism); (2) the guidelines for
permissible aggression (the rules of chivalry); (3) the
need for clear-cut standards of good and evil (the laws of
the Church); and (4) the issue of fairness, whether it be
individual or social (Frey, 1983, p. 32).

To help children understand that justice is seldom a
simple matter, the teacher says, they study historical
events from divergent viewpoints. In their unit on the
Norman Conquest, for example, the class hears different
accounts, one written by Normans, another by Saxons.
First-hand experience is used to help students "empathize
with, not just learn about, a particular group." To enter
into the life of a monk, for example, the classroom becomes
a Scriptorium. Students look up examples of initial letters, Gothic alphabets, and marginal decorations. They

learn calligraphy and the use of gold leaf. The manu-
scripts they produce through their slow, painstaking efforts "give them a great sense of achievement and appreciation of the artist monk" (Frey, 1983, p. 33).

The history of the period is also personalized by
reading aloud fine historical fiction. The book that made
the deepest impact on her fifth graders, teacher Frey says,
is Barbara Leonie Picard's One Is One (1965). The protagonist, a boy reared to regard knighthood as the only
admirable life for a man, finds himself drawn instead to
the peace of the monastery and the beauty of art. Mocked
by his brothers, however, he reluctantly becomes a knight.
But appalled by the brutality of battle and the horrible
aftermath of war, he finally returns to the monastery to
become a creative artist. This book, says the teacher,
stirs discussion of the difference between physical and
moral courage--and the difficulty of moral choices. One Is
One also reminds us of a larger point made by Kevin Ryan
in a later chapter: that good literature, in the hands of
a sensitive teacher, is an unexcelled resource for moral
education, one that both enlightens the mind and touches
the heart.

An ethics teacher at Fieldston (Sommer, 1983) re-
counts a project which sent sixth graders into a nearby
Jewish home for the aged. Interviewing people, the teacher explains, helps to counteract stereotyping by enabling
children to learn about people as individuals. In the
home for the aged, they "learn from its residents what it
has meant to be Jewish and to grow old in contemporary
America. The children get first-hand descriptions of
pogroms, culture shock, poverty, and the Great Depression." Back in the classroom, the students compare their
preconceptions of the elderly with their newfound knowl-
edge--and their particular learnings about the immigrant
elderly.

Most schools, unfortunately, are light years away
from making the whole academic curriculum serve the cause
of moral development. But any teacher in any school can
develop an "ethical eye" that spots the opportunities for
moral reflection and discussion. One second-grade teacher
saw just such an opportunity during a science project
which had the class incubating 20 chicken eggs. She had
suggested to the class that they might wish to open an
egg each week to monitor the embryonic development.
Later that day, in his reading group, seven year old

Nathaniel confided to his teacher: "Mrs. Williams, I've
been thinking about this for a long time--it's just too
<u>cruel</u> to open an egg and kill the chick inside!" Mrs.
Williams listened without comment and said she would
bring it up for discussion with the whole class.

When she did, there was some agreement that Nat's
point was worth thought. But many children said they
were curious to see what the embryo looked like. Nat replied that being curious wasn't a good enough reason for
killing a chick: "How would you like it," he said, "if
somebody opened your sac when you were developing because
they were curious to see what you looked like?" Anyway,
he argued, the library must have pictures of chick embryos; that would be a better way of finding out what
they looked like. But, countered some children, they
wanted to see the <u>real</u> chick. "Is it alive?" became a
question. Some said it wasn't alive until it hatched;
others said it's alive now, and it <u>is</u> a chicken.

Mrs. Williams asked the children to think about the
issue overnight, and they would reach a decision as a
class the next morning. By that time a majority of the
children had come to feel that Nat's objection should be
honored; they should not open the eggs.

The potential moral learnings here are many: that
all life, even that of a chick embryo, is to be taken seriously; that just wanting to do something isn't a good
enough reason for doing it; that when a member of the
group has strong feelings about something, he has a right
to express them and others an obligation to listen; and, if
possible, a conflict should be solved in a way that tries
to meet the needs of all parties (the class did, in fact,
search for pictures of chick embryos in the library).
These learnings were possible because Mrs. Williams took
time to allow her children to come to grips with a difficult
moral dilemma arising from the real life of the classroom.
As a side point, it is worth noting that teachers find real-
life dilemmas like this one are far more effective in engaging children's thinking and feelings than are "canned"
dilemmas from a book or kit.

Elementary schoolchildren are not too young to begin to learn the skills of rational decision making, which
many philosophers and educators (see, e.g., Hall & Davis,
1975) believe is a more thoughtful, systematic approach to
solving moral dilemmas than simply tossing children a
problem and having them debate it. Consider, for example,

the dilemma of eleven year old Hank (an actual case): He has just made friends with two boys after a month of painful lonesomeness at a new school. Walking home from school with Hank, these boys steal a package from an apartment mailbox, open it at Hank's house to find two gold medallions, and laugh when Hank says he thinks they should return them. Hank wants to keep his new friends, but he thinks stealing the medallions is wrong. What should he do?

Rational decision making teaches students to ask these questions: What are the alternatives? What are the likely consequences of each alternative for the various people involved? What are the values involved in each course of action? What is the best solution--the one that maximizes the good consequences and is most consistent with the important moral values? Hank, for example, might tell his parents about the problem, and they might talk privately with the boys about returning the medallions. That wouldn't get the boys in trouble, might have some positive influence on their future behavior (at least with Hank), and would keep alive Hank's chance of a continuing friendship.

The advantage of moral dilemmas is that they create conflict between and within students, and this disequilibrium causes students to revise and improve their moral reasoning. An extensive research literature (see Lockwood, 1978; and Leming, 1981; for reviews) documents that, typically, about half the students in any given class advance roughly one third of a stage on Kohlberg's moral reasoning scale as a result of sustained participation in moral dilemma discussion. But a steady diet of moral dilemmas, aside from being boring, distorts the moral life; it obscures the fact that doing the right thing is usually more like resisting a temptation than solving a difficult dilemma. In most moral situations, there is a clear right choice: I shouldn't shoplift the tape at the music store; I should tell my mother the truth when she asks where I've been; I shouldn't join in teasing a retarded boy, or throwing stones at a stray dog; I should help out around the house when I'm asked; I shouldn't cheat on a test or copy someone else's homework; I should keep a promise to go somewhere with a friend even when a better offer comes along. Moral reflection in the classroom, whether through story, Socratic questioning, or didactic instruction, should teach children how to act in clear-cut situations like these--for such actions will constitute the greater part of their characters.

Moral reflection should also teach children that while it is often easy to know what is right, it is usually harder to do it. Children should talk about why they (and other people) sometimes cheat, lie, put people down, or fail to be fair even when they know they shouldn't. What factors (self-interest, peer pressure, anger, anxiety, low self-esteem) lead them to do such things, and what helps them stay on the straight and narrow? Children need to be moral psychologists who understand human weakness and wrongdoing, as well as moral philosophers who can say what's right—and they need to be challenged to develop the self-awareness, self-discipline, and strength of will that will help them hew to the right course.

All of this is a tall order, and it should come as no surprise that teachers, even the best ones, usually find guiding moral reflection to be the hardest part of moral education. It involves many sophisticated skills—framing the moral issue, Socratic questioning, paraphrasing responses, making connections among the various contributions, drawing out and challenging children's reasoning (rather than settling for mere opinion), to name just some of them. Most teachers have rarely seen such skills modeled in their own education and will need much time, patience, and practice to develop them. But the effort to do so is clearly essential, since moral reflection is at the center of the moral enterprise.

Participatory Decision Making

Based on his work with high schools, Clark Power has observed that it is easy to get students to agree about moral rules ("Don't steal," "Don't cheat") but much harder to develop moral norms that students feel obligated to follow in their behavior. A true norm is a moral standard to which children will hold both themselves and each other accountable ("Hey, you're not following the rule!"); rules become norms when they are internalized and taken seriously. Norms create a support system that helps students practice living up to their moral values. And that process of putting belief into practice is the way, for all of us, that a value becomes a virtue.

Participatory decision making, the fourth process of elementary school moral education, provides a motivational push to go from judgment to action. It does so by requiring children to participate in making decisions (e.g., about fair rules or solutions to classroom conflicts) to which they are then held accountable and which can eventually become operative group norms. Piaget (1932) was one of the first to argue for this kind of participatory governance of the classroom. If children are truly to understand the origin and purpose of rules (people make rules to help them live together), Piaget reasoned, they must have a hand in making and discussing rules. Otherwise, rules will remain external to the child's mind and have little inner power over behavior.

What is essential, however, is not any specific set of governance procedures but rather a spirit of participation and shared responsibility for the classroom. In setting rules, for example, teachers have several options. They may wish to take a highly structured approach: distributing a list of "expectations" ("I expect you to work to the best of your ability, speak courteously to me and each other, and respect others' property"), and then ask, "What specific rules do we need to make sure these things happen in our classroom?" Or the teacher may post rules ("Raise your hand to speak," "No put-downs," "Keep hands and feet to yourself") and ask the children, "Why is each of these rules important? What do you think is a fair consequence for breaking them?" Or rules can be introduced by the teacher on the first day and discussed later in the week at a class meeting ("How are the class rules working so far? Can they be improved to make them work better?"). Whatever the approach, teachers should understand that they are not turning the class over to the children, but are using their moral authority to guide children in taking on an important responsibility: thinking and working together to make the classroom a good place to be and learn.

Does it work? My favorite story of this theory in practice comes from a young teacher, Debbie Wilcox, who spent a full year after graduating from our program in that pedagogical purgatory known as substitute teaching. She was soft-spoken, slight of build, and stood barely five feet tall, but she knew what she was doing. In November of that year, she was called by the principal of a fairly tough city school and asked to take over a class

of 26 third-grade children; the regular teacher, who found
them "impossible to deal with," was taking a six-week mental health leave. The children wore their notorious reputation like a badge, greeting teacher Wilcox on her first
day with the announcement, "This is the bad class of the
school."

This teacher called a class meeting and immediately
shared the responsibility for discipline and order with the
children. She asked: "What rules are necessary in this
room? Why do we need them? Should everybody have to
obey rules?" A flurry of opinions followed these questions.
The meeting ended with consensus on a rule suggested by
a child: "Care about each other." That became the class
ethic, the source of specific rules and the yardstick
against which behavior would be measured in future discussions.

Steadily, teacher Wilcox reports, children improved
in their conduct. "They tried to get their schoolwork in
on time. A 'give it to me, it's mine' attitude gave way
to more open sharing. More and more children participated
in class meetings and learned to listen quietly when someone else was speaking." When someone violated an agreed-
upon rule or the general expectation about caring--as did
three boys throwing spitballs--the teacher called an on-
the-spot class meeting and confronted the problem: "What
are you doing? What rule did we agree to?" Serious behavior problems became almost nonexistent, however, and
"many children actually began expressing a liking for
school." The daily class meetings, teacher Wilcox believed,
had done a lot for their self-esteem; they gave each child
"a place, a group of people, who believe that he is worthwhile enough to be listened to."

Teacher Wilcox's dramatic success in turning around
a terrible situation became the talk of the school. But
there is more to the story. At the end of the six weeks,
when the regular teacher was about to return, two children came to Debbie Wilcox and said, "Miss Wilcox, we
don't want to lose our class meetings. Will you teach Mrs.
Blodgett how to do them?" Miss Wilcox said she would see
what she could do.

Mrs. Blodgett listened politely but did not institute
class meetings. Later that year, Debbie Wilcox was called
to the same school to substitute teach in another classroom.
She happened to pass by the room where she had spent
those six weeks. The children were behaving badly, and

the teacher was yelling. She learned from other faculty
that this third grade was once again the "bad class" of
the school.

Children's morality, as a teacher once said to me,
"takes a lot of slow to grow." While it is growing, it is
very fragile, very much in need of support structures that
hold it together. The class meeting, the supportive moral
community it created, and the strong, respectful moral
leadership of teacher Wilcox were clearly all necessary to
help the third graders consolidate the fragile gains they
had made in their social-moral behavior. Indeed, even
after moral values begin to take root in a child's character, the surrounding moral community of the classroom and
school remains an important support system. Learning to
act consistently on the basis of our best moral reasoning
is a process that is never finished, and children, like
adults, need all the help they can get.

Let me repeat that there are many ways to foster
responsible participation in the classroom, and that teachers should begin slowly, with whatever they are comfortable with, and gradually branch out. Giving children a
bigger voice in the classroom can, for example, start with
something as simple as a suggestion box. It can expand
to include teacher-student learning contracts, small-group
brainstorming on ways to solve a persistent classroom problem (such as people not following directions), a "conflict
corner" where two students go to work out an interpersonal
conflict, a teacher-moderated "fairness committee" to propose solutions to a classroom problem (e.g., name calling),
written or oral student feedback on a curriculum unit
("What did you learn? How could it have been improved?
How can we make the next unit better?"), and regular class
meetings. Class meetings can be weekly or daily, and
run on a consensus model (everybody agrees on the decision), a voting model (majority rules), or a voting-by-
consensus model (vote only if all agree to support the outcome). Voting can be open (to encourage taking a public
stand) or by secret ballot (to minimize peer pressure).
Through any and all of these methods, teachers can send
the message that they value the viewpoint of the child.

John Dewey urged educators to help students see
the links between learning and life, between the affairs
of the classroom and the affairs of the wider world. Participatory decision making offers obvious opportunities:
Just as societies have laws, classrooms and schools have

rules; just as lawmakers discuss and debate what are good laws, we discuss and debate what are good rules; just as adults are citizens with responsibilities to society, students are citizens of the classroom and school. One fifth-grade teacher helped his children make connections like these as they studied the birth of the nation's democracy. Together, they organized their own "constitutional convention"; it drafted a "Classroom Constitution," complete with a Bill of Rights and what the students regarded as an improvement over the U.S. Constitution--a Bill of Responsibilities.

Participatory decision making, then, has many benefits. It contributes to character by helping children apply their moral reasoning to their behavior and their social environment. In a democratic society, it has a special value: teaching democracy <u>through</u> democracy, training an active citizenry by having children be active citizens in the life of their school.

It should be clear from the foregoing discussion that there are many points of overlap among the four spheres of moral education I have described. When Sister Barno had her fourth graders work cooperatively on their Mexico project, she was simultaneously fostering social community and the self-esteem that comes from a shared success to which all have contributed. When the teacher with the incubating chickens had her second graders debate the pros and cons of opening the eggs, moral reflection took the form of participatory decision making. When Debbie Wilcox used class meetings to help her third graders bring order to their classroom, she was building social community, self-worth, and moral reasoning at the same time that she fostered participatory citizenship.

These four processes not only reinforce each other; each, I would submit, is necessary to the full success of the other. Moral discussion, especially debate, is very difficult when social community is weak, when students don't know or like each other, and is shallow without opportunities for application to real-life decision-making. Class discussion is "all talk" if children never work together on substantive tasks. Cooperative learning doesn't realize its full potential if children don't participate in planning and evaluating their joint endeavors. And participatory decision making, without the group spirit that is born of cooperative activity, can turn into a forum where students argue for their "rights" with little thought to their obligations or the good of the whole.

The classroom, of course, is part of a larger social ecology--the school. All of the four processes of moral education can and should be carried out in the larger school in a way that supports and extends their occurrence in the classroom. Social community can be fostered through all the ways described by Ed Wynne (Chapter 4) in his call for a greater emphasis on traditional school spirit and a healthy identification with the collective. Cooperative work can take the form of cross-class projects such as a camping trip or fund-raiser. Cross-age tutoring and community service projects will develop altruistic helping relationships. School assemblies can be used to foster moral reflection--as, for example, when one school brought in police, a judge, store owners, and consumers for an assembly on shoplifting. Student councils (with rotating representatives elected from each classroom) and special task committees (to reduce vandalism, improve bus behavior, clean up the school grounds) offer students opportunities to participate in decision making and take a larger responsibility for the school as a whole.

A word about obstacles. The school as a system must provide more support than it now does for the person on whom all of this ultimately depends--the teacher. Right now many teachers feel very little support from either school administrators or parents; lack of support is right behind discipline as a reason for leaving the profession. And teachers certainly don't get much support for making moral education a priority in the classroom. Here is a fifth-grade teacher speaking about obstacles to just two of the moral education processes 1 have recommended:

> It has taken a long time for me and my students to learn to have effective group discussions, and 1 still feel this is a problem. There is a trust level that must be built anew each year, and the kids have to learn discussion skills. These days discussions are rarer in early grades, thanks to the movement back toward cognitive performance, achievement testing and the ever-decreasing verbal interactions in most families--all of which rob time from discussions and make the teaching of discussion skills more difficult.

> Democracy in the classroom, which 1 consider important, is time-consuming and

cumbersome. Authoritarianism is expedient.
When one feels the pressure of time and the
burden of material-to-be-covered-by-June, it
is hard to justify the time it takes to create
and operate a democratic environment unless one is truly committed to this process.
Democratic participation is vital to moral
development, but it requires constant attention and a large revision in role and attitude
for many teachers (Smith-Hansen, 1984, p. 3).

The large revision in role and attitude of which
this teacher speaks will come only when we give teachers
the support they now lack, not before. With that support,
I think the task of moral education is one that most teachers will take up willingly, at least at the elementary
school level, where the natural bent of teachers is a concern for the whole child. Indeed, even now, as I hope
this chapter attests, many individual teachers are doing
character education with imagination, dedication, and skill.
They have shown us that we have the means to help our
children toward moral maturity if only we muster the will.

REFERENCES

Canter, L., & Canter, M. Assertive discipline. Los
    Angeles: Lee Canter & Associates, 1976.

Cole-Farris, P. The socio-moral core of the elementary
    school curriculum. Moral Education Forum (Summer
    1983), 9-13.

Frey, G. The Middle Ages: The social studies core of
    the fifth grade. Moral Education Forum (Summer 1983),
    30-34.

Hall, R., & Davis, J. Moral education in theory and prac-
    tice. Buffalo, N.Y.: Prometheus Books, 1975.

Johnson D. W., & Johnson, R. T. Learning together and
    alone. Englewood Cliffs, N.J.: Prentice-Hall, 1975.

Kegan, R. The evolving self. Cambridge, Mass.: Harvard
    University Press, 1982.

Knowles, R. T., & McLean, G. F. (Eds.). The philosophical foundations of moral education. Washington, D.C.: University Press of America, 1986.

Kohlberg, L. Essays on moral development, vol. 1: The philosophy of moral development. San Francisco: Harper & Row, 1981.

Leming, J. Curriculum effectiveness in moral values education: A review of research. Journal of Moral Education, 10, 1981, 147-164.

Lockwood, A. The effects of value clarification and moral development curricula on school-age subjects: A critical review of recent research. Review of Educational Research, 48, 1978, 325-364.

Moral Education Forum, summer 1983.

Piaget, J. The moral judgment of the child. New York: Free press, 1965 (originally published 1932).

Picard, B. L. One is one. New York: Holt, Rinehart & Winston, 1965.

Raths, L., Harmin, M., & Simon, S. Values and teaching. Columbus, Ohio: Charles E. Merrill, 1978.

Selman, R. The growth of interpersonal understanding. New York: Academic Press, 1980.

Smith-Hansen, P. A moral education program for the fifth grade. Unpublished paper, State University of New York at Cortland, 1984.

Sommer, P. Children as historians. Moral Education Forum (Summer 1983), 33-44.

8

Moral Education in the
Junior High School

Clive Beck

The importance of moral education is particularly clear at
the junior high level (grades 7-9, average age 12-14
years). Fortunately, it is also a stage when most educators and parents are willing to concede time for moral
education activities: The "basics" have been taught in
some measure, and the precollege pressure has not yet
begun.
    The field of moral education is, of course, vast.
We can here only take up a few issues and make a few
practical suggestions. In particular, the focus in the
final three sections of this chapter will be on the study
of moral issues, rather than moral education in general.
This narrowing of focus to study activities is because of
limitations of space alone, and does not reflect on the importance of the rest of the moral education program of the
school. The "integrative model" of the person and of moral
education developed in the present volume is one I en-
dorse: all aspects of the person--thoughts, feelings, be-
havior--must be attended to in moral education.[1]
    The main theme running through the chapter will be
that moral education in the junior high school must be
grounded in the life needs of the young adolescent students. Accordingly, we will begin with a brief overview
of the situation in which these students find themselves.

THE WORLD OF JUNIOR HIGH SCHOOL STUDENTS

These young people, at early adolescence, are being given more responsibility for their lives, facing new questions and having new experiences. They are beginning to choose their way of life, whereas before much of it was chosen for them.

Junior high students are thinking about what kind of job they want. This is necessary both so they can select suitable school subjects and job training, and to give them a sense of direction and meaning in life. If they can see the necessity of schooling partly in job terms it helps them to go along with its more difficult aspects. To a degree, also, these students are free to choose other elements of their way of life: sports, friendships and group life, movies, TV, music, reading of different kinds, the clothes they wear. Possibly they can now buy a Walkman or a ten-speed bike with their own money. Perhaps they can give up (or take up) a musical instrument without much adult control.

At this age, students are very concerned about their self-image. Rapid changes in bodily size and appearance, together with greater social interest, result in a need to rationalize their changing self and see it as acceptable. Strong feelings, again both internally and externally triggered, lead to questioning about the nature of their personality and the meaning of their life.

Health, physical and mental, is also a preoccupation of these young people. Physical and emotional changes make them aware of the possibility of change, and they fear abnormality. They also sense that they may have some control over their health: They are hearing about fitness programs, proper nutrition, dental hygiene, how to overcome stress. And probably their parents are giving them increasing responsibility in health matters.

Friendship patterns are changing. Being accepted by their peers takes on much greater importance, and many of their activities are directed toward that end. Sexual relationships become a distinct possibility, requiring a set of attitudes and verbal responses even if only negative ones for the time being. Thoughts of marriage begin to crop up, even (or perhaps especially) when there is as yet little experience of close heterosexual friendship.

Access to alcohol and drugs is now a reality. Although it might be difficult, they could if they wished experience such things; and in many cases it would not even be difficult. This accessibility along with the interest in self-image, group life, and health constitutes a new life situation.

Family relationships are of pressing interest to young adolescents. Most still have strong emotional ties to their family, but potentially competing relationships are developing. There is a growing sense of a need to strike out on their own, perhaps encouraged by their parents. The thought of one day leaving home may be entertained from time to time. And issues of parental authority arise constantly.

Because of increased independence and heightened social interest, students of this age are concerned about the community setting: happenings at the local mall, movie theaters nearby, neighborhood youth centers, the local police station. Racial, religious, and class conflicts take on a personal meaning, since they may now have to respond on their own initiative (although often with peer group support). As they build their distinctive interests, personality, and way of life, these young people are developing ideas about life in society, at a local level at least.

Perhaps the most urgent concern of young adolescents is to maintain a sense of meaning in life. There is a fear of finding themselves in limbo: not children, not adults, not working, not married, not voting, not dependent, not independent, not achieving anything (except make-work school tasks). What is their place and purpose? Some of their other concerns are heightened and distorted (from an adult point of view) in attempting to gain a sense of meaning or to escape a sense of meaninglessness.

THE INTERFACE OF ADOLESCENT AND ADULT WORLDS

In morally educating young adolescents, we adults must recognize the legitimacy of their needs and interests, while at the same time helping them accommodate to our interests as far as is justified and to the many values that should be shared by all members of society.

Our task is to help students develop a total value system which, as well as serving their distinctive needs for independence, identity, self-respect and so on, gives

room for general moral and societal values such as reliability, honesty, fairness, tolerance, loyalty, participation,
cooperation, and sharing. Pursuit of these values, in appropriate ways, benefits both the adolescents themselves
and society as a whole.

In the past, in moral education programs, we have
often given almost exclusive attention to the general needs
of society, especially the adult world, and neglected the
distinctive needs of adolescents. We have sometimes even
questioned the morality of adolescent desires and aspirations. We have not recognized that the needs of adolescents are in large measure legitimate, and moral requirements must be tailored to meet them.[2]

A central focus, then, of a moral education program
in the junior high school must be the world--including the
interests--of the students. The main reason for this has to
do with justice: A truly moral education must promote the
well-being of the young person and other members of society alike. But another, practical reason is that unless
we meet students on their own ground we will fail in moral
education. We will fail, first, because we will not engage
their attention or enthusiasm and, secondly, because we
will be going against a fundamental educational principle,
namely, that one must start from where people are. Dewey,
of course, told us this long ago, and Piaget and Kohlberg
(in the field of moral education) have continued to make
the point.

Where, specifically, are young adolescents? In the
previous section we saw that they are largely absorbed in
learning how to run their lives, choosing a way of life
(including school subjects and a possible future job),
achieving an identity acceptable to themselves and others,
establishing good friendship, family, and neighborhood relationships, working out how to deal with sexual relationships now and in the future, working out how to maintain
physical and mental health, establishing attitudes and
practices with respect to alcohol and drugs, and trying to
maintain a sense of meaning in life.

Where most young people are is in a state of rough
balance between concern for themselves and concern for
others, especially their family and friends (which is precisely where most adults are). In the world of the young
adolescent, as we have seen, there is strong interest in
being responsible, doing work, getting on well with one's
family, having good friendships, living a meaningful life.

Helping them satisfy their concerns is not giving in to a lesser morality but helping them achieve legitimate life goals which, of course, are partly self-interested.

The position 1 would recommend we adults adopt is that adolescents are our moral equals. This is not simply the view that they are "of equal moral worth," which is relatively easy to accept. It is the stronger position that they are "as good at morals" as adults, and their moral thought and behavior is on average as appropriate as that of adults. Insofar as their morality differs from that of adults it is not due to a lesser capacity but to differences in the life circumstances in which they find themselves and to which their morality is more or less appropriately adapted. Stages of morality may be traced but they are stages of change associated with changing life circumstances, not stages of improvement.

One can, of course, always live better as an adolescent. Moral development in the sense of improvement is possible at a particular age. However, it is equally necessary for both adolescents and adults. Adolescents do not stand in greater need of moral improvement.

If one grants that adults are not, on average, more moral than adolescents, what place is there for moral education conducted by adult teachers? Normally in education we assume that teachers have greater knowledge and skill than their students, which is why they are teachers. What is the situation in the case of moral education?

To begin with, as we have noted, there is always the possibility of moral development (in the sense of improvement) at a given age. Adolescents, like adults, can become more altruistic, sensitive, thoughtful and wise, and more skillful in giving expression to their morality. Accordingly, the need for moral education certainly exists.

In society as it is presently structured, adults are cast in the role of teachers. They have the authority and the professional training and status. They are the ones who are expected to organize educational programs. In most cases, young adolescents who attempted to take on such a role would be rejected, by peers and adults alike, as precocious and presumptuous; and besides they would not be paid for their activities or even given time to perform them. Adults, then, must engage in formal moral education if it is to take place to a significant degree under present social, political, and economic conditions.

While adults are not in general better at morals than adolescents, particular teachers may through training and selection emerge as "moral experts" (just as we have literature, history, and mathematics experts in the school). They may be better at morals than most adolescents and fellow adults, and have a great deal to teach.

Besides moral development at a given age, adolescents must eventually go on to a morality appropriate to adulthood. If they are to live well as adults, and fulfill the responsibilities assigned to them, they must take on the way of life of an adult and the corresponding moral behavior. Now, adults are in a good position to initiate adolescents into the responsibilities and way of life of adulthood, since we are there already. In this area we often have greater knowledge and skill than students.

While there is room for moral education by adults, however, we must tread carefully. In many areas, especially those having to do with moral development at an age level, we may have less knowledge and skill than our students, even though custom and politics assign us the role of teacher. Even where we do feel we know more, either because ethics is our teaching field or because we know about the adult way of life, we should adopt an interactive teaching mode since adolescents already have many insights into the adult world and its problems. We must resist the temptation to push students into the adult mode of conduct just because it suits our interests: Our concern should rather be for the whole, including ourselves. We must as far as possible allow students to enter adulthood in their own way, so that their needs for identity and relative independence are met.

We must keep constantly in mind that initiation of young people into an adult mode of life is only one part of the story. The adult way of life must itself be under constant scrutiny to see if it can be improved. In a great many ways adults and adolescents should be exploring precisely the same societal issues. The significance of the adult–adolescent distinction should not be exaggerated. A key principle of moral education is that of "teachers and students learning together." In many cases, we do not "know the answers" beforehand: We must search for them together.

Part of the teacher's role may be to help liberate adolescents, since potentially such a change has enormous advantages for both adolescents and adults: Adolescents

could live fuller, more interesting lives and adults could
have better relationships with adolescents and also benefit
from their aid in societal projects. It is important, however, that we not jeopardize their well-being by pushing
too quickly or in the wrong directions. We could destroy
a way of life--adolescence, which for all its problems is
at least a way of life--before we have established a satisfactory new way of life--adulthood-at-an-earlier-age. A
key principle here, once again, is that teachers and students must work together to ensure that both the speed
and the direction of change are appropriate. Eventually,
however, it is possible that the moral orientations we now
describe as "adult" will become common at a much earlier
age, as they were in some communities and eras in the
past.[3]

A CONCEPTION OF MORALITY FOR USE
IN MORAL EDUCATION PROGRAMS

In what has been said so far a conception of morality for application in moral education programs with junior
high students (and others) is starting to emerge. The
time has come to spell it out more systematically.

Morality is based largely in human needs, of oneself and others. It is grounded in goods such as friendship, fellowship, self-respect, health, happiness, fulfillment, a sense of meaning in life. Following Aristotle,
there is a strong emphasis here on human nature and basic
human desires and tendencies.[4]

Many moral and social values, then, such as self-
control, truthfulness, promise keeping, loyalty, fairness
and so on are largely means to ends rather than ends in
themselves. They should be seen (and taught) as components within a total value system, the ultimate purpose of
which is to enable humans, individually and as groups,
to achieve human goods. This in no way diminishes the
importance of moral and social values but shows that they,
like all other values, must be weighed against one another
rather than be seen as absolutes.

Members of subgroups (such as adolescents) have a
right to pursue their distinctive interests rather than subordinate them completely to general societal values. They
also have a responsibility, of course, to integrate their
values with others as much as possible and look for areas
of shared values.

Morality in both its foundations and its daily implementation involves feelings, desires, and life forces (such as those we have noted in young adolescents). It is "a work of life, not of death."[5] It is not purely mental. The mind does not simply control feelings in morality; rather the two are constantly interacting or working together to give direction to life and moral motivation.[6]

Moral autonomy is an important ideal, and the notion of the child as moral philosopher is crucial.[7] However, young adolescents are dependent on their peers, their parents, and their teachers for moral support, encouragement, and guidance. They should be basically in control of their own lives, but it is rare that they will be able to think or act completely by themselves, nor is it clear why that would be a laudable moral ideal.[8]

Religion plays an important role in morality for many people, but it is possible to be moral without being religious. This follows from the rootedness of morality in human nature and human life. One could develop a broad definition of religion according to which it would be necessary to be religious in order to be moral.[9] But in the everyday sense of religion there is no necessary connection between the two. For a great many people, however, their religion is in fact the mediator (in part at least) of their morality, and if they lost the one the other would suffer, temporarily and perhaps permanently.[10]

Ethical questions are objective. Here we part company with "values clarification" and other relativist positions. Moral issues are deeply embedded in the hard realities of life, and no matter how much we clarify our values, we can still be wrong, objectively. For example, we may firmly believe that it is always wrong to tell lies, but one day come across a case where, given all the facts, we are forced to admit that telling the truth would be wrong, since it would clearly do more harm than good. This does not mean that the same things are right or wrong for everyone: Relevant differences abound in circumstances and temperament. But for a given person or group in given circumstances one can in principle objectively determine which actions would be better and worse morally.

Moral questions are enormously complex, but nevertheless soluble in many cases. Morality has often been seen (and taught) as a matter of following a few simple rules, the main obstacles lying not in finding out what is right but in bringing oneself to do what one knows to be

right. The view I have presented, rather, is that moral
questions are difficult--hence the need for moral education--
but that humans have the capacity to weigh a wide range
of considerations and, in many cases, arrive at sound conclusions.

THE PRACTICE OF MORAL EDUCATION

In the present context, we only have room to high-
light a few elements in moral education, ones which follow
from preceding discussion and are especially relevant in
the junior high school. The following are some key principles and strategies.

Teachers (including administrators) and students
are growing together; they are engaged in joint inquiry.
On many matters students know as much as teachers and
on some they may know more (e.g., bullying, fighting in
the school yard, parent-teen-ager relationships, early
teen-age sexual needs). The teacher's input may be quite
strong: information, ethical theory, tough questions, possible answers, persuasive arguments. But it is given as
grist for the mill, not as the last word.

Teachers should embody in their behavior and the
way they run the school their view of how one should live.
This view, however, is constantly developing. It is not
the established "right" way: We do not yet know fully
what that is. Furthermore, it is a view that the students
are helping to develop. School behavior and organization
should, for teachers and students together, be an ongoing
experiment. Modeling sound attitudes and behavior is an
important aspect of the teacher's role, but it should not
become a vehicle for indoctrination through the transmission of unquestioned moral beliefs.

The school as an institution should be used to illustrate some of the "hard realities" of life. It is unlikely
that we will be able to make the school a great deal better than other societal institutions, since it is inextricably
bound up with the rest of society. But we can discuss
why the school is the way it is, in terms of embedded injustice, the bureaucratization of society, cultural inertia,
parental, teacher, and student convenience, institutional
imperatives, sexual discrimination, age discrimination. We
should work with the students to try to correct moral
wrongs in the school; but it is crucial that, in addition,

we help them understand situations of this kind and how
to make the most of their lives within them. The school is
an ideal laboratory for learning both how to change an institution and how to live with what (for the moment at
least) cannot be changed.

The discipline system of the school should be used
to help students and teachers learn how to create sound
power structures and how to live within them. Students
should have genuine involvement so better decisions are
made and students gain a deeper understanding of the issues. Teachers should not be afraid to exercise authority
when appropriate--e.g., stopping a fight, punishing use
of prejudiced language, insisting that homework be done--
but should see the explanation and discussion of their actions as a major means of moral education. Teachers
should not be embarrassed to be "in charge," since this
is their assigned leadership role and does not necessarily
imply superiority.

Participation in curriculum discussion and decision
making is an essential tool of moral education in the
school. Students need to understand why learning is
necessary, why particular branches of learning are important, and what is the place of the school in the total
cultural, economic, and social fabric of society. Obviously, once again, these are questions to which many teachers have only very sketchy (and perhaps incorrect)
answers, and which must be addressed jointly with the
students whose experiences and interests are crucial data.

The quality of social experiences in the school
should be enhanced, both by increasing the opportunities
for social interaction and by including the study of friendship and other human relationships in the curriculum.
The school is a setting in which students can make a
great deal of progress in relationships with both peers
and adults. This is so because of the large amount of
time spent in school, and also because of the many contacts it provides beyond the immediate family and neighborhood. Making room for genuinely social occasions and
improving the quality of interactions should be an integral
part of the moral education program.[11]

There should be extensive study of morals in the
school. If students and teachers are to benefit substantially from other aspects of the moral education program,
they must grow in their moral knowledge and understanding. Of course, moral discussion can take place as issues

arise incidentally in the life of the school, and also in the context of decision making about school organization, social life, and curriculum. But the issues are so many and so complex that there is need for a more systematic treatment, whether in separate courses or within other school subjects.

TOPICS AND THEMES FOR THE STUDY OF MORALS

The study of morals, as we have noted, is just one part of a school's moral education program. However, it is a very important part; and working out its content helps give direction to the total program. The following are some suggested topics and themes for junior high school, grouped according to the subject areas in which they might be incorporated.

The word "values" is used in the lists below rather than "morals." This is because it is a more familiar word to most students and teachers, and does not have the somewhat negative connotation of "morals." However, moral issues relevant to this age group would still be covered under these topics.

Social Studies
  What are values? What is morality?
  Differences in values
  How to solve value problems
  Self and others
  Extended families and close communities
  From inner group to global community
  Values, regionalism, and patriotism
  Values, religion, race, culture
  Richer and poorer countries
  Values and politics
  Values and commerce

Language Arts and/or Literature
  Values and communication
  Values and the mass media
  The aesthetic side of life
  What is a good book, a good film?
  Indoctrination through literature
  Freedom as a theme in literature
  Suffering as a theme in literature

Guidance, Life Skills, Human Relations

   Friendship
   Friendship and love
   Values and Sexuality
   Sexism
   Family relationships
   Marriage
   Values and school
   Getting the most out of school
   Choosing a career
   Finding values in a job
   Choosing a way of life
   Enriching a way of life

Health, Physical Education

   Values and health
   Holistic health
   Values and stress
   Values and coping
   Values and sport
   Values and fitness
   Values and spectator sport

While the above topics have been listed under school subject areas, most of them could easily be studied in a separate "morals" or "values" course or in courses other than the ones indicated. In schools with a religion program, many of the topics could be incorporated into that subject. Another possible approach is to focus on a new topic throughout a grade level every three or four weeks and have different aspects of it dealt with in a variety of school subjects. The important point is that by some means or other most of these topics (and others) should be studied in depth during the junior high school years, rather than just touched on briefly and superficially or neglected entirely. Because the field of morals is so complex, students need the opportunity to build cumulatively a comprehensive system of moral ideas, principles, and skills.[12]

There are, of course, other ways of organizing the content of a moral studies program. One could study theories of ethics, such as absolutism, relativism, utilitarianism, and intuitionism, looking at the strengths and weaknesses of each and working out their implications for everyday life. Again, one could focus on traditional moral virtues, such as responsibility, thoughtfulness, generosity, fairness, loyalty, courage, self-control, and honesty. The reason for the above selection of topics is to emphasize the practical value of morality in students' lives, as discussed in earlier sections. It is intended, however, that ethical theories and moral virtues would still be considered at length while studying the topics listed above.

SAMPLE STUDY UNITS

The following are sample study outlines that might be used with junior high students.[13] While learning materials for these topics would normally contain many more ideas, examples, questions, and activities than can be included here, these excerpts will serve to clarify the approach to moral studies recommended in earlier sections. In the next section we will analyze further the pedagogy underlying these units.

MYSELF AND OTHERS

Idea for discussion: "We should look after our own needs to a considerable extent and the needs of others to a considerable extent." e.g. (i) In helping a friend with schoolwork, we should not normally spend so much time on it that our own work suffers badly. e.g. (ii) Parents should make sacrifices for their children, but should also look after their own development.

Questions: What do you think of these examples? Do you agree with the general principle? Why?

Activity: Think of situations in your own life where you have to decide how much to look after your own needs and how much to look after the needs of others. In each case, what do you do, what should you do, and what will you do next time?

Activity: Make a list of reasons (if any) why we should look after our own needs; make a list of reasons (if any) why we should look after other people's needs.

Idea for discussion: "A major task of morality is to work out ways to help others and ourselves at the same time." e.g. (i) A parent of a young child tries to find activities that are interesting and enriching to both parent and child. e.g. (ii) In choosing a career, we look for one that is both interesting to us and of some help to other people.

Questions: Can you think of other examples? Do you
agree with the general idea?

Question: What should we do when it is "either him or
me," my life or his, and no "third way" is possible?

FRIENDSHIP

Idea for discussion: "People need friends for many reasons, e.g. to keep them company, to help when things
go wrong, to share feelings, to help them do things they
could not do alone."

Questions: Can you think of examples where people seem
to need friends for reasons such as the above? Do you
agree that people need friends?

Idea for discussion: "Some people seem to get along well
without 'close friends.' Instead they have acquaintances,
work companions, social companions, clients, neighbors,
and so on." Do you agree? How important is it to
have close friends?

Idea for discussion: "We often have to work at friendships."

Questions: Do you agree that we have to work at friendships? If so, how far should we go in trying to keep a
friend? Can you think of examples?

Key question: Should we try to keep up friendships when
circumstances change? e.g. (i) You have been close
friends with someone who was a neighbor but moves to
another part of the city, ten miles away. e.g. (ii) Two
people become friends while working in the same company. One of them gets a different kind of job in another company.

Idea for discussion: "Friendship is a wonderful thing,
but we should not expect too much of it: friends sometimes take advantage of each other, aren't completely
loyal to each other, aren't completely frank with each
other."

Questions: Do you agree that these things sometimes happen? If so, do you still think friendship is worth it?

Activity: Make a list of the various kinds of things
people can contribute in a friendship (e.g. jokes, good
conversation, money, other friends, invitations to parties). What if one person seems to contribute more to
the friendship than the other? Is that OK?

FAMILY

Idea for discussion: "The family serves a wide range of
values, such as affection, protection, and health care,
training in life skills, social and intellectual training,
cultural, moral, and religious training, a home base, a
sense of belonging, privacy, material needs."

Questions: Do you agree that the family serves these values? If so, which ones and how well does it do so?
Discuss examples of each kind.

Activity: Can you think of (hypothetical) cases where
young people should reduce contact with their family?
If so, in what ways should they reduce contact, and in
what ways should they try to maintain contact? Can
you think of (hypothetical) cases where young people
should increase contact with their family? If so, in
what ways?

Principle for discussion: "Insist, firmly and quietly, on
being treated more or less as an equal in the family."

Questions: Do you agree or disagree with this principle?
Why?

Activities: Make a list of things we can still learn from
our parents in our teens; make a list of things our
parents can still learn from us.

Principle for discussion: "Don't try to change members of
your family: accept and enjoy them (as much as possible) as they are."

Activity: Work out ways people might accept and enjoy
their family more. Do you agree with the principle?
Why?

Idea for discussion: "Family relationships present many
difficulties: e.g., sibling rivalry; parent-child rivalry;
emotional blackmail; people who are different but have
to live together; shift in the parental role as the children become adults."

Questions: Can you think of examples of these difficulties
(not in your own family)? Can people live with these
difficulties while staying close to each other? Do you
agree that these difficulties occur? If so, do you still
think close family contact is a good thing?

GETTING THE MOST OUT OF SCHOOL

Principle for discussion: "Take control of your own schooling. Don't just drift along. Work out what you are

doing at school and why. Then, work out how to get the most out of school."

Questions: Do you agree with this principle? Why?

Activities: Work out what possibilities there are for students in your school to make decisions about their schooling. Make concrete plans to take more control of your own schooling (if you think you should).

Principle for discussion: "Students should take part in curriculum and program decisions, such as decisions about what subjects are available; decisions about the way subjects are selected for individual students; choice of suitable textbooks; choice of effective learning activities and methods; allocation of time and facilities for social, cultural, artistic, and sporting activities."

Questions: Do you agree with the principle? Why? If so, what should the school do about it, and what should you do about it?

Idea for discussion: "School should help you in your present way of life. You should be getting a lot out of it now."

Questions and activities: Do you agree with this idea? Why? If you do, make a list of ways school could help you in your present way of life, and make concrete plans to get more out of school now.

Idea for discussion: "School should help you prepare for your future way of life."

Questions and activities: Do you agree with this idea? Why? If you do, make a list of ways school could help you in the future, and make concrete plans to get more out of school to help you in the future.

Activity: Interview, by yourself or with other students, one or more teachers in the school to find out their views on the nature and value of their teaching subject(s).

CHOOSING A CAREER

Idea for discussion: "If possible, we should choose a job that serves many values, such as enjoyment, a sense of achievement, contributing to society, status and recognition, money, security, friendship, personal growth, a sense of belonging, physical exercise."

Questions: Can you think of jobs which you would like that serve many or all of these values? Do you agree with the general idea?

Activities: Make a list of the main interests and activities you think you will have in your life in adulthood.
Then, think of jobs that (i) will leave you time for
these interests and activities, (ii) will help you pursue
some of these while not at work.

Idea for discussion: "Sometimes people have to choose a
job 'just for the money,' e.g., if there are very few
jobs; if one's main interests are painting, writing, or
studying; if one doesn't have the qualifications for a
more fulfilling job."

Questions: Do you agree with this idea? Can you think
of (or imagine) people whose work is very separate from
their private life? Could even these people get more
out of their job?

Idea for discussion: "Job security is an important consideration in choosing a job; but how important it is
depends on our temperament and circumstances."

Activity and questions: Make a list of jobs of varying
security in terms of (1) the possibility of being fired or
laid off and (2) the possibility of not making much
money at all (e.g., artistic professions, some businesses).
Work out the advantages of the more risky jobs and the
disadvantages of the more secure jobs. How important
is job security to you? Should people sometimes choose
an insecure job for the good of society? Do you agree
with the general idea?

METHOD IN THE STUDY OF MORALS

    The sample outlines we have just reviewed illustrate
several aspects of method in the study of morals. To begin with, they underscore the importance of structure in
moral studies. We need to plan discussions carefully (in
consultation with students) so students have a sense of
"getting somewhere." It is easy in a subject where everyone is interested and has something to contribute for study
to deteriorate into a swapping of anecdotes. Students become discouraged if they feel they are just going around
in circles. Accordingly, it is important to move from one
clearly identifiable topic, principle, concept, or example
to another. Often, of course, the plan will have to be
set aside; but it is essential that it be there initially.
    Perhaps the most striking feature of the sample
units is the extent to which they give suggested answers

to the questions raised. Great care is taken to leave
students free to disagree, propose alternatives, or make
modifications, but in the end the materials--or the teachers through the materials and other comments they make--
propose certain ideas as more worthy of consideration than
others. The approach is open but not neutral.[14] <u>Moral
content is being advocated</u>, at least at a general level.
Implicitly, then, this approach rejects "discovery learning," since answers are often suggested beforehand rather
than being simply discovered by the students; and it rejects a "values clarification" approach, since it assumes
that some answers are objectively better than others and
that moral inquiry is not merely a matter of becoming
clearer about and more committed to one's values. The
teacher has something to say, and argues that certain
ideas are right and others are wrong.

How, then, do we escape the charge of authoritarianism in teaching morals? We do so in part by ensuring
that students <u>also</u> have plenty of opportunity to suggest
answers, to advocate and argue for moral content. As
noted earlier, the teacher's views are grist for the mill,
and further grist is provided by students. In part, also,
we avoid authoritarianism by ourselves introducing plausible counterarguments and alternative positions. These are
thoroughly explored, precisely because they may be correct and our views mistaken. Nonauthoritarian teachers
are not ones who refrain from advocating moral views, but
ones who are aware that they may be wrong and so are
willing to consider plausible alternatives.

The method of moral studies I am proposing requires
moral advocacy; however, it does <u>not</u> involve suggesting
answers at a specific and personal level. The examples
given and solicited--about friendship, family, career
plans--are usually somewhat hypothetical, and no attempt
is made to tell individuals what they should do in specific situations. The teacher and the class simply do not
have enough information about the circumstances, temperament, and needs of individual students to offer such advice; nor is it appropriate to pry too much into individual
lives. This imposes a limitation on the discussions, but
it still enables the group to refine general and intermedi-
ate-range principles which individuals can then apply.

Another feature of the method implicit in the materials is its <u>realism</u>. It constantly gives both sides of
the story--positive and negative--with respect to schooling,

families, and even friendship. This is in line with principles discussed earlier in this chapter. Students must not be sold a bill of goods about morality or the world. They must find out about the hard realities of life and, in that context, and in the light of facts about their needs and the needs of others, forge a satisfactory way of life. The brighter side, however, must also be presented, not only because it is there but also in order to give students a solid basis for hope.

It is apparent from the sample units that many teacher skills are required in studying morals in the manner proposed. The teacher must be able to move constantly back and forth between principles and examples; utilize the students' insights, weaving them in with textual and other materials; bring in other principles and examples to give new angles on issues; inject general ideas and historical cases when the discussion has bogged down in anecdotes; move quickly on when a general principle or question arouses no discussion; steer discussion carefully away from unduly personal or sensitive areas. Teachers must master these skills and sensitivities at least in some measure if they are to deal with the topics under consideration.

Finally, given that the approach being recommended involves some degree of moral advocacy, it is essential that teachers be growing in their own moral knowledge and understanding. To a large extent this will happen naturally as a result of classroom discussion, daily life experience, and joint decision making about how the school should be run. But it can be furthered through discussion with peers, reading, attending university courses and professional development programs, and thinking through the issues more deeply by oneself. Happily, growth of this kind, which is so crucial to one's role as a teacher of morals, is also of central importance in one's own attempts to live life well: Teachers will be enriched through their moral education activities.[15]

In conclusion, I wish to emphasize once again that study of morals is only one part of a total moral education program, the broad shape of which was explored in earlier sections of this chapter (and has been developed at length in other chapters of this volume). While study of morals is a key activity, it must be complemented by many other experiences in the daily life of the school.

NOTES

1. For an outline of this "integrative model" see Chapter 1 of this text. On the role of the school climate in moral education see especially Clark Power's chapter.

2. In this chapter, I take a position on adolescent morality which, given prevailing views in developmental psychology, is unorthodox. It differs in emphasis from the account provided by several other writers in this volume. Readers should be aware of this as they read the present chapter. The more usual view is that children and adolescents are, on the average, less moral than adults. While I disagree with this view, I must concede its general currency.

3. For a study of the development of the modern phenomenon of "childhood" as we know it in the West, see Philippe Ariès, Centuries of Childhood: A Social History of Family Life, trans. Robert Baldick (Knopf, 1962). For a discussion of adolescence as "optional," see Carl Bereiter, Must We Educate? (Prentice-Hall, Spectrum, 1973).

4. On this feature of morality and its basis in Aristotle, see John Farrelly, "The Human Good and Moral Choice," in D. Schindler, J. A. Mann, and F. A. Ellrod (eds.), Act and Agent: Philosophical Foundations of Moral Education (University Press of America, 1984).

5. Emile Durkheim, Moral Education, trans. E. K. Wilson and H. Schnurer (Free Press, 1961, p. 87).

6. For an elaboration of this point, see Sebastian A. Samay, "Affectivity: The Power Base of Moral Behavior," in D. Schindler, J. A. Mann, and F. A. Ellrod (eds.), op. cit. Lawrence Blum, in Friendship, Altruism and Morality (Routledge & Kegan Paul, 1981), shows how mind and emotion are integrated in morality.

7. On the concept of the child as moral philosopher, see Lawrence Kohlberg, The Philosophy of Moral Development (Harper & Row, 1981, pp. 14-16).

8. Durkheim, op. cit., shows that moral autonomy must be qualified and developed with reference to the larger society. Madhu Prakash, in Chapter 4 of the present volume, argues for the necessity of considering the community context in moral education. Carol Gilligan, in In a Different Voice (Harvard University Press, 1982), questions the appropriateness of complete moral autonomy as an ideal.

9. For suggestions along these lines, see Wilfred Cantwell Smith, Faith and Belief (Princeton University Press, 1979); James Fowler, Stages of Faith (Harper & Row, 1981, Part I); and David Schindler, "On the Integrity of Morality in Relation to Religion," in D. Schindler, J. A. Mann, and F. A. Ellrod (eds.), op. cit.

10. On the importance of religion for the morality of particular people in a specific era, see Durkheim, op. cit., especially p. 19.

11. For practical suggestions on how to promote friendship in the classroom, see Tom Lickona's chapter, above.

12. On the need for an extensive, systematic treatment of morality in the high school, see Robert Starratt's chapter, below.

13. Excerpts are included with permission from Values and Living: Learning Materials for Grades 7 and 8, Clive Beck, OISE Press, Toronto, 1983.

14. Paul O'Leary, in a book review in Canadian Journal of Education, 9(2), Spring 1984, pp. 235-37, provides an excellent discussion of the limitations of an excessively open approach to moral inquiry which he, following E. Pincoffs, refers to disparagingly as "quandary ethics."

15. On the preparation of teachers of moral education, see Kevin Ryan's chapter, below.

9

Moral Education in the High School Classroom

Robert J. Starratt

After some years of practicing their craft, teachers develop increasingly sensitive intuitions about the young people they work with. Sometimes that involves distinguishing between a youngster who is lying about his reason for missing homework and a youngster who, with a similar story, is telling the truth; sometimes it involves the second sense that a youngster has the answer to the question, but has to tug it out of the molasses of her fluid thinking. At other times, that intuition can lead a teacher to spot a youngster who has come to school after a fight with his or her parents, or to come up with just the right balance of firmness and affection when a student is acting up in class.

This chapter reflects teachers' intuitions about moral education in the classroom. It will focus on practice or on principles derived from practice. Except for references to essays in earlier volumes of this series,[1] it will not contain scholarly references because it will reflect teachers' craft experience. Readers, however, may discern the footprints of John Dewey throughout the essay; he said most of this years ago.

The three or four years of high school make up one of the crucial developmental periods of a youngster's life. For most teen-agers, they enter high school as children and leave as young adults.[2] During those years the potential for psychological and intellectual growth is enormous. The young person during that time also crosses the threshold of social responsibility: after 16 they can be

sent to "adult" prisons; in some states they can drink after their eighteenth birthday; after 18 they can vote and
register for military service. Some youngsters marry and
bear children during these years. Whether all of this implies that they have become adult moral agents, however,
remains to be seen. One thing is certain: The family,
the school, and other socializing agencies such as churches
should assume collective responsibility for nurturing the
growth of teen-agers toward moral maturity. This does
not deny that, ultimately, the adolescent must be responsible for fashioning his or her moral life. The church, family, and school engage the youngster in a social conversation and encourage him or her to channel energies and
explore the positive options toward life-giving choices.
This chapter will explore how such nurturing might take
place in high school classrooms.

ASSUMPTIONS

For effective practice of moral education in a high
school classroom, many preconditions need to be in place.
A school board or superintendent cannot simply mandate
the moral education of the students. They also have to
mandate the means to accomplish that difficult task. Some
preconditions for moral education include the following:
School-wide goals which clearly articulate the moral ideals
and principles which are sought; teachers who are convinced of the importance of moral education and who have
developed some skills in promoting the moral growth of
youngsters; classroom pedagogy and curricular units which
are sensitive to stages of moral growth (including cognitive, emotional, religious, and social dimensions); an approach to morality as both individual and social, and
nuanced by gender; a school climate that reinforces classroom learnings; organizational flexibility, in schedule and
finances, which supports special projects in moral education, such as community service projects, or a community
speakers' forum.

This chapter will assume that all these preconditions are satisfied. Such an assumption obviously flies in
the face of the real world of the public school. Institutional obstacles to moral education abound. Simply to
move a proposal on moral education through the byzantine
bureaucracy of a moderately sized school system requires

political skill, patience, and dogged persistence. On the other hand, there are many examples of individual teachers as well as whole school faculties who have strong commitments to the moral education of their students. This chapter will not attempt to document all of the obstacles to moral education in the public school. Nor will it attempt to suggest ways to overcome these obstacles. Rather, it offers a view of what is possible to achieve. Armed with this view, perhaps other educators will join the struggles to bring about all or some of the above preconditions for moral education in their school system. At a minimum, this chapter may suggest specific practices to individual teachers who behind their classroom doors have been striving quietly and unobtrusively to promote the moral growth of their students while at the same time maintaining the ongoing mastery of academic skills and understandings.

GUIDING PRINCIPLES

Behind the intuitive practice of teachers, one can uncover or discover principles that inform that intuitive practice. In most cases teachers have not taken the time to articulate these principles, nor are they inclined to do so. They are too busy for such heady matters. Furthermore, their practice is never uniform; they are always responding to an individual youngster in a moment that is colored by six or seven circumstances that call for a highly particular response. Hence the guiding principles are sometimes discarded in favor of a response that appears more idiosyncratic.

Therefore, the following list of ten principles may never be implemented in the same way by any two teachers, nor by the same teacher in the same way on any given day. They are offered, nevertheless, as general principles which some of the most effective educators seem to follow.

Teaching morality in the classroom should be an explicit, intentional, planned activity.

This guiding principle does not rule out the intuitive response to an individual situation. For example, if a fight breaks out just before class begins, the teacher has to respond to that unplanned situation. The teacher can use that opportunity to bring the combatants to an experience of reconciliation. This guiding principle, however, states that the teaching of moral behavior and attitudes should not simply depend on ad hoc situations; the whole class needs to learn how to seek and accept reconciliation after many kinds of painful conflicts or misunderstandings. Such learnings can be planned for the whole class and need not depend on a haphazard instance in which only a few students are involved.

Walter Nicgorski and Frederick Ellrod, in their essay "Moral Character,"[3] cite a multitude of good traits of character, for the formation of which life in the classroom provides ample opportunity: truthfulness, patience, perseverance, respect, courage, cooperation, impartiality, justice, etc. Almost every day in the classroom, youngsters will be called on to continue to exercise these virtuous habits. Perceptive teachers will reinforce the formation of these habits with individual students, and will also develop learning units which bring the whole class to reflect on the importance of these virtues.

This guiding principle also accepts teaching of morality by example. Many teachers believe strongly that the example of adults who exhibit moral maturity is the best way to teach morality. Besides the collective and individual example of teachers and parents, some teachers use biographies of highly moral people, such as Gandhi, Lincoln, and Thomas More, to illustrate and embody the best expression of human living. Some would argue that the presentation of heroic individuals--perhaps saints-- when coupled with several more practical didactic strategies, is a more complete way to teach morality. Instead of presenting a minimalistic morality ("How far can I go before it becomes 'wrong'?") this approach presents high ideals, the pursuit of which will bring the truest satisfaction of a moral life. This first principle argues for the explicit treatment of moral issues and moral behavior, using a variety of stimuli, some derived from classroom incidents, some from simulations, some from the good example of teachers and other adult role models.

Moral education should be coordinated both horizontally (across academics in the same grade) and vertically (showing development in each discipline from the tenth through the twelfth grade, one building on the other).

This guiding principle urges that, where appropriate, the nurturing of moral attitudes and behaviors be echoed or repeatedly dealt with in several courses within the same academic year. Such repetition will mutually reinforce, from class to class, the learnings being sought. For example, a student who hears of the injurious effects of racial stereotyping in his or her science, literature, and social studies classes is more likely to grasp that notion than if only one teacher dealt with it. This implies that there is some planning going on between teachers of various disciplines in the same grade level for such mutually reinforcing classroom learnings.

Moreover, this guiding principle suggests that the curriculum be sequentially planned so that the more basic and easily grasped moral issues be dealt with in the earlier grades, with the more difficult ones tackled in the upper grades. This allows youngsters the space to deal with those moral notions with which their emotional and intellectual development is most able to cope. Too intense an exposure to very complex moral issues with which youngsters are not psychologically equipped to cope will only drive them to defensive reactions, such as ridicule, denial, or avoidance of that issue.

Since adolescents are not yet adults, but on the way to becoming adults, basic predispositions to adult moral behavior should comprise the focus of moral education. These predispositions include self-esteem, empathy, altruism, caring for others, and the use of their talents for building up the community.

Readers of the above-mentioned volumes on the philosophical and the psychological foundations of moral education will hear echoes in this particular section, namely, that a limited focus on justice is inadequate as a basis for moral education; moral education must include those foundational values, understandings, and attitudes which provide the necessary freedom in which moral choices become possible. Moreover, moral education must point beyond justice to love as the richer more fully human foundation for moral behavior.[4]

This guiding principle helps the teachers set realistic goals in their efforts at moral education. Some moral dilemmas tax the intelligence of highly educated adults. Expecting a 14 year old to argue the principle of double

effect in distinguishing between euthanasia and the acceptable practice of removing extraordinary life support
systems from a dying person may be asking that youngster
to understand something that perplexes mature adults. A
class discussion in the tenth grade of just war theories
and nuclear disarmament may be asking youngsters to
reason at a level of abstraction well beyond their capa-
bilities. In his essay "Moral Education in the Junior
High School," in this volume, Clive Beck argues that there
are appropriate ways to raise these larger issues for
younger students. Teachers will have to test this out with
their students. At the very least, however, teachers can
build a strong foundation for such mature levels of moral
reasoning and moral choice by nurturing the predispositions to such moral reasoning and choosing. By helping
youngsters confront concrete and specific issues, such as
lying to one's parents about where one goes on Saturday
nights, or about cheating on homework, teachers help to
develop analytical reasoning skills while at the same time
helping their charges develop more responsible attitudes.

Besides focusing on reasoning skills on more concrete and immediate questions, educators following this
principle will devote considerable time developing an even
more essential foundation for moral behavior.[5] One can
easily see that what constitutes the great dividing line
between moral behavior and immoral behavior comes down
to conflicting sets of attitudes: selfishness, self-centered
fixations, insecure self-images, lack of empathy, on the
one hand; on the other we find attitudes of self-esteem,
a trusting openness to others, a spontaneous liking of
people, a sense of altruism, a feeling that the forces at
work in one's life are basically benign and trustworthy.[6]
If the significant adults in a youngster's life teach that
the world is a jungle, then the youngster will live by the
law of the jungle. If the significant adults in a youngster's life teach that the essential purpose and meaning
of human life involves the creation of harmony and community among people, then the youngster will be more likely
to assume responsibility for making that happen.

This point perhaps deserves further elaboration.
Teachers enjoy a certain distance from the hurly-burly,
stress-filled, ambiguous life of "normal" adult life precisely so that they can see what is happening beneath the surface of that world. They are supposed to read a lot, reflect a lot, try to make sense out of all the smaller pieces

of the puzzle and see the larger pattern. They are supposed to have, as well, a more refined sense of traditional human values, and be able to explain the difference
between what appears immediately attractive and what is
of enduring and, perhaps, of profound human value.

So the distance is important. No matter that the
movers and shakers in society condescendingly disparage
the work of teachers. No matter that some shortsighted
citizens want teachers to turn their attention to the most
immediate symptom of malaise, whether it be drugs, teen-
age pregnancy, delinquency. While they cannot ignore
these symptoms, they have to deal with the more basic
realities of the intelligibility and trustworthiness of life.
If they deal with these well, then the children they teach
will have a chance to function with sanity and integrity
and humanity as adults. That, at least, is what seems
to be society's intuitively held belief about teaching, despite the periodic stridency over more immediate crises.

It is important for a teacher, therefore, to discern
the intelligibility and trustworthiness of life, important to
acquire a larger and deeper perspective on human values,
important to have a sense of one's own sanity and integrity and humanity. For they are supposed to help young
minds and hearts develop these very same things.

Sometimes parents' moral assumptions seem quite
different from those of the schools. They seem to assume
that it is a dog-eat-dog world, that it will always be a
power struggle between the haves and have-nots, that people are basically untrustworthy and dishonest, that having much is the criteria of being much, and that the purpose of living is to acquire as much power, prestige,
wealth, and social prominence as one can. A school
which functions on those assumptions will destroy itself.

Let me quote a teacher whose moral assumptions are
quite different.

When I teach I spend a lot of time--many
would say too much time--repeating a few
simple principles. (1) The greatest wealth
and power in human society is what's inside us. (2) Our talents of intelligence,
artistic or athletic ability, craftsmanship,
practical organizational skills, etc., are
gifts given to us. They are to be cherished
and developed first and foremost as gifts for

the community, not primarily as our exclusive private property to be exploited for our own self aggrandizement. (3) Sharing our wealth, especially our interior wealth, is the most enriching experience a human being can have. (4) We should forgive others as we would want to be forgiven. (5) A commitment is a promise; honor it. (6) Don't take life for granted, make it happen.

Countless opportunities to practice these principles arise during the course of a normal week. We take time to reflect on the practical consequences when these principles are followed and when they are not followed. Sometimes it gets a little painful, but most of the time these practical activities lead us to insight and--I hesitate to use such a romantic word--joy.[7]

Moral questions should be related to the lived experience of adolescents.

This guiding principle leads teachers to strive always to illustrate a more general moral issue with examples drawn from adolescent experience, or to draw out of the concrete adolescent experience general moral principles.[8] For example, specific instances of selfishness in a family situation at home can illustrate how destructive of relationships such repeated selfish behavior can be. Using an example of theft in school, perhaps when someone's locker has been broken into, teachers can help youngsters perceive how destructive of trust among the student body such events can be. Indeed, where theft is a common occurrence in a school, students will need to realize how such actions, if allowed to continue, will poison the whole environment of the school. Teachers can help students to take positive steps to reduce or eliminate theft in school. They can also, perhaps, help students explore the possible reasons why a fellow student would steal: reasons such as anger on the part of a student from a poor family toward students who appear to have so much better clothes and so much more money to spend. Other adolescent experiences, such as sexual stereotyping or exploitation, scapegoating, drug abuse, parental conflicts, family break-up through divorce, the use of violence in obvious or subtle forms, anxiety and shame over one's physical appearance, not knowing how to belong to a group--these and countless other realities in the experience of students can provide any number of opportunities for leading students to reflect on the moral qualities and consequences of their actions.

Learning from mistakes is at least as important as learning from successes.

Principled moral choices are frequently developed from experiencing the disastrous consequences of the opposite. Teachers who respond to moral mistakes and failures in their youngsters only with punishment are missing a great opportunity to help them learn from their mistakes. When a youngster is caught in a lie, or apprehended in a cheating incident, the perceptive teacher uses it as a therapeutic opportunity. Sanctions can be imposed, but more important than the external conditioning they provide is the effort to help the youngster see why that behavior is morally wrong, and to see why its opposite (telling the truth, or achieving a good grade through one's own effort) is so much more humanly satisfying and indeed productive of better results for oneself and others.

During adolescence, youngsters are experimenting with various adult responses to situations in their life. Choosing how one will be accepted by the group--for example, through pulling down others in order to promote one's own image, or through doing something that benefits the group--will have real consequences for that youngster in establishing habits of social interaction. Since much of their social growth will result from raw experimentation, one can predict by the law of averages that half of their experiments will be infelicitous. The natural pain such trial-and-error learnings bring with them will frequently lead them to avoid such choices in the future. Adolescents can be helped enormously, however, by teachers who expect that they will make mistakes, who can respond sensitively to their feelings of awkwardness and insecurity, who will see such experimentation as necessary and indeed as healthy, and who will help them reflect on the consequences and on the underlying moral goodness or foolishness of their choices.

These kinds of reflection sessions can take place on a one-to-one basis outside of the classroom where a certain privacy and personal sensitivity are called for. But frequently they can take place in the classroom when the particular moral issue has broad applicability to adolescent experience and will not embarrass any one member of the class. This consideration leads to the next guiding principle.

Moral education must involve dialogue and disagreement.

If teachers simply lecture their students about moral principles they will have little impact. Students need time to appropriate ideas, values, attitudes; time to question socially approved standards; time to disagree with teachers, and to take apart an argument and put it back together. They need to integrate newly found ideas, values, and attitudes with their past experience and previously held ideas, values, and attitudes. Therefore, they need to test and clarify their understanding in dialogue with another person or in talking with a group of people. They need to be able to engage in exchanges such as, "If that's the case, then what about this instance?" or "While your analysis makes sense, if you look at it from this perspective you end up with a different feeling for that choice."

Furthermore, adolescents will be jolted into a new perspective much more easily by another adolescent than by a teacher. When students argue a point in class, it forces them to consider other points of view; it leads them to search for higher principles or concepts that will embrace what appear to be opposing perspectives. The emotional tone of a discussion or argument among students differs considerably from an exchange with a teacher, and that emotional tone qualitatively enhances the understanding that is gradually taking place. Besides the substance of what is being learned, students are also gaining a very important side-benefit; namely, that they are learning how to think for themselves, how to pursue a moral issue through listening to several points of view, how to change one's mind, or alter an opinion in the light of more persuasive viewpoints, etc. In such ways they are learning how mature adults explore moral issues.

Morality can be rehearsed.

Some people think that spontaneity and honesty are violated if human exchanges are rehearsed. Others believe that moral choices are so unique that one has to examine all the unique nuances of a given situation before deciding the moral thing to do. Both perspectives have some merit, but they do not rule out the benefits that can result from simulating or rehearsing moral decisions.

Most youngsters find role playing rather easy and indeed enjoyable. A creative teacher can set up a typical adolescent situation (say, a fight, an interracial hassle, a cheating incident, a dating scene) and let the students debate with the moral choices involved. This can be especially valuable in a school where particular moral issues are in fact at stake, such as in a school being integrated through busing, or in a school experiencing ethnic tensions, or in a school with rampant drug abuse.

Such role-playing exercises must be followed by extended debriefing sessions in order to allow students to describe their feelings during the exercise, to look at the potential consequences to themselves and others of the choices they made in the role playing, and to use the specific case to draw out some general conclusions. Teachers need to exercise care in setting up role playing so that unwarranted pressure is not brought to bear on students who do not or cannot handle the emotions such exercises bring on.

In these simulations, teachers can help students develop basic skills needed for moral behavior. Such skills might involve being able to confront a peer who is bullying a younger student, or to confront (respectfully) an adult who is treating someone unfairly. Other skills include being able to tell the truth when under pressure by others to lie, the skill to withdraw from a group that is doing something one considers morally indefensible, the skill to use humor as a healing exchange or to bond a relationship stretched by misunderstanding, skills to accept defeat or a failure by putting it into a larger perspective (as one parent put it to his children, "Cope, don't mope.").

This principle follows the more general principle that we learn best by doing, by putting into practice an idea or principle. Through exercises which simulate typical adolescent moral dilemmas and begin, in the upper grades, to tackle some adult moral dilemmas, youngsters can learn the lessons of moral behavior while still in a relatively protected environment. In that environment their mistakes do not punish them as they do in a real situation. In the school environment the satisfaction of

altruistic behavior can be savored and such attitudes take
root before being exposed to the potentially withering cynicism of the streets.

Parents must become involved in their children's learning of morality in the classroom.

Teachers can suffer frustrations in trying to develop
healthy moral attitudes in youngsters when their parents
are teaching quite opposite attitudes at home. Examples
of such attitudinal conflicts between home and classroom
include racial, sexual, and ethnic stereotyping; conspicuous
consumption; alcohol abuse; dishonesty on taxes; environmental issues. The teacher needs to enlist the support of
the parents right from the start. The school's administration should encourage frequent exchanges between parents
and teachers. Parents should see the school's efforts at
moral education in at least as favorable a light as the
programs in computer science and consumer education.
The skillful teacher will go beyond simply informing
parents of his or her efforts in the classroom. The teacher
will suggest a series of exercises or discussions at home
that parallel what is being treated in the classroom, and
will provide parents a weekly list of suggestions for ways
to reinforce what is being taught at school. In those
cases where the parents disagree with a position the teacher might take, they would be urged to communicate that to
the teacher and indicate how they deal with that issue
with their son or daughter. As long as such disagreements can be discussed and dealt with in an adult, reasonable fashion, those very disagreements may help the
youngster see more clearly the values that are at stake.
The experience of disagreements with parents leads to the
next principle.

Moral issues frequently require intensive research.

While some moral choices are open to relatively
simple analysis, many involve very complex consideration.
For example, it is easy to say that it would be morally
wrong for me to bash in someone's head because their family came from a different country than my parents. It is
not so easy to say whether it is morally wrong for me to
bash in his or her head when our country is at war with
their country and I am attacking their village. Considera-

tions of the theory of a just war now enter in, as well as the moral guidelines for soldiers in battle.

When the moral issue moves from an individual, personal moral issue such as lying, to a moral issue regarding social justice, the need for serious study increases exponentially. The attempt of various churches in the United States to examine the morality of nuclear arms and the ethics of capitalism are good examples of moral issues that demand extensive study, debate, reflection, and research. Here, the principle urges the teacher to discourage facile, platitudinous rhetoric when students are debating a moral issue. Too often the positions held flow out of an uncritical ideology instead of a consideration of the human factors at stake. One of the results of following this principle in the classroom is the unmasking of positions masquerading as moral statements that are in fact self-serving rationalizations, ideological slogans, or simply flabby or fuzzy logic.

One of the better pedagogies in this regard is to expose students to opposing extreme positions on a moral issue. This helps to define by contrast the limits of the terrain being explored and to point toward the probable middle ground where reasonable disagreement can be expected. Not only does such exposure to different points of view clarify the values at stake; along the way, students will be gaining important analytical and critical skills for taking apart and constructing moral arguments. Furthermore, they will grow to understand that almost all important moral issues have several sides to them. This understanding will nurture a caution against simplistic answers, as well as a habit of serious study when moral issues are debated.

This principle also cautions the teacher to beware of do-gooders or reformers who frequently end up doing more harm than good because they never stopped to study the realities they thought they were dealing with. It means, of course, that the teacher also must do the painstaking research necessary to raise the moral issues intelligently for the students.

Proactive moral behavior and citizenship behavior are the goals of moral education in the classroom.

This guiding principle leads the teacher to stress that kind of moral behavior that seeks the good, rather

than that which simply avoids the bad. Some forms of
moral education seem to concentrate on resisting temptation, or keeping oneself clean from the contamination of
immoral action, as though being moral was equated with
simply not being immoral. A teacher could concentrate,
for example, on avoiding racial stereotyping and never
really bring about racial understanding. That comes only
when people from different racial backgrounds mix and talk
to one another. One can teach teen-age boys to avoid explicit sexual overtures to their girlfriends. The problem
for the boys then becomes what they are supposed to do on
a date when their avoidance training actually works. Who
helps them develop healthy options for communicating with
such strange, exotic creatures?

This guiding principle is derived from the understanding that if people are involved in healthy behavior
that is satisfying and fulfilling, they won't have the time
or the inclination for unhealthy behaviors. If you want
people to avoid sin, give them lots of satisfying experiences with virtue. Hence, the teacher will spend much
more time in the classroom effort at moral education providing experiences of moral behavior. Instead of lecturing on the evils of selfishness, they will provide opportunities for youngsters to share something that is theirs,
whether that is a material possession or a talent. Instead of inveighing against stealing, they will expose
students to the satisfaction of giving gifts to one another.

Furthermore, the teacher must go beyond teaching
for moral exchanges between individuals. Moral education
that stops there is incomplete. The class has to deal with
the need for proactive citizenship behaviors. Quite simply,
democracy will not be worth preserving if the majority of
the citizenry does not care about the larger common good.
One strength of some countries is the acceptance of pluralism and the right of the individual to pursue happiness.
This can turn into a liability, however, when it is used
to justify a "me first" kind of individualism.

Hence, moral education in the classroom has to lead
students beyond proactive moral exchanges between individuals to concern for the common good of the community.
This inescapably flows into citizenship concerns. The
classroom has to explore the meaning of the common good
as it applies to the environment, the economy, criminal
justice, labor laws, international relations--in short, to all
major areas of public policy.

Such classroom discussions will require prior research, exploring major policy options, weighing of the consequences of each course of action, looking at the special interest groups supporting one policy over another. It will help to study those instances where citizen action won out over narrow, selfish concerns in order to discern effective political procedures. Youngsters need to have some sense that they can make a difference in their communities. Likewise, they have to develop a sense of responsibility for the quality of life in that community.

In order for this higher level of moral education to work, however, all the teachers in the school have to agree on its importance and have to develop a plan for its accomplishment. Year-by-year citizenship goals need to be spelled out, with all disciplines assigned some responsibility for promoting some target learnings. A moment's reflection would surface several examples of public policy concerns in science, in social studies, etc. Even the mathematics departments can take on some citizenship tasks, for example, using accounting principles for filing tax returns, using statistics to document unfair labor practices, using computers to work on community problems.

When a faculty takes on this task, their sense of mission as teachers takes on a whole new feeling. Normally teachers believe that they are helping youngsters grow into becoming good human beings. But when they can work together with other teachers to encourage this kind of larger moral concern, then their work becomes enormously enhanced in value. They are playing their part in building up the quality of life for everyone.

CLASSROOM SCENARIOS

What follows are simple examples which may illustrate how moral education can be conducted in a high school classroom. They are meant to be suggestive, not exhaustive. Some will indicate how several disciplines might lend themselves to an appropriate effort at moral education. Others will indicate that the normal classroom interaction, whatever the subject under study, can provide opportunities for moral education.

Exercises in and for Self-esteem

These exercises can take place in a variety of settings, either in a language arts class, a group counseling

session, a communications course, or in almost any classroom where the teacher is trying to build up teamwork and
a spirit of cooperation and respect. It is assumed that
some time for teachers and students to get to know one
another will have elapsed. Beyond the exercises mentioned
below, readers are encouraged to refer to Lickona's essay
in this book for further suggestions on this important topic.

In one exercise, students are assigned to groups of
six or seven. Each youngster writes his or her name on
the top of a blank page and passes it to the person on
the right. That person puts down something likable about
the person whose name is at the top of the page. When
that person is finished, he passes the sheet to the person
on the right who also puts down something likable about
the person whose name is on the top of the page. This
continues until each person in the group receives the sheet
with his or her name on the top. The exercise can stop
there, with each student encouraged to save their own
sheets, perhaps pin them up on the wall of their room at
home.

Some teachers post those sheets all around the room
for a week. Other teachers will continue the exercise,
encouraging students to elaborate on what they put down
on the sheet of paper. After everyone has had their say,
the teacher encourages each student to reflect more often
on their good qualities and to take the time in the future
to tell people more spontaneously what they like or appreciate about them.

Some teachers will encourage youngsters to write a
letter to each of their parents, telling them of all the
things they like about them. A notice is mailed home to
each parent, asking them to write a letter to their son or
daughter telling what they especially like about him or
her. One of the ground rules is that the letters cannot
contain negative criticisms. These letters not only can
bring youngsters to a new feeling of self-acceptance; they
can unblock communications between themselves and their
parents.

Other teachers, once they get to know their students
well, will try to find at least one positive thing every
week which they can praise each student for. Frequently
this will involve something in the homework, or in tests
and quizzes or classroom responses. Sometimes it will involve something very simple such as "You look really happy
today. Thanks for bringing that into our class." Some-

times it will involve something the youngster has done around the school, such as performing in a play, or playing well in the basketball game. In this way, teachers can let the students know that they are special, and that the teachers care about them. These moments of recognition are precious for an adolescent who, despite the outward show of indifference, is very insecure underneath.

Another way of promoting self-esteem is to set each of the students a challenge for the semester, some project or other which will stretch them a bit. By letting each student know that the teacher believes in his or her ability to complete the project, and encouraging each student during the time of the project, the teacher is helping to build up greater confidence. When these projects are able to tap into some of the unique talents, experiences, and backgrounds of the students, they will benefit all the more. For example, some students may be talented musically or artistically and can use that talent in the project. Others may have come from a foreign country and can bring something from their culture to enrich the project. In all these ways teachers are able to say to their youngster, "You are a special person. You have something to offer to your world." They will also be helping these youngsters to experience the enormous satisfaction of doing something that expresses their uniqueness.

Finally, some teachers will arrange some projects to be completed by a team of two or three youngsters. As they work on the project, the teacher will encourage the teams to appreciate how each person on the team has something to offer to the project. Care must be taken both to avoid artificiality or giving compliments where they are not deserved, as well as to rein in some of the stronger students who will dominate a team and control what the team does in a project. By teaching teamwork, they can help students grow accustomed to expect that every member of the team will contribute something, and to recognize that in almost every instance each person has something to offer. Such exercises also help to develop attitudes toward collaboration, a healthy balance to the sometimes excessive attitudes of competition.

Using Talents for the Community

The last exercise involving teamwork touches upon some learnings that overlap with our next classroom scenario. In this classroom, the teacher repeatedly attempts

to emphasize that everyone has been given talents, not as
their exclusive private possessions, but primarily for the
enrichment of the community. All too often, youngsters
are taught by their parents to exploit their talents in order to get ahead, to get to the top of their class, to be
the star of the show, the captain of the team. Frequently
youngsters believe that their talents are to be used
against others, to beat them out in a competition for a
prize, be it valedictorian of the class, a scholarship to
college, or the lead part in the play. This is not to
deny that competition is a reality in school or adult life.
Rather, the lesson to be learned in this instance is that,
first and foremost, talents belong to the community and
are to be used to enrich and build up the community.
Interscholastic competition in athletics, debates, and other
activities are not sublimated forms of violent warfare between schools, although some coaches and adults sometimes
give that impression. Rather they are celebrations of the
talents young people possess, expressed through the ritual
of games and contests. Most athletes after a hard played
game are genuine when they congratulate members of the
opposing team: "That was a great curve ball you threw
in the third inning." "You faked me into the bleachers on
that end run." "That hook shot from the corner was a
classic." They know from the experience of the game itself what their opponents' talents are, and they can tell
them openly how much they admire particular skills those
players exhibited during the game.

One easy application of this principle in the classroom is to provide time for the faster students to tutor
the slower students. The teacher will have to manage
such arrangements carefully, however, so that the slow
students do not feel patronized. Every opportunity must
be sought, moreover, to enable those slower students to
make their own contribution to the class. Although it
smacks of stereotyping, there is some validity to having
the slower student in language arts repay the one tutoring
him or her in grammar by showing that student how to
change a carburetor in his or her car, or by sharing a
new recipe in the home economics class. It is a rare
youngster who has no talent, however unusual, to contribute to the class, whether that is in exchange for help received from others or not.

Some teachers will teach this lesson by rotating responsibility for changing the classroom displays and posters

among teams of students. Others will make teams of students responsible for keeping the classroom tidy and the desktops clean. Others will simply hold a short skit every week, with a different team of students responsible for providing the weekly melodrama, musical, or farce. The limits to the variety of activities teachers can use to teach this lesson are set only by the teacher's imagination and the talents of the youngsters in the classroom. By having repeated experiences of being expected to share their talents freely on behalf of others, students will gradually develop a disposition to do this as a matter of course.

Putting the King on Trial

In social studies classes, one lively way to engage students in debates of moral issues is to stage a trial of some famous person in history. Assign a team of students to be the prosecuting attorneys, another to be the defense attorneys, another to be the jury. Provide all the students with a variety of source materials and have them prepare for the trial. The teacher will have to provide some instruction in courtroom procedures, rules of evidence, etc., and will probably have to preside as the judge. Members of either prosecution or defense may play the role of witnesses called before the court. Examples of such trials could be the following: Teddy Roosevelt on trial for needlessly starting the Spanish-American War; Martin Luther for supporting the Peasants Uprising; General Custer for his attack on the Indians at the Battle of Little Big Horn; Fidel Castro for turning Cuba into a Communist country.

In the research required to prepare the trial, as well as the lengthy debates during the trial, students would be exposed to a variety of moral issues seen from a variety of perspectives. The jury, especially, would be required to make a moral judgment. Not only will the students grasp an historical moment more completely; they will likewise be forming more mature habits of moral reflection.

Literature as Exploration of the Human Heart

In literature classes, whether involving dramatic or narrative literature, many opportunities abound for consideration of moral choices faced by the characters in the story. Whether the character be Huckleberry Finn, Bo Radley in To Kill a Mockingbird, Ralph in Lord of the

Flies, or Othello, the youngsters can be led first to appreciate why the characters behaved as they did, then to
discuss the moral options open to them; and then to consider analogous moral choices which they have to face in
their own lives.

Exposure to the larger-than-life characters in the
literature will gradually form a more compassionate understanding of the potential in human beings for greatness as
well as for foolishness and evil. Such experience with the
stuff of human life may gradually lead them to forgive
themselves and to forgive others for the stupidity and
harm that we needlessly bring on ourselves. With care
not to destroy the aesthetic integrity of the literary work,
teachers can legitimately use literature as a basis for discussions of moral issues that touch upon the lives of the
students in class.

Being Gifted by the Poor

Assuming that a school has a community service
program, students will need some setting in which they
can process their experience in that program and draw
some explicit learnings from their experience. Frequently
those settings are classrooms.

Sometimes a community service experience can be an
emotionally upsetting experience for a youngster. It may
have involved working with disabled children or with
feeble, elderly people in a nursing home for the first time.
The student may need time to sort out the feelings which
the experience occasioned, and to express them to the
group. Only after the youngster's own feelings have been
dealt with can that youngster begin to appreciate the persons they are serving in the program. Frequently this
will involve a needed breaking away from stereotypical
ways of perceiving "those people."

Teachers and students can then try to describe the
people they work with, their circumstances, their strengths,
their liabilities. Again and again, teachers need to encourage the youngsters to listen carefully to what people
in their program are really saying, and to understand
what life looks like through their eyes. The usual response of the student is to want to do something to help.
Frequently there is little they can "do" except listen, be
present, share a little of themselves with their people.
One important learning outcome of such gradual coming
to know and appreciate those they work with is that

they, the students, are receiving as much, if not more, from the people they are supposed to be serving. Again and again, this has been the most rewarding outcome of moral education efforts, whereby youngsters can see that they are gifted in the act of service of another person. When that other person is poor, or sick, or handicapped or in some way is culturally defined as having less than the students, then the students' superficial understanding of wealth, health, and happiness gets shattered and they are freed to perceive that these are a matter of the human heart, not of money, youth, and external definitions of joy. That experience, more than any other, helps them to ground their moral conscience on a desire to share the riches of the human heart and spirit.

Citizenship in Practice

Teachers should be encouraged by the administration to take up in the classroom matters of significance affecting the whole school. Students should be encouraged to govern themselves, as much as that is possible. Hence, if there are problems with theft, students should be encouraged to come up with ways to counter that. Likewise, with drugs, with cheating, with violence, with racial or ethnic conflicts, with difficulties between the students and administration. Some form of classroom discussion can be explicitly requested by the administration if a serious incident has occurred in the school. Suggestions can be collected and passed on to the student government and administration.

Every two or three years the student handbook should be evaluated by a faculty-student committee and be revised. The revisions should then be discussed in class, so students have a better sense of what various rules mean and why they have such-and-such sanctions attached to them. These discussions certainly need to take place with every entering ninth- or tenth-grade class, so that every student has some sense of how the school community has decided to govern itself. Some classroom time, moreover, needs to be given to student representatives from the student government to explain what that organization has been doing to enhance the quality of life around the school.

In some schools, every class is given the assignment of making some contribution to the life of the school during the course of the year, contributions such as decorating

the school for Thanksgiving or Christmas, running a special assembly promoting community service, or organizing a
parents day at the school, etc. By having such responsibilities, students come to the gradual recognition that the
life of the community requires everyone's participation,
that everyone has something to offer, that everyone can
make some difference to the community.

CONCLUSION

This chapter has presented but a few pieces to a
much larger mosaic of moral education. This assumes that
the family is engaged in a variety of ways in moral education. Likewise the extended family, the neighborhood,
the local church or temple--all nurture in appropriate
ways the moral growth of youth. In schools, activities
outside of classrooms as well as inside have their part to
play. The examples of classroom activities presented here
are but a few of the potentially countless ways moral education can be conducted in the classroom. The ten guiding
principles were offered precisely because it would be impossible to elaborate more than a handful of classroom
scenarios. Those principles can guide the intuitions of
the experienced practitioner in the classroom to carry on
that most important part of the profession of educating
youth, the learning of virtue.

NOTES

1. Act and Agent: Philosophical Foundations of
Moral Education and Character Development; Psychological
Foundations of Moral Education and Character Development
(Washington, D.C.: University Press of America, 1986).
2. Margaret Gorman, "An Integrating and Integrative View of the Developing Moral Person," in Richard T.
Knowles, Jesse A. Mann, and Frederick A. Ellrod, Psychological Foundations of Moral Education and Character Development (Washington, D.C., 1986).
3. Walter Nicgorski and Frederick E. Ellrod,
"Moral Character," in David Schindler, Jesse A. Mann, and
Frederick E. Ellrod, Act and Agent: Philosophical Foundations of Moral Education and Character Development (Washington, D.C., 1986).

4. William F. Kraft, "An Integrative Theory of the Moral Person," in Knowles et al., op. cit., Chapter 7.

5. Sebastian Samay, "Affectivity: The Power Base of Moral Behavior," in Schindler et al., op. cit., Chapter 3.

6. Ernest Becker, Escape from Evil (New York: Free Press, 1975), pp. 327–46.

7. Robert J. Starratt, "On the Interior Life of a Teacher," California Journal of Teacher Education, 9(2), 1982, pp. 36–37.

8. While agreeing with Clive Beck's suggestion that moral principles can be derived from adolescents' experiences, I would also use life experiences to illustrate already accepted moral principles.

Part IV
Beyond the School

10

Character Development in the Family

Thomas Lickona

While most ~~writing~~ *knowledge* about character development centers on the role of the school, classic wisdom holds that the family is the primary moral educator of the child. There are common sense reasons why this should be considered true. A parent's socializing influence begins early (at birth) and endures, since at least one parent is usually with a child throughout the child's growing years. Because they are a constant presence, parents are uniquely able to surround a child with a spiritual heritage that supplies a larger vision of life's meaning and an ultimate reason to lead a good life. Finally, parents are an important affective influence. Children need a parent's love to feel valued--a pre-condition for valuing other people. And the affective relationship between parent and child deepens the impact of the parent's values and personal example.

Teachers have long recognized that character begins at home. That is why they greet with some ambivalence the Gallup Poll finding (1976) that more than 80 percent of parents with school-age children want the schools to teach "morals and moral behavior." One group of teachers opined, "Parents are copping out. They want schools to do a job they ought to be doing themselves."

In truth, moral education is the responsibility of all the social institutions and groups--school, family, church, youth organizations--entrusted with the care of the young. But clearly the family has a central role. How can parents carry out their role in a way that contributes to the character development of their children?

253

This chapter offers one set of guidelines, ten major concepts or "big ideas" that can guide parents in their work of trying to raise moral children. Many of these ideas are ancient wisdom; some build on contemporary psychological research. All are informed by my interviews of parents, in which they have shared memories of their childhoods and accounts of their own efforts to raise good children.

Table 10.1 Raising Good Children: Ten Big Ideas

---

1. MORALITY IS RESPECT
2. A MORALITY OF RESPECT DEVELOPS SLOWLY, THROUGH STAGES
3. FOSTER MUTUAL RESPECT
4. SET A GOOD EXAMPLE
5. TEACH BY TELLING
6. HELP CHILDREN LEARN TO THINK FOR THEMSELVES
7. HELP CHILDREN TAKE ON REAL RESPONSIBILITIES
8. BALANCE INDEPENDENCE AND CONTROL
9. LOVE CHILDREN
10. FOSTER CHARACTER DEVELOPMENT AND FAMILY LIFE AT THE SAME TIME

THE CORE OF MORALITY IS RESPECT

Before parents can develop morality in their children, they need to be clear about what it is. The first big idea says that the core of morality is respect--for oneself, for other people, and for all forms of life and the environment that sustains them.

Respect for ourselves requires us to treat our own life and person as having value. That is why it is wrong to engage in self-destructive behavior. Respect for others requires us to treat all other human beings as having worth, dignity, and rights equal to our own. That is the heart of the Golden Rule, a moral principle that can be found in religions and cultures all over the world. Respect for the whole complex web of life prohibits cruelty to animals and calls us to act with care toward the natural environment, the fragile ecosystem on which all life depends.

To say that the core of morality is respect is not to deny that there are other moral values to be taught to

As another example of the utility of a developmental perspective, consider a later stage, Stage 3 of moral reasoning. At Stage 3, the central question for the child is, "What do other people think of me?" "Being good" now means earning the esteem of others by being a "nice person." But in the early teens, Stage 3's strength--caring about others--becomes its weakness. Adolescents care so much about what others think, that "everybody's doing it" begins to seem like a good reason for going along. Meeting children where they are during this vulnerable period means providing support. Support includes supervision, authoritative rules that are in the child's best interest (such as, "No drinking," "No unsupervised parties"), and ongoing dialogue about moral issues that helps the teenager understand the parent's views and identify with and feel accountable to the family's values. These parental measures offer young teenagers prudent protection against rising peer pressure and their own developmental immaturities. (See Lickona, 1985, and Kohlberg, 1984.)

At the same time, a developmental approach would encourage parents to make reasonable concessions to teen conformity. Since peer acceptance is so important at this stage, parents who oppose all aspects of peer culture are ignoring developmental reality as much as parents who treat their teens as fully autonomous moral agents. A developmental perspective suggests allowing adolescents "safe conformity" in areas such as music, dress, and hairstyle, while countering negative peer influence in the area of moral values. Finally, a developmental view shows that progress beyond Stage 3 involves developing a greater measure of moral independence--from both parents and peers. Thus, even as parents use their personal authority to offset peer pressure, they must also use the "natural authority" of higher moral reasoning, making clear to children the rational basis of parental positions on moral matters such as shoplifting, sex, drugs, and drinking. Ultimately, rational self-guidance must replace a parent's guidance and control.

Elsewhere (Lickona, 1985) I have detailed various ways parents can try to foster their children's moral growth at each developmental stage. Here I wish only to indicate that a developmental perspective is a helpful part of a parent's total approach to nurturing a child's moral development.

FOSTER MUTUAL RESPECT

One of the most important lessons a parent can teach children is that morality is a two-way street. Respect is reciprocal. "Do unto others as you would have them do unto you."

The first step in teaching this lesson is to treat children with respect. Treating children with respect means treating them like persons. As one mother said, "I have to remind myself that my children are human beings, not puppets waiting to be manipulated by me." Treating children like persons means trying to be fair with them. In the area of discipline, as the mother of a five-year-old and a seven-year-old says, being fair means "asking for and at least considering my kids' opinions when setting up rules and consequences." And in the everyday discourse of the family, respecting children means speaking to them with the same courtesy adults demand of them in adult-child discourse.

It is a mistake, however, to believe that children will automatically return the respect shown to them. Many adults do not automatically reciprocate the respect extended to them. So there should be no surprise when children, who are at immature levels of development, speak and behave disrespectfully. Teaching a morality of respect requires that adults constantly hold up to children the standard of respect and insist that they meet it. If a child lapses into disrespectful talking, a parent can respond in any of several ways, all of which send the same message: "Am I talking to you in a disrespectful tone of voice?" "Can you talk about this in a respectful way, or do you need to go to your room and calm down?" "I respect myself too much to allow anyone to talk to me in that way."

Mutual respect is never more important than it is in adolescence. Although some conflict between parents and teenagers is inevitable, respect appears to have widespread efficacy in calming the troubled waters. One study of 656 Swedish adolescents (Pikas, 1961) found that they were more likely to accept parental authority when they thought it was based on rational concern for their welfare. Parents who take pains to make clear the rational basis of their concern are showing one form of respect for their teenager.

TEACH BY EXAMPLE

The fourth big idea about parenting for character development is one of the oldest: Set a good example.

In the interviews I conduct with parents, I ask, "How did your parents influence your moral development?" Far and away, the most common answer I get speaks of the example a parent set. One man, for example, remembers how his parents "were always helping out others in the community. They were generous to others in need, even when they had little for themselves." A young woman recalls the time when she was seven and her family had just moved into an all-white neighborhood in Philadelphia. Soon thereafter, a minority family tried to buy a house on the block, and the neighbors circulated a petition against it. "My mother was the only person who refused to sign," says this young woman, "and when the family moved in despite the petition, she made a cake to welcome them."

Besides trying to be good role models themselves, parents can make use of other sources of positive moral examples: children's books featuring kind and caring characters (such as C. S. Lewis's The Chronicles of Narnia and the new Value Tales biographies of great humanitarian figures); stories of heroism on the part of children or teenagers; newspaper articles about a good deed performed or a service rendered; and examples of good deeds that we come across in our own experience. Wise parents also limit their children's exposure to bad examples, which means, among other things, controlling television. Sullivan (Chapter 12, this book) calls our attention to television's power to promote consumerism and materialism, and a spate of empirical studies document the contribution of TV violence to aggression among children (see, for example, Television and Behavior, 1982). In a world in which children are surrounded with negative moral examples, parents must assume the role of managing the moral environment to reduce exposure to destructive examples and of mediating their influence through discussion with their child.

TEACH BY TELLING

The fifth big idea is also drawn from the wisdom of the ages: Teach by telling. This is the notion that it's not only important to practice what you preach; it's also important to preach what you practice.

Direct moral teaching often takes the form of explaining things to children. Why is it wrong to call people names? Because name-calling hurts; the hurt is inside where it can't be seen, but it's real. Why is it wrong to lie? Because lying destroys trust, and trust is the basis of any relationship. Why is it wrong to cheat? Because cheating is a lie--it deceives another person--and it's unfair to all the people who aren't cheating. Why is it wrong to steal? Because there's a person behind the property, and stealing violates the rights of that person.

Is there research evidence that direct moral teaching has positive effects on the character of children? Baumrind (1975), in a review of the literature, concludes that, at least within American society, families who maintain and communicate a strong belief system are able to keep their children from destructive drug use and radical alienation. Döbert and Nunner-Winkler (1985) report that parents who frequently "moralize"--point out the moral issue in a situation--have children who are more likely to act on their best moral reasoning than parents who do not do this kind of teaching. Smart and Smart (1976) cite a similar finding in the realm of moral conduct: teens whose parents discussed their misdeeds with them and communicated standards clearly were much better able to resist temptation than those teens whose parents did not communicate in this way.

Direct values transmission can also take a broader form: that of seeking to pass on to children a spiritual heritage, a coherent vision of life that speaks to its ultimate purpose. I interviewed a mother, a Catholic, who has three children in the public schools, and asked her, "What values or heritage do you hope to pass on to your children that you don't expect them to get from school?" She answered, "Faith in God. The value of an interior life. Prayer. A religious view of the universe." In answer to the question: "How does your faith in God translate into what you teach your children about morality?" she said:

> If you see God as the center of things, it
> affects everything. It affects why you
> behave in certain ways and not others.
> There is a standard of behavior. It comes

partly from people who have tried to discern the mind of God over the ages.   We
also have our own hearts to listen to.
There is someone who has created us to
behave in a certain way, so much so that
if we don't behave in that way, we are
unhappy, we create problems for ourselves.
We are called to goodness, to live our
lives according to a very high standard.

This mother wants to pass on to her children a God-
centered view of the universe. She wants them to understand that God has made them for goodness, that He calls
them to a high morality, that, indeed, they cannot be
happy unless they are good.

How is the teaching of this vision made concrete in
the life of the family? The mother described a family tradition that is rooted in their religious beliefs. On the
first night of each week, they have a "fasting dinner"--
usually a piece of fruit for the children and a cup of
broth for the parents. The meal begins with a prayer,
written by the oldest child:

Lord, we pray for all the hungry people
in the world, that they may become well
and fed, and that the pain they suffer
will be lifted from their hearts--and that
all people in the world will turn their
hearts to generosity and compassion.

The money saved by not having a regular dinner is put
in a jar and sent at the end of the month to Oxfam, an
organization dedicated to relieving world hunger. Sometimes at the meal, the mother or father will read a letter
from Oxfam reporting progress in relieving hunger in one
part of the world or the outbreak of a new crisis somewhere else. Says the mother, "It helps us to be aware of
how much suffering there is, and what we can do to help.
We want the kids to know that God calls us to love our
neighbor, wherever our neighbor is, and that we are all
members of the same human family."

In the largest sense, how do such spiritual traditions (and there are certainly spiritual traditions other
than the one illustrated here) contribute to the moral formation of a child? They offer the child a meaning system,

a view of life and our relations with each other, in which
doing the right thing and being a good person are of central importance. By making morality central, such traditions increase the likelihood that children will come to
take morality seriously, act upon their best moral reasoning, and try to lead a good life. If many young people
today are awash on a sea of relativism, it may be because the significant adults around them do not seem to
stand for or believe in anything, do not offer a world
view that grounds morality in something larger and answers the question, "Why be moral?"

HELP CHILDREN LEARN TO THINK FOR THEMSELVES

Teaching children what to believe gives them important moral content. But they need to think about that
content, to exercise and expand the structures of their own
moral reasoning. The sixth big idea is that we raise
moral children by empowering them to think for themselves.
A father describes how his parents did that:

> Whenever I did something wrong, my par-
> ents didn't just demand that I stop my be-
> havior. Instead, they almost always
> asked, "How would you feel if someone did
> that to you?" That gave me a chance to
> reflect on whatever I had done and how I'd
> like to have it done to me.

> I feel this has helped me throughout my
> life. Now I always try to stop and ask
> myself that question before I do something
> rather than after the fact.

This man's parents taught him two very important
moral lessons. First, take the time to think. Second,
put yourself in the other guy's shoes. Neither of those
things comes naturally to children.

An important part of helping children learn to think
is helping them develop a moral imagination--an ability to
see the consequences of their behavior. Consider the following example. John is seven years old. Each morning
he and his sister walk two blocks to get the bus to school.
One day the bus driver reported to John's parents that
John and two other boys had been throwing stones into the

road as cars were driving by. John admitted to his mother
and father that he had thrown the stones. Here is the
conversation that followed:

Father: John, what might happen as a result of your
    throwing stones in the road while cars are going by?
John: The driver might stop and yell at us. Are you
    going to spank me, Daddy?
Father: No, but I think we should talk about this some
    more. What might happen if you frightened the driver?
John: He might go off the road and hit a tree.
Mother: And if he hit a tree?
John: He'd get hurt.
Mother: How would you feel if you were the driver?
John: I might hurt all over with a broken leg.
Father: And how can you prevent that from happening,
    John?
John: Not throw stones.
Father: (short silence) You know, your mother and I feel
    very bad that you were throwing stones in the road.
    We want to hear from you what you intend to do about
    this situation.
John: I won't throw stones in the road again.

     In their handling of this situation, John's parents
used questioning to engage and develop his powers of moral
thought. Rather than tell him why his actions were wrong,
they got him to do the thinking about the possible consequences of his actions. Rather than forbid him ever to do
it again, they got him to make his own statement about
the right course of action in the future.
     To the best of the parents' knowledge, John did not
throw stones in the road again. What if he had? His
parents might begin by asking him what he had promised,
whether he had kept that promise, and what would be a
fair consequence for breaking the promise. Then together
they could agree on a fair consequence for not keeping
his resolution. This approach to handling a rule violation
requires that children apply their moral reasoning to the
problem at hand.

HELP CHILDREN TAKE ON REAL RESPONSIBILITIES

     In 1975 Harvard anthropologists John and Beatrice
Whiting published the results of their study of six cultures.

The cultures differed in a number of characteristics, such as social organization and level of technological development. The Whitings found that in some cultures children were more altruistic (made more responsible suggestions, were more helpful to adults and peers), while in other cultures, children tended to be egoistic (sought help and attention for themselves).

The factor most strongly related to differences in children's altruism was the degree to which children were assigned responsibilities that contributed to the maintenance of the family. The more children had to tend animals, take care of younger children, do chores, and so on, the more altruistic was their behavior in other situations. The most egoistic children in the study were those from the United States sample. Their only obligations in the home typically consisted of keeping order in their own rooms, a duty unrelated to the welfare of others in the family.

The moral of the Whitings' study is obvious: Children become responsible by having responsibility. They learn to care by performing caring actions. Such responsibility training can start early. Says a father, "When our daughter was little, we started her in with emptying the wastebaskets. She could look and see all those baskets she had emptied around the house; that was a visible contribution she had made." I interviewed a mother in Chicago who has three sons; her system is to start them doing chores at age two and to add a chore each year. Her two-and-a-half-year-old puts the pillow in place when she makes the bed and pushes the button to start the dishwasher. At age three, he will help to set the table. Bradley, the four-and-a-half-year-old, sets the table, "dust-busts" the hall, and cleans out the downstairs bathroom sink and toilet. Don, the six-year-old, vacuums the stairs, makes his bed, washes the upstairs sink and toilet, scrapes the dishes, loads the dishwasher, and pours the milk at the table each night. ("There are some spills," his mother says, "but he's so proud.")

This mother made it clear that she had a double agenda: preventing sexism as well as fostering responsibility. "I'm really concerned about what their idea of a woman is. I don't want them to think of women as servants. That's the way my brother, who is a lawyer, treats my mother. It is also the way my father treats her."

Responsibility training need not stop at the family doorstep. Children can learn about being a responsible member of the neighborhood by visiting or doing some other kindness for an elderly neighbor. A mother remembers her training in helpfulness:

> I come from a Quaker background. There
> was a lot of emphasis in our home on ser-
> vice to others. I can remember coming
> home from school when I was just a little
> girl and my mother saying, "Susan, Mrs.
> Flannigan"--an old lady who lived down
> the street--"has been alone all day, and
> I'm sure she would like to talk with you
> for a while." I remember asking now and
> then why I had to do this, and other kids
> didn't. My mother said that what other
> kids did didn't matter--that I should do
> all that I was capable of doing.

BALANCE INDEPENDENCE AND CONTROL

The eighth big idea is that effective parenting bal-ances two things that are always somewhat in tension: the child's desire to be independent and the parent's need to exercise control.

Baumrind (1975) offers a good operational definition of this balance. Labeling it "authoritative" parenting (as contrasted to "authoritarian" or "permissive" parenting), she writes:

> Authoritative control includes the following
> attitudes and practices: The child is
> directed firmly, consistently, and rationally;
> the parent both explains reasons behind
> demands and encourages give-and-take; the
> parent uses power when necessary; the
> parent values both obedience to adult re-
> quirements and independence in the child;
> the parent sets standards and enforces
> them firmly but does not regard self as in-
> fallible; the parent listens to the child but
> does not base decisions solely on the
> child's desires (p. 130).

A number of studies support the efficacy of the authoritative balance. Middleton and Putney (1963), for example, report that parental discipline that is seen by teenagers as either very strict or very permissive is associated with lack of parent-child closeness and with the child's rebellion against the parent's views. Baumrind (see Maccoby, 1980) has produced similar evidence from her studies of children that began when they were nursery schoolers and followed them until they were nine. The most self-confident, socially responsible children had authoritative parents. Baumrind also reports briefly (1975) a study of 103 tenth-graders. Among these adolescents she identified a small group, 15 students, that she labeled "Principled Humanists." These were highly achieving, highly responsible teenagers who said they felt good about authority arrangements in their families and--what is germane to the present issue--described their parents as "firm but democratic."

In a family intervention study, Azrak (1980) found that many parents felt rejected when their young adolescent child began to pull away from close family ties. But he also observed that teens showed less resistance to parental discipline and more willingness to listen to parents' moral reasoning when parents explicitly addressed separation issues (e.g., "We understand your desire to spend more time with your friends . . ."). When teenagers feel recognized as independent, maturing persons, they are more willing to accept the moral guidance they still need.

LOVE CHILDREN

At any stage of development, morality builds on love. A parent's love contributes to a child's character development in at least five ways. First, a loving parent helps a child feel valued as a person. Coopersmith's research (1967) with pre-adolescents finds that high self-esteem children, who are better able to stand by their own judgment and have an easier time making friends, come from families which show their children lots of love and appreciation through everyday expressions of affection and concern. (Children with low self-esteem, Coopersmith found, tend to have parents who are highly critical of them and treat them as a burden.)

Second, a loving parent models a way of treating others. Consider the following passage from the autobiog-

raphy of Christiaan Barnard (1974), originator of the
heart transplant:

> Whenever we were ill, my father got up at
> night to doctor us. I suffered from fester-
> ing toenails that pained so much I would
> cry in bed. My father used to draw out
> the fester with a poultice made of milk
> and bread crumbs, or Sunlight soap and
> sugar. And when I had a cold, he would
> rub my chest with Vicks and cover it with
> a red flannel cloth. Sunday afternoons we
> walked together to the top of the hill by
> the dam. Once there, we would sit on a
> rock and look down at the town below us.
> Then I would tell my problems to my father,
> and he would speak of his to me (p. 21).

This son is clearly learning to care by being cared
for. He is learning that other people--their needs, their
feelings--are important. He is learning that human relationships, and all that they require of us, are to be taken
seriously.

Third, a loving relationship gives a parent clout
in the face of competing moral influences. Children care
about their parents' expectations when they know they are
loved. Reflecting on how she made it through the teens,
one mother said: "I knew that whatever I did, I wanted
to be able to look at myself in the mirror and my parents
in the eye at the breakfast table. I cared about what
they thought, because I knew they cared about me."

Fourth, love plays a role in the development of
moral reasoning. Holstein (1972) compared "successful
fathers" (morally principled themselves and whose 13-year-
old children had progressed to a conventional morality of
caring about the expectations of significant others) with
"unsuccessful fathers" (principled themselves but whose
13-year-olds' moral reasoning still showed a self-centered
orientation). Holstein asked children in both groups to
rate how often their fathers showed affection to them or
spent time with them. Successful fathers were seen as
much warmer and much more involved with their children.

Finally, love promotes parent-child communication,
which is likely the key variable mediating the relationship
between love and moral reasoning development. When com-

munication is good, parents obviously have a better chance of developing their child's ability to take the perspective of others and think about moral issues. When the lines of communication are open, a parent is able to offer moral counsel when the need arises.

Realizing the importance of communication, wise parents create situations that are likely to bring it about. When a colleague's son was nine, he worried that they didn't talk much, didn't seem to have much in common. What would it be like, he worried, when Dan became a teenager? So the father began to take his son out to breakfast every Saturday morning--just the two of them. He promised not to admonish Dan for anything he said, or said he had done, as they chatted over eggs and home fries. "It's amazing what I learned," the father says, "and it's been good in making Dan feel open about talking to his mother and me about all sorts of things: school problems, girls, sex, fears. . . ." The father added that Dan is now a freshman in high school and a lot busier, but they still go out to breakfast many Saturday mornings. Because of this tradition, which is clearly a tangible expression of the father's loving interest in his son, the father will have a channel of moral influence all through the teen years.

FOSTER CHARACTER DEVELOPMENT AND A HAPPIER FAMILY LIFE AT THE SAME TIME

The tenth big idea is this: Helping children grow morally and making good families are really opposite sides of the same coin. The same approaches that help children develop morally will also help families manage their conflicts constructively and enjoy a greater measure of happiness.

One particular strategy that pays these double dividends is a "fairness approach" to conflict. A fairness approach has three parts: (1) trying to achieve mutual understanding (which involves taking the viewpoint of other persons involved in the conflict); (2) arriving at a mutually agreeable solution to the problem (which fosters fair moral reasoning); and (3) holding a follow-up meeting to evaluate how the solution is working (which fosters accountability to the family agreement).

An example of the fairness approach comes from a single-parent mother whose two boys--Phillip (seven) and

Ben (five)—"went bananas" every time the mother tried to talk on the phone. Yelling at the boys and punishing them had not improved their behavior. Finally, the mother tried a fairness approach. This is the dialogue that ensued:

Mom: In a fairness discussion, the three of us will work together to solve the problem.
Ben: I don't get it.
Phillip: If you keep your big mouth shut, you might understand, dummy.
Ben: You shut up yourself!
Mom: I want both of you to be quiet and listen. Now, the problem is that it upsets me when you guys get wild when I'm on the phone and I can't carry on a conversation. What are your feelings about this?
Phillip: Are you going to tell Daddy about this?
Ben: Are you?
Phillip: I haven't been so bad.

The mother comments: "This type of reasoning on the part of the children went on for what seemed like an endless time. It was very hard to get the idea of the meeting across to them. I was astonished to see how punishment-oriented they were." But she persisted, saying again, "We need to come to an agreement that is fair for all of us. I want to understand your feelings about this problem." Finally, there was a breakthrough:

Phillip: Mom, I hate it when you get on the phone and talk forever. It really makes me mad.
Ben: Yeah, the other night you talked on the phone when you said you would play a game with us, and then there wasn't time.
Mom: You feel I spend too much time on the phone?
Phillip: I could never stay on the phone as long as you do, and I wouldn't want to.
Ben: You don't love me when you're on the phone.
Phillip: She always loves us!
Ben: You're not home that much, Mommy, so when you are you should want to be with me.

"The more we talked," the mother says, "the better I understood their feelings of rejection when I talk on the phone. I explained that I often do get carried away—but that with working and going to school and taking care of our home, I hardly have time to see my friends, and this is often my only way of keeping in contact with them."

Once they understood each other's feelings, Phillip, Ben, and their mother were able to work out a fair solution to the problem. They came to this agreement, signed by all and posted:

1. If Mom has promised to do something with us, she will tell the person she is busy and call back later.
2. We will make a list of things to do while Mom is on the phone.
3. Mom will make her calls shorter.
4. If Mom has to be on the phone for a longer time, she will tell us, and we will behave.

"During our follow-up meeting two days later," the mother says, "we agreed that we had stuck to our plan. The kids played together or did things independently while I was on the phone, and I made calls shorter. We also agreed that there had been less arguing and less hassle."

Table 10.2   Steps in a Fairness Discussion

A. Achieving Mutual Understanding
   1.   State the purpose of the discussion (to find a fair solution).
   2.   State intent to understand each other's feelings about the problem.
   3.   State your feelings about the problem.
   4.   Ask your child for his or her feelings about the problem.
   5.   Paraphrase your child's feelings to show understanding.
   6.   Ask your child to paraphrase your feelings.

B. Solving the Problem
   7.   Together brainstorm fair solutions to the problem.
   8.   Agree upon a solution that everyone thinks fair; sign a "fairness agreement."
   9.   Plan implementation of solution and follow-up; evaluate discussion.

C. Evaluating the Solution
   10. Hold a follow-up discussion to evaluate how the solution is working.

At any developmental level, a fairness approach fosters moral growth in several ways. It creates a positive moral atmosphere in the family by making fairness and caring shared norms. It shows that reason rather than power can be used to solve conflicts, and it teaches responsibility by making children active partners in the solution of conflicts. Done repeatedly, it will help children develop a problem-solving approach as a stable disposition of their characters. And by solving conflicts, it will make the family a more loving, mutually supportive environment, which in turn will increase a child's openness to the family's moral influence.

These, then, are ten ways a parent can approach the task of trying to raise moral children: Think of morality as respect, meet children where they are developmentally, promote mutual respect, set a good example, teach values directly and try to pass on a spiritual heritage, stimulate children's moral thinking, give them meaningful responsibilities, balance independence and control, love them, and foster a positive family life and a child's character development at the same time. The research and common observation suggest that these approaches do indeed have a salutary effect on the development of morality in children.

Anyone who is a parent, however, will long for a note of realism. We can do all of these things and still be confronted with children who seem to lack the virtues of thoughtfulness and responsibility we work so hard to foster. I have a friend, the mother of a four-year-old, who says, "God sends us children to teach us humility. One minute Jason is cooperative and helpful, and I think I'm a success as a parent. The next minute he's acting like a rotten kid, and I feel like a total failure." In this connection, three things are helpful to keep in mind. First, children are developing; many of the self-centered, irresponsible things they do are the product of their developmental immaturity. Second, children come into the world with at least the beginnings of their moral personality; some are more easily socialized than others. Third, much of a child's character lies in the region of mystery. There is certainly not a one-to-one correspondence between what a parent does and the kind of human being a child turns out to be.

That said, it is nonetheless true that children are greatly influenced by those around them, and parents have

the potential of wielding more of that influence than anyone else. For this reason, schools and churches cannot
afford to neglect parents; they are indispensable partners
in the enterprise of moral education. Unfortunately, in
recent years, parenting has not been a source of much social status. In order to build a good and just world,
however, society must vigorously support parents in their
efforts to bring up good and decent children. Parents must
know that they are engaged in the most important work
there is: raising up new human life.

REFERENCES

Azrak, R. Parents as moral educators. In R. Mosher
(Ed.), Moral education. New York: Praeger, 1980, pp.
356–365.

Barnard, C. Selections from One life. In J. L. Milgram
and D. J. Sciarra (Eds.), Childhood revisited. New
York: Macmillan, 1974, pp. 11–30.

Baumrind, D. Early socialization and adolescent competence. In S. E. Dragastin and G. H. Elder (Eds.),
Adolescence in the life cycle. New York: Wiley,
1975, pp. 117–143.

Coopersmith, S. The antecedents of self-esteem. San
Francisco: W. H. Freeman, 1967.

Damon, W. The social world of the child. San Francisco:
Jossey-Bass, 1977.

Döbert, R., and Nunner-Winkler, G. Moral development
and personal reliability: The impact of the family on
two aspects of consciousness in adolescence. In M.
Berkowitz and F. Oser (Eds.), Moral education and
application. Hillsdale, N.J.: Lawrence Erlbaum Associates, 1985, pp. 147–174.

Gallup Poll. Annual Survey of Attitudes Toward Public
Education, 1976 (reported in New York Times, April
18, 1976).

Holstein, C. The relation of children's moral judgment level to that of their parents and to communication patterns in the family. In R. C. Smart and M. S. Smart (Eds.), Readings in child development and relationships. New York: Macmillan, 1972.

Kohlberg, L. Essays on moral development, volume 2: The psychology of moral development. San Francisco: Harper & Row, 1984.

Lewis, C. S. The chronicles of Narnia. New York: Macmillan, 1952.

Lickona, T. Raising good children. New York: Bantam Books, 1985.

Maccoby, E. Social development: Psychological growth and the parent-child relationship. New York: Harcourt Brace Jovanovich, 1980.

Middleton, R., and Putney, S. Political expression of adolescent rebellion. American Journal of Sociology, 68:527-535, 1963.

Pikas, A. Children's attitudes toward rational versus inhibiting parental authority. Journal of Abnormal and Social Psychology, 62:315-321, 1961.

Selman, R. The growth of interpersonal understanding. New York: Academic Press, 1980.

Smart, M. S., and Smart, L. Families and developing relationships. New York: Macmillan, 1976.

Television and behavior: Ten years of scientific progress and implications for the 80s. National Institute of Mental Health report. Washington, D.C.: U.S. Government Printing Office, 1982.

Value Tales. (Series of 27 books for children.) La Jolla, Calif.: Value Communications, Inc., 1979.

Whiting, B., and Whiting, J. W. M. Children of six cultures. Cambridge, Mass.: Harvard University Press, 1975.

11

The Role of Religion in Character Development

Thomas C. Hennessy

The position upheld in this chapter is that religion can be and actually is a strong and preferred factor contributing to good character development if religion is taught and accepted in a certain way. No claim is made that this positive relationship between religion and good character development always takes place, only that it often does. Admittedly, it is easy to point to anecdotes in the lives of some who did not integrate their religious knowledge and practice with their other behaviors.

This chapter is devoted to only certain aspects of religion in relation to character development. It is impossible here to give adequate attention to many religions and religious education issues which could be sources of inspiration and empowerment to lead a good moral life. Hence, the meaning of grace, the meaning of the magisterium, the place of authority in one's life, religious scriptures, prayer, liturgy, the importance of the study of the life and teachings of Christ and other religious leaders, and related important issues cannot be considered herein. Readers who seek a recent overview on the content of religious education and related issues are referred to the "Apostolic Exhortation on Catechetics" by Pope John Paul II.[1]

In view of my own background, the reader should understand that what I mean by religion is most proximately the Christian religion and, more specifically, that which is expressed in the teaching and practices of the Roman Catholic Church. Of course, the applicability of what is

said from my frame of reference should be generally trans-
ferable to other groups. For instance, all religions seek
to impart to others their specific doctrines, believe that
these doctrines, correctly understood, assist in character
development, and welcome the best teaching devices to assure instructional improvement as means toward achieving
their ultimate goals. In fact, a seminary professor in a
Protestant mainline denomination wrote of an earlier version of this chapter: "I fully support your thesis as
would [members of our denomination] in general."

AN ADDITIONAL DIMENSION TO MORAL EDUCATION

Most of the moral education programs currently in
place employ as their basis for human development various
perspectives that flow from philosophical and nonreligious
humanistic education. Thus, the application of the concepts of justice, civic education, reciprocal understanding
of the rights of others, logical reasoning, and the like,
play important parts in major moral education programs.
All these approaches can and do offer considerable insights to the young people who participate in the programs.
Yet religious perspectives on human behavior offer a
much deeper foundation than the above approaches because
they deal with the deeper aspects of our nature, our quest
for the transcendental, for the will of God, for salvation,
and for a future life. Furthermore, religious perspectives
provide a deeper view of the person since the person is
viewed in relationship to God, and human behavior is seen
as being judged ultimately not just by humans but by the
Maker of all. A few examples of the religious viewpoint
in relationship to human rights, the basis for justice, and
forgiveness for personal misdeeds should illustrate the
deeper religious dimension; they are offered below.
Respect for each individual's rights is a frequent
theme, even a given, in moral education discussions. When
such discussion probes into the basis for respect for the
individual's rights, recourse is had to a philosophical review of human achievements and abilities, such as abstraction, reflective thinking, and human creativity in
works of art and music. These points are well taken, but
the religious perspective, in my judgment, is deeper and
more integrated. In the religious approach one can see a
pattern behind the special human potential to achieve as a

gift of the Creator of all, and can link it with an overall goal, life now and in a future life. Hence, the rights of the individual are seen as flowing from the universal Creator, not only from a human law or from even an outstanding human document such as the U.S. Constitution.

A second example of the way the religious goes beyond a humanistic perspective concerns the general norms of morality and justice which one uses as a basis for justifying or condemning actions. In practice many of these programs use Rawls's Principle of Justice, the Golden Rule, positive law, or the moral and other effects of one's actions as a basis for decision making. All of these are good sources for determining one's actions or for evaluating them after they have been completed, but they are all based upon human resources, though many see them as reflecting elements of "natural law." For those who can turn to a religious background, however, there is an additional source for decision making and evaluation: declarations of the will of God as revealed in a general code for human behavior in the Bible (e.g., the Decalogue) and in other sources such as in tradition. Various religious groups offer differing views of the ways of interpreting the Scriptures and give different degrees of value to religious tradition. Thus, the religious person in using the Golden Rule and other sources for conscience formation has also the sense of security derived from a further religious source of guidance, with which God's blessing is associated and which can provide a whole integrated context of reinforcement. Adherence to the religious perspective does not make life easier--usually the situation is just the opposite--but those who follow it are deeply convinced that they are doing the correct thing and carrying out in daily life their religious commitment. Their conviction based on faith is not just an additional factor in their lives; there is a qualitative difference which aids also in resisting group or peer pressure and social patterns.

A third special element that religion can provide to the moral approach is the sense of true forgiveness during liturgies of atonement and reconciliation for those truly sorry for misdeeds and truly determined to reform. Those especially who have offended others gravely by injustice or offended the commands of God have a means of being reconciled. An awareness of this instrumentality as a part of God's ecclesial and social providence consoles and reinforces one who is aware of his or her weaknesses.

Thus an evil or immoral action does not necessarily con-
demn one forever to alienation with no hope for reconciliation through remorse and penance. Mary Magdalen and
the Good Thief had a direct message of forgiveness. A
sacramental faith offers the same sense of relief from sin
and the restoration of friendship, once one has truly
turned from grave misconduct. Various religions have
their own means for assuring those truly repentant of God's
forgiveness. But even the best of the moral education programs in themselves have no adequate resource for the
need for forgiveness other than that of self-forgiveness
and forgiveness from the person or persons offended--which
are also important aspects of the problem of one's reconciliation.

     While only three examples of the special contribu-
tions that religion can offer to buttress and deepen character education programs have been offered above, they
could be multiplied. Yet in most cases, the messages regarding standards for human behaviors as urged by religious sources do not differ from those which depend upon
philosophical and humanistic sources. But, as indicated
below, there are times when the standards differ.

VARIANCE IN MORAL AND RELIGIOUS STANCES

     A few cases where religious positions may differ
among varied denominations and differ from positions taken
by those relying on philosophical and other sources can be
briefly reviewed. The recent series of Baby Doe cases are
an example. A child is born with numerous defects which
may be temporarily repaired through delicate operations
but which will guarantee only a difficult and relatively
short life for the child. Some legal authorities believe
that there is an obligation to operate and do all that can
be done for the child. Yet many theologians have regularly held that there is no obligation to take extraordinary measures such as a medical operation to prolong life
though they would insist on "ordinary care" and would
not accept the deliberate neglect of the child that would
lead to death by starvation. Another example is that of
recent "right to die" and "death with dignity" themes,
reactions to excessive prolongation of a terminally ill patient's life through use of highly sophisticated machines
out of concern about medical malpractice suits. Again,

religous traditions tend to see such artificial, extraordinary means as not obligatory. In cases such as those cited above, the religiously oriented person accepts the theologian's tradition over approaches that rely upon legal and other sources.

There are special cases where there seems to be conflict within the religious tradition regarding its authentic teaching. The present confusion concerning contraception is such an example, and it is too complicated to consider here. Suffice it to say that in such types of genuine uncertainty, one should follow the dictates of one's own, well-informed conscience.

The position that has been developed in the preceding paragraphs is that for the reasons proposed, at least in theory, religious education (even if its message is not always certain) should be, for religious people, the preferred basis for character development over the various nonreligious philosophical and humanistic-based programs. Of course, the religious-based program can be used in conjunction with other programs as there is nothing inherently contradictory and much that is mutually complementary in the several approaches. Now a legitimate question arises: If the position stated above is correct in theory, how does it work out in practice? This challenge is examined in the following section.

THE PROBLEM

Critics of religion often point to certain behaviors of religious adherents as a means of condemning religion. For instance, in the past, Christians mistreated Jews; Moslems and Christians assaulted each other; various Moslem sects warred against each other; and Protestants and Catholics persecuted each other. Today, the picture is no different as one looks to conflicts in Northern Ireland, Lebanon, Israel, and Iran-Iraq. Likewise, the cases of the regular churchgoing religious adherent who is revealed to be a corrupting force in politics or whose decisions were influenced by bribery, are unfortunately all too numerous. Furthermore, general studies of those who demonstrate racial or other prejudice, obtain a divorce and remarry, seek abortions, or cheat in schoolwork, usually conclude that there is no pattern marking one of the different groups as significantly superior to the other groups. Religionists' behaviors do not vary differently from those of the nonreligionists. Hence the natural question arises: How can one maintain that "religious education can be a superior basis for character development?"

THE ROOTS OF A SOLUTION

Some thirty years ago, Gordon Allport, in his classic work, The Nature of Prejudice,[2] was concerned about the same issue. His summary statement of the problem is that religion

> makes prejudice and it unmakes prejudice. While the creeds of the great religions are universalistic, all stressing brotherhood, the practice of these creeds is frequently divisive and brutal. The sublimity of religious ideals is offset by the horrors of persecution in the name of these same ideals. . . . Churchgoers are more prejudiced than the average; they also are less prejudiced than the average.

In his treatment of the problem, Allport offered the salutary basis for distinctions about religious groups. He noted that the faith "is the pivot of the cultural tradition of a group." And one might add that in many cases there are economic factors, such as employment, training opportunities, and housing conditions, which are summarized in terms of religion or presumed religion. For instance, many of the extremists in Northern Ireland may be regarded by the press as either Catholics or Protestants; yet in fact many of them have rejected the tenets of their religion, though they perhaps remain attached to their traditional attitudes and labor under the cultural and economic environment of their peers.

For a solution to the problem of the apparent discrepancy in research concerning the amount of prejudice in churchgoers, Allport referred his readers to some unpublished research conducted in a university seminar. The research was done by a Catholic priest and a Protestant clergyman who probed the prejudices of small samples of their own flocks. In each church those tests were divided into two groups, the more versus the less devout or religious. The summary of the studies, which admittedly lacked the sophistication of most of the research with which Allport dealt, is as follows:

> In both studies, the same result occurred: those who were considered the most devout, more personally absorbed in their religion, were far less prejudiced than the others. The institutional type of attachment, external and political in nature, turns out to be associated with prejudice.

Allport concluded that it is important in dealing with religion to distinguish between two types of religious adherents. One type belongs to a church "because its basic creed of brotherhood expresses the ideals one sincerely believes in" (the "interiorized" or "internalized" religious adherents). The second type belongs to a church "because it is a safe, powerful, superior in-group" (the "institutionalized" adherents). He reported the former group to be associated with tolerant, nonprejudiced attitudes; the latter group was characterized by an authoritarian character and "linked with prejudice." Whether this distinction is true of all religions is another issue, but it is this writer's contention that the distinction provides a key to an understanding of failures of some to act consistently with beliefs, and contains a key that can open the door to religious educators for assistance in development of adherents from belief to behavior to character.

The implication of the Allport report as summarized above is that those who are charged with the teaching of religion should give special importance to efforts to interiorize religious beliefs. If that is done, there should be obvious results in students' moral thinking and behaviors. Hence, we look next at important research which, focusing on Catholic schools, has included sections that pertain to religious education and correlates of religious education.

RELATED RESEARCH FINDINGS

This section is devoted to a summary of several research studies that included segments on character development and religion. The research material is contained in reports about the general state of Catholic education in both nationwide and inner-city samples; prior media attention to these reports has focused on academic achievements and has neglected references to character and internal religious development. The brief review below looks to appropriate sections of the classic studies by the Greeley-Rossi study, the Notre Dame Study, National Catholic Education Association reports, and the Inner-City Schools study. As with all research, there are certain limitations regarding methodology in each of the studies. As our conclusions are based upon the cumulative pattern of the research findings, the limitations in the individual studies are not here a major concern.

The Greeley-Rossi study,[3] released in 1966, was based upon 2,753 interviews taken in 1963-64, and supplemented by two thousand questionnaires. Their findings include the conclusion that, in the moral and religious area, Catholic education is most effective among those who have had a complete Catholic education, from elementary school to college, especially if they have come from homes that are strongly religious. Furthermore, they found that "Those . . . who attended Catholic colleges have significantly lower scores . . . for anti-Semitism, anti-civil-liberties attitudes . . . and religious extremism." This writer interprets the Greeley-Rossi findings as emphasizing the importance for character development of consistent, relatively school-intensive learning (the "full treatment" of elementary-school-to-college Catholic schooling is best) that is complemented by related practices and teachings in the home environment (especially "from homes that are strongly religious"). When parents make a partial attempt toward Catholic education (i.e., their children attend Catholic schools for only a part of their education), the effects were not as obvious as in the other cases. The challenge to parents who seek religious education for children but who, for one reason or another, cannot do so, is to attempt to match in some way the learning conditions which the Greeley-Rossi report found favorable for moral and religious growth; these conditions for learning are reviewed below in the section on Modern Religions Education.

The Notre Dame Study of Catholic Elementary and Secondary Schools in the United States, entitled Catholic Schools in Action, and edited by Reginald A. Neuwien, was also published in 1966.[4] The study was based on responses to a special questionnaire administered to 14,519 male and

female students in Catholic schools. One of the many pertinent findings of this study was that the students who had
the deepest awareness of the implications of religious doctrine were those who were instructed in the new catechesis
or kerygmatic method. The researchers were convinced that
"54% of . . . elementary school students and 59% of . . .
secondary school students reflected" their receiving the
new catechesis or kerygmatic emphasis in their questionnaire responses.

As considerable emphasis in the Notre Dame Study was
placed on the new catechesis or kerygmatic approach to
religious instruction, a brief explanation of that approach
seems appropriate. It is described in the report:

> [It] is a combination of the intellectual
> and practical emphases and at the same
> time is quite distinct from both. It is in-
> tellectual in that it leads the student to
> probe deeply into the origins and mean-
> ings of . . . religion; it is practical in
> that it aims explicitly at helping the stu-
> dents to live fully the Christian message.
> However, it differs from them and tran-
> scends them in that it emphasizes the
> beauty and the joy of Christian faith at
> the very moment it seeks its truth. It
> emphasizes that the Christian religion is
> not something simply to be known or even
> merely to be practiced; it is rather a
> total spirit, or better, an inspiration or a
> life process. It is a view of the [fully
> developed, integrated] Christian person, as
> it were, from within. . . . By recogniz-
> ing and responding to the "good tidings"
> of the gospel . . . the Christian [can]
> enter into a living awareness of the mys-
> teries of his faith.[5]

In their enthusiasm for this new approach,* the authors of the Notre Dame study predicted that "the next

---

*The kerygmatic approach is supplemented in other
recent religious education trends. For instance, the "revisionist" religious educators, such as Thomas Groome,[6]
emphasize the need for critical inquiry regarding religious

generation of students in the Catholic schools will have a much better understanding of their religion than those of former generations had." In 1983, Francis D. Kelly reported an analysis of inventories administered for more than seven years to more than five hundred thousand eighth-grade students (Religious Education Outcome Inventory, the REOI) and to twelfth-grade students (Religious Education Outcome Inventory of Knowledge, Attitudes, and Practices, the REKAP). Though the report showed the pupils' inadequate grasp of religious or dogmatic technical terms, Kelly confirmed the Notre Dame prediction in stating that the students:

> have caught quite well the essential kerygmatic message of Christianity: God's unconditional love for all persons and his personal care of each individual, as well as . . . the redemption and salvation brought by Jesus, God's Son. Catechetical materials affected by the renewal have emphasized these points over the past 15 years and the results are a cause of encouragement. The data indicate that the young people's basic perception of the Christian Message is positive and hopeful.[9]

The concepts that are emphasized in the kerygmatic-catechesis approach to religious instruction are reviewed later in this chapter as we summarize what research has taught us regarding religious education.

The Notre Dame study was generally corroborative of the Greeley-Rossi report with regard to the relationship of the family to religious education. They found that "supportive" families "take considerable interest in religion,

---

tradition and human experience. In addition, the "reconceptualist" religious educators, such as Gabriel Moran, seek to understand one's own tradition and, as well, to understand "to whatever degree possible the religious life of other people"[7] and so is very acceptable to those whose primary concern is the ecumenical movement. However, for all its attractiveness, the reconceptualist approach is "still in its infancy," according to Scott[8] in the sense that it has not yet been widely applied in the literature and especially in religious education textbooks.

and they make prayer and discussion of religious topics a regular part of the home life." An interesting related finding concerning the social class of the parents was that:

> upper class status is associated with less
> prejudice toward minority groups and more
> frequent Mass attendance, whereas middle
> and lower class status reflects stronger
> support of religious vocations and of
> Catholic family values as measured by at-
> titudes toward divorce and mixed marriage.

The report of the study brought home the importance of home and family complementarity through the observation that there is an obviously strong relationship between active encouragement of religion in the home and the religious attitudes of children. The report mentioned certain practices that encouraged religion among children:

> family prayer, commemoration of religious
> feasts, and discussion of religion. The
> families where these are a part of daily
> life or where they occur very frequently
> . . . [have] children whose attitudes and
> values set them apart from those in whose
> home religion is relatively weak. Parents
> who may have expected the Catholic school
> to assume full responsibility for the total
> religious formation of their children will
> perceive how essential is the collaboration
> of home and school.

The third pertinent research report is Inner-City Private Elementary Schools: A Study by J. Cibulka, T. O'Brien, and D. Zewe.[10] Reported in 1982, the study used data from 54 inner-city, predominantly Catholic schools in eight U.S. cities. The schools were E.S.E.A. Title I schools whose students were at least 70 percent minority. One of the areas upon which the report focused was that of social behavior, especially behavior toward adults in school, peers, and behavior at home. Teachers, principals, and parents were surveyed for information about social behavior. In general, the schools reported relatively few discipline problems, although some school officials reported that some individuals displayed disruptive patterns regarding "cooperativeness with school authorities and respect toward their peers." This finding suggests that the students in the school were typical children who displayed the usual range of problem behaviors, and so cannot be termed "elitist" in the usual sense of that term.

The Inner-City Private Elementary Schools study contains a pertinent report from parents who had a child in one of the targeted inner-city schools. Parents were asked to respond regarding their child's behavior since enrollment in the school. Thirty-five percent (1,412 parents) stated that the behavior was greatly improved; 32 percent (1,287 parents) said somewhat improved; 28 percent (1,112 parents) said the behavior was not changed; 4 percent (139 parents) said the behavior became worse.

The Inner-City report differed from the Greeley-Rossi and the Notre Dame findings in one special area, the influence of the home. Using statistical regression techniques, the study came to two important conclusions: (1) In the case of their students, "Family background factors do not overwhelm school impacts" and (2) "Quite the contrary, school factors appear to compensate for family background deficits." Where the other two research reports emphasized the importance of the home for collaboration with the school regarding behavior, the Inner-City report viewed the behavior-oriented factors within the school as of primary importance.

The four pertinent school factors viewed as the basis of the success of these schools were: "strong instructional leadership, a concept of shared work, a safe school climate, and clarity of mission and shared purpose." Many good public schools share these characteristics but the details of the fourth factor, clarity of mission and shared purpose, was distinctive of most of these predominantly religious schools. That factor was explained as involving combined efforts by administration and faculty for quality education, a supportive learning environment, shared "religious values and, more broadly, a moral concern for one's fellow human beings."

The importance of shared religious values in the Inner-City schools was confirmed in "repeated emphasis" in interviews with administrators, principals, and teachers. Furthermore, 94 percent of the parents of the pupils in the schools asserted that "learning moral values is essential" for their children. Since the majority of the pupils in these schools were not Catholic--the high percentage of non-Catholic pupils in Catholic inner-city schools is a recent development--they represent a "pluralistic" population. Hence, it would be hard to say that the shared religious values flow from home or parish traditions or beliefs though there very likely existed some shared moral values flowing from their basic Christianity. However, of the 63 private inner-city schools studied, 56 were Catholic, and 7 were either Lutheran or community-type (i.e., formerly Catholic schools which were taken over by the local community, usually with assistance of their former directors and usually retaining most of the school traditions). Their religious education (and undoubtedly factors that flowed from religious education like shared values, moral concerns, high ideals) was the main factor that influenced the good behavior of the children, since other elements in the curriculum were those which were required by the education departments of the various states.

Before ending this section on pertinent research, the reader is referred to a study which has not yet been fully published at the time of this writing. The Catholic High School: A National Portrait,[11] published by the National Catholic Educational Association. The 1985 volume contains only Part I of the study; it reports results of in-depth surveys of 910 principals of Catholic high schools. The section in the report that refers most directly to the content of this chapter is in Chapter 5, Religious Education. That chapter indicates that principals report strong emphasis in their schools on the three dimensions cited as central in To Teach as Jesus Did:[12] message (the teaching-learning of Christian doctrine); community (fellowship in the life of the Holy Spirit); and service to the Christian and to the entire human community. The principals ranked among their educational goals "building community" first and "spiritual development" second and reported that nearly half (46 percent) of their senior students were engaged in some kind of volunteer service programs. The reader is referred to the forthcoming Part II of this report for factual data based upon in-depth surveys of principals, teachers, and students in Catholic high schools in 1983. It should be interesting to determine whether the contents of this, the latest and most extensive survey of Catholic high schools, support the contentions of this chapter; especially interesting should be the data on students, such as their integrating religious beliefs into their lives.

In summary, a theme in the Greeley-Rossi, the Notre
Dame, and the Inner-City studies is that the contemporary
type of religious education is effective as judged by the
depth of knowledge (Notre Dame study) and the behavior of
pupils receiving it (Inner-City study). Below, we try to
identify and examine some distinctive factors in contemporary religious education which presumably were reflected
in the three studies. These factors are emphasized here
as a basis for the benefit of schools and teachers who have
not yet adopted the newer methodologies, but also for their
potential as guides for parents of children who are not
now receiving a Catholic education. Such parents can
adapt these factors in whole or in part in their attempts
to increase their children's religious and character literacy.
Most of these factors are incorporated in the section below
on modern religious education, in which there is a description of some methods used by the new catechesis or
kerygmatic approach.

ON INTERNALIZATION/INTERIORIZATION OF RELIGION

Before describing teaching methods, it seems appropriate to discuss the goals of the methods. The research
reports summarized above and reflection on learning problems of the young, together with the material presented
from Allport, suggest a need for an analysis of the problem of "interiorization" and possible means toward achieving it. That problem is an aspect of the more general
concern about how we adopt our values in life. Throughout this volume and the companion volumes the issue of
the imparting, teaching, or transferring of values from one
person to another is often implied and sometimes addressed.
Unfortunately, there are no necessarily effective formulas
for value transfer or for the interiorization of religion.
Nevertheless, there are some observations that can be made
concerning the facilitation of the process of interiorization.
The observations center upon the awareness of this factor
and upon the use of the best possible instructional methods
or strategies as described in the next section, entitled
Modern Religious Education.

Effective teachers or parents are aware of the distinction between those who have internalized their religion,
as opposed to those who have not. Hence, such teachers
and parents bring to their work an intensity and care that

befits the importance of religious education. Their empathy with the young is transparent and their affection genuine, even if at times they show "tough love." They work hard to develop healthy self-images among the young, and they uphold high, though realistic, goals for them. They are open in dealing with them, and do not refrain from revealing much about themselves. Once such parents and teachers have established a genuine relationship with the young, the sharing of religious values is facilitated since the young like to imitate the ways of thinking and acting that characterize those whom they admire. This intergenerational condition has probably been experienced by the reader, but there is no guarantee that it will be experienced by even those who are regarded as most admirable adults. That this happens sometimes but not at other times is part of the mystery of human relationships; there is no ready formula to explain it. However, the combination of the competent, conscientious teacher working toward interiorization of religious values, and use of varied modern teaching methods is likely to provide the best conditions for success.

MODERN RELIGIOUS EDUCATION

An older generation recalls religious education as consisting of dull lectures, the memorization of formulas, and the questions and answers of the catechism. Because of the importance placed by many generations on memorization, another generation tried to do away with that part of religious learning. Both extremes are clearly erroneous. Memorization of truly important materials has its place in religious education, as it does in history or in chemistry, but neither should it take first place in the learning hierarchy.

In the earlier approach to religious education when pupils were not engaged in memorization, they received a great many lectures or sermons on the topics that were regarded as important. Of course, the use of the lecture or verbal explanation of an issue continues to play an important part in all learning. However, contemporary religious education attempts to appeal to all human ways of learning, not only directly to one's memory and cognitive abilities. Some of these newer ways of teaching are described briefly below. Of course, these methods or

strategies of teaching are well known to modern professional teachers, but even they may take the occasion to
reflect on their use of these various methods, particularly
in relation to religious and value concepts. Furthermore,
the methods or strategies described briefly here may be a
source of information to parents who seek a greater variety
in religious instruction at home. The summary of newer
methods is, of course, incomplete, and presumes an in-
depth knowledge of appropriate religious material, careful,
prayerful preparation of the content of the lesson or unit,
and skillful use of the traditional chalkboard as a means
of emphasizing and clarifying the ideas being presented.
The following teaching methods, as alternatives to memorization and lecturing, will be briefly described: use of
visual materials, choice of the best possible printed material such as textbooks, lectures in an original and/or
personal vein, and group learning methods, including discussion. Fieldwork, such as appropriate volunteer service,
is another learning strategy and is described in a separate section.

Use of visual materials as a teaching methodology is
greatly assisted by developments in modern technology.
Reproductions of art masterpieces, film strips, educational
movies, and cassette video recordings are all available for
the illustration of Biblical materials, for historical and
geographical presentation of important religious places.
They can be presented on overhead projectors, opaque
projectors, video and film projectors. A wealth of visual
material is now available from many distributors, for instance, on the Land of the Bible, the Sacraments, religious
shrines, missionary activities, religions of various peoples,
and religious art. Most schools and religious education
centers have at least some of these visual materials in
their own collections, or they can be borrowed from a local
religious education center. The materials are usually accompanied by helpful teachers' guides. While most teachers
are aware of these instructional opportunities, parents
whose children are not receiving regular religious education in school or in successful religious education centers
should seek the loan of such materials for use at home.

The choice of the best possible printed materials,
such as textbooks, is an important decision made well
ahead of actual instruction. A careful evaluation of all
available materials, such as those housed in a diocesan
or college religious education center, includes a considera-

tion of the age and academic level of the students, as well as the correctness and attractiveness of the printed contents. Special care must be exercised in selection of textbooks because of the numerous defects that have been found in many of them. Many educators, including this writer, view it as a mistake to omit using a textbook. It is a definite advantage to learners to have their knowledge reinforced by written material. The textbook can be used as a regular source of ready reference for important religious information; it is likely to be retained by students if it is clearly written, well illustrated, and attractively printed. The need for the textbook and other printed materials is as important for home instruction as it is for learning and instruction imparted in schools.

Lectures in an original and/or personal vein are important in religious education. Every effort is made to dramatize the message, so as to avoid boredom. The teacher investigates all possibilities of visual materials as a means of increasing attention to the content of the lecture. Without getting into "ego trips" or centering the lecture on one's own history, it is appropriate that the teacher explain what the doctrine, sacrament, or unit being explained means in his or her life, or in the lives of others. Thus, the teacher is a "witness" to faith. Perhaps in the past lecturing and teaching have been too impersonal and thus the application of the doctrine was too difficult for students. For very specialized material, a guest lecturer may be invited. These days it is more and more likely that a full, appropriate lecture may be available on videotape, and the presenter may be a national figure with outstanding charismatic appeal. Alert religious education teachers are aware of these possibilities. Parents who are directing the religious education of their children can also be informed of these possibilities by ongoing contact with a religious education center and can be assisted in obtaining a loan of them.

In the attempt to dramatize lectures in religious instruction, a veritable gold mine is available in material culled from church history. This writer can recall still, some fifty years later, the sense of inspiration felt in a high school senior religion class which contained numerous units on church history. This was intimately linked with explanation of the various church doctrines which had been challenged in the course of the centuries. Of course, inspiring and dramatic incidents in the lives of saints and other exemplary figures in the history of the church fitted well into this course, and sparked the imagination of many students. There are as many heroic religious figures in the church today and in the recent past as there ever were, and their stories can be incorporated in lectures. The lives of such people as Dorothy Day, Mother Teresa, Pope John Paul II, Gandhi, Albert Schweitzer and countless missionaries (some of whom may be available for personal appearances as they make visits back to their "native air") are as appropriate as the stories of figures in the Scriptures. In using such history and such lives of exemplary people, care must be exercised to present well-established dimensions of their lives and to choose illustrations and conditions with which the young can identify.

Whether the regular presentation is by the teacher, a guest lecturer, or a videotape, it is important that religious education sessions be concluded with a question-and-answer period. This enables the teacher to respond to the intellectual challenges that are imparted, to clear up obscurities, and to encourage a deeper interiorization of the religious education message.

Discussions have come to play an important part in modern education. Unfortunately, some of those who use discussion in religious education do not realize the importance of preparation for profitable discussion sessions, for instance, by selection of challenging "stimulus" questions or even minidramatizations. The discussions in large or small groups may follow an instructional session, and they may be directed toward personalizing the main thrust of the instruction. Successful discussions are not used as an excuse for the teacher's lack of proper class preparation. A skilled discussion leader knows when to redirect the flow of the participants from detours and tangents. Discussions may be enlivened by use of specially prepared panel groups and by role playing, techniques which are developed at length in books on group guidance. Many group discussion leaders find it helpful to conclude the session with a summary of the varied viewpoints, the range of feelings expressed by the participants, the new knowledge or appreciation achieved, and such conclusions as the need for further information on specific topics.

As students in religious education become accustomed to the potential of discussions, they become more personally involved. They find that the general religious teachings can be discussed in personal terms with the group. (However, successful discussion leaders are on their guard to avoid some of the excesses of the values clarification movement in which pupils were put under great pressure to reveal personal matters and to declare their values when they did not care to do so.) If a healthy relationship develops between the teacher or discussion leader and the group, the discussion period of the religious education program can become a time of deep interiorization of religious and moral insights. In discussions as in lectures, the teacher or leader can model this interiorization through giving oral religious witness by stating precisely what the doctrine or subject being taught means in his or her life. Thus, in a real way the teacher or discussion leader becomes the role model to the learner in his or her internalization or interiorization of religion.

Evaluation of success regarding the various teaching methods described above and of genuine interiorization is extremely difficult and in the long run can be adequately tested only when one is faced with difficult choices later on in one's life. Yet, for practical purposes of evaluation we must be satisfied with the intermediate indicators of success that can be derived from external behaviors and well-tested knowledge as in the research reported in the earlier section on related research.

Now let us turn to two topics that are often elements of programs in moral education and character development to see how syllabi in religious education often deal with them. Thereby we can illustrate the special dimension that religious approaches offer as compared with humanistic approaches. We look to religious treatment of the themes of justice and of volunteer service to others.

JUSTICE AS A THEME IN RELIGIOUS/CHARACTER EDUCATION

Due perhaps to its emphasis in the Kohlberg paradigm of moral education, justice is a theme or important element in most programs of character education. The purpose of discussing justice in this section is to illustrate its relationship to various other important themes in a religious education and to illustrate the potential for integrated, religiously oriented character development through concern for justice and its correlates.

The justice movement among religious people has received special emphasis in recent years from publicity about injustices accorded minority groups (Japanese-Americans in World War II, American Indians, Blacks, Hispanics, working people, Jews, women, religious groups) and from reflection upon a series of important religious documents. For instance, Pope Leo XIII, as far back as 1891, wrote an encyclical, "Rerum Novarum," concerning injustices incurred by many workers in industry. In spite of numerous other important religiously oriented documents protesting injustice, there are some who see the concept of justice as a secular notion and thus a governmental concern and as opposed to that of charity (in the sense of love, not in the sense of alms giving) as a religious concept and so a concern of the churches. As a corrective of this view, the U.S. bishops recently asserted that justice and charity "are part of Christian social responsibility and are complementary. . . . Justice is the foundation of charity. . . . It is impossible to give of oneself in love without first sharing with others what is due them in justice." [13]

Many classical religious treatises on justice are found under the heading of duties of which the main categories are duties to God, to self, and to the neighbor. The focus of this section is upon the last category, duty to the neighbor, seen in the same perspective as one views oneself as made in the image of God, redeemed by Christ, and called to an eternal destiny. Hence, even in one's thoughts as well as one's words, all human beings are worthy of the respect we give ourselves. Their spiritual and moral health, their intellectual and cultural status, their material and physical necessities (food, health, housing, employment, health facilities, schooling, etc.) are the concerns of all who would be religious.

A development in recent years of the religious approach to justice on the part of religious persons is the more universal application of the principles of justice. "All people" and "neighbors" are really seen as embracing those who live anywhere and everywhere in the world, not just those who live next door. More and more, we are recognizing that we cannot just say to the ill housed and hungry at home or abroad, "Be warmed and be filled, and go in peace" (James 2:16). The call for human justice demands that feelings and convictions regarding justice be translated into actions. These may involve going abroad as a member of a team that assists refugees, raising funds for those exiled by an unjust government, protesting housing conditions, writing to legislators to correct unjust working conditions, attempting to help others both to be just to their employer and to seek justice for coworkers, seeing that procedures that exist to protect the rights of others are carried out exactly, writing or teaching as clearly and as strongly as possible on the theory and practice of justice, doing one's best to exemplify just practices in dealing with peers or with students, or being sensitive and sensitizing others to the need for ethics in professional and other human behaviors. The person who has deliberately adopted a sense of justice will consciously reject opportunities to defraud others. The just person is sensitive to the real scandal given to the young when adults boast of their "putting something over" others, whether the other be the government, the boss, or another.

Does justice mean something different to the person with a religious rather than a restrictively humanistic philosophy? Externally, their behaviors should be equally just regarding individuals and social structures. But the religiously oriented person has the conviction that his or her norms are given by a higher absolutely loving, absolutely just Authority, and so has an additional source for confidence and motivation concerning the meaning and importance of justice in his or her life.

VOLUNTEER SERVICE AND RELIGIOUS/
CHARACTER DEVELOPMENT

Mention was made above of the fact that many religious education programs now incorporate a segment of fieldwork in their syllabi. Let us examine that aspect of religious education as an element of character development and see how it compares with similar fieldwork that is primarily humanistic.

Together with teaching doctrine and building faith commitment, the ideal of serving others is emphasized as a goal in current religious education literature. The basic note is that, since Jesus Christ came to serve, not to be served (Matt. 20:28), His followers are called upon to show love for Him through service of others. Thus, from their earliest years, children can be prompted to "perform acts of kindness and compassion in the home and neighborhood."

It is increasingly becoming the practice of religiously oriented schools to induct pupils gradually into the concepts of service of others. The concepts that are involved are based upon the earliest Christian traditions, such as the instructions to new converts given by Sts. Peter and Paul that they take care of the poor (Galatians 2:10) and the very existence of deacons whose work was to "serve" the community (Acts 6:2). The tradition of hospitality was important in the various monastic institutions of Europe, and the nursing care of the sick and infirm was fostered not only by the humanistically motivated Florence Nightingale in Switzerland but by numerous religious women such as, in the United States, Mother Alphonse Hawthorne (Servants of Relief for Incurable Cancer), St. Elizabeth Ann Seton (Sisters of Charity), and Mother Angeline McCrory (Carmelite Sisters for the Aged and Infirm), who founded congregations whose work included service for the sick, the poor, the aged. Hence, Catholic Christians are not newcomers to the concept of service of others.

Concepts of service are based not only upon example and tradition, but upon Church teachings related to the development of a social conscience. Concern for others, based upon an awareness of human dignity, is the theme of numerous papal and bishops' documents which assert that religious people cannot turn their backs upon those who need special help. Instead, as individuals, they are asked to recall that the spirit of Christian faith is love of God as demonstrated to neighbor, that love is demonstrated more by deeds than by words, and that some practical actions of service should characterize the lives of all committed Christians.

Local conditions play a large part in the details of volunteer service opportunities. Some areas have a large number of elderly citizens who need help; there are the sick, the poor, the disenfranchised, the imprisoned, the disadvantaged, the handicapped. Many religious schools and religious organizations focus upon one or more of these groups. Those who do this volunteer service work believe that they are carying out the Second Greatest Commandment as enunciated by the Lord, to "Love your neighbor as yourself."

Whatever the type of volunteer service in which young people are engaged, and whatever the school they attend, it is important that their service activities be supervised and coordinated by someone who has and shares a mature view of service. Just doing the volunteer service isn't enough. The supervisor of volunteers, as a mature person (whose age is not important), can help others share a sense of respect for different ways of living, different ways of practicing belief in God, and different ways of expressing one's thoughts and feelings. Weekly group meetings of those doing service work can help all involved increase their sense of the wide range of local living conditions and human problems. Through insights achieved in the meetings, the volunteer service and its meaning can become personalized and interiorized. Discussions of volunteer work and sharing experiences may help to inspire some with goals of a lifetime service to others. Others may gain from the volunteer service a determination to do all they can as activists or legislators or perhaps just as voting citizens to right wrongs and improve the lot of people in need.

Service to those in need is by no means the exclusive prerogative of religious persons. Service clubs and service activities exist in public as well as in religious schools and in numerous nonreligious and religious organizations. Indeed, the recent increase in this kind of activity, especially for the handicapped, is viewed by some as among the more optimistic signs of our civilization, as foreseen by Father Teilhard de Chardin when he spoke of humans' likely "spiritual evolution." The importance of service as an aspect of adolescents' growth to genuine maturity is recognized in Ernest Boyer's[14] recent recommendation that service activities be incorporated into the school curriculum as a requirement and that academic credit be awarded for this work. In view of the increasing pervasiveness of volunteer service in our culture, the question arises: How do the religious and the nonreligious service programs differ?

Some of the ways in which the religiously oriented service volunteer differs from his or her counterpart who is primarily humanistically oriented have been implied above. While their external behaviors may be practically identical, the origin of their inspiration and their habitual view of the person of the client differ. The interpretation of experiences and the relatedness to the later living of one's life are likely to be influenced by the presence or absence of an important ingredient, one's belief in God, as a living and personal influence in our life, and the related belief that "Whenever you did it [feed the hungry

. . . take in the stranger . . . clothe the naked] for the least of my brethren, you did it for Me" (Matt. 25:40). The religiously oriented volunteer, somehow and mysteriously, sees Christ the Lord in the hungry, the stranger, the naked, and in that frame of mind, gladly extends help to those who represent Him.

In summary, this chapter has attempted to answer several important questions regarding the position that religious education is the preferred way to character development. The questions and answers follow. (1) In theory, why is religious education the preferred method? Briefly, the reply is that the religious perspective, including the nature of the person and the ultimate basis for responsibilities, extends to and moves the total human person more deeply than do other approaches. (2) Can one account for the differences in the behaviors of religious persons? In response, we used Allport's report of the positive effects of those who interiorized religion, in contrast to those in whom religion was less interiorized. (3) Are there research studies which confirm the position taken in this chapter? In reply, we turned to three research projects of the predominantly Catholic schools which attested to the moral development of pupils in the schools. (4) What is meant by the kerygmatic, or catechesis, approach to religious education, as used in some of the research, and how is it achieved? The term was explained, and recent teaching methods for personalizing and interiorizing religious teachings were reviewed. (5) Since many moral education programs emphasize justice, how does the religious approach to justice differ from others? The response emphasized the dignity of the person as provided by a religious vision. (6) How does the religious basis for volunteer service differ from that of other approaches? The reply is that there is a long religious tradition of seeing the Lord in those in need, and that there is an increasing awareness among religious people that the neighbors they should love as themselves are all fellow inhabitants of this globe.

NOTES

1. Pope John Paul II, "Apostolic Exhortation on Catechetics," Origins, 9 (1979), 343.
2. Gordon W. Allport, The Nature of Prejudice (Reading, Mass.: Addison-Wesley, 1954), p. 444.

3. Andrew M. Greeley and Peter H. Rossi, The Education of Catholic Americans (Chicago: Aldine, 1966), p. 168.

4. Reginald A. Neuwien, ed., Catholic Schools in Action (Notre Dame, Ind.: University of Notre Dame Press, 1966).

5. Ibid., p. 152.

6. Thomas Groome, Christian Religious Education (San Francisco: Harper & Row, 1980).

7. Gabriel Moran, Interplay: A Theology of Religion and Education (Winona, Minn.: St. Mary's Press, 1981), p. 37.

8. Kieran Scott, "Three Traditions of Religious Education," Religious Education, 79(3), Summer, 1984, p. 337.

9. Francis D. Kelly, "Evaluating Our Catechetical Efforts," Momentum, May 1983, pp. 13-14.

10. James G. Cibulka, Timothy J. O'Brien, and Donald Zewe, S. J., Inner-City Private Elementary Schools: A Study (Milwaukee: Marquette University Press, 1982).

11. The Catholic High School: A National Portrait (Washington, D.C.: National Catholic Educational Association, 1985).

12. To Teach as Jesus Did (Washington, D.C.: United States Catholic Conference, 1973), p. 9 (No. 30) and passim.

13. Sharing the Light of Faith: National Catechetical Directory for Catholics of the United States (Washington, D.C.: United States Catholic Conference, Department of Education, 1979), p. 94.

14. Ernest Boyer, High School: A Report on Secondary Education in America (New York: Harper & Row, 1983), pp. 202-15.

12
Television as a Moral Educator
Edmund V. Sullivan

If you ask the average teacher what he or she competes with for the minds and hearts of children as far as education is concerned, do not be surprised by the answer: television. This would not have been said of radio sixty years ago, which prompts a second question: "Why this difference between media?" One tentative answer is that Western culture has come increasingly under the influence of commercial interests outside both home and school, so that both parents and teachers compete with a new constellation of socialization agents in mass media personalities. The transmission of culture through socialization agents is a relational activity where the new generation comes into contact with the older one's cultural myths, values, and so on. The process is a dynamic interchange and in a sense there can be a reciprocity of roles between the generations. The older generation generally attempts to duplicate itself (that is, social formation or socialization) and the newer generation tends to forge changes in predominant cultural images (that is, transformation or social change). This process is dialectical and it should not be surprising that the valences change. It is safe to say that, in general, the older generation tends consciously or unconsciously to reproduce some of its dominant, accepted "cultural myths," the predominant cultural images by which a culture represents itself (Sullivan, 1980).

Culture is mediated; that is, its symbols and images are passed on by institutions. Obviously, the most important mediating institution in the socialization of children was the family structure. In simpler cultures it has been historically the only mediating device for cultural transmission. The second major mediating institution has been the school. Before the advent of the modern era, schools and family were the two main cultural mediators; that is, they carried or mediated the cultural messages to the younger generation. As already indicated, the twentieth century has seen a complete reversal of this process. In our own time, the family has been devastated as a cultural mediating device. Parents essentially relinquish this role to the schools where possible. This cultural transformation is quite complex and I cannot deal with this dramatic change for our present purposes. What I would like to call attention to is the advent of a new major mediating device for socialization in the twentieth century, that of the mass media. We will be focusing upon it in this chapter because it carries, in an unequivocal manner, the message of the central myths of "commodity culture."

When compared with parents and schools, the mass media—that is, newsprint, comics, radio, and television—are, at the same time, more anonymous and democratic. As opposed to parents, who concentrate their efforts on their own children and possibly their neighbors', the mass media are directed to a wider range of people, but with patently more utilitarian motives. In essence, the media are supported by modern advertising, whose main message is to sell products as commodities to people on a large scale as the correlate of mass production. It can be seen in some of the early advertising journals that the media were to conflict with the family. The advertising business both welcomed the demise of familial authority and, at the same time, was careful not to demystify all authority:

> Rather it pointed toward the commodity market and its propaganda to replace the father's authority. Business was to provide the source of a life-style, where before the father had been the dictator of family spirit. (Ewen, 1976, pp. 131-32)

The decline of direct parental authority can be seen in all of Disney's comics, where there is a total absence of parental figures. It is indicative that this should go unnoticed (Dorfman and Mattelart, 1975).

This chapter will self-consciously concentrate on television as a moral educator. This does not ignore the fact that we are presently in the midst of what appears to be another information revolution in the development and penetration of the computer technologies into our culture. I have discussed some specific issues around this phenomenon elsewhere (see Sullivan, 1983b). One thing is certain, the computer will not replace the television as a medium. Rather, it is an amplification and extension of television. Therefore, to restrict our discussion to television is simply to provide a focus for the reader in a chapter that will consider a medium as a powerful device for cultural transmission.

The average person takes television for granted. It is a household expense, like a car or a toilet. Yet it is much more important as a moral influence than we care to think because it is a symbol-making medium. As such, one should not discount its influence. Rose Golsen, in How Television Works and Works You Over, makes a penetrating observation:

> The power to dominate a culture's symbol-
> producing apparatus is the power to create
> the ambience that forms consciousness itself.
> It is a power we see exercised daily by
> the television business as it penetrates
> virtually every home with the most massive
> continuing spectacle human history has ever
> known. Wittingly and unwittingly, this
> business and its client industries set the
> stage for a never ending performance strip-
> ping away emotional associations that cen-
> turies of cultural experience have linked
> to patterns of behaviour, institutional forms,
> attitudes, and values that many cultures
> and subcultures revere and need to keep
> vigorous if they are to survive. The daily
> consciousness-raising sessions transmitted
> by television demonstrate the narrow range
> of alternatives selected by a handful of
> people as eminently worthy of attention
> and collective celebration. (Golsen, 1975,
> pp. 14-15)

MEDIA AND THE MORAL ACT

To speak of the mass media as a moral educator is to indicate that a particular type of communication system has the capacity to influence moral actions. To talk of a moral act being influenced, it is necessary to clarify the nature of the act being influenced. I have elsewhere indicated that the defining characteristics of a human act are its features of consciousness, intentionality, intention, responsibility, and significance (Sullivan, 1984). My own treatment of these features shares striking resemblances to Caputo, Samay, Nicgorski, and Ellrod in Volume 1 of this series, Act and Agent: Philosophical Foundations of Moral Education and Character Development and Knowles's treatment of human action in Volume 2, Psychological Foundations of Moral Education and Character Development. For my purposes here, I would like to amplify on the last two features since they define human action as at once moral and communicative.

Responsibility is one characteristic of a "human act" insofar as one is accounting for the actions of a person in terms of their desires, intentions, and purposes. Of necessity, in humans this involves the negative pole of action, that is, reflection. "Responsible action" has, therefore, as part of its ongoing process, a reflective component which in ordinary language we call deliberation (Sullivan, 1984). It follows that a fundamental condition of education is the fostering of moral conduct, which by my definition, is responsible action. The attribution of responsibility for an action is canceled altogether if it can be shown that the behavior was not governed, at least in some aspects, by intentions (Taylor, 1964). The deliberation involved in the reflective component of human action opens up the question of the autonomy or freedom of human action. The notion of a "deliberate action" assumes that, after the process of deliberation, there is a motive force which carries that action to some outcome or completion. Education is, in the best sense, the cultivation of responsible moral agency.

There are those who venture that education in goodness must mean education in value realization and that authentic moral education must involve the removal of all inertial obstacles which tend to block or deflect the positive direction of moral action. One of the issues that we must face in this chapter is whether the mass media foster

responsible moral action (i.e., are educational) or are inertial obstacles (i.e., miseducational) in relation to responsible human action. Before going into this issue, let
me turn to the feature of the human act as significant.

Elsewhere, I develop the notion that a human act
has a sign quality that makes it simultaneously an act
and an expression (Sullivan, 1984). Therefore, the sign
quality of a human act puts it in the category of a communicative event. A human act is not an isolated event,
but rather, relational. Therefore, there is no such thing
as a significant act in itself. The meaning or significance
of a human act is the place that it occupies in a network
of relationships (Chein, 1972). I assume, after Geertz
(1973), that significant human action is cultural action.
"Man is an animal suspended in webs of significance he
himself spun, I take culture to be those webs" (p. 5).
This notion will take on a deeper meaning later when we
consider Paolo Freire's notion of "cultural action for freedom" (Freire, 1974). What is important now is to establish
in the mind of the reader that "moral conduct" or "responsible action" exists within the framework of communications. My task will be to assess how mass communications influence moral actions.

MIRRORING: THE POSSIBILITY THAT
WE BECOME WHAT WE BEHOLD

It is often said that morality is fostered by good
example. It is also said that evil is fostered by bad example. There is an intuition here that we are strongly
influenced by the company we keep. There is also inter-
jected into this discourse the idea that individuals can
rise above their surroundings. This is usually said to
someone who cannot avoid bad company, as it were. What
is implicit in all of this is the belief that a moral point
of view, or lack thereof, is mediated through social influences. There is nothing astounding here, except that we
tend to forget the effects of normative influence. In some
working-class families, one of these influences is the television which interacts with the children more even than do
their parents (Sullivan, 1980). Although the school still
plays a significant role in the legitimation of culture, it
now has a contender in television. For example, before a
child reaches the age of 20 in this country, he or she will

have seen 350,000 television commercials. The average child, it is estimated, will have seen 20,000 commercial messages each year or more than three hours of television advertising a week (Sullivan, 1980). One might say that children keep a good deal of company with the ethos of consumption, for television is a mirror of commodity culture (Sullivan, 1980).

In order to consider the effects of social influences on moral character, one must not fall into the trap of thinking that those being socialized (children) are <u>passive</u> and those socializing (parents) are <u>active</u>. It is a mixture of both, as any parent will attest. What is important to consider from the side of such cultural socialization agents as parents, teachers, and mass media personnel is the extent to which they encourage a sense of agency in those whom they would try to influence. We should, therefore, judge socialization agents, such as parents, schools, and mass media, on their power to influence or detract from the development of moral agency (i.e., capacity for responsible action). While it can be said, in some instances, that parents and schools are frequently impediments to the fostering of responsible action, they are not the issue here. This chapter concerns the role of television in the fostering or impeding of moral agency. In this notion of mirror, it will be helpful to introduce the idea of images and imagining.

A mirror is a reflector. It can give us images of ourselves and our surroundings. When you look in the mirror, what you see is not yourself but your image or reflection. Depending on the qualities of the mirror, you may appear fatter, thinner, taller, or smaller; you may be flattered or miffed. The image may start you on a regimen of eating or not eating; the reflector can encourage or discourage certain types of action. Similarly, socialization agents are reflectors or mirrors of cultural codes. One part of a cultural code is its moral code, which signals whether actions are good or bad, worthy or unworthy, etc. As I said earlier, human action is embedded in webs of significance, part of that web being a culture's moral code. As it has developed in North America, where consumption is the major cultural action fostered for the attainment of the good life, television does reflect a moral code.

As a technological device, television has been around since 1925. It was not until the 1940s, however, that the

advertising industry saw the commercial possibilities that
this medium offered (Mander, 1978). Mander goes so far
as to say that television is the invention of modern advertising. Of all the other media mentioned, it is the most
active in the creation of images while reducing its watch-
ers to a relative state of passivity (Sullivan, 1980). For
example, whereas in radio you must create your own images
since only the audio is supplied, television does both.
That it works best for a viewer who is seated and in a
dark room, aids in the achievement of a passive state.
From there, Mander points out

> Every advertiser, for example, knows that
> before you can convince anyone of anything
> you shatter their existing mental set and
> then restructure an awareness along lines
> which are useful to you. You do this with
> a few simple techniques like fast-moving
> images, jumping among attention focuses,
> and switching moods. There's nothing to
> it. (p. 197)

The socially constructed nature of television makes
it more of a private event, even though the viewer-listener
is receiving communications. A morally responsible actor
is not a private actor. As I have already said, a human
act is an expression which has as one of its distinguishing
characteristics, significance. Significance implies that
moral action has a public nature. It is a premise of
commercial television that the viewer is a consumer rather
than an actor. Whereas a responsible actor deliberates,
reflection is the enemy of commercial interests. Modern
advertising is designed to short-circuit reflection and deliberation, because your judgment may arrive at a different
conclusion than the product being advertised.
    There are some research indications that television
viewings tend to disengage analytical thinking (Nelson,
1980). This finding does not mean that it is impossible
to be analytical while viewing, but it is not a normal
outcome of conventional viewing:

> Thus, as viewers, it is possible to watch
> television in an analytical-critical frame
> of mind: noticing specific camera angles,
> camera distances, sound-image and rela-

tionships, the use of moving camera, etc.,
and determining the extent to which such
techniques constitute to over-all meaning.
This kind of attentive viewing engages both
hemispheres rather than putting one on
"hold" [the left]. Yet the typical viewing
situation is one which discouraged this
kind of critical attentiveness. (Nelson,
1980, p. 30)

TV AND THE DECLINE OF PUBLIC LIFE

Moreover, the advent of commercial television as a
cultural institution follows a steady development that can
be characterized as a decline in "public life." This decline has been building up since the nineteenth century
(Sullivan, 1983a). The paradox here is that the decline
in public presence is synonymous with the steady advance
of communications technologies, which presently have
reached revolutionary proportions. What has increasingly
occurred since 1945 is the indirect mediation of significant
events through the new technologies provided by the media.
Without other forms of public expression, these vicarious
events become our public rituals. We depend on them as a
means of communication with a wider world than our own
immediate surroundings. The turning point for this was
the assassination of President Kennedy in 1963 (see Goethals,
1980). Television was the focal point for a national ritual.
It has increasingly taken on this role since that time.
With satellite communications the viewing audience for
major public events, such as a royal wedding, is greater
than for any prior events in the whole history of the
human race.

We are now in the midst of what is being called a
"communications revolution." It is a revolution because we
are said to be moving, in a rather dramatic fashion, from
an industrial to a communications society. There are some
indications that something of the nature of a "cultural
revolution" is taking place. Increasingly, our way of life
and our cultural interests are being molded by the new
communications technologies. Many North Americans, at
least, wake up to early morning programming via TV,
commute in a car where a radio gives them traffic reports,
news, and financial information, etc. Some watch children's

programming, soap operas, game shows, health, beauty, and exercise programs, etc., during the day. Some watch the evening news, more will congregate to watch programs such as "Dallas," or detective crime stories. The less socially sensitive members of the family may tune out the spuriously public event of night-time TV watching and tune into another world offered by the Walkman. Others will read a newspaper. Some will leave the room and go to their new personal computer to play games. In sum, examples underline the dependence that our culture is developing on communications technologies. It is likely, in a typical North American family, that each individual in that family will have been spoken to by TV figures more than they have spoken to one another.

Moreover, what is interesting and important to note about these communication technologies is that the programs and the commercial interests which sponsor them proceed on the assumption that there is a public to be formed (i.e., a passive public) to certain commercial and consumption values. Kavanaugh (1981) refers to these values as the "commodity form." What is very evident in conventional commercial programming of whatever variety, be it news, soap, game shows, etc., is that there is no expectation that you will go out into the streets and do something other than consume the advertised products. In fact, the main objective of a network such as CBS, be it radio or television, is to keep the viewer or listener tuned in, in order to hear the commercials. Many programs have a hooker advertisement for some of the fare to be seen later than evening. Richard Sennett makes the same point:

> The mass media infinitely heighten the
> knowledge people have of what transpires
> in the society, and they infinitely inhibit
> the capacity of people to convert that
> knowledge into political action. You cannot
> talk back to your T.V. set, you can only
> turn it off. Unless you are something of a
> crank and immediately telephone your
> friends to inform them you have tuned out
> an obnoxious politician and urge them also
> to turn off their T.V. sets, any gesture of
> response you make is an invisible act.
> (Sennett, 1978, p. 283)

In the process of discussing the new technologies of mass communications we have moved to the opposite of public expression, that of the <u>privatizing</u> of consciousness and human experience. It seems contradictory to say, for example, that a viewer, having increased access to world events via the evening news, should be privatized in terms of her or his own consciousness. Nevertheless, there is a paradox here which needs elucidation. The media give viewers access to many events outside their immediate awareness, but in a form that leaves one as a private spectator to the events seen. The viewer is asked to make no public commitment on the basis of the communication. It is done in the privacy of one's own home; therefore, at the level of structure, it is a private experience.

Television, as already indicated, is also monological in form. There is the program communicator and the listener. People are not encouraged to discuss and problematize what they are seeing or hearing. For each viewer or hearer it is a private and intimate event between the communicator and the individual. For this reason I call this an event of "privatized consciousness." Because of its privatized nature, public mass communications avoid public scrutiny. The television is as familiar to the family as the family pet; it's taken for granted. At the same time, it is the reflector or mirror of the most powerful commercial interests of our culture (Smythe, 1981).

Let me now make some summary statements before proceeding to some new issues. I have characterized the human act as conscious, intentional, intending, responsible and significant (cf. Sullivan, 1984). I have specifically elaborated the characteristics of responsibility and significance because they amplify the <u>moral</u> and <u>public</u> nature of human action. A moral act is a responsible act that involves deliberation in order for it to be called a free act. It is public because it is an expression that opens on a "world": it is significant. It seems to me that the task of the moral educator is to foster institutions which encourage human acts which are responsible and significant. Part of that moral education is to eliminate or, at least, raise the problem regarding those institutions that reduce us to irresponsibility and insignificance and encourage us to be patients rather than human agents (Sullivan, 1984).

Because of the powerful influence of television as an inertial obstacle to human agency, there is a positive case to be made for problematizing this medium as part of a program in moral education. Let me now suggest some parameters for the development of a problem-posing experience with television.

THE MORAL ACT AS CULTURAL ACTION

The idea that a moral act is responsible and significant assumes a "culture" which can enhance or deplete one's responsibility and significance as a moral actor. In other words, moral action is not simply an individual action; it is at the same time cultural action (Sullivan, 1984). Moral action and the development of character must be seen as a gift from one's society or culture (Nicgorski and Ellrod, Volume 1): the formation of character takes place within the womb or matrix of one's culture. Every culture produces a set or cluster of images which, in some way, characterizes the important concerns that culture must deal with in order to be called a culture. There are images for social maintenance and social change, which can be combined or separate. Either way, these images become part of the symbolic system of the child as he or she moves toward adulthood. Television is a medium par excellence of these images (Sullivan, 1980). The issue of control over our symbol-making capacities has some important consequences for the cultivation, or lack thereof, of moral action. Every stable culture has within it dominant symbols which rehearse why a culture is what it is and also symbols of what it ought to be. Thomas Groome refers to these symbol systems as stories and visions. The story is the linkage of the past into the present. The vision is the linkage of the present into the future. These are not distinct, but the dynamic interplay of humankind's need for stability (story) and change (vision). It is in this interplay that cultural values are created, maintained, and altered. Elsewhere I refer to the cultural story as its habitus, or that dynamic within a culture that preserves our cultural memory.

Through the stabilizing aspects of the cultural story or habitus, individuals are given a continuity with the past. This perception of order and continuity is buttressed by "ideological symbols" which give a sense of stability and inevitability to a particular cultural synthesis. To live is to change, however, and any culture which denies this will eventually die. A culture's vision is its ability

to continue coherent change. I call this vision the cultural project. The project is that dynamic within a culture that augments a future; it is the work we do today
for a tomorrow. Because of the transformative nature (i.e.,
challenged form) of the cultural project or vision, members are given a projection into the future. This perception of cultural change is buttressed by utopian symbols
(i.e., the net yet) which give a sense and direction to
cultural change. A culture's perspective or value consensus lives ambiguously within this story and vision.

It is important to understand that these symbol systems are not separate at the level of practical life. Any
culture is a complex mixture of a dominant story and project and nondominant alternatives. Western culture, in our
case North American culture, is the receiver of a dominant
story and project that has been developing over several
centuries. While I cannot go into the complexity of this
history, I would like the reader to attend to the contemporary version of that dominant myth (i.e., cultural story
and vision) as it is reflected in the culture's most important medium of communication, television. It is here that
one can see rehearsed our culture's habitus and project
(i.e., ideological and utopian symbols).

Let us first notice that the communicator addresses
us on the TV as individuals, rather than as groups, and
that the individual, for all intents and purposes, is a
receiver of information. We are individuals who have a
right to own, a duty to consume, and the cultural task of
believing that this is the best of all possible worlds. It
is the cultural story of consumer capitalism; its main cultural memory is that we have consumed yesterday and
therefore have a right, indeed an obligation, to consume
today. We also come to learn that there are those who
know more and those who know less; as a viewer, we happen to be the one who knows less.

We are never asked to use our judgment: We are
to rely on the judgment of "experts." With rare exceptions,
they never problem pose their expertise so we, in effect,
accept their judgments as absolute. At the level of viewing we come to realize that although all people are equal,
some nevertheless are more equal than others. Thus merit
becomes an essential caveat to our notion of equality.
Therefore, at the level of media images, men are said to
be equal to women. At the same time, the portrayal of
men's roles, in contrast to women's, shows the male species

to be more important and significant. The same applies
when capital and labor, whites and blacks, first and third
world, are considered (Sullivan, 1983a). Further, one of
the dominant actors within our culture is not a person but
technology.

Although it is not a person it is personified and we
come to believe that technology accomplishes cultural tasks.
For example, a multinational such as United Technologies
presents advertisements depicting technology as a cultural
actor and transformer of our world. Here we come to believe that technology creates culture, rather than being
the by-product of a cultural consensus. What is absent
from all of these commercials is the "human agency" and
judgment which decides how our technological inventions
come to fruition. For example, nuclear reactors don't just
happen, but are the outcome of human decisions, which are
not shown in these commercials (Sullivan, 1983a).

The cultural vision or project of the dominant myth
is the idea of <u>progress</u>. Progress symbols project the vision that we go forward gradually but inevitably. The
mass media encourage us to think that we can move forward best by not questioning the integrity of the dominant
cultural story. Thus the agents of utopian change remain
the same as the agents of the cultural story. They are
capitalist white men from the first world. Progress achieves
equality by molding all within the confines of the dominant
myth. This is done by exploiting nature or manipulation.
It is the cultural myth of mastery over stewardship.

In addition, the utopian symbol of progress constantly erodes the cultural story by tying it to the "myth of
consumption." The products or the effects that we have
acquired from products are constantly eroded by new products for consumption. Thus, the car, toothpaste, or stereo
that we bought yesterday is no longer adequate, given the
new line of commodities. The only stability in the story
is the process of consumption itself and not the products.
Although it is never the center stage of TV programming,
it is intimated that lethal armaments, although undesirable,
are inevitable necessities for the maintenance of progress.

I might add that all of this cultural myth making
can be done in the privacy of your own living room. It
is best done when the communication is private and unquestioned. Thus, a public political life in which we
make judgments is not encouraged. The TV frequently
eclipses the need for public rituals that go beyond address-

ing the individual by providing quasipublic events, such as the football Super Bowl. It is interesting that a sports event of this kind could assume such prominence. However, upon closer scrutiny, it becomes clear why this is so. The event extols the nation with a flag ceremony, male dominance, technology, competition, and merit rewarded in the games "star" system. There is even a moment of "ideological silence" to pray for the people of Poland.

Commercial television,* then, if looked at carefully, allows one to codify the dominant cultural story and vision. It is the dominant story and vision because commercial television is the forum for the most powerful commercial interests in our society. They sponsor the programs. It is within this dominant story and vision that we individually and collectively attempt to make our way as responsible and significant moral actors.

What I would like to consider now is the extent to which the dominant cultural story and vision increase or detract from our capacities to be moral actors within culture.

CONSUMER CAPITALISM: THE DOMINANT
CULTURAL STORY AND VISION

May I say at the outset of this section that it is essential for people to have a sense of order (i.e., habitus) in order to perform responsible action. Freedom is built on an ordered social fabric (Marris, 1974); a sense of order is the matrix for responsible and significant action. Simone Weil, the French philosopher, dramatizes the need for a stable social fabric:

The first of the soul's needs, the one which touches most nearly its eternal destiny, is

---

*Given that there is now a new mode with cable television, one can ask whether there will be significant shifts as a result of noncommercial ventures. At this point, I would speculate that cable television will not change the offerings significantly. The same group that produce commercial programs provide programs for cable. Culturally, I do not think cable television is shifting the media industry significantly.

> order; that is to say, a texture of social
> relationships such that no one is compelled
> to violate imperative obligations in order
> to carry out other ones. It is only where
> this, in fact, occurs that external circum-
> stances have any power to inflict spiritual
> violence on the soul. (Weil, 1971, p. 18)

Weil is saying that a culture's "sense of order" is
an antidote to violations of the soul which, as she states
it, are the negations to one's sense of responsible moral
action. I maintain that the dominant story and vision of
commercial capitalism has progressively eroded our moral
sense in the twentieth century. The dominant story and
vision of the mass media mirror is not moral action, but
consumer action. The intent of a commercial is not to encourage you to be a moral agent. Its objective is to pene-
trate any sense of order or resistance you might have to
the message and thus render you a passive subject with
consumption needs.

Media carry the messages of legitimation and mass
media, as we shall see, help to manipulate public opinion
into consumptive patterns of commodity culture. Stuart
Ewen gives a current history of the new mass media and
its systematic attempts to manipulate public opinion through
advertising. In North America, a significant turn of
events took place around 1920. Up to that time there was
a considerable amount of labor unrest, which focused upon
both working conditions and wages. Concentrations of
wealth (e.g., those of Rockefeller and Ford) increased the
resentment against these "captains of industry." By 1920
North American labor was receiving better wages and there
were significant attempts to bring the working people in
line with industry.

One of the carrots was to sell labor on the idea of
the need to consume products. With higher wages, it was
found that labor could buy more products and this stimu-
lated industry. The question was, how could the mass
population come to accept poor working conditions which
many industrial jobs have as a natural outcome of mass
production? The consensus was to draw the attention of
the public away from the alienating production process and
focus it upon the attractiveness of the products to be consumed or purchased as the outcome of that process. To
this day, it is extremely rare for an advertisement to
show a product in the making.

This refocusing away from production to products was to be accomplished through advertising. The legitimacy of the capitalist world order would be achieved not by coercion symbolized by the presence of the "captains of industry." Rather, a more anonymous group of people (the ad men and women) would achieve this through the manipulation of the public's consciousness on a mass scale. Ewen calls advertisers the "captains of consciousness." The message would be common to the population at large. In essence and in all of its guises, that message would be the advertising pitch for the consumption of products. We seem to take all of this for granted for in advertising we live and move and have our being, but one must realize that this is an invention of the twentieth century (Sullivan, 1980).

Cultural stability is accomplished through the education of our children, yet in a real sense children bring new realities into our world. In one sense, there is a feeling of hope for the new generation in our elders. This occurs partly by accident through a certain slippage in the socialization process. As we have already indicated, parents and schooling are partly responsible for the reproductive process of culture, but in the twentieth century a significant new organ of socialization has, in some significant ways, replaced, or at least encircled, these traditional socializers. In 1964, television as a medium created the "child market" which specifically pitches its programming at children from 3 to 11 years of age (Golsen, 1975). Television enters almost every home, rich and poor alike, and makes no literacy demands (Mander, 1978). It is, if I may be facetious, a very democratic instrument. In their own distinct way, all of the mass media serve the cause of consumer culture. As Dorfman and Mattelart point out about the Disney comics:

> As we have observed, all the relationships
> in the Disney world are compulsively con-
> sumerist; commodities in the marketplace
> of objects and ideas. The magazine is
> part of the situation. The Disney indus-
> trial empire itself arose to service a so-
> ciety demanding entertainment; it is part
> of an entertainment whose business it is
> to feed leisure with more leisure disguised
> as fantasy. The cultural industry is the

sole remaining machine which has purged
its contents of society's conflicts, and
therefore, is the only means of escape into
a future which otherwise is implacably
blocked by reality. It is a playground to
which all children (and adults) can come,
and which very few can leave. (pp. 306–
307)

At this point, I would like the reader to understand
that I do not believe that people are inherently passive
and pacified by consumer images. We bring to these media
a certain complicity with our dominant culture:

It is obvious that as children, teenagers,
and adults, audience members come to the
TV tube with rich past experience, with
commodities-in-general. They have observed and evaluated old and new models
of products on the street, in the homes of
friends and peer group members, and on
the persons of people they see at the job
front, the school, and in all other social
relationships (including transportation
vehicles). They will also have discussed
with family members, friends and strangers
the merits and demerits of the old and new
models in any of a thousand different social contexts. (Smythe, 1980)

At some level we must assume responsibility for the
lives we lead or are prepared to tolerate. It would be
educationally dishonest to blame the mass media for our
passivity before commercial images of the good life. At
the same time, we cannot ignore the power of the mass
media as a powerful instrument for value formation within
our culture today. Moreover, educators must come to terms
with the fact that a medium such as television is a moral
education into the dominant cultural story and vision of
North American culture. It is the bard for the glorifica-
tion of technological wizardry, consumption, competition,
individualism, narcissism, etc. (Sullivan, 1983c).
The anchorpersons for the evening news are now assuming the legitimacy of cardinals in time past. Walter
Cronkite was revered more than presidents and trusted

more than clergy. This new class of experts extol the values of expertise and technology. Technological experts are constantly marched out to explain to the unwashed public the significance of an event. This is not restricted to the news. A football game is a national ritual for those in the U.S.A. The Super Bowl pulls out all the stops on the wonders of science and technology. Statistics, experts, bards of the turf all converge on the event, the game proper being a small portion of a larger extravaganza (Sullivan, 1983c). If McDonald's does it all for you and Walter Cronkite says "that's the way it is," where in this discourse is the opening for your own capacities for critical judgment on cultural events? Without a sense of resistance to our present dominant cultural forms, our capacities for moral actions are rendered inert. This is irresponsibility and social anomaly.

NONDOMINANT CULTURAL STORIES AND VISIONS: CULTURAL RESISTANCE TO THE DOMINANT FORMS

The general description of the dominant cultural story and vision does not exhaust the stories and visions within a complex culture such as our own. There always exist within a culture oppositional stories and visions. Normally, these currents are contained and do not challenge the dominant myth (Sullivan, 1983c). In the normal course of events, the dominant cultural form is said to be hegemonic (see Gramsci, 1971). Hegemony refers to a form of ideological control in which dominant social practices, beliefs, and values are reproduced and solidified through a range of institutions (e.g., schools, church, and, in the present case, television). The hegemonic presence of the dominant cultural story and vision is not restricted to only mass media communications. Hegemony, because of pervasiveness, relates to all major spheres of social existence. It is convenient here to consider what Kellner (1978) identifies as the four major ideological realms: (1) the economic realm, which encompasses the ideologies of production, exchanges, distribution, etc.; (2) the cultural realm, encompassing the ideologies of culture, values, mass media, etc.; (3) the political realm, encompassing ideologies of the state, legal-judicial system, police, military, etc.; and (4) the social realm, encompassing ideologies of the private sphere, family, education, social groups, etc.

If the powerful legitimations of modern capitalism exert themselves with such a dominating force (i.e., hegemony) in all ideological realms, it would seem that there is no room for any independence from this pervasive consciousness. To say that our personal worlds are not powerfully determined (i.e., reproduced) under the hegemony of capitalism would be patently naïve. Almost all social classes in our society adopt the powerful consumer values of the dominant culture, even if some of those classes are hardly in a position to consume. Nevertheless, we do see breaks in the dominant form. Sartre (1968) in defining his notion of the human project declares that, "every man is defined negatively by the sum total of possibles which are impossible for him; that is, by a future more or less blocked off" (p. 95).

How could this be if the hegemony we have just spoken of is all pervasive? Left at this point, we are locked into a total determinism of reproduction ("Whatever has been will be"). Raymond Williams (1973) introduces the notion of "oppositional forms" to the dominant ethos as a way of handling this problem:

> We have to think again about the sources
> of that which is not corporate of those
> practices, experiences, meanings, values,
> which are not part of the effective dominant
> culture. We can express this in two ways.
> There is clearly something that we can call
> alternative to the effective dominant culture
> and there is something we can call opposi-
> tional in a true sense. The degree of ex-
> istence of these alternative and oppositional
> forms is itself a matter of constant histori-
> cal variation in real circumstances. (p. 206)

Williams (1973) identifies two oppositional forms to the hegemony of the dominant culture. A residual is in essence a carryover from a previous historical period. The presence of a residual form is indicative that some experiences, meanings, and values which cannot be expressed or verified in terms of the dominant culture are, nevertheless, lined on the basis of the residue of some previous social formation. A certain nostalgia for a past cultural synthesis can be laced with romantic utopianism or a cultural pessimism. Values conserved from a previous epoch are remembered and extolled. A sense of history or lost history is intimated in the rejection of the anomaly of the present dominant commercial form. This nostalgia can be held with a sophisticated criticism of present values and, in many cases, a repulsion at the moral outcomes of our present cultural values. I consider the general orientation of the Wynne article (Chapter 4 above) to be exemplary of a residual value system. Without being the slightest bit pejorative, one could characterize a residual position as both reactionary and conservative. It is reactionary in the sense that a residual system is a reaction to a dominant system or process. It is conservative in the sense that certain historical values are considered to be worthy to be conserved (i.e., respect for parents).

To speak of an "emergent form" in opposition to the dominant culture is to assume that new meanings and values, new practices, new significances and experiences are continually being created (Williams, 1973). The emergent form, like the residual form, questions the dominant cultural images but does not retreat from those images to an earlier cultural synthesis. What we see in emergent forms is the culture's development of a new set of moral concerns that have not been on the culture's moral agenda up to now. The concerns of ecologists for the environment, feminists for gender domination, the peace movement, etc., are some of the new moral agendas that our culture is facing. The stories and visions for these nascent concerns are in the making and are thus emergent.

To be a moral actor within these types of concerns demands new responsibilities and significances. Part of the problem of realizing new moral responsibilities is the veritable crowding out of these oppositional images within the media organs of the dominant culture (see Cover, 1983; Kavanaugh, 1983; Slinger, 1983). The onslaught of mass media images acts as a veritable eclipse, overriding oppositional images. If one thinks that part of what constitutes a moral action is deliberation and critical reflection, then it is necessary to come to terms with factors which discourage deliberation. Why deliberate when there are "experts"? Does not TV extol the value of expertise in its day-to-day programming? Television suggests that technological expertise makes unnecessary our need for deliberation and reflection. Technological experts are not only there to sell products in the programming. The experts are constantly marched out to explain to the audience public the meaning of events. This hermeneutical exercise is what Paolo Freire (1974) calls "naming the world." The main function of the larger commercial venture, of which programming is only a part, is to make you a consumer rather than an actor. Advertisers frequently talk about "penetrating an audience" (Ewen, 1976). The image it conveys to me is that of an invader. At the level of culture it is what Paolo Freire (1974) calls "cultural invasion":

> Cultural invasion, which like divisive tactics and manipulation, also serves the end of conquest. In this phenomenon the invaders penetrate the cultural context of another group, in disrespect of the latter's potentialities, they impose their own view of the world upon those they invade and inhibit creativity of the invaded by curbing their expression. (pp. 150-51)

I call the reader's attention to the last sentence in the above quote where it is indicated that creativity is linked to expression. I have already indicated that moral action is an expression which must have significance and responsibility (i.e., deliberation). In order for moral action to be significant, it is necessary to reflect and deliberate on those institutions which culturally act as a narcotic on moral awareness. This moral awareness is what Freire (1974) calls "critical awareness." It is a reflective cultural action (praxis) which poses problems about one's circumstances and is open to new ideas and new ways of looking at "taken for granted" cultural realities. The normal communication framework of TV is monological in nature. Critical awareness through the problem posing of media programming moves the situation to that of a dialogue. Linguistically, education for a critical (deliberation) consciousness has, as an essential ingredient, dialogue with one's world and events. This renders the person involved in this dialogue less prone to hyperbolic images to mystify events in the world (McDonald's does not do it all for you).

THE FORM OF A CRITICAL PEDAGOGY

Within our culture today there are emergent themes
which are oppositional to the dominant social mythology of
capitalism. Frequently these oppositional forms are not
coordinated into a larger social expression of opposition
(i.e., a movement). Thus, many oppositional strains within
our culture exist as independent expressions of oppositions
(e.g., ecology, labor concerns, third world solidarity movements, peace movements). At times, these oppositional
strains converge on a social concern (e.g., peace movement
activities), but this is the exception rather than the rule.
In addition, the mass media accent their differences and
cover up their similarities as oppositional currents to the
dominant social mythology of capitalism. Rather than being viewed as resistance to the dominant myth, these oppositional strains are frequently characterized within the
mass media as simply deviance from the accepted cultural
norm (i.e., hegemony).
     In a very real sense, the pervasive onslaught of
images acts as a veritable eclipse, trivializing oppositional images. The media act as a "cultural invader"
(see Freire, 1974), that is, because they rule culturally oppositional forms of their creative significance within the
dominant culture. I use the term creative significance because as moral agents our expressions must have (and be
seen to have) the qualities of significance and responsibility (i.e., deliberation). In order for oppositional expression to be significant, it is necessary to reflect and deliberate on those institutions which act in culture as a narcotic to critical oppositional awareness.

Culturing of Resistance

One must accept, as a given within present day
popular culture, that the mass media are a popular molder
of the dominant cultural values of capitalism. It is,
therefore, politically obtuse to treat the media as a peripheral concern in a liberatory educational praxis. It is
now possible to use media programming as a curriculum for
a critical pedagogy of our cultural values. With video
playback machines, the viewer now has a chance to control
and edit dominant images and reflect on their influence
for mounting the oppositional currents. Therefore, a critical media pedagogy confronts dominant images (i.e., resistance) rather than withdrawing from them (as if ignorance

could detract from their cultural power).   With a playback, the viewer assumes a modicum of control so as to gain a footing to problem pose dominant images (see Freire, 1974).

This media image should be problem posed in groups where people can have a dialogue about the cultural realities that form their awareness.   The normal viewing of TV, for example, does not allow dialogue and usually the viewers do not converse with one another (i.e., monological). Under the hegemony of the mass media, we have been cultivated as passive consumers of information.   Therefore, a critical pedagogy of the mass media would be a culture of resistance to the dominant cultural myths of liberal capitalism.   The need for a critical pedagogy, of course, will only be experienced when there is a sense that the dominant cultural myths are problematic to human survival and enhancement.

What I am saying may first appear contradictory, given that the media communications system is a veritable communications eclipse around transformative and oppositional cultural stories (habitus) and visions (project). The cultural domination of the media presents a practical problem for oppositional currents within mass culture. Problem posing a medium such as television has the effect of giving one easy access to the dominant myth making in our culture.   Since we are culturally saturated with these stories and visions, it is important to assess the effect they have on us.   This is a first step in a problem-posing process (i.e., critical awareness).

To explore media images further, one does not have to devise complicated learning processes.   For example, a simple way to problem pose television programming is to ask, "what is left in and what is left out of a program? Who benefits from what is left in and what is left out?" These probes are purposively simple because they tap into what Gramsci (1974) calls the public's "good sense."   This is there to be developed and does have to be contained. One can see this good sense, or critical ability, when you ask children to do some reflection on TV commercials.   You can see this "good sense" when you problem pose soap operas in a women's reflection group.   It is a latent awareness, in the viewers, that media images conceal more than they reveal and that the concealment serves to subjugate the viewers' awareness of real social processes.

Developing Societal Projects

Developing resistance to media images as a critical pedagogy cannot be an end in itself. The culturing of resistance can be only one aspect of a deliberative moment in critical pedagogy. In a certain manner of speaking, resistance is a negative moment which has the potential to reveal the normally concealed condition of domination. To reiterate, domination or oppression operates when the agency of one's person or group (i.e., their consciousness, intentionality, intentions, responsibility, and significance) denies that of the other person or group. This situation for those dominated turns its agent conditions listed above into their opposite. Thus, for consciousness we have repression or concealment, for intentionality we have withdrawal or privatization, for intentions we have an absence of goal orientation or rootlessness, for responsibility we have dependency, and for significance we have meaninglessness or anomie (Sullivan, 1984). This is the condition of the consumer vis-à-vis the mass media.

The education of resistance to mass media images simply names the oppression and codes existing power relations. Thus reflection on the media cannot be considered as complete unless it opens on and is motivated by the domain of politics in the public sphere (e.g., schooling, state apparatuses, work settings, etc.). The latter cannot be done in front of a television. It is in the public sphere that the world can be named and this is where the action of agents (not consumers) becomes cultural action that has significance (it means something). McDonald's will not do it all for you anymore than Walter Cronkite could have told us, without question, that "that's the way it is." A critical pedagogy serves the educational function of helping actors to "name the world" with their own reflective judgment.

A FEW EXAMPLES

I close with a selected set of examples which are only suggestive of the particular form that a critical pedagogy of mass media might take in specific instances. It seems to me that it is possible to use the media in an infinite number of ways for cultural reflection. One can raise questions about peace, ecology, health care, sexual stereotyping, corporate images, labor images, to name a

few. I will here suggest three areas in which the reader
must realize are my own idiosyncratic examples.

Children's Values

The case can be made that children's cultural values
can be strongly influenced by a medium such as television
(Sullivan, 1980, 1983a,b). A teacher who would like to
have children reflect critically on their values concerning
consumption, sex roles, sports, attitudes toward violence,
etc., can easily utilize popular programming. One could
take the Saturday morning children programming and explore values in our culture. Commercials can be reviewed
and heroes and heroines can be discussed as a way that
children will see the images which are considered important within our culture. When the media are problem posed
in this manner, children can achieve a certain distance
from the emphasis on consumption, competition, and violence which is so pervasive on commercial television's
children's programming (Sullivan, 1980).
This is the place where children can explore alternative cultural options to their media images (e.g., peaceful resolution to problems, cooperation vs. competition).
It is a place where children can explore the limitations of
TV cultural images while watching popular programs. This
can be done by editing commercials and programs. Since
a video playback machine can freeze frames, one is allowed a modicum of control over images for more conscious
deliberation of dominant cultural images (i.e., agency).
Surprisingly, children have what Gramsci (1971) calls the
"good sense" to assess commercial images critically which
saturate the programming directed toward them in the media.

Women's Issues and the Mass Media

The women's movement is one of the emergent oppositional forms dealing with exploitation along gender lines.
Careful attention to the media presentation of sex roles
indicates the dominant values of commodity culture vis-à-
vis women. A judicious editing of advertising can be very
revealing when considering the exploitation of women as
commodities. The recent film Killing Us Softly is a collection of advertisements which has the dramatic effect of

coding the attitudes of modern advertising toward women. Women are constantly depicted as fickle, temperamental, and sexual objects. In conventional advertising there is no sense of a project for women. Women exist for the project of men. They are constantly pictured as adornments to commodities or to men. A sustained look at modern advertising also reveals the high tolerance that our culture has toward violence to women. The recent documentary film of the National Film Board of Canada, Not a Love Story, illustrates the extension of this violence into pornography where women are perceived as desiring the violence that men visit on them for their sexual pleasure. Advertisements appear to be a very good revelation of the exploitation of women by the male cultural project.

But the exploration of gender relations does not have to be restricted to advertisements. Soap operas, situation comedies, and detective stories can be equally revealing. For example, even where women are acting as detectives (e.g., "Policewoman," "Charlie's Angels," "Lobo," etc.), they, more than men, use sexuality to lure criminals. Men are also seen as the dominant intelligence in the police hierarchy (e.g., Charlie's Angels always calling in to the anonymous Charlie). Soaps also show women as either very naïve or as vicious schemers.

The exploration of sex roles through the media can be a critical pedagogical exercise for both men and women who are trying to transform the present gender hegemony. What the media reveal about sex roles is the powerful exploitation images that our culture has toward the sexes. This type of coding helps to name and clarify the oppressive structures of gender that saturate popular awareness and resist transformation.

The Coverage of Labor Issues

In a very interesting study entitled, Television: Corporate America's Game, rank-and-file workers from three unions studied television programming. They concluded that all major networks illustrated a favorable bias in reporting management issues. There was also a very marked positive aura for corporate activity. In addition, in regular programming there was a predominance of models from a professional class (e.g., doctors, lawyers, psychiatrists). Crime was invariably blue-collar crime and law enforcement was usually carried out against working-class people or unemployed marginals.

What is important about this type of study is the consciousness raising that this activity had for rank-and-file union members. It dramatized labor's uphill battle in having its agenda presented fairly and accurately by media coverage. It also shows how labor resistance and initiatives are trivialized and made to appear deviant by media coverage. Thus, when a union withholds its labor it receives the appellation "strike," which has a violent connotation. There is no comparable violent symbolism for a "runaway corporation," which can affect more people than a strike.

The above examples are only illustrations of how a study of the media can be part of a consciousness-raising critical pedagogy. The resourceful reader can think of many more examples. My one major conclusion is that media communications must be an essential part of a critical pedagogy. We can ignore it only at our moral and political peril.

REFERENCES

Chein, I. (1972) The Science of Behaviour and the Image of Man. New York: Basic Books.

Cover, J. (1983) Theological Reflections: Societal Effects of Television. Religious Education, 78(1), pp. 38-49.

Dorfman, A., and Mattelhart, A. (1975) How to Read Donald Duck. New York: International General Press.

Ewen, S. (1976) Captains of Consciousness. New York: McGraw-Hill.

Freire, P. (1974) Cultural Action for Freedom. London: Penguin (paperback).

Geertz, C. (1973) The Interpretation of Culture. New York: Basic Books.

Goethals, G. I. (1980) The T.V. Ritual. Boston: Beacon Books.

326 / Character Development

Golsen, R. (1975) The Show and Tell Machine. New York: Delta (paperback).

Gramsci, A. (1971) Selection from Prison Notebooks. New York: International Publishers.

Kavanaugh, J. (1983) Capitalist Culture as a Religious and Educational Formation System. Religious Education, 78(1), pp. 50–60.

Kellner, D. (1978) Ideology, Marxism and Advanced Capitalism. Socialist Review, 8(c), pp. 57–58.

Leiss, W. (1976) The Limits to Satisfaction. Toronto: University of Toronto Press.

McLean, S., Ellrod, F. E., and Schindler, D. (1986) Act and Agent: Philosophical Foundations of Moral Education and Character Development. Washington, D.C.: University Press of America.

McLean, S., and Knowles, R. (1986) Psychological Foundations of Moral Education and Character Development. Washington, D.C.: University Press of America.

Mander, J. (1978) Four Arguments for the Elimination of Television. New York: William Morrow.

Marris, P. (1974) Loss and Change. London: Routledge and Kegan Paul.

Nelson, J. (1980) Fine-Living: TV and the Brain. In-Search, pp. 26–32.

Sartre, J. P. (1968) Search for Method. New York: Vintage Books.

Sennett, R. (1978) The Fall of Public Man. New York: Vantage Books.

Slinger, P. (1983) Television Commercials: Mirror and Symbol of Societal Values. Religious Education, 78(1), pp. 29–37.

Smythe, D. W. (1981) _Dependency Road_. Norwood, N.J.: Ablex.

Sullivan, E. V. (1980) The Scandalized Child: Children, Media and Commodity Culture. In J. Fowler and C. Brusselmans (Eds.), _Toward a Moral and Religious Maturity_. New Jersey: Silver-Burdett, pp. 549–573.

Sullivan, E. V. (1983a) Mass Media and Religious Values. _Religious Education_, 78(1), pp. 13–24.

Sullivan, E. V. (1983b) Computers, Culture and Educational Futures: A Critical Appraisal. _Interchange_, 14/31, Toronto.

Sullivan, E. V. (1983c) Commonsense and Valueing. _Religious Education_, 78(1), pp. 5–12.

Sullivan, E. V. (1984) _Critical Psychology: Interpretation of the Personal World_. New York: Plenum Press.

Taylor, C. (1964) _Explanation of Social Behaviour_. New York: Routledge and Kegan Paul.

Television: Corporate America's Game. A Study Conducted by International Association of Machinists and Aerospace Workers, the International Union of Operating Engineers and Bakery Confectionary and Tobacco Workers.

Weil, S. (1952; 1971) _The Need for Roots_. New York: Harper-Colophon Books.

Williams, R. (1973) Base and Superstructure in Marxist Cultural Theory. _New Left Review_, pp. 3–16.

13

The College Experience and Cnaracter Development

Walter Nicgorski

While public criticism, disaffection, and self-doubts have plagued U.S. primary and secondary schools, especially the state-supported ones, higher educators seem to "stand tall," much more respected, assured, and secure.[1] In fact, if one were to listen to certain higher educators, their problems, insofar as they have any, are the results of the failures of precollege education. Higher educators are generally quick to join the chorus of critics of primary and secondary schools. They seem slow to notice, if they do at all, problems in their own house. The aura and prestige of a college education, including its power as a credential for position and professional school, and the prevalent social and athletic glitter of the college experience contribute to mask the widespread failure of U.S. higher education to serve undergraduates well.

BUSY ABOUT OTHER THINGS

The same forces in society which generate understandable pressure on the basic educational system to teach fundamental skills well and to build those character traits (such as honesty, orderliness, and industriousness) that both will reduce costly disruption as crime and vandalism and support a lawful, orderly society, can readily if inadvertently pose obstacles to adequate service to undergraduates, especially service to their character development. Higher education has become, in the words of a recent report sponsored by the U.S. government, "an integral part of our economic progress and national well-being."[2] This is so partly because numerous functions have fallen to higher education, including vocational training, research, and graduate and professional education, and also because ever larger numbers of U.S. citizens are enrolling in institutions of higher education. These institutions, as well as the students and their parents, feel the pressures from the competitive, fast-moving society around them. These are pressures on the institutions to do many things well while handling large numbers of students; such institutions are to provide efficiently the specialized expertise and education the surrounding society is seeking. It is easy then for institutions of higher education to be swept up into the society's pursuit of usually immediate and tangible goals and to come to measure their own success in the commonly understood terms of growth of budget and physical plant, range of programs, numbers of degrees awarded, and notable research contributions. Warren Bryan Martin, long experienced in higher education, has stressed the degree to which the "crisis" of the U.S. college enters the campus from the surrounding society. "Educators tout the contributions of scholars and basic research to society." On the other hand, added Martin, these same educators "are reluctant to acknowledge . . . that society is often active while the college is reactive; society contributes or corrupts while the college receives and reacts. Crisis breeds crisis."[3]

Barry O'Connell, a college teacher, also found the disorder and incapacity of higher education related to the wider moral disorder of the society. To those students in search of ideals and models, colleges and universities, especially the elite ones, offer "an adult culture which nearly mirrors the society at large." What students find is that

> Teaching is, for the most part, honored
> mainly in public relations releases. The
> highest rewards go to those who pursue
> their special fields as intensely as possible.
> Faculty members appear primarily devoted
> to professional advancement and uninter-
> ested in a community of teachers and
> learners. The education of people for life
> in a democratic society is scarcely attempted.

> The proffered education is instead directed
> to reproducing the academic profession or
> to enhancing some student's competitive
> edge in the mobility race. Departments
> reign supreme, and the question of cur-
> riculum is relegated to their supervision
> with an occasional gesture toward a gen-
> eral, integrated education.[4]

Similarly, a recent report by the Association of American
Colleges found the key to curricular disintegration in "the
transformation of the professors from teachers concerned
with the characters and minds of their students to professionals, scholars with Ph.D. degrees with an allegiance to
academic disciplines stronger than their commitment to
teaching or to the life of the institutions where they are
employed."[5] Insofar as these descriptions, which few
would dispute, represent conditions in higher education,
it is not surprising that graduates of such institutions in
large numbers find that their college experience, in the
words of a recent Harvard report on its own graduates,
has had "little influence on present friendships, or on
moral, political, or religious perspectives," and "little
lasting effect on their moral and ethical views."[6]

The loss of interest and then, capacity, of U.S.
higher education for a moral mission of broad personal
development for its students is a story that slowly but
steadily unfolds throughout the twentieth century. One
way of measuring what has happened is to recall, as have
Boyer and Hechinger in a recent Carnegie Foundation essay,
the emphasis of the nation's first colleges on preparing
leaders, notably for the religious and educational communities, and on instilling in their students "piety, loyalty,
and responsible citizenship."[7] Throughout the nineteenth
century, the dominant form of U.S. higher education was
that of the small liberal arts college marked by a closely
woven community and characterized above all by a sense
of moral responsibility to convey the prevailing moral vision and principles to the leaders of the next generation.
A significant element and symbol of that moral mission was
a final course in ethics and moral philosophy required of
all students and given in most nineteenth-century colleges
by the president of the college.

Today higher education is, of course, on a much
larger scale and has the potential for a broader moral

horizon and the utilization of better methods of moral development. There is no need or justification for a nostalgic fixation on the nineteenth-century model. Nevertheless, the approach of the early U.S. college can be instructive in some respects: first in the very genuine concern of these institutions for the moral or ethical dimension of college education; secondly in the conscious and unconscious recognition of the role of community in education; and third in the close relationship between a liberal education emphasizing the humanities and the moral mission of the college.

The slow erosion of interest and competence in such matters came close to passing unnoticed amidst those notable achievements of twentieth-century higher education, such as more education for more people, expansion of physical plants and range of specializations, significant and abundant research results bearing on the defense, health, and welfare of the nation. While such achievements were prized, institutions usually continued to pay their rhetorical respects to the emphasis on liberal humane learning and the moral and citizen development of an earlier day. There were, of course, protests and countermovements to one or another of the effects of the main drift of higher education in this century, toward the model of the highly specialized, fragmented research university which the Germans had seemingly perfected early in the nineteenth century. After World War I, concern for "the values of the West" and their transmission, and a sense that the university's soul was being drawn to other tasks gave rise to the Western civilization sequence at Columbia University and became the seedbed for the Great Books movement in higher education. Later in the century large universities experimented with residential colleges and other efforts to build living and learning communities within the large institution now come to be called "the multiversity." Such endeavors and movements did not have much effect and perhaps tended to reassure all too many that whatever the defects of some institutions, higher education was richly pluralistic with a pedagogical style and curriculum to suit nearly everyone's taste. It was then that the Berkeley outburst of the 1960s and similar student discontent throughout the nation exposed to all who would look closely, how the nation's higher education had lost interest in and contact with undergraduate development.

Significantly, the Berkeley student rebellion occurred at an institution that had what all other universities aspired to obtain: resources, facilities, and with these the capacity to attract one of the best research faculties in the world. The ideal of Berkeley reached beyond universities. Earl McGrath, former U.S. commissioner of education, and Warren Bryan Martin have argued persuasively that the ways and values of the great research university have worked throughout the century to undermine the confidence and useful traditions of the nation's liberal arts colleges.[8] Overall, Berkeley was where higher education saw itself moving and wanted to be. Old Mr. Chips, one on one with a student, and a college president teaching ethics, is where the nation had been.

The most penetrating analyses of the student discontent and activism represented and symbolized by the Berkeley outburst have revealed what Eugene Miller, a professor of political science, observed in 1971 in its immediate aftermath. Miller found that students of the time had concluded "that 'the system' is repressive and rotten," and they longed for something better.

> Yet the university offers little guidance on this most urgent matter. It can train students to make a living and to contribute to the smooth functioning of the system. It cannot guide their deliberations about the best way of life for man and society because it is largely indifferent to questions about the goodness or justice of things. Students have charged, quite properly, that American higher education is "one-dimensional," that it trains young people to accept things as they are without imparting a vision of a higher good. It is hardly surprising that many of the best students have repudiated a system of education that fails to satisfy their deep longing for answers to the most serious questions. Nor is it surprising that they have devised their own answers, which they insist upon uncritically and even self-righteously. Young activists are quite properly to be blamed for plunging heedlessly into action on behalf of shallow and

immature conceptions of what men need or
what the good life is for man and society.
Yet critics should remember how little guidance these young people have received from
their teachers in these matters.[9]

Although Berkeley and related events opened to view the
moral incapacity of modern higher education and the luster
of the research multiversity is now gone or at least tar-
nished, it is far from clear that change is in the air in
higher education. Many find the situation today as bleak
as did Nevitt Sanford, a widely respected scholar of student development, who in 1982 wrote that "if the university
has any noble purposes, or any purposes beyond preparing
students for vocations, keeping the wheels turning, and
maintaining the standard of living, there does not seem to
be anyone around to say what these purposes are. . . .
Nobody is telling students," continued Sanford, "that they
ought to do better or be better persons, or suggesting
what is better; nor do students have much opportunity to
learn from the example of their elders."[10] And now the
challenge is a little different from that of the Berkeley
days, for the students of the 1970s and 1980s seem much
more affected by what one commentator has called the "new
meism or narcissism" and "an almost singleminded concern
with material success."[11]

Despair is, of course, pointless and by definition
hopeless. The widespread awareness of deficiencies first
occasioned by the Berkeley outburst can be seen as a
hopeful sign and perhaps yet a springboard for reform.
The essential task in reform, whatever its specific shape
in different contexts, is to prevent undergraduate education from being neglected or distorted under the direct or
indirect influence of the model of higher education found
in the modern multiversity as an impersonal, fragmented,
sprawling enterprise for enlarging and transmitting human
knowledge. Stated positively, the essential task is to
protect and extend the conditions for and commitment to
the full human development of undergraduates, at the heart
of which is their character development. Whatever institutional context the reformer faces, there will be vested
interests, obstacles in established modes of organization,
support for the status quo in the encompassing society and
the special skepticism higher academics have for the task
of moral or value education. No one then can possibly

expect that the road to reform will be short and easy.
Modest changes that enhance the capacity of an institution
to engage in character education would often be all that
could be expected at this time, and such developments
would usually have to be woven into the fabric of specific
institutional configurations and histories. Those proponents
of moral education who have not the tolerance for compromise and incrementalism will find little hope and likely do
little good. What is possible and desirable is that each
institution that professes to educate undergraduates, however constrained by its own history and ambience, place
itself on that road moving in the direction of full assumption of its moral responsibility to human development.

In the following pages this chapter will present
three broad strategies for effective character education
during the college years. Although each of the strategies
will be illustrated by model practices or policies, the emphasis is on strategies in order to keep before the various
readers the importance of shaping specific policies and
practices in the light of the opportunities and constraints
of differing institutions. The three strategies explored are
(1) the recovery of commitment in colleges and university
to the moral development of undergraduates as a high or
central priority, (2) provision for the intellectual grounding and consolidation of the moral dispositions and habits,
and (3) support for the development and strengthening of
a healthy, affective direction in students. The latter two
strategies are to shape and focus the means used to provide character development appropriate to this time of life.
The first strategy, the recovery of commitment, is a necessary step to engage in significant efforts under the latter
two.

RECOVERY OF COMMITMENT

Is character development an appropriate goal of the
undergraduate college years? The inability of higher educators and their institutions to respond with a decisive
affirmative poses the major obstacle to the college's renewal as a moral educator. What prevents a clearly affirmative response are first of all doubts, if not dogmatic
denials, that the university or college is capable of moral
direction and then questions about whether there remains
any character development to be accomplished after the
high school years.

Skepticism regarding anyone's capacity to know
about the right and the good and the relativism implied
in such skepticism have posed obstacles to programs for
moral development at all levels of education. The question
usually asked is whose values are to be taught. Widely
present in higher education is the view that insofar as
colleges and universities consider morals or values they
are to do it solely in an uncommitted neutral spirit of inquiry and/or in the objective manner of looking at values
as sociological facts, data to be accounted for in good empirical theory. It is not surprising that in the intellectual centers, namely the colleges and universities, from
which skepticism and relativism emanated to touch all of
society over the last century, doubts and denials of anyone's capacity to direct moral development are especially
strong.[12] Those doubts and denials are yet strong despite
the fact that the last generation has witnessed a persistent
and powerful assault on the intellectual and personal adequacy of relativism and the often associated pretense of
value neutrality or value freedom.

What has, however, come to be more clearly recognized and acknowledged is the fact that those apparently
dominant characteristics of higher education and modern
science--openness, inquiry, objectivity, and explanation as
styles and goals--are hardly value neutral and in fact
entail some commitments to what is good and worthwhile.
So too the implicit values in the common support for human
rights and a democratic society have been brought more
into the light.[13] In discipline after discipline and thus
in the university itself, the inconsistency between the
claim of ultimate relativism and value neutrality on the
one side, and lived practices and procedures on the other
has been exposed to open criticism in the last generation.

Scholars themselves, in a number of fields, have
become the leading critics of the pretense at value neutrality and value freedom that so captured circles of learning thirty years ago. This direction of scholarship is especially evident in political science among the students of
Leo Strauss, and in psychology and education among the
followers of Lawrence Kohlberg. It receives support from
the Frankfurt school's impact on philosophy and social
science as well as from new understandings in the history
and philosophy of science on the intellectual and social
frameworks in which science is done. Likewise the emphasis of phenomenology on seeing any person's perspective

as rooted in time and relatedness and the associated new
vigor of personalism in philosophy have converged with
such otherwise seemingly disparate developments to bring
some change in the atmosphere of higher education.

Although these developments of what many have
called a postpositivistic period do not necessarily overcome
the pervasive skepticism and relativism about moral knowledge, the recent critiques of the claim of value-free objectivity have enhanced the possibility that intellectual
circles, including colleges and universities, will be more
open in acknowledging their values, more forthright in
fostering those values, and more concerned with the in-
eluctable value-dimension of life. This is more receptive
ground for efforts at character development than concerned
higher educators faced in an earlier time. It is now
easier--though yet ever so difficult--than it has been for
some time to find higher educators who are willing to affirm that character development is a proper and even
leading concern of their institutions.

There are, however, other reasons and powerful
prejudices supporting the view that character development
is an inappropriate goal for undergraduate education.
These consist primarily in the belief, not without some
basis, that character development belongs primarily to the
family and the earlier school years. Character seen as a
set of formed habits and dispositions is taken to be largely fixed by the onset of the college years. Those years
are then more properly employed in coming to possess an
expertise and the appropriate skills of a life's career.

This outlook underestimates both the potential moral
growth of the undergraduate years and the danger of
divorcing during these years vocational and skill-oriented
education (including a presumed value-free education in
such liberal arts as those of reasoning and writing) from
moral education. Socrates's legendary struggle with the
Sophists represents a well-known effort to overcome that
divorce. The characteristic gift of human beings, argued
Socrates, the power of reason and speech, must be utilized,
not simply to enlarge a person's power and dominion
through, for example, the mastery of rhetoric, but also
and primarily to find and understand life-directing values
such as justice. Socrates was a college educator or perhaps one of the first adult educators, for he directed his
efforts at those who were interested in power and seeking
the skills for success in the political life of Athens.

Socrates apparently thought that the moral inquiry
he provoked and conducted was not only appropriate but
in fact necessary for these young men. His judgment on
their potential for moral growth and its critical importance
to their well-being and that of their society is supported
by many contemporary studies of the college student. Psychologists have identified specific development tasks appropriate to the college years.[14] Others have documented not
only cognitive, but moral development, during this time of
life.[15] John Whiteley's recent studies led him to affirm
these expectations from various developmental theories
claiming, what appears sound to many experienced college
educators, that the transition from late adolescence to
early adulthood provided an "unprecedented opportunity for
character development."

> The press of ethical dilemmas in our so-
> ciety, the failure of most institutions of
> our society to help young people learn to
> surmount the transition from late adoles-
> cence to early adulthood all combine to
> create an opportunity for colleges and uni-
> versities to offer educational programs
> which give students their first real oppor-
> tunity to think through their own moral
> and ethical beliefs.[16]

Character development is then a wholly appropriate objective for colleges and universities. They are called upon
to contribute in a distinctive way to the development of
the responsible moral agent. What good is there to all
the skills, fine tastes, and learning that can be endowed
on students if they are used selfishly or destructively?
No less than Socrates and this nation's first college educators saw moral development as the central and highest
purpose of higher education.

Although it is wrong to believe that where there is
no explicit and widespread agreement on first principles
and goals a community or institution cannot develop at all
or progress in a sound way, clear and explicit commitment
to any goal is a considerable advantage if not a requisite
for attaining it. Thus an institutional commitment to character development as a primary purpose of undergraduate
education is an important step in overcoming the distrac-
tions from and resistance to a serious concern with moral

development in the college years. Colleges and universities will not much improve as moral educators if they cannot publicly state their purpose as such, show its curricular impact and use it openly in evaluation or assessment of their work. Moral or character education is generally more explicit in statements of the overall goals of colleges and universities than in curricular requirements or standards for evaluation. What mention of this purpose is there frequently reflects the concern of founders of the institution in the eighteenth or nineteenth centuries. Consistent explicitness throughout should be the goal.

Few institutions have been as explicit, and as consistently so, as Alverno College in Milwaukee in the design and explanation of its competency-based curriculum for liberal education. At Alverno, "valuing" is one of eight competencies that mark the goal of liberal education and that include such traditional measures as powers of analysis and communication and such untraditional ones as social interaction. What is notable about Alverno's approach is that valuing ability is not simply a goal; it is translated into specific achievement levels, and treated as a skill that pervades all parts of the curriculum from history to art. Success at valuing is regularly assessed for all the students, and institutional success at developing this competency is acknowledged by Alverno to be a key test of its relatively new program.[17]

Many institutions, in a post-Watergate trend, have acknowledged anew the importance of moral development and accordingly have given some recent attention to the curricular implications of such a commitment. Harvard, in the remaking of its core curriculum, has required a number of credits in courses where moral analysis is practiced. Other institutions have required or welcomed specific courses on value analysis or ethics, often tying these to specific professional specialties; examples are the well-known courses on business and medical ethics.

For most institutions the recovery of commitment to character development to the point where it can be genuine, explicit and consistently so, is a tall order indeed. Even modest curricular requirements, such as a value-analysis dimension in some courses or a specific ethics course, need the support of a communal commitment at which most colleges must work. More ambitious and extensive efforts such as that at Alverno require a consensus around an even stronger commitment. Faculty development is necessary to encourage as well as to sustain a communal and institutional commitment to moral education.

In most settings it will be difficult to proceed with such development without administrative leadership, but it should be remembered that the building of faculty concern and some commitment to moral education might encourage or at least allow administrative leadership at a later stage. Interested faculty members can, at a minimum, launch informal faculty seminars or reading groups to consider writings, both classic and contemporary, on the overall nature and purpose of undergraduate education. Such faculty groups seem the best initial place to talk through the perceived tension between "real substance" or the hard stuff of college and university learning and the soft stuff or even "therapy" in which some faculty and administrators place moral concerns and those questions of relevance and life-relatedness which students often have. Such faculty groups also seem the appropriate initial forum for efforts to reach across the many disciplinary and departmental barriers and especially across the gap between the traditional humanities and the social sciences which has opened in this century. The aim, of course, is to forge an alliance in which character development in the college years would be seen as a common challenge on which all resources and expertises of the faculty would be brought to bear.

When faculty actually become committed to and engaged in moral education, there will be need for another kind of faculty development, one that emphasizes the continuing broad growth of the faculty member as a person and as a possessor of the necessary skills. The object of such development would be to enhance the faculty member as moral educator, as one better prepared to function both as a model and a catalyst for moral development. This faculty development will need to overcome the prevailing tension among higher educators between disciplinary expertise and "professionalism" on the one hand and pedagogical awareness and skills on the other. Insofar as the higher educator is a master of a field, be it eighteenth-century British history, sociology of the family, or the philosophy of Spinoza, he is not likely to be concerned with, and his teaching informed by, an understanding of stages of student development and appropriate pedagogical techniques. This kind of faculty development clearly requires a stronger institutional commitment in terms of resources and faculty time. Workshops, retreats, time off for study, and leaves for personal and pedagogical development are some of the chief means that would need to be used. If an institution is seriously committed to the moral development of its students, it must at some point be systematic and professional in evaluating not only students in this respect but also faculty members in terms of their contribution to this high-priority institutional goal. Such evaluation is a form of consistency with explicit and important goals.

The conclusion of Boyer and Hechinger's recent Carnegie report calls for a recovery of commitment to moral development among college educators. This report, <u>Higher Learning in the Nation's Service</u>, reviews the many ways that higher education has served the nation and understandably looks favorably on those activities of the multiversity, such as research for the national well-being and consultantships and other involvement in government by higher educators. Near the end, however, the report tells readers:

> Education's primary mission is to develop within each student the capacity to judge wisely in matters of life and conduct.
> This imperative does not replace the need for rigorous study in the disciplines, but neither must specialization become an excuse to suspend judgment or interfere with the search for worthwhile goals.
>
> . . .
>
> As we look to a world whose contours remain obscure, the time has come for higher learning to adjust, once again, its traditional roles of teaching, research, and service. In so doing, it should affirm that at the heart of the academic enterprise there is something more than the heating system or the common grievance over parking.
>
> The center holds because the search for truth leads to the discovery of larger meanings that can be applied with integrity to life's decisions. This, we conclude, is higher learning's most essential mission in the nation's service.[18]

For many the question will be not whether the college years are opportune ones for character or moral development or whether the college and university should be concerned with this development. The question rather is what sort of thing should be done? How does one begin to assume the challenge? Formal programs in moral education or value development have been rare in higher education and have not commanded the interest and ingenuity applied to those intended for other levels of education. Authoritative examples of successful efforts are not in view. Also, many of the past practices of early colleges and those of religiously affiliated institutions seem too indoctrinative for the college years and for contributing to effective moral agency in contemporary pluralistic society. Then too as the college years come far along in human development and are for most at the end of formal education, whatever is right to do in the college years for moral development necessarily depends on the state of readiness of students; this, of course, will reflect their distinctive backgrounds, including their prior education and their inherent abilities.

These challenging difficulties should not prevent the effort to set directions, to determine policies and programs appropriate to a context, and to be prepared to change in accord with the results of evaluations. The strategies and sample policies which follow can be conceived as the sketch of a model for character development during the college years. The model is built on the assumption that the students coming to college have experienced the shaping of character, including the tuning of the dispositions through the efforts of parents and educators at the earlier levels of schooling discussed in previous chapters in this volume. This means that young people would arrive at college with good character traits such as the classical virtues, including willpower, and a positive but not naïve feeling about themselves and the world around them. The task of the college experience, then, will be to see that that character, like a healthy young tree, matures or spreads itself into a new range while deepening its roots. The college's task is to facilitate the rooting and maturing of character. This rooting is primarily a process of intellectual grounding and consolidation. The maturing is above all a firming and refining of character through testing and practicing it with new people and in novel situations, in wider circles than those in which it was first formed.

INTELLECTUAL GROUNDING AND CONSOLIDATION

To be concerned with character development in the college years is not to abandon the powerful view that college should be primarily an academic experience, specifically an exercising and development of the intellect. Rather it is to set the highest of expectations for intellectual endeavor in those years. Decisions on right and wrong have already been made and fallen into patterns for the young student. Character is there, but the influences of others--peers, family, and community--have operated strongly in the making of this first form of character. The college years come at a time when the personal dynamism to autonomy is usually at a peak. Scratch the surface of those college students who deny it and you will find them in agreement with the great many who confess that they are deeply concerned to understand for themselves who they are and who they are in the process of becoming. Whether they are disposed to affirm who they are and thus the moral universe in which they have been formed or to strike out anew in directions alien to their elders and forming communities, the significant fact is that they are proclaiming their own readiness to examine and think through the situation and then to affirm or deny accordingly. Character, an important dimension of each person's being, can be affirmed in this process or eroded or shattered by the alleged discovery that it has no intellectual moorings. Character development in the college years turns critically on the young person's efforts to make sense of the world.

Bettelheim has written that the human being's "greatest need and most difficult achievement is to find meaning in life." He speaks of the diminishment of will to live when meaning cannot be found.[19] It is likewise clear that one draws back from living in a certain way, with, that is, a certain character when it cannot be anchored in a meaningful view of the world. College years usually see the first earnest expressions of the need for self-attained meaning and the first earnest efforts to pursue it. The need and quest of this time is almost always directed at ideas, and it is with ideas, synoptic and synthetic, that people through the ages have found meaning that has quickened their will to live and their determination to live in a certain way. E. S. Schumacher has written of the importance of education's leading students to work out a metaphysical position which provides the basis for ethics and direction in life.[20] Students seek, and need, even more than they seek, this "connected" or "philosophical" view which John Henry Newman also made the chief object of a university education.[21] Thus for students with a religious upbringing or touched by some religious faith the college years necessarily become an occasion for working out a first personal integration of faith and such knowledge of the world they have been able to attain. The meaning one finds can ground and support character. Many have attested to the truth of Luther Weigle's observation that moral character is surely established when it is wedded to religious faith.[22]

Colleges and universities support character development above all by providing the conditions, stimulus, and guidance favorable to the undergraduate's search for meaning. For an institution not to take that quest seriously is to stifle character development in those years or to abdicate its influence on the search to sources (e.g., the media, peers) less equipped to provide constructive direction. The search for meaning, even when it reaches its college-level terminus by affirming a healthy character, is not usually a smooth and easy process. The search is often disorienting and appears to involve setbacks to moral development. Contemporary observers, Carol Gilligan and William Perry most notably, have explored the basis for the disorientation and moral relativism that sensitive parents and teachers have long known to be a part of the college experience of many. Gilligan explained

> The notable achievement of the adolescent
> mind is the capacity for reflective thought,
> the ability to include, among the facts of
> experience, the activity of thinking itself.
> When thought thus turns inward and begins
> to examine its own constructions, it calls
> into question knowledge formerly taken for
> granted, including the knowledge of good
> and evil. To think about morality is to
> confront the problem of judgment and
> thereby to discover the inevitable limita-
> tions of knowledge itself.[23]

The familiar "crisis" of the college years often is provoked by or centers on an ethical or moral issue. A

disparity between the will and inclination of the student
and the moral or religious norms of the family, community,
and college frequently leads to a shaking or loss of confidence in the framework of meaning provided by these em-
bedding communities. It would be romantic and utopian in
the worst senses of these words to suppose that these
crises pit unselfish pure idealism against unresponsive,
staid institutions. It would be unwarranted to suppose
such crises represent a necessary stage in moral development. In fact, it is probably the case that the lack of
preparation of parents and other institutions, including
colleges and universities, to cope with and direct moral
development helps bring on such crises and surely contributes to making the passage through them more dangerous and morally disorientating than need be.

In fact, the noted "crisis" often seems to reflect an
acute case of the common need of young persons developing
to autonomy to make a tradition their own. It is only in
making sense of traditional ways in a context of a meaningful world that one makes them one's own. Central and
most important to any cultural tradition are moral and
ethical norms, the same norms that often "rub or pinch"
the late adolescent or young adult. These then would
seem natural points at which to begin inquiry into the
values and entire outlook and understanding of the dominant culture. Moral tension and moral perplexity must be
utilized to facilitate the search for meaning, and an initial task in that search is to see fairly and quite fully
the understanding (namely the very vision or telos and
metaphysics) that supports a traditional moral code. Discussion of moral dilemmas that grow out of the materials
(history, literature, philosophy) of an education in the
humanities as well as those that spring from direct experiences, including those of TV and the cinema which attract and grip college students, should be allowed and
encouraged to move to high levels of abstraction and uni-
versality, for the students are generally in search of
grounds and structures of meaning that will sustain one
or another resolution of a dilemma.

A crisis in the process of happening often has too
many side-effects to be developmentally fruitful or educationally productive. Better then for a college or university to anticipate the interrelated moral and intellectual
needs of the students in a structured way than simply to
boast of its responsiveness through special "rap" sessions,

crisis centers, and counseling offices, though all of those unquestionably would have their place. There is much to recommend a structured response in the form of a curriculum that invites students, in Alexander Meiklejohn's apt phrase, "to think their way into the common life of their people."[24] This means giving the student's emerging cognitive powers the opportunity to encounter the best that has been thought and written in a tradition, its moral, philosophical, and spiritual classics. Such experiences offer the student the best materials for working out the issues of meaning and the ground of moral norms. Courses of study like that provided at St. John's (Annapolis and Santa Fe) and in the Program of Liberal Studies at the University of Notre Dame are based on the reading and discussion of the great books and are conducted with, among other purposes, a special interest in the variety of answers given to the Socratic concern with "how life should be lived." More common and also in the process of restoration in recent years is the development of core courses or core requirements that emphasize an encounter with the classics of the tradition. The renewed strength of such requirements is testimony to the portion of truth in Robert Hutchins's provocative statement that the elective system represents a moral failure.[25]

A curriculum centered on the classics is not only a fitting response to the students' quest for meaning at this time; it also presents a proper framework for faculty and institutional humility about the fundamental issues of life and society. The faculty and the institution, at the college level, are not simply transmitters of a society's moral code or socializers for the society, but they themselves are also to be involved in personal growth and in that way enhance their capacity as leaders in the moral development of a society and culture. There are no better sources for working out such a multilevel agenda of development than the best thinking of a tradition approached in a spirit of common inquiry with a lively interest in its applicability to the present and future.

Whether the moral heritage in classic works or contemporary moral dilemmas are being explored, much is lost if it must be done in a lecture format with a large audience of students. Classroom-discussion approaches in contexts where there is also much opportunity for one-on-one work are clearly those most conducive to moral growth, for this teaching, just as personal counseling, can be sensitive to the specific needs and level of understanding of individual students. The prospective declining college student pool of the late 1980s and early 1990s and the resulting lower enrollments for some institutions could be turned to good purposes if faculty modes of teaching and counseling undergraduates were allowed to take a much more personal dimension.

A structured curriculum can assist a student's search for meaning by increasing the probability that the student will be better prepared to face and understand the challenges to a tradition that spring from his personal life and specific historical period. Before developmental theory led most to appreciate the importance of conflict to the process of personal development, John Stuart Mill had stressed the utility to personal and societal growth of a teacher representing forcefully a viewpoint out of general favor in the society and perhaps one with which he or she disagreed.[26] To struggle with error and see it as error is to come to a real and personal possession of the truth. The intellectual struggles through conflicts and dilemmas toward meaning even when provided and prepared for by a curriculum and institution, can still be very trying experiences. As the college student undergoes these intellectual challenges in which his or her very character is at stake, he or she will also be moving in new and wider circles of experience and people. As the student searches for intellectual grounds for character, the college or university should be striving in every way to support that character by strengthening its affective aspects.

DEVELOPING AND STRENGTHENING THE AFFECTIVE DIRECTION

Students must be encouraged to love the good and the right even as they are in the process of trying to understand such notions better and to find the grounds for them. The dual process of loving even as one searches for greater precision and depth of understanding is an initiation into one of the best conceptions known of a healthy adult life. If, when the college years arrive, a student has the budding virtues of due self-esteem, self-control, concern for others, and an interest in and attraction to principled ways of ordering human communities and settling human conflicts, the college's challenging task will be to sustain an environment that helps those emerging virtues become the settled dispositions of adult life. Where the student is not already so favorably predisposed, the college must hope and strive to stir some latent inclinations to a life richer than one of simple self-aggrandizement.

Students, like most human beings, are enmeshed in specific contexts and concrete relationships. Although ideas at this stage of their lives have a greater power than ever before, what they often may be attracted to and even love are not ideal notions of justice and goodness as such but these qualities as instantiated in lives of people with whom they interact. Those who do seem to delight in ideas or abstractions run the risk in the moral realm of being akin to the proverbial lover of humanity who could not tolerate individual persons. Thus interaction with others can be viewed not only as the source of and support for models of good character but also as the testing and practicing arena for those good ideas and good qualities that require practice to grow into the effective virtues of good character.

There are, in a student's life, three types of interaction to which a college should especially attend if concerned with the affective side of the student's moral development. These are: (1) the student's encounter with teachers and staff, (2) the relationship with peers, and (3) the experience with the world outside the college or university.

Teachers and Staff as Models

College students, especially those in a residential college, have often found their first adult models outside their families in the faculty and staff whom they encounter and can observe with some regularity. The encounter with such models comes at a point in their personal development when there seems to be an especially strong interest, even a fascination, with how active lives in the workaday world are put and held together. This fascination is understandable because college students are usually turning over in their minds their possible roles in the larger world, and they are also often found wondering how the learning from book and the classroom really relates to life beyond school.

Such wonder about the artificiality of the school atmosphere and even their own "youth culture" is especially
focused on moral ideals and principles. Students, at least
the best disposed of them, hope that such ideals and principles are not the mere stuff of school, but there are
plenty of warnings, often given by their own parents,
that the "real world" will be different. Thus it is especially important for the student to find adults who manifest good character amid the struggles, ambiguities, and
even the full responsibilities of family and citizenship, in
that "real world." Students need more than moral dilemmas,
the questioning of their moral traditions, and being pressed
to a search for moral ground and ultimate meaning. Some
evidence of this need is found in evaluation interviews of
students who had participated in the Sierra Project, a
concerted character development effort at the University of
California at Irvine. After their experience in the project,
some students indicated that its emphasis should be shifted
in some measure from "moral conflict induction" to "moral
conflict resolution" and that more models of "mature moral
reasoning" had to be put before them in order to achieve
increases in their moral growth.[27] Similarly biographies,
autobiographies, and other historical accounts that exemplify moral maturity or excellence should not be neglected
in the selection of curricular materials. College youth
have not outgrown the need for moral examples.

The legitimate and necessary concern with the character of faculty and staff should not be narrowly focused
on a single type of person or limited, as such discussion
of faculty role models has often been, to the classroom
teacher. Suffice it to say that both developmental theory
and common experience indicate that it is healthy in the
late adolescent passage to adulthood to encounter some
diversity of types of integrated personalities. Such experience tends to make the process of growth and integration more personal and genuine and less simply one of
imitation and conformity; it also provides for a less abrupt
passage into the variegated pluralism of much of modern
society. In fact, in the current state of society, institutions of higher education will have little difficulty in providing variety of types of adults in the faculty and staff
positions. This caveat against narrowness or singleness
of type is probably applicable only to certain smaller
church-related colleges. The challenge for most of higher
education will be how to maintain a standard of character

in the selection and development of faculty and staff in
the light of the often deeply cutting pluralism of the surrounding society and the tendency of the legal system to
protect broadly diversity of life-style as a civil right.

The modern obstacle, of course, to the faculty is
assuming and maintaining the large responsibility as moral
models which seems to fall naturally to them is found in
that changed conception of the college and university high-
lighted earlier in this chapter. The faculty member has
come to be defined and thus to understand him/herself
more as a purveyor of specialized expertise and information and less as a developer of persons. Nevitt Sanford
wryly observed that however rampant the faculty "examples
of competitiveness and acquisitiveness, absorption in narrow specialities, virtuosity untempered by humane feeling
. . . students rarely get to know their professors well
enough to consider them as models. 'Getting them off the
subject' went out of fashion some time ago."[28]

In all institutions of higher education but especially in larger ones, staff--notably those with responsibilities
in residence halls and counseling centers--spend substantial time with students. Their relationships with students
are often more continuous than those of faculty, and such
staff are frequently better positioned to interact with students at times of important personal decisions or even at
times of crisis. No institution serious about the character
development of its students could possibly ignore the important position of many staff members as models and educators.

The call here for undergraduate faculty who will
assume their responsibilities as models and otherwise also
embrace a vocation as a developer of human beings is not
a call for incompetence in field or discipline or the modest
abilities of a genial Mr. Chips or "guru"-inspired indoctrination. Education's history is dotted with instances of
abuse of the teacher's power, where personal dominance
has suffocated or otherwise distorted the genuine human
development of the student. Faculty should, of course, be
expertly prepared in a field and among the genuinely
brightest of the society; there is need too for proper distance and professionalism in faculty-student relations.
Such objectives in faculty recruitment and development
must, however, be tempered by attention to the overall
goals of undergraduate education, including that most important one of character development and by a recognition

of how a faculty member's life and actions can play a necessary and important function in moving toward that goal.

Peer Group as Source of Models and Opportunities of Practice

It is a commonplace among the reflections of college alumni and students to observe that they have learned more during their college years outside the classroom than in. Of course, the learning at issue in this common reflection is not the techniques or information of a major field or profession. Such matters are properly and ordinarily learned in the classroom, library, or laboratory. Rather what has been learned outside the classroom is something coextensive with or overlapping what could be called moral education. What is learned seems to include how to get along with people, how to cope with difficulties, and how to make some sense out of life.

Much has been written about the peer pressure, and most of that is negative. But there can be a positive side to peer pressure; it can assist the right dispositioning or affective direction and keep moral development on track. The heavy and often illegal drinking as well as academic cheating among college-age youth is regularly attributed in large part to peer pressure, but it is clear that groups in which service-activities are widely undertaken or in which serious and engaged study is common tend to have the effect of setting such behavior as a norm for individuals who enter their spheres. At the least unhealthy peer pressure can be diffused by the introduction to the group of models who mitigate the negative pressure, thus reducing its force. Peer pressure works because it provides the emotional support of relevant models and these are especially potent at the less secure and assured times of personal development.

Nor is it at all adequate to see the influence of the peer group as an emotional or affective factor that is an obstacle to academic or intellectual development. That education outside the classroom that has been referred to as so potent is, after all, much more than a compulsive force to conform. Peer education is a noteworthy reality because interaction with peers is for most more natural and easy than with others. Peers are "on the same wavelength." People tend to work out important issues with those to whom they can talk and listen. Thus peers have a special access to the process of character development. Peer interaction may have limitations as a mode of moral education; peers, for example, may be too alike and reinforcing to create the Socratic disequilibrium often necessary to moral growth. Nevertheless peers are clearly a powerful force, not only by their pressure or collective modeling but also by their thinking and conversation. Although peer influence seems a major way that the moral attitudes and values of the wider society continue to work within the college or university, institutions are not helpless regarding this dimension of the moral environment. Through admission policies, the structuring of social settings and programs, such as the location and nature of student centers and lounges and through curricular and other efforts to affect the conversation of peers, educators can have some effect on the nature of the college experience with peers. Most institutions so totally abandoned the concept of in loco parentis in the 1960s and 1970s that they lost substantial control of the students' environment and with it control over the forms of peer interaction.

The community that forms around a residence hall or a common curriculum will have the shared experiences that activate peer group discussion and cooperation. Such a peer group's impact as a moral educator can potentially be much greater than if it simply reflected attitudes and values from the media and other sources outside the college or university. So it is the living together and learning together communities like those of the Sierra Project at the University of California and of James Madison College at Michigan State University that provide very desirable settings for moral development, settings rarely able to be attained and maintained in contemporary higher education.

Peer groups of the college years also provide opportunities for free commitment and action in small societies much akin to those of the adult world. These vary from personal relationships to leadership responsibilities in a fraternity or a campus service organization. These experiences of relationships and in new roles are, for better or worse, going to have some impact—very likely a significant one—on the affective disposition that is brought to the continuing task of moral development. Such experiences can, for example, enhance or diminish self-esteem;

they can, at this still formative stage, open one to the beauty and virtues of others or sour one on human relationships. Experience in different roles tends to enlarge one's perspectives on moral issues, and that often is a condition for moral development.

Cutting across involvement with peers as well as with faculty and staff are opportunities for participation in college and university governance. Common experience and the findings of scholars of moral development from Aristotle to the present indicate that the sharing of real responsibility for the direction of common affairs is conducive to moral and personal growth. Thus experiences that range from service on a dormitory judicial council to participation in a university senate are among the most significant for moral 'growth that an undergraduate can have. Such student sharing in governance is a sensitive matter in nearly all educational institutions, and one need not be dogmatically and single-mindedly democratic to recognize an educator's responsibility to seek ways for meaningful student and faculty participation in the making of institutional policies.

Experiential Learning

Some college educators have long sought to give their students wider experiences with the world outside the college than those provided by peer group communities. Thus internships, apprenticeships, and work-study programs are well established in higher education. Like peer group communities though on a different scale, these provide diverse opportunities for functioning in various roles as well as tests of initial and provisional commitments.

Recent developments in experiential learning have emphasized the objective of a greater social awareness, and through field experience and service have attempted to bring home the reality of problems and potential tasks in the social and political sectors. The importance of such wider experiences for moral development cannot be underestimated. These experiences have the capacity not only to build self-esteem but also to provide more concrete and immediate objects of a healthy affective direction. Such experiences and appropriately guided reflection on them increase the possibility that the late adolescent will move from a concentrated concern with acceptance of self

by others, self-achievement—albeit by rules of fair play—
and a heavy appetite for entertainment, to a habit of service, empathy with the disadvantaged, and sense of responsibility for the shape and direction of the wider society.

Well-structured programs in experiential learning,
integrated with the college curriculum, can make a very
special contribution to attuning the student's moral reasoning and character to the specific moral challenges of
contemporary society. One such program is the Pulse Program at Boston College, an effort to place students in social service agencies and political action groups in conjunction with the study of significant works concerning the
pursuit of justice and peace. American University's Washington semester serves the students of many colleges and
universities by providing internship and other experience
in national government, joined with study and reflection
on the operation of that government. These are but two of
the more notable programs from a large number in place
that might be examined by institutions interested in a
more experiential dimension to their curriculum. Some institutions have made experiential learning and/or community
service time a graduation requirement. In fact, a strong
case has been made for a national universal service requirement (between ages of 16 and 24) as a way of check-
ing "the sense of entitlement . . . so widespread today."[29]

Recent programs in experiential learning have often
been resisted or accepted reluctantly in a qualified way
by college and university faculty. While there may be
instances when such programs deserve resistance because
they have been hastily conceived or are improperly partisan or even ideological in thrust, resistance frequently
seems to reflect a much too narrowly intellectual or career-
ist approach to the development of the college years. If
proponents and opponents of such programs meet on any
ground, it is likely to be the apparent ground of compromise, namely, that experiential learning is good and a
proper endeavor for higher education only insofar as reflection upon the experiences is a requisite part of the
program or course. Raw experience, if that were possible,
is worthless in terms of education and development. Reflection upon experience would usually entail discussion
and articulation of the significant aspects of the experience. Such reflection is really a mode of appropriating
experience to one's self-definition and search for meaning.
The ground of compromise proves here to be the wisest

among all the possible courses. Experience, especially in
the college years, must be integrated with the wide and
deep search for meaning at that time.

This felt need for the integration of experience with
thought calls attention to the fact that intellectual development ought not and cannot take place independently of a
broad personal development and that moral development involves both of these forms of growth. In the light of that
awareness it is not surprising that one of the most discerning scholars of the college experience, Douglas Heath,
has found that such measures of intelligence as scholastic
aptitude do not predict success in adult life when success
is measured in terms of a standard of maturity. That
standard for Heath was composed of reflective intelligence,
ability to combine a variety of views, stability, and a
character marked by empathy, altruism, and self-direction
in accord with broadly humane values. College students
already high in this maturity tended in later years to enjoy such fruits of success as higher competence in performing a job, greater job satisfaction, and greater vocational
adaptability. Heath's recommendation from his studies is
to urge attention to the development of the whole, integrated person and so to assist college students toward a
maturity of balanced growth as a thinking, feeling, and
relating person.[30] This chapter has contended that the
character development of college-age students is advanced
by attention to the strategies of encouraging and supporting an intellectual consolidation and grounding of character and of strengthening the healthy affective dimension of
character. It is very clear that these strategies overlap
and must work in tandem thus reflecting the unbroken
wholeness of a student's life.

The college or university clearly has the opportunity to provide the capstone to character development in
the schooling years. When these institutions fail to make
their special contribution to the character development of
their students they not only fail the individuals involved
but also fail to reach in this important respect the leadership of society. Among those pursuing undergraduate
education are the future leaders of every sector--business,
the professions of medicine and law, the media, government
officials, writers, and teachers. Here is a key leverage
point for the moral quality of our or any modern society.

NOTES

1. Three recent reports are welcome exceptions to the tendency to spare education during the college years from the critical scrutiny usually turned upon primary and secondary education. These are Involvement in Learning: Realizing the Potential of American Higher Education, issued by the National Institute of Education in October 1984; To Reclaim a Legacy, issued by the National Endowment for the Humanities in November 1984; and Integrity in the College Curriculum, issued by the Association of American Colleges in February 1985. William Bennett's widely noted critique of higher education in his Harvard address of October 1986, the Carnegie Foundation's 1987 report on the undergraduate experience, Ernest L. Boyer, College: The Undergraduate Experience (New York: Harper and Row, 1987), and Allan Bloom's The Closing of the American Mind (New York: Simon and Schuster, 1987) appeared while this chapter was in press.

2. Involvement in Learning, p. 5.

3. Warren Bryan Martin, A College of Character (San Francisco: Jossey-Bass, 1982), p. 178.

4. Barry O'Connell, "Where Does Harvard Lead Us," Working Papers: Toward the Restoration of the Liberal Arts Curriculum (New York: Rockefeller Foundation, 1979), p. 70.

5. Integrity in the College Curriculum, p. 6.

6. Harvard President Derek Bok, cited by O'Connell, p. 74.

7. Ernest L. Boyer and Fred M. Hechinger, Higher Learning in the Nation's Service (Washington, D.C.: Carnegie Foundation for the Advancement of Teaching, 1981), p. 9.

8. Earl J. McGrath, Values, Liberal Education, and National Destiny (Indianapolis: Lilly Endowment, 1975). See also Martin, A College of Character, passim.

9. Eugene F. Miller, "Activism and Higher Education—A Socratic View," Journal of General Education, 23 (October 1971), 214.

10. Nevitt Sanford, "Foreword," in John M. Whiteley, Character Development in College Students, Vol. 1: The Freshman Year (Schenectady, N.Y: Character Research Press, 1982), p. xix.

11. Arthur Levine, When Dreams and Heroes Died (San Francisco: Jossey-Bass, 1980), pp. xvi-xvii.

12. See the discussion in Edward A. Purcell, Jr., _The Crisis of Democratic Theory_ (Lexington: University Press of Kentucky, 1973) and the earlier popular discussi in Walter Lippmann, _The Public Philosophy_ (New York: New American Library, 1955).

13. A fuller discussion of this takes place in the following places in the first volume of the series, of whi this is the third. See Frederick A. Ellrod, "Contemporar Philosophies of Moral Education," David Schindler, "On th Foundations of Moral Judgment," Walter Nicgorski, "Envir ment: The Social Dimension of Moral Development," in David Schindler, Jesse A. Mann, and Frederick A. Ellrod (eds.), _Act and Agent: Philosophical Foundations of Mor Education_ (Washington, D.C.: University Press of Americ 1986).

14. See for example Richard T. Knowles, "The Act ing Person as Moral Agent: Erikson as the Starting Poin for an Integrated Psychological Theory of Moral Develop ment," and Margaret Gorman, "Life-long Moral Developmen in the second volume in this series, of which this is the third. Richard T. Knowles, Jesse A. Mann, and Frederic A. Ellrod (eds.), _Psychological Foundations of Moral Edu cation_ (Washington, D.C.: University Press of America, 1986).

15. The most noted study is William Perry, _Forms of Intellectual and Ethical Development in the College Years: A Scheme_ (New York: Holt, Rinehart, & Winston, 1970). See also Carol Gilligan and J. M. Murphy, "Moral Development in the Late Adolescence and Adulthood: A Critique and Reconstruction of Kohlberg's Theory," _Human Development_, 23 (1980), 77–104. Mary Brabeck, "Intellec tual Development During the College Years: How Strong I the Longitudinal Evidence" (unpublished, 1983).

16. Whiteley, p. 5.

17. Margaret Earley, Marcia Mentkowski, and Jear Schafer, _Valuing at Alverno: The Valuing Process in Lib eral Education_ (Milwaukee: Alverno Productions, 1980).

18. Boyer and Hechinger, pp. 60–62.

19. Cited in Martin, p. 105.

20. E. S. Schumacher, "I. The Greatest Resource— Education," _Small Is Beautiful_ (New York: Harper & Row 1973), pp. 72–94.

21. John Henry Newman, _The Idea of a University_ (Notre Dame, Ind.: University of Notre Dame Press, 1982 pp. 33, 77, _passim_.

22. Cited in William E. Chapman, Roots of Character Education (Schenectady, N.Y.: Character Research Press, 1977), p. 19.

23. Carol Gilligan, "Moral Development in the College Years" (unpublished paper, 1978), cited in John M. Whitely, Barbara D. Bertin, and Bridgette A. Berry, "Research on the Development of Moral Reasoning of College Students," New Directions for Higher Education (San Francisco: Jossey-Bass, 1980), 31, 37.

24. Alexander Meiklejohn, The Liberal College Boston: Marshall Jones Co., 1920), p. 27.

25. Robert Hutchins, "Morals, Religion, and Higher Education," The University of Chicago Round Table (January 15, 1950), p. 29.

26. John Stuart Mill, On Liberty (Indianapolis: Bobbs-Merrill, 1956), pp. 45-55.

27. Loren Lee, "Five Years Later: Retrospective on a Moral Community," in Whiteley, p. 239.

28. Sanford, in Whiteley, p. xix.

29. Levine, p. 137.

30. This aspect of Heath's work is so summarized in Norman A. Sprinthall, Barbara D. Bertin, and John M. Whiteley, "Accomplishment After College: A Rationale for Developmental Education," NASPA Journal, 20 (Autumn 1982).

14

The Moral Education
of Teachers

Kevin Ryan

The education of teachers is one of those perennial problems, like insensitive social service agencies and cost
overruns for military equipment, over which there is much
hand wringing and editorial writing, but seemingly little
progress. Regularly, national commissions study the issues and regularly national magazines pinpoint the problems. Although there are variations, the same targets
keep coming to the surface: The people who are becoming
teachers are not the right ones; the people who are currently preparing the teachers are not the right ones; and
the ideas that one group is teaching the other group are
not the right ideas. Occasionally, the more philosophical
reports identify a more fundamental villain: the public,
which does not care enough about education to bring about
a fundamental change. Still, however, teacher education
continues with its many critics, few advocates, and at
what is widely acknowledged to be a low level of resources.
    Each year the more than thirteen hundred institu-
tions that are authorized to prepare teachers graduate approximately 180,000 people to fill the ranks of the nation's
schools. So, although the institution of teacher education
may appear friendless and vulnerable to almost continual
attack, as an institution it seems rather robust and enduring. And given the facts that most thoughtful people
are convinced that there must be something by way of professional knowledge that the ages of schooling have taught
us which should be known by future teachers, the institution of teacher education would appear to be inevitable:
At least, it seems inevitable for the foreseeable future.

The perspective of teacher education as a large, diverse, and survival-oriented institution is important to keep in mind as we discuss the redirection of teacher education. And, although many despair at what they see as the magnitude of such an institution, teacher education has, in fact, changed direction several times in the recent past. For example, in the past twenty years, the education of teachers has changed in at least two very fundamental ways: One change has been the shift in teacher education from a largely lecture hall-dominated activity to heavily field-oriented. The other change, which is basic to the central thesis of this chapter, the education of teachers for character education, has been the increasing technification of teacher education. By this I mean the shift in emphasis away from the teacher as a special representative of the larger society conveying to the young the society's values to the all but exclusive view of the teacher as a technician concerned primarily with the transfer of information, be it the alphabet or calculus. And, while it is questionable just how effective teacher education programs of the past were in molding teachers as character developers, it contributed actively to the teachers' expectations and visions of themselves as a moral force in the lives of students. Education textbooks were continually reminding future teachers of the important moral roles that they were to play in the lives of children. The emphasis given to philosophy of education (before it became conceptual analysis), and the history of education, brought the teacher-in-training regularly in contact with the normative and ethical nature of the teacher. In this pre-1960 world of teacher education, professors and students existed in an intellectual environment which, while hardly homogeneous, was rather clear and definite about that for which teachers were to stand, and against what sorts of things they should stand. Teachers were expected to be in loco parentis authorities and speak for the community about what was or was not considered to be correct.

At the same time that the rather well documented value divisions surfaced in U.S. society,[1] teacher education turned to science for the answers to its core questions, "What is a good teacher?" and "How is a good teacher produced (formerly, 'educated')?" To oversimplify the situation, professors of education, who formerly professed about the values that teachers must stress to develop in the young the seeds of their own growth and the general

health of the democracy, now taught them skills and tech
niques of teaching. The moral and value dimension of
teaching receded, giving its space in the curriculum, and
presumably the mind of the future teacher, to techniques.
This new view sees teaching as human behavior and sees
the job of the teacher educator to identify the teaching
behaviors that bring about good results with children.[2]
Being a rather simplistic application of the scientific
method, what is "good" (as in "good results" and "good
behavior") is limited to what is readily observable.
Scores on standardized achievement tests, such as the
Scholastic Aptitude Tests, are highly observable. Such
scores became the measure of effective teaching skills and
indeed, of the good teacher. Because teaching a child
how to be a good citizen or to know when to put his or
her own self-interest aside for the interest of the group is
difficult to measure, this aspect of education did not receive much attention. Teacher education, then, has become largely a curriculum of skills and techniques, such
as learning the appropriate "wait time" after asking a
question, and using the appropriate nonverbal cues to
foster positive interpersonal behavior. What the "positive
in "positive interpersonal behavior" means is rarely clear
    While some of this undoubtedly is important for
teachers to know and do, this advance in teacher education has not been without its cost. Either directly or in-
directly, this dominant view of teaching-as-applied-science
has driven out the value dimension. At present, it is
highly likely that a young person studying to be a teach
er will be innocent of the traditional and still existing
role of moral educator and character developer. If young
teachers have views about this dimension of their new
role, then it is likely that they evolved these views outside the context of teacher education.

BECOMING A MORAL EDUCATOR

    Critical to the argument being advanced here is the
assumption that the elementary- and secondary-school
teacher is a moral educator, a developer of character. I
seems a brute fact that if children are put in the hands
of teachers at five years of age, until age 17, for six to
eight hours a day, five days a week, forty or so weeks a
year, then the adults who teach in the schools will have

some impact on the students' view of what is right and
wrong, what is good and bad, and what is praiseworthy
and what is blameworthy. This is based, in turn, on
the observation, first, that the life of the classroom and
the playground is rich in ethical issues and tests of character, and second, that the teacher is at the center of
much of this activity. They are figures of power who reward certain students and punish others. Not only do
they specify what and how students know, but they decide
whether or not they really know it. "Shall I bring out
the ethical issues that permeated the Civil War?" "Is
Julius Caesar to be read in my class for imagery and
structure or do I help the students come to grips with
Brutus's struggle of conscience over the assassination of
his legitimate leader?" In addition, teachers set standards and enforce rules. They are continually dealing
with issues of fairness and justice and sometimes mercy.
Even if they work hard not to take stands on moral issues,
the teacher's own values and moral priorities are continually on display to students. Like it or not, the teacher
is de facto a moral educator. The teacher is intimately
involved in the development of character.

A second assumption is that children's character is
affected by schooling. For many years there has been
controversy among certain social scientists over whether or
not the schools have an effect on students' character or
values or morality. Hyman and Wright's recent book,[3]
which synthesizes many studies in this area, provides
strong evidence to the positive effects of schooling on values and puts this somewhat precious argument to rest.
Like many such issues, however, our best evidence may be
our personal experience. Did the kindnesses and generosity
of certain teachers and the unfairness and thoughtlessness
of others affect us? Did their example make us desire to
be in our own lives one way or another? Were our moral
standards, our sense of right and wrong, affected either
positively or negatively by schooling? An assumption of
this chapter, then, is that children cannot but be affected
by the people and the moral environment with which they
are surrounded. Our central purpose, however, is not to
establish the moral nature of teaching, but to explore what
teachers should know and be able to do to promote moral
development and character development. And it is to this
that we now turn.

What the teacher should do to be a positive force i
the lives of young people has been a theme running throu
several of the earlier chapters, in particular, the chapte
dealing with the content and instruction at various levels
of schooling (Chapters 7, 8, and 9). Here we wish to
elaborate those teacher skills and behaviors as matters to
be given direct attention in the selection and preparation
of teachers. Seven areas of competence are seen to be
necessary if the teacher is to deal adequately with the
role as developer of character and as a moral educator.
They are: First, the teacher must be a positive model of
good character and of the moral person. Second, the
teacher must see the development of the student's moral
life and character as a professional responsibility and
priority. Third, the teacher must be able to engage the
student in moral discourse. Fourth, the teacher must be
able to articulate clearly his own moral viewpoint on a
range of ethical and value issues. Fifth, the teacher mu
be able to help students empathize with the moral world
others. Sixth, the teacher must be able to establish in
the classroom a positive moral climate, an environment of
communal support and concern. Seventh, the teacher shou
be able to provide the students with the opportunity for
tivities in school and in the community that will give the
experience and practice in behaving ethically and altruis
tically.

The Teacher as a Model

Not long ago, the dean of the college of education
at a large state university told me that the aspect of his
job about which he was most uncertain was having to tes
tify to the state that his institution's graduating teacher
were of "good character" and prepared to be a positive
moral force in the lives of students. His state, like mos
others, has a law requiring that all teachers of the youn
be persons of good character. Also, the codes of educati
in most states require the school to promote moral values.
The way in which the people are assured of this is by
delegating the responsibility for this judgment to the inst
tution preparing these teachers. The dean lamented that
not only did he rarely come to know any of the teacher
candidates, but that he doubted if many of the faculty
were seriously concerned or attending to this aspect of

their students' development. Still, each graduation time
he signed a statement for the state Department of Education
attesting to the good character of three or four hundred
graduates who were applying for certification as teachers.

Although the determination of which teacher candidates are of good character may have degenerated into
empty ritual in some places, the question of whether or
not a teacher is an adequate role model for the young is a
real and pressing one. Further, this question goes to the
core of the distinction made earlier between the teacher
and the technician. Someone who is simply involved in
the technical transfer of information or skills has no particular need to be of good character. On the other hand,
the fact that children spend such a great deal of time with
teachers during very formative years and that teachers'
lives are so readily available suggests that teachers ought
to be models for students. Our own memories of being students and for some of us our experiences with our own
children attest to how carefully children observe the character and moral behavior of their teachers. "Are they
playing favorites?" "Are they impatient?" "Are they selfish or generous with their time?" "How do they behave
with other teachers?" "Do they gossip?" This attention
of the young with the noncurricular facets of teachers was
well captured a few years ago by a cartoon in The New
Yorker, which showed a young, modishly dressed father in
his easy chair startled by his third- or fourth-grade
daughter's reply. "What did I learn in school today?
Well, I learned that Paris is groovy. Amsterdam is crazy
wild. And that Miss Featherstone isn't sure if she is
really going to marry that guy with the leather jacket who
picks her up every afternoon with his motorcycle." Who
the teacher is and for what he or she stands counts.

If one accepts the thesis that children are a community's most important natural resource, then it seems reasonable that a community and, in particular, the parents
in that community have the right and the responsibility to
know something of the character of those to whom they
have entrusted the nurturance of their young. Because
few people feel that they are what they should be and are
as good as they ought to be, this idea of the teacher as
moral role model is unsettling. Indeed, the very idea of
being a moral role model puts our teeth on edge. Still,
it is the intention of the law and the suggestion being
made here that young people assuming teaching positions

be of good character and be people whose lives are head
in a positive direction; not that they be saints or moral
works of art. The rub, of course, is who is to judge
what is a "good character," and what is a "positive dire
tion." In a society such as that of the United States,
which is pluralistic in the extreme, the decision is not a
simple one. Two judgments or decision points need to
come into play. The first takes us back to the dean of
the school of education. While he personally may be in
weak position to make the necessary decision, college fac
ulty members should be in a strong position to make such
a judgment. As a result of contacts in courses and field
experiences (in particular, student teaching), the faculty
who have responsibility for the prospective teachers ough
to be ready to make a judgment on the character of the
future teacher.

Second, the local community ought to judge whether
or not this is the type of teacher it wishes to have work
with its young. Our tradition is for local control of the
schools, because people at the local level have the large
stake in the issue. Also, local community people are accustomed to taking responsibility for rather lofty issues,
such as "What is most worth knowing?" and translating
their answers into curricular policy. Of course, there is
in this suggestion the possibility of abuse. The communi
can define "good character" in an excessively narrow way
as was the case in an earlier U.S.A. where teachers were
not allowed to dance or smoke in public. On the other
hand, the teacher has at least two protections here, besides moving on to another school district. Usually, he
she has the protection of a professional association commi
ted to protecting teachers' rights. And, second, as a cit
zen he has the protection of the courts against arbitrary
and unjust decision by a local community. There should
no doubt, however, that this is a tender area with no
guarantees. Educators and community people must make
these judgments of character and values, but they must
do this with sensitivity and justice. As with so many a
pects of life in a democracy, people are thrown back on
their good judgment and goodwill.

The Teacher's Commitment to the Moral Realm

Beyond accepting the responsibility of being a mod
for young people, the teacher needs to have an active

commitment to students' development of character. This does not mean that the teacher, particularly the public-school teacher, should be committed to the spread of sectarian religious views or to specific moral ideologies. Nor does it mean that moral reform or character development is the teacher's single, consuming passion. Rather, the teacher ought to see this domain as an integral part of his or her work and one that he or she is ready to embrace. For instance, in teaching Huckleberry Finn, the teacher is ready to have the students grapple with Huck's dilemma of whether or not he should do what he "knows" to be wrong, to help Nigger Jim gain his freedom, or obey the law of the land and turn Jim in. And the teacher is ready to respond to a classroom situation where children are being abusive to one another. He or she is ready to promote the development of certain personal and society-enhancing virtues, such as courage and kindness. In planning instruction, one seeks opportunities to bring out and examine the legitimate points which relate to the ethical domain.

Commitment does not mean obsession. Rather, the teacher committed to the moral realm is one who should balance this commitment with other responsibilities as a teacher. The learning of crucial skills must not be sacrificed in order to belabor ethical issues. The commitment must be fair and balanced. At a more fundamental level, though, the teacher must demonstrate a commitment in the small, everyday acts of the teacher: preparing classes carefully; correcting papers; being available to students having trouble, either academic or otherwise; using sick days as they are meant to be used, not to extend a vacation. It means living out one's responsibilities as a teacher. Or, more simply, doing the job correctly.

The Teacher and Moral Discourse

The teacher must be able to engage the student in moral discourse. Without this, the possibility of students acquiring the skills and habit of moral discourse is low. By "moral discourse" we mean dealing with the "oughtness" of life. Students need to become skillful and, thus, comfortable dealing with questions such as "What is the right thing to do?" and "What is really of value?" To be a citizen, to be a human being, one must be able to deal with the oughtness questions of life.

There are three aspects to the teacher's focusing on moral discourse. The first relates to the students' cognitive moral development. The work of Lawrence Kohlberg and his colleagues has in recent years drawn attention to stages of moral reasoning.[4] This work suggests that for children to advance through the various stages of moral development, they must be confronted on a regular basis with moral questions and, further, they must have plentiful opportunities to grapple with the moral complexities involved. In this sense, moral discourse is the vehicle for moral maturity.

While Kohlberg and his colleagues see the necessity of the moral discourse and have developed procedures and materials to facilitate such discourse for children at all levels of schooling, others focus directly on the process of moral reasoning.[5] In recent years a number of educators have been attempting to teach the skills of moral reasoning. In effect, they appear to be attempting to distill the skills that are at the core of ethics and to adapt them to school-age children. Second, then, there are sets of skills that are targeted for elementary, junior, and senior high school students. While this subject is typically the province of social studies, elementary-school teachers are learning how to teach these skills of ethical reasoning and argumentation to students.

A third and final aspect of the teacher's attention to moral discourse is that this attention points out to students that the ethical and moral realm is accessible to reasoned inquiry and is for the teacher an area of intellectual priority.

The Teacher's Own Moral Views

In the 1960s and 1970s the most talked about approach used with students to involve them in the moral domain was called values clarification.[6] Few movements in education are as clearly described by their titles as values clarification. The role of the teacher is simply to let children clarify their own values. An important element in this process is for the teacher to be neutral about his or her own values, so as not to inhibit the child's deliberations about what it is he or she really values. The major developers of values clarification justify this downplaying of traditional values and focusing on the self-discovery of values by quoting the psychologist John Gardner: "Instead of giving young people the impression that their task is to stand a dreary watch over the ancient values, we should be telling them the grim but bracing truth that it is their task to recreate those values continually in their own time."[7]

It is not coincidental that this movement gained force during a period when the value consensus in the country began to come apart at the seams, when families were divided over moral positions related to the Vietnam War, when recreational drugs became widely available, and when the traditional views of human sexuality were assaulted from many sides. One can only speculate that teachers as a group were probably just as morally confused about these issues as the rest of society. Where once teachers felt relatively safe sharing their moral views on issues of the day, now in the midst of a cacophony of new moral assertions, teachers began to feel unsure. They sensed no particular moral authority to speak for the community's values, because these values seem so suspect or so clouded. More and more teachers began to believe that while the moral domain was an important one, it was essentially a private domain. Hence, the appeal of values clarification. The teachers could present children with value issues, let them grapple with the issues, but the teachers did not have to take a moral position themselves. Indeed, they are directed not to make their views known.

At the same time that values clarification came on the educational scene, and very much related to the same set of social events, there was a new cry against the school as a source of indoctrination.[8] Teachers and schools were characterized as places where children were shaped according to the values and needs of the immediate society. Many teachers responded to this negative charge of "value inculcation" and indoctrination by keeping their moral views and values to themselves. As suggested earlier, they retreated to become technicians passing on information and skills, or so it seemed.

The view taken here is quite different. The teacher is a conscious part of society's process of character development. We see teachers sharing with parents a deep responsibility to pass on to children a moral vision of the world. Therefore, it is important for teachers, as part of their conscious function as models, to be able to express themselves on moral aspects of life in and out of school.

And, to the degree that they reflect the positive value consensus of their communities, they should attempt to inculcate these values in their students. Further, teachers should feel responsible to oppose behavior that opposes these positive values of the larger community. Students who bully one another should be reprimanded. Students who cheat should be punished. Students should be clear about what the larger community values and does not value. To do less is to rob children of society's precious legacy.

There is, of course, implicit in this view the possibility of irrational indoctrination. Moral views, like religious faith or political preference, only have validity and meaning if they are arrived at freely. It is imperative that the teacher, while making it clear he has particular views, does not force these views on students. Students always have the right to reject a value position. On the other hand, they do not have the right to behave immorally, especially if their immoral behavior offends others. Again, openly presenting one's moral views requires good judgment and balance on the part of the teacher. While there are dangers of abuse here, there is an even greater danger of making the teacher a moral eunuch.

Empathy and the Moral World of Others

Shedding the insulating, but selfish view of childhood is fundamental to gaining maturity, moral or otherwise. Children coming from the shelter and particularity of their homes must learn to appreciate the psychological world of others. The capacity to feel the distress of others and to be able to put oneself in another's shoes is integral to developing character and moral maturity. An important aspect of the teacher's work is to provide experiences for the children that allow them to grow out of their limited, self-centered world.

Literature and history traditionally have been supported as curricular components because they allow children to experience a range of life situations in a sheltered way. The stories, factual and fictitious, confront us with human problems and events that call for some action. Early we learn of treachery from the wolf in Little Red Riding Hood and of the dangers of giving oneself completely over to pleasure from the example of two profligate Brothers Pig.

Later, we learn about the complexity of moral decisions as we struggle with Lincoln both to preserve the Union and to abolish slavery. We become a young foot soldier with the protagonist in The Red Badge of Courage and feel through him both the shame of cowardice and the flush of heroism. These experiences not only confront us with troubling issues, but they give us the opportunity to see the world from the perspective of others. Few adolescent, white teenagers are quite the same after reading The Autobiography of Malcolm X or Claude Brown's Manchild in a Promised Land. In addition to this, virtues that have been important to the survival of the race, such as kindness and willingness to take on hard work, are presented to the young in vivid ways for their appraisal and emulation.

The opportunity for role taking, for viewing the social and moral situation from the eyes of another, is part of the same emphasis. Students need to be encouraged to examine situations from the perspectives of different actors.[9] Having students struggle with moral dilemmas and take different roles in social and moral situations is one valuable way, but so, too, is using the events of classroom life. Helping other classmates to share the sorrow of another student can be an important learning experience. Getting students to see how their seemingly innocent behavior impinges on other students aids them to acquire a larger sense of group membership. An important contributor to this sense of empathic appreciation of the lives of others comes from nonacademic experience inside and outside of schools, a topic to which we now turn.

The Teacher and the Classroom's Moral Climate

From 5 to 17, much of the child's life is spent in classrooms and the environs of school. No other setting except for the home has such a pervasive impact on the child's character and moral development. It is not only that children spend so much time in schools, but that the time is so crowded with people and events. Our early successes and failures, our friends and enemies, are found there. We are punished unfairly and just as unfairly rewarded there. We are made a fool of there. We are cruel to another child there. We feel emotional love and smoldering rage in those classrooms. While we usually conceive of classrooms as places of intellectual learning,

actually classrooms are bubbling cauldrons brimming with
social and moral matter. And the teacher is expected to
be in charge of all of this. Therefore, it is important
that teachers be able to establish an environment that
constructively channels the social and moral learnings of
young people. It is equally important that teachers help
minimize the problems that arise in classrooms, problems
that if allowed to get out of hand can turn the lives of
children into Lord of the Flies nightmares.

From the time they begin school until they graduate,
students need to be taught the skills of living in a community. They need to learn how to support the group and
be supported by the group, how to lead and how to follow,
how to stand up for their rights and how to defer to the
needs of others. These crucial learnings are not inborn.
What is not learned at home must be supplied by teachers.
In effect, this means that teachers continually must be in
the act of creating and maintaining a moral and communal
environment.

The Teacher and Moral Action

Being a person of ethical standards, teaching ethical
ideas and skills, and maintaining a moral climate are crucial activities of the teacher, but they are not enough.
While the teacher is active here, the student is, in a
sense, passive. Students need to be immersed in activities
that will give them opportunities to behave morally and
practice virtues. The teacher, then, must also make or
take advantage of experiences that will promote desirable
qualities in students.

Modern society can be described as information-rich
and experience-poor. This is particularly true for young
people who increasingly live in their own socioeconomic
ghettos, be they Scarsdale or Spanish Harlem. Television
and film provide young people with enormous amounts of
information about how the very powerful and rich live and
it gives them a ringside seat at wars and bedroom intima-
cies. There are few adult activities that remain secrets
for children of the television age.[10] As realistic as the
information seems, however, it still offers only vicarious
experience. Youths have passively received it, rather
than having been part of it. They have been information
consumers, rather than involved actors. Indeed, the

information-dispensing activities of school tend to perpetuate this direction. Given the realities of modern life, schools need to stress active learning on many fronts, but not more than in the realm of character development. First, in schools and then in the larger community, teachers need to give children opportunities to engage in activities that give them practice at being virtuous, whether this means being helpful to an intellectually slower classmate or gracious in defeat on the sports field. Students can be given responsibility for certain classroom chores, such as feeding the animals or helping teachers maintain their records.

It is outside the school, though, that some of the potentially most rich experiences come. Teachers should be able to weave children into their communities, so they see themselves, they define themselves, as contributing members of a community. Giving children opportunities to be of service (which perhaps began in their classrooms) can start quite early in the school life of a child, opportunities such as having children take on as a class project the cleanliness of a neighborhood park or as individuals to visit regularly the home for the elderly couple in need of someone to run errands or do small chores.

There are two emphases to such outreach activities. One is to provide social service[11] and the other is to be involved in social action, often social reform.[12] Certainly in the elementary years and particularly in the high school years, young people should be given the chance to learn how to contribute to the lives of others. Through such activities, children develop not only a truer picture of the world, but they also develop a sense of self-worth. They can contribute to others. They are not trapped in themselves, as mere takers. Although service is an important habit to form and there are many skills children learn in the process of helping others, at a certain point in their development they need to transcend simply giving service, but take a hand in improving political and institutional structures. While maintaining and enriching the social fabric is not to be dismissed casually, it is not enough. Students need to see the necessity for continually addressing social problems and for learning the skills for making positive change. Although all students may not be mature enough to engage in social change activities, some are and should be encouraged to involve themselves. School government is one obvious and easily available arena, but so are community political campaigns and environmental improvement efforts.

In the entire area of moral action, the teacher must be more than a mere broker who places challenges in the paths of students. Often students are overchallenged. A young woman working with retarded children becomes revolted by their personal habits and frightened by the angry outbursts of some. A young person becomes frustrated and discouraged by inability to help a blind person for whom he or she wants to be useful. The teachers need to help the student acquire new skills for their work. Leaving students alone simply to learn by doing may lead to unpleasant and unintended learnings.

While described singularly, it should be clear that these seven areas of competence are related, and often overlapping. A teacher cannot truly develop students' capacity for moral discourse if he or she is not committed to the moral realm. The teacher cannot expect to involve students effectively in moral action projects if s/he him/ herself is not a good model.

The Content to Be Taught Teachers

If the competencies above represent what the teachers' skills and attitudes ought to be, the content speaks to what they are trying to teach, to what they want students to learn. The competencies themselves give a strong indication here. Students should understand the differences between good and evil. They should take moral issues seriously. They ought to be able to discuss problems rationally that emerge in their own lives. They must be moving and growing continually during their years of elementary and secondary school toward the development of their own views on ethical matters. They should know how to be part of a democratic community. And, finally, they need to acquire that skill and perspective of being a contributing member of society. They must feel their connectedness to others and be ready to contribute to the well-being of others.

Many of the above competencies are process skills, such as knowing how to reason through an ethical problem and how to ensure that the views of the minority are heard respectfully. Another and perhaps more helpful way to look at the goals of the teacher as character developer is to identify the characteristics of students that we, as a society, find desirable. What is meant here is that com-

munity members and educators should specify the positive
qualities and dispositions and habitual behaviors they
wish to foster in the child. Candidates for inclusion
might be teaching children how both to cooperate and compete, knowing the necessary skills of each and the situations where each is most appropriate and, especially, how
to strike a balance between the two. Another strong candidate for inclusion is persistence. North American children of the middle class live in a world of comfort and
ready gratification. Children and adults alike live off
the fruits of the culture's past intellectual and physical
efforts. To maintain our society and to extend its benefits
further and to others will require that the inheritors of
our world know how to delay gratification and persist at
difficult tasks. A third candidate is charity. Children
come to school still quite self-centered and they need to
learn to extend their concern for and love of self to others.
These habitual behaviors or virtues, and others, should
become the content of schooling.

Much of what the teacher studies should be focused
on how to develop these virtues in the young. Teachers
at different levels should be learning the literature and
history that supports these virtues. Methods courses
should deal with how most effectively to engage children
in activities that give them experiences that help promote
these virtues. Field experiences should expose them to
teachers who are exemplars of effective teaching of these
selected qualities and virtues. And, teachers in training
should be expected to practice how to teach and to promote
them. For experienced teachers, a major agenda item for
their own professional development and as part of their
in-service education should be work on how most effectively
to convey this character-developing content.

TEACHING TEACHERS THEIR ROLE
IN CHARACTER DEVELOPMENT

It is always tempting when writing about the education of teachers to take the high ground of "ought to be,"
the never-never-land where only the best and the brightest
are selected for long and exacting and well-funded teacher
preparation. While such an exercise is often good for the
soul, the aftermath tends to be discouragement and paraly-
sis in the face of the real world. On the other hand, it

is easy to suggest that, having laid out seven areas of teacher competence, courses be designed or modified to prepare new and experienced teachers in these competencies. While one approach leads to cynicism, the other could well reinforce the technique-is-all mentality mentioned earlier. Perhaps the most honest way to address the issue of how to help teachers with their work as developers of human character is to return to the dean of the school of education and his struggle with his question of how he is going to be confident that he is graduating teachers of good character and who will have a positive moral influence on youth.

The first thing the dean might do is share the problem: raise the issue of character development and the teacher's role with the faculty. The simple act of showing the flag of concern is an important step. By posing the problem to the faculty, the dean is both legitimizing the question and setting the stage for ideas and suggestions to emerge. Implicit in this suggestion is the belief that only the faculty can effect change in this arena, and, therefore, they must be involved in generating solutions to the problem. But first, the dean (or whoever is in authority) must establish it as a priority and then create the conditions for the issues to be addressed. There are a variety of mechanisms that could be used, such as faculty retreats, study groups, weekend workshops, and a series of special meetings. It would seem important, though, for the dean carefully to create conditions for faculty to come together in a supportive climate and for a sustained period of time.

Once brought together, the emphasis should be on faculty members sharing their own experiences, questions, and ideas. While there may be some value initially in providing information and perspectives, the major focus ought to be on the faculty's thinking together. The target of the discussions ought not to be outward, on the moral foibles of current world leaders or the characterological deficiencies of their students, but rather inward on their own world. Instead of addressing the moral lapses of the current administration, they might talk about the moral climate of the school. Instead of dealing with international power politics, they might deal with bullying on the playground or the heavy load new teachers are required to carry. Instead of talking about the world's haves and have-nots, they might focus on the haves and the have-nots around them. The important thing is to address issues in the moral realm that affect them personally and passionately, and about which they have, or might, develop a personal stake. It is somewhat hollow to have faculty incensed about hunger in Ethiopia, while local issues such as abuse of library privileges, sloppy teaching, and character assassination of students or their administrators go unchecked. But, while the most pressing moral problem for the faculty might be that their program is composed of "cake courses" that leave the students ill-equipped to teach, this might not be the best initial issue with which to deal. The faculty will need, first, to engage an ethical agenda and learn to talk with one another before getting to areas where their individual or collective oxen are being gored. Nevertheless, to involve faculty in an ethical agenda, it might be useful to have the faculty struggle with hypothetical moral dilemmas and to have them role play ethical problems. Gradually, though, the moral discussions should come closer to home, examining the qualities of the environment they have created for their students and themselves.

Once the faculty has seriously begun examining the values and moral messages that exist in their own hidden curriculum, it is ready to address how the formal curriculum can prepare teachers for their role as developers of character. Competencies, such as those mentioned above, become candidates for inclusion in the student's program. It is important, though, that this goal is not reduced to a mechanical process of stuffing information and training into specified courses. In the same manner that the faculty initially needed to invest themselves in the centrality of the moral domain to the life of the school and of character development to the teacher's role, this, too, must happen with teacher education students. Many students may need help to become committed to this facet of the teaching profession. Here, as with their professors, simulation and role playing may play an important part. In addition, regular opportunities to talk and work with elementary and high school teachers who are particularly effective as character developers can be quite important for the student's growth. In addition, students should be urged to take advantage of opportunities to address the moral needs of their own collegiate community through such programs as student associations, peer counseling, student-faculty committees and social action efforts.

A major and essential part of the college education of a future teacher is devoted to liberal studies. For a secondary-school teacher, over three fourths of a four-year program are devoted to general education and the student's subject matter concentration. Also, most future teachers have had substantial exposure to liberal studies during their high school years. In fact, the formal coursework of teacher preparation represents a very small portion of that required of the future teacher. And it is in this dimension of the student's education that he or she comes into the most intimate contact with our moral tradition. It is this exposure to and reflection upon our culture's literature and history which represents our greatest opportunity to prepare our teachers to take on the role of character developer and moral educator. Without being brought into the great moral conversations of our heritage and without being given the chance to come to their own judgments of these conversations of value, future teachers become little more than technicians. Of course, it is not enough simply to require future teachers to take a prerequisite number of courses in the arts and sciences. On college campuses today, many liberal arts professors appear to be unconcerned with or loath to bring out the moral dimension of their fields of study. They are more concerned with issues of form and structure than they are with the substantive meaning the content might have on the lives of students. This insistence, then, on the necessity of a strong liberal education component to a teacher's preparation assumes that a vital concern for ethical and value questions be a part of this liberal education. Again, being responsible for the total preparation of future teachers, it falls to our dean of the school of education to assure that the future teacher's liberal education is contributing to their moral growth and understanding.

While all the faculty within and without the school of education should be sharpening the student's capacity for moral discourse, consideration ought to be given to requiring all future teachers to take a course in ethics as part of their preparation to teach. Such a course should not only teach them how to engage in discussing more issues, but also convince them of the centrality of moral issues to civilized life.

In-Service Teacher Education

The education of teachers does not end with graduation from college, of course. Teachers, perhaps more than any other professional group, need to be continuous learners. Experienced teachers, however, have particular problems in this area of character development. A prime consideration is that the great majority of the teachers now serving in our schools have gone through teacher preparation programs that were silent about this dimension of their work. Other than a smattering of values clarification and cognitive moral development theory, teachers, by and large, have been left on their own. Many teachers, of course, have come to teaching out of moral commitment and they see their efforts to help children develop virtues and moral maturity as an integral part of their work.

Still, these teachers, and certainly the others, need education and support for this responsibility. Those in charge of in-service education, such as the superintendents in public schools, might take many of the same steps that our hypothetical dean of education has taken. They need to raise the question publicly and request that the teachers come together and address these concerns. They should work with staff and teacher leaders to assure that the setting for discussing these issues and concerns is conducive to honest, nonthreatening, and productive thought. They should do what they can to ground the discussions in the ethical dilemmas and problems of character development that actually impinge on the teachers. The moral climate within which the teachers work should not be immune to those deliberations. In fact, for many teacher groups this is exactly the place to begin, because for many this is the seat of their discontent.

The issues of addressing the character developmental needs of experienced teachers, as opposed to preservice teachers, are affected by a number of factors. Major among them, of course, is the maturity and professional experience of the people involved. Also, recognizing that teacher preparation is, by necessity, general, aiming to prepare the future teacher for a variety of settings, in-service training should be specific. It should concentrate on the immediate and particular circumstances of the teachers' schools. Of special significance, though, is the current morale of teachers. For a variety of reasons, including their deteriorating economic situation, the high levels of disruption and delinquency in schools, soured management-labor relations between teachers and their administrators and communities, and the general low regard the public currently has for schools, teachers feel discouraged and unappreciated. In this type of climate, moral abuses, such as unnecessarily taking sick days and simply not performing at a professional standard, are encouraged. It seems especially necessary, then, in working with experienced teachers to give some sustained attention to the moral climate and the human relations in their workplace. To do less would be an exercise in artificiality. Because so much of what is troubling the nation's schools is a moral malaise, teachers, who are on the front lines of our education system, have a special stake in and responsiveness to these issues.

CONCLUSION

Socrates believed that the role of education is to make people both intelligent and good. A major goal of teacher education, the education of a professional teacher, is to prepare them to be skillful teachers. It has been argued in this chapter that the emphasis in teacher education in recent decades has been on preparing the skillful teacher and that has been done by focusing on the technical end of the teacher's role. Using Socrates's formulation, we have concentrated on making the teacher intelligent about instructional technique and ignored the teacher's responsibility to foster the good. This dichotomy, while currently operational, is a false one. In the name of education, the teacher cannot accept one part of the role, helping to foster intelligence, and reject the other part, fostering goodness. In a similar sense, the teacher cannot take on the partial role of fostering goodness, while ignoring or downplaying technical skill at teaching. In effect, the teacher's first moral obligation is to teach well. If the teacher is denying students the opportunity to become intelligent, there will be little fostering of the good. Teacher education, then, needs to recapture the Socratic ideal of education and to help teachers in their work to make students both intelligent and good.

NOTES

1. T. Smith, "General Liberalism and Social Change in Post World War America," Social Indicators Research, 10, January 1982.

2. B. Skinner, "The Shame of American Education," American Psychologist, 39(9), pp. 947-954, 1984.

3. H. Hyman and C. Wright, Education's Lasting Influence on Values (Chicago: University of Chicago Press, 1979).

4. L. Kohlberg, Philosophy of Moral Development (New York: Harper & Row, 1981); J. Reimer, D. P. Paolitto, and R. Hersh, Promoting Moral Growth (New York: Longman, 1983).

5. J. Fraenkel, How to Teach About Values: An Analytical Approach (Englewood Cliffs, N.J.: Prentice-Hall, 1979).

6. L. Raths, M. Harmin, and S. Simon, Values and Teaching, 2nd edition (Columbus, Ohio: Merrill, 1978).

7. J. Gardner, Self-Renewal (New York: Harper & Row, 1964), quoted in Raths, Harmin, and Simon, Values and Teaching.

8. N. Postman and C. Weingartner, Teaching as a Subversive Activity (New York: Delacorte, 1969).

9. Robert E. Selman, The Growth of Interpersonal Understanding (New York: Academic Press, 1980).

10. K. Moody, Growing Up on Television: A Report to Parents (New York: Times Books, 1980).

11. E. Doyer, High School: A Report on Secondary Education in America (New York: Harper & Row, 1983).

12. F. Newmann, Education for Citizen Action: Challenge for Secondary Curriculum (Berkeley, Calif.: McCutchen, 1975.

Epilogue
A Practitioner's View
M. Donald Thomas

THE AMERICAN ETHOS

As superintendent of schools in Salt Lake City, I enjoyed my conversations with Henry Y. Kasai. He often spoke of the Japanese character. His words still linger with me in South Carolina. "Our imperial ancestors," Henry once said, "founded our empire on a basis broad and everlasting and it has deeply and firmly implanted virtues." He once showed me a letter, written fifty years earlier. He did not know who had written the letter. In it, the writer, probably in his late years, recalled the joys and sorrows of his life. One statement summed up his personal philosophy: "Everyone can live in this world respectably. At least everyone should make it a respectable living place."

Moral education, civic learning, ethics instruction, character education, value analysis--call it what you will-- the aim of these programs is the same: to teach each of us to live respectably and if Japan has "deeply and firmly implanted virtues," so do we have important ethical principles embedded into our national character. Such principles are written into the basic documents of our nation.

They are a set of principles against which we can measure if we are creating a respectable living place.

I certainly do not wish to suggest, as Ryan and Lickona have, that the transmission of a moral code to the young may be genetically based. At the same time, I do not subscribe to the position that morality is situational. I agree with several of the authors who see ethical relativism as part of the problem and not the solution. I also reject the Skinnerian belief that we are at the mercy of the forces around us. I agree with those who say that individual responsibility for moral behavior is possible and also is the cornerstone of a good and safe society. Further, I believe that there is, in our country, a common ethical ethos and that it is the responsibility of the school to impact that ethos into the behaviors of the young. It is the basis of character for all of us.

An examination of our basic documents, a careful study of our history, and an analysis of the attributes of our moral heroes leads me to conclude that we, as a nation, are committed to the following:

1. Belief in the worth and perfectibility of human life on this earth;
2. Conviction that democratic societies have more to offer than totalitarian ones;
3. Faith in reason and in the orderly solution of conflict between individuals and between nations;
4. Respect for knowledge and a strong commitment to educate all;
5. Protection of personal liberties within limits established by law;
6. Equal protection under the law and equal opportunity for personal and economic success.

From these fundamental principles we can establish codes of conduct, criteria to examine moral behavior, the oughts of our society. Following a study of these principles, the Salt Lake City School District developed a set of criteria for moral behavior:

1. Each individual has dignity and worth.
2. A free society requires respect for persons, property, and principles.
3. Each individual has a right to learn and the freedom to achieve.

4. Each individual, regardless of race, creed, color, sex, ethnic background or economic status, has equal opportunity.
5. Each individual has the right to personal liberties.
6. Each individual is responsible for his or her own actions.
7. Each individual has a responsibility to the group as well as to the total society.
8. Democratic governments govern by majority vote and protect minority rights.
9. Democratic societies are based on law.
10. Problems are solved through reason and orderly processes.
11. An individual should be tolerant of other religious beliefs and should have freedom to exercise his or her own.
12. Each individual has the right to work, to pursue an occupation, and to gain satisfaction from personal efforts.

Our ethos has sustained us for more than two hundred years. It is a balance between individual rights and the public good. While it respects diversity, it extracts conformity in some areas. While it encourages freedom, it places restrictions on all members of society. While it provides equal opportunity, it expects individuals to take advantage of existing opportunities. It has a fine and delicate balance. It works well.

CHARACTER DEVELOPMENT

Good citizenship is understanding and appreciating these ethical principles. It is also having congruence between the principles and one's personal behavior. In simple words: We ourselves must do what others are expected to do.

Character development is not an easy task, and it cannot be done by the schools alone. As this book indicates, it is a job for all of us—schools, parents, institutions of society, leaders, churches, media, and anyone else who comes in contact with our children and youth. Moral behavior in a democratic society is "the living" and not the message.

The conditions which require us to give greater attention to character development are adequately covered by Edward A. Wynne. Data related to violent crime, suicides, drug use, and illegal behavior clearly indicate basic ethical principles are not being learned by our young people. For them there appears to be no coherent set of values which are "deeply and firmly" implanted in their character. Nor are there sufficient models for them from which to learn appropriate moral behavior. Those who are not convinced by Wynne may wish to read Amoral America by Benson and Engeman (Hoover Institute, Stanford University, 1975). The same case is also made by an array of sociologists, psychologists, human behavior specialists, and educators. The case is not only convincing, it is overwhelming. Wynne is also correct, I believe, in his position that character is conduct. And therein lies the nation's dilemma: the inability of individuals and institutions of society to conduct themselves in congruence with the ethos of the nation. The case was well stated, long ago, by Gunnar Myrdal.

If we are to be effective in the development of character, our first responsibility is to create schools of character. They are schools in which the adults teach, govern, and conduct themselves in congruence with the ethical behaviors they wish to establish in the students. They are schools in which morality is lived and not only verbalized. They are schools in which adults conduct themselves respectably.

What is needed in many of our schools is a moral confrontation--an examination of the moral behavior we expect of our young and the morality of the school itself. As with other institutions of society, schools often are a contradiction; there is a serious difference between professed ideals and actual behavior. If character is to be developed in students, the school itself, the people who work in it, must conduct themselves as men and women of character. The words of John Ruskin in his essay "On Education" are still appropriate today:

> Education does not mean teaching people
> what they do not know. It means teach-
> ing them to behave as they do not behave.
> It is not teaching the youth the shapes of
> letters and the tricks of numbers, and then
> leaving them to turn their arithmetic to

roguery, and their literature to lust. It
means, on the contrary, training them into
the perfect exercise and kingly countenance
of their bodies and souls. It is a painful,
continual, and difficult work to be done
by kindness, by watching, by warning, by
precept, by praise, but above all by example.

Fortunately, schools of character can be established.
It is not easy, but it can be done. A good example is
South High School in Salt Lake City. With the help of the
Danforth Foundation, the school established the democratic
ethos as the psyche of the school. The common ethical
principles extracted from basic documents became the criteria against which everything was measured: the operation of the school, the conduct of classrooms, the behavior
of students and adults, and the values expressed in the
curriculum, both formal and informal. South took seriously the advice of Professor Isaac Scheffler of Harvard University, proffered at a conference sponsored by the National
Endowment of Humanities in Denver in 1977:

The challenge of moral education is the
challenge to develop critical thought in
the sphere of practice and it is continuous
with the challenge to develop critical
thought in all aspects and phases of schooling. Moral schooling is not, therefore, a
thing apart, something to be embodied in a
list of maxims, something to be reckoned
as simply another subject, or another activity, curricular or extracurricular. It
does, indeed, have to pervade the whole of
the school experience.

The moral nature of South High School is best expressed by Principal LaVar Sorensen:

South is an inner city school that works
well. It has high achievement, high attendance, high public confidence, and high
confidence in itself. It has low vandalism,
few incidences of student violence, almost
no problems related to drugs, and is a

is a consensus that the school has an obligation to impact common moral values into the lives of its students. I would add to that that the school also has the obligation to set a moral example through its governance, its reflection of values, the actions of adults, and the expressions of a basic set of ethical principles.

Similarly, the authors do not engage in extensive debate over methodologies for teaching ethical behavior. Lickona, Beck, and Starratt concentrate more on getting the job done than on definitive ways of getting it done. There is, however, in their statements a set of basic beliefs:

1. The practice of moral behavior is the responsibility of both students and the adults who teach them.
2. Moral education is a process of joint inquiry--a search for moral responsibility.
3. Moral education is more than the study of ethics; it is the totality of what one experiences in school.
4. Moral advocacy is an appropriate teacher behavior.

If there is anything lacking in this book, it is a reluctance on the part of the authors to identify and advocate a common set of values as criteria against which we can examine moral behavior. This reluctance is common among college professors. They are extremely sensitive to the issue of indoctrination. They would rather discuss the search for truth than identify what truth has already been established. To me, the position is clear. The national experiment is based on something. The basic ethical principles articulated earlier in this chapter are part and parcel of U.S. character. They are the fundamental beliefs of a democratic society. They are to be established in the life of a school the same as teaching students to read, teaching an appreciation for good literature, or developing outstanding athletic teams. They are principles for which we need no apology. They are as fundamental as the alphabet or the numbers needed to learn arithmetic. Without a common set of values, in any society, little else is possible. Indoctrination is more a question of methodology than it is a selection of what we will teach. Further, moral behavior requires criteria against which it can be examined, be it the Ten Commandments, the fairness test of the Rotary Club, or a set of ethical principles extracted from basic documents of our nation.

It is my belief that we can successfully implement moral education programs in our schools. At the same time, I agree with Lickona, Hennessy, Sullivan, Nicgorski, and Ryan that moral education belongs to everyone; school, home, church, and other institutions of society. Each has a responsibility for transmitting our moral values to the young.

There is a saying in Polish: "Everywhere is good, but at home it's better." In moral development, the home is the primary source of influence. A great deal of one's character is formed prior to the school experience. This does not, however, relieve the school's obligation to be a moral exemplar, to support moral growth, and to accept a responsibility for moral education. The sooner practitioners accept this, the better our schools will be.

MORAL EDUCATION OF TEACHERS

The final chapter by Ryan may very well be the key to all that we are attempting to do--the moral education of teachers. What he says about teachers in the generic sense applies equally well to administrators, counselors, coaches, librarians, and specialists of all kinds. Schools will not be able to be effective in moral education until colleges prepare moral teachers. "Teacher education," he writes, "then, needs to recapture the Socratic ideal of education and to help teachers in their work to make students both intelligent and good."

From Ryan's point of view, the current problem in the moral education of teachers is ". . . the shift in emphasis away from the teacher as a special representative of the larger society conveying to the young society's values to the all but exclusive view of the teacher as a technician concerned primarily with the transfer of information." Prior to this shift: "Teachers were expected to be in loco parentis authorities and speak for the community about what was or was not considered to be correct." Teachers were expected to teach by personal example and were considered to be models for young people both in intellectual development and in moral behavior. Character development was as important as learning the alphabet.

Given the current social conditions (Wynne) and understanding the influence of school on moral development (Power), and having the tools to establish moral education

(Lickona, Beck, and Starratt), there should be no question that each teacher should be "a moral educator, a developer of character." Further, there is little reason to disagree with Ryan's seven areas of competence which are necessary if teachers are to be moral educators.

These competencies, however, are not sufficient. Teachers must have an understanding of and an appreciation for the history of this nation. From it they can obtain the criteria for moral development--against which they can measure the moral development of the school and the student. Even more important, these are the criteria needed for one's personal character development. They are the U.S. ethos.

CONCLUSION

It is my hope that this book will assist school leaders to take a greater interest in citizenship education. By building individual character we create schools of character. Schools of character can then evolve into a nation of character.

Ryan, Lickona, and Johnson have provided a sufficient rationale for a more aggressive leadership in character development. Wynne, Prakash, and Power provide an adequate understanding of the cooperative nature of schools. Lickona, Beck, and Starratt explore realistically the teaching of moral development. Lickona, Hennessy, Sullivan, and Nicgorski put into proper perspective that moral education comes with the territory in every function of society. And finally, Ryan rightly articulates that moral education is not possible without teachers being moral exemplars.

The authors have done their work. It is now time for educators to do theirs. School personnel must accept and carry out their responsibility to transmit moral values to the young. To avoid doing so is to misunderstand the purpose of schooling.

Like Henry Y. Kasai, we who are in education must know and live by the "deeply and firmly" implanted virtues of a democratic society. When we have learned to live respectably, we can then make schools a respectable living place for our students. Moral education will then have been established.

Index

About the Contributors

KEVIN RYAN is a faculty member in the School of Education at Boston University. He has written widely in the areas of moral education and teacher education, having published 12 books and more than 50 articles in the last 18 years. His textbook in education, Those Who Can, Teach is currently going into a fifth edition and is the most widely used in the field. Dr. Ryan has taught on the faculties of Stanford University, University of Chicago, Harvard University, and Ohio State University. He has received an award for recognition of service from the American Association of Colleges of Teacher Education and the Medal of Service from the University of Helsinki. He was awarded the Alfred North Whitehead Fellowship at Harvard during the 1970-71 academic year and a Fulbright Senior Research Fellowship to Portugal in 1980.

THOMAS LICKONA is a developmental psychologist and professor of education at the State University of New York at Portland, where he has done award-winning work in teacher education. In 1983, Dr. Lickona's research reached a wide public audience with the publication of Raising Good Children: Helping Your Child Through the Stages of Moral Development (Bantam). Dr. Lickona's 14 years of work in teacher and parent education include experience as a family counselor and as a consultant to Harvard University's Center for Moral Education and to schools across the country. Lickona is currently the president of the Association for Moral Education.

EDWARD A. WYNNE is a professor of education at the University of Illinois at Chicago. In addition, Wynne is a lawyer, having served in the federal government prior to turning to university-based research and teaching. He is the author of six books, and more than 70 articles, reports, and chapters. He is, also, editor of Character II, a bimonthly newsletter about public and private policies shaping the character of young Americans, and Coordinator of "For Character," a Chicago-based area school recognition program. Recently, Professor Wynne was the editor for the widely distributed "Thanksgiving Statement" entitled Developing Character: Transmitting Knowledge.

HENRY C. JOHNSON, JR. is a professor of the history of education at Pennsylvania State University. Dr. Johnson holds advanced degrees in theology from Nashotah House and in education from the University of Illinois. He has authored various publications dealing with the history of education, having given particular attention to the impact of science on American educational thought and practice. Professor Johnson is chairman of his university's Interdisciplinary Symposium on Problems of Value and was recently president of the Middle Atlantic region of the Philosophy of Education Society.

MADHU SURI PRAKASH is an assistant professor of education at Pennsylvania State University and a Spencer Fellow at the National Academy of Education. A public policy analyst, Dr. Prakash has presented and has been published on the topics of ethics and moral education. Currently, she is working on a manuscript entitled Four Conceptions of Excellence. As part of her work on the subject of excellence, Prakash is also doing research on "Teacher of the Year--Awards for Promotion Excellence on Teaching."

CLARK POWER is an assistant professor at Notre Dame University and a faculty member in the Program of Liberal Studies. Professor Power holds a doctoral degree in education from the Harvard Graduate School of Education. A developmental psychologist, Clark Power has spent ten years studying and working with young people in schools and other settings. His primary focus has been on aiding young people in establishing a moral environment. Professor Power is currently working on a book with Lawrence Kohlberg and others on this topic.

CLIVE BECK is a philosopher of education at the Ontario Institute for the Study of Education in Toronto, Canada. A native of Australia, Dr. Beck has been for many years a major spokesman in North America for a more conscious effort to teach the skills of ethical reasoning. With Edmund Sullivan, he developed a special course for the teaching of ethics to high school students. Until recently, Professor Beck was director of a project with the Ontario Ministry of Education. The purpose of this very successful project was to develop a wide range of materials for teachers to use in the moral and character development of elementary and high school students.

ROBERT J. STARRATT is a Jesuit priest and a professor of education at Fordham University. In addition, he is director of the Center for Non-Public Education at Fordham. His publications range over various topics, including education leadership, teaching as a moral enterprise, curriculum renewal, and education for citizenship. His best-known work, which he coauthored with Thomas Sergiovanni, is now in its third edition: Supervision Human Perspectives (McGraw-Hill, 1982). Professor Starratt has conducted workshops and seminars for educators in Canada, Australia, India, Japan, Hong Kong, and the Philippines. He has participated in numerous symposia, seminars, and conferences in the United States, including the Annual Association of Independent Schools, and the convention of the National Catholic Education Association.

THOMAS C. HENNESSY is a Jesuit priest and the recently retired dean of the School of Education at Marquette University. Prior to assuming the deanship at Marquette, Fr. Hennessy was for 20 years a faculty member at Fordham University, where he served as a professor of education and director of the W. A. Kelly Counseling Laboratory. Now back at Fordham, he is teaching courses in business ethics. Father Hennessy has edited five books and numerous articles on education. His particular focus has been the various approaches to character and moral education and more recently the relationship of religion to these topics.

EDMUND V. SULLIVAN is a developmental psychologist on the staff of the Ontario Institute for Studies in Education. He currently holds a joint professorship of applied psychology and history and philosophy. Professor Sullivan has previously taught at Harvard University and Simon Fraser University. Sullivan has written widely in the fields of education, religion, and child development. His most recent book, Interpretation of the Personal World: A Critical Psychology, was published by Plenum Press in 1983.

WALTER NICGORSKI holds a degree in political philosophy from the University of Chicago. From 1979 to 1985, Professor Nicgorski chaired the Program of Liberal Studies at the University of Notre Dame, in which he continues to teach. He is also a member of the graduate faculty of government and international studies. His articles on classical and American political theory have appeared in Political Theory, Review of Politics, Interpretation, and many others. In 1976, he coedited bicentennial essays under the title, An Almost Chosen People: The Moral Aspirations of Americans. In addition, he has held a Lilly Endowment faculty fellowship for the study of the American history of liberal education. Professor Nicgorski has just completed a year as a National Endowment for the Humanities Research Fellow at Cambridge University.

M. DONALD THOMAS is a senior partner, Harold Webb Associates, Winnetka, Illinois. He was formerly deputy superintendent for public accountability for the state Department of Education in Columbia, S.C. His experience as a school administrator is extensive, including positions as superintendent of schools in California, New York, and Illinois and most recently chief school officer of Salt Lake City. Thomas is also a nationally recognized authority on a number of educational policy issues, in particular, citizenship and character education. To date, he has published more than three hundred articles and has written three booklets in the Phi Delta Kappa Fastback Series.

ROBERT COLES is among America's leading intellectuals. As a medical doctor and child psychologist, Dr. Coles has brought to his studies of youth broad-based scientific training. However, a distinguishing characteristic of his studies is their grounding in the humanistic tradition. In 1973, Dr. Coles was awarded the Pulitzer Prize and the McAlpin Medal for his series of volumes, Children of Crisis. Since 1963, Dr. Coles has been a research psychiatrist at Harvard University Health Services and a

lecturer on general education. Four years ago, Coles received the prestigious MacArthur Prize Fellowship. He is a
contributing editor to American Poetry Review, Literature
and Medicine, and New Oxford Review and for many years
he has been a regular book reviewer for The New Yorker.
A Fellow of the American Academy of Arts and Sciences,
Robert Coles has in the last dozen years received more
than thirty honorary degrees for his work.